OVERLY MEDICATED.

Based on a true story.

Lewisham. Overly Medicated

Amazon publications and Shaun Lewisham enterprises

2013

Steven Webb asserts the moral authority to be identified as the author of this work

ISBN: 9781468081350

Printed and bound by Amazon.

SHAUN LEWISHAM ENTERPRISES

All titles available from www.amazon.co.uk

CONTENTS

PROLOGUE

BOOK ONE: HOOLIGAN.

CHAPTER 1.   **PLANNING.**   **6-19.**

CHAPTER 2.   **RIOT.**   **20-41.**

CHAPTER 3.   **WALKER.**   **42-58.**

CHAPTER 4.   **NATALIE.**   **59-69.**

CHAPTER 5.   **PREGNANT.**   **70-84.**

CHAPTER 6.   **CEREMONY.**   **85-109.**

CHAPTER 7.   **VICTORIA.**   **110-125.**

CHAPTER 8.   **DOMESTICITY.**   **126-135.**

BOOK TWO: THROUGH THE LOOKING GLASS

CHAPTER 9.   **SILKS.**   **136-159**

CHAPTER 10.   **ECSTASY.**   **160--171.**

CHAPTER 11.   **DRUDGERY.**   **172-181.**

CHAPTER 12.   **BUSTED.**   **182-193.**

CHAPTER 13.   **BETRAYAL.**   **194-203.**

CHAPTER 14   **RECKONING.**   **204-212.**

CHAPTER 15.   **SINGLE.**   **213-220.**

CHAPTER 16.   **JUNKIE.**   **221-232.**

CHAPTER 17.   **CYCLES.**   **233-237.**

CHAPTER 18.   **DUBLIN.**   **238-254.**

CHAPTER 19.   **MURDER.**   **255-263.**

CHAPTER 20.   **ABYSS .**   **264-278.**

BOOK THREE: MIND OVER MATTER

CHAPTER 21.   **MADNESS.**   **279-294.**

CHAPTER 22.   **DARKNESS.**   **295-316.**

CHAPTER 23.   **RECOVERY.**   **317-331.**

CHAPTER 24.   **RETURN.**   **332-342.**

CHAPTER 25.   **STUDENT.**   **343-351.**

CHAPTER 26.   **POISE.**   **352-366.**

CHAPTER 27.   **PSYCHIATRY.**   **367-376.**

CHAPTER 28.   **ETHICS.**   **377- 397.**

CHAPTER 29.   **PROFESSIONAL**   **398-410.**

CHAPTER 30.   **KATHY.**   **411-419.**

CHAPTER 31.   **PROSPERITY.**   **420-433.**

CHAPTER 32.   **SCHISM.**   **434-448.**

CHAPTER 33.   **REMOVED.**   **449-471.**

EPILOGUE

To Shorty, whose love guided me like a beacon through the dark times. To my mother, who wasn't so soft when the going got tough and proved a rock of support.

To Silks the man that taught me to: 'Get a Grip!'

And finally to Langley and the lads, you know who you are, raise a glass boys. We made it! Love and respect xx

S.LEWISHAM 2011

PROLOGUE: 2010

The volcano in his head finally erupted. "Shut the fuck up and get the fuck out!" He raged. The large man`s patience was finally exhausted as he directed his frustration at another of his indolent staff team. He liked to promote a culture of free expression, but sometimes that meant the irreverent drivel they spouted, turned his head in the wrong direction, causing a brief moment of apoplexy before a fleeting moment of serenity would relaxingly descent.

The door shuddered violently in its frame as he slammed it shut with equal ferocity. The unfortunate target for his angst scuttled hurriedly away from his assault, their eyes rooted to the floor, relieved that the door was now a physical barrier preventing another assault. The rest of group assembled in the adjourning office breathed a collective sigh of relief that the storm had finally broken, releasing the cloud of tension that'd hung tangibly in the air. The big man would brew for twenty minutes, muttering to himself in his office, before he ventured out full of smiles and enthusiasm with a fresh wave of motivational speeches to rouse the underpaid workers to greater heights of productivity.

Walker sat down and rubbed his temples to ward off the drum-beat that was increasing in intensity behind his eyeballs. He sipped at his coffee, savoring the taste. The flavour acting as a trigger, reminding him of the path he'd walked along to reach the *pinnacle* of his nursing career.

The shrill ring of the phone interrupted his daydream and the peace and quiet that had provided momentary shelter from the outside world was shattered. Walker sighed and picked up the handset, his hands slightly shaking, a reaction to the overdose of caffeine and anger that was now fading into the distance. He composed himself and took a deep breath."Hello Temple Court. Gary Walker speaking. How may I help you?"

This was the existence of Gary Walker; manager of Temple Court, a home for people with serious mental health disorders that no other home in the locality could cater for. Twenty residents lived there, myriad sad tales from disjointed pasts. Clients who had been released from Ashworth Maximum Security Mental Hospital. Deemed cured of the acute phase of their collective psychosis that had led them to commit some heinous crimes. But not *cured enough* to live independently in the community, without twenty four hour supervision under home office approved risk assessment.

Walker`s day entailed a daily ritual of running battles; sporadic scuffles with his nurses, support staff, the people that lived there and senior management who didn't care about his daily tribulations and stresses as long as the 'Yankee Dollar' kept rolling in.

Gary Walker was 43 years old: big, broad shouldered and shaven headed. The last profession people assigned to him was that of a Mental Health Nurse. His life had been complex to say the least. He'd experienced problems with both his head and his heart. Football hooliganism and crime had been a way of life. Just about everything he touched managed to turn to shit. But by some means he'd managed to keep ahead of the game; but the game was getting harder and increasingly demanding. People and organisations were asking awkward questions about his past. He couldn't remember the last time he'd slept well and woken with a peacefully fresh mind.

The doors in his mind were slowly slamming shut behind him and the pressure mounting. Cider and vodka had offered him counsell in the past. Drugs had always provided him with an escape route: the pills, wraps and joints had once offered him respite from the harsh reality of the outside world. Walker shook his head and dismissed his past indiscretions. "Weak heart talk." He muttered to himself. "That thinking isn't goings to help the situation. Think rationally, calm down, deal with the problem and find a rational solution."

Walker's problem was he lived life with his heart on his sleeve, a daily dose of paranoia in his mind and a constant thought that the world was out to get him. He was a decent man, but prone to burst like a bottle of Coke that had been shaken to the point of detonation. He sighed and drummed his hand on his desk, blinking into the screen of his lap top as he prepared another spurious risk assessment. All words and no substance for a client who's lack of social skills lent itself to him dragging off the occasional female into dark alley or two.

A Phil Collins song played a cross his thoughts as Walker reflected on the pertinence of the words............

"Oh think twice, just another day for you and me in paradise............

Book One: HOOLIGAN
CHAPTER ONE:
PLANNING.1987

Walker's excitement couldn't be contained any longer, this was the big day. Wolves were due to play at newly promoted Scarborough, their first match of a brand new season. Walker and the lads were travelling there to join in the fun. They'd already rampaged through a succession of seaside resorts, causing more damage than Hitler's Luftwaffe had managed before the RAF blew them out the sky during the wartime blitz. It must be the sea air that turned the Wolves lads into marauding Viking's, summerised Walker as he reviewed the scrap book containing press reviews of their past activities. There was a definite lack of entertainment to be found on the grey polluted industrial streets of Wolverhampton in 1987. They had to find their entertainment elsewhere; it was simply a matter of priorities.
'Bring out your riot gear, Wolves are here, Wolves are here'. The battle chant echoed through his memory, bringing a smile across his face as he picked up the phone and punched in a number. Walker sighed, strumming his fingers impatiently against the wall as he waited for an answer. "Pick up the phone man," he said aloud. "Fuck me, what's he up to?"
"Hello," Walker`s irritated thoughts were interrupted by the voice on the end of the line.
"Hello Mrs. Harris, could I speak to Pete please?" Walker said, understanding the premise of good manners and respect. Mrs. Harris was a kindhearted lady who'd decided that Laura Ashley was the height of haute couture; she always made an effort to make Harris's friends feel welcome when they arrived at her front door and she had a particular soft spot for Walker. When the door to the Harris's household opened, she would be standing in the doorway; armed with a cheeky smile and a look of defiant mischief in her eyes, while his old man would glance up from his paper and grunt an unintelligible greeting.
 Mrs. Harris would always offer you a cup of tea and a sandwich. Some parents would view their children's friends suspiciously, fortified in the belief that anyone under the age of 23 was subversive and a threat to national security. They would stare down their aquiline noses with a

look of lasting distain and a prejudicial attitude that immediately reinforced the us and them mentality that existed in the battle between the generations, and alienated Britain's youth from the generation that should had provided a positive role model for them. "I'll just get him, is that Gary?" she enquired. Her tone was neutral, she wasn't really concerned with the callers identity. Peter Harris liked to know who he was talking to, or he'd grumble under his breath about being disturbed by people he had little desire or motivation to communicate with.

"Yes, its Gary," Walker answered." Let him know I'm bored and looking for him to come out and play."

Mrs. Harris laughed down the phone. "Like nice boys I hope Gary? I'll just go and get him for you."

After about minute or so, a tired sounding voice, heavy with sleep yawned down the phone.

"Yes Walker, yam up early ay you mate what's occurring?" Harris never sounded like Harris when he spoke on the phone. It was like talking to an impostor.

"Come on Harris," Walker said impatiently."Get your arse out of bed, let's have a few beers before we go into town and meet the lads. Get a head start and all that."

"Go on then." Walker could sense Harris's smile on the other end of the line." Give me half an hour to get my shit together and I'll meet you down The Woods mate." Harris replied, the smile was now clear in his voice. He was waking up to embrace the day, and the semblance of excitement was starting to nestle in his stomach.

The Woods, was the name appointed to their local; a pub they used regularly ,an ugly edifice that was built in the fifties and dominated the social life of the residents that lived on the nearby council estate. It sold a decent pint and experienced an occasional brawl over the weekend. It was a decent venue with good customers, punters who enjoyed a bet over the deal of a card, a game of darts, listening to the juke box, getting drunk and spending their weekly wage packet on honest, no thrills entertainment. The Woods was a typical 'there'll always be an England' pub that can be found on many estates in many cities up and down Great Britain. The only black spot when Walker assessed his surrounding, was a few of the darters that drank there insisted on supporting highlighted mullets. It made them look like southern slack jawed red necks, and they were deluded in their thinking that they were making a positive fashion statement. Walker managed to kept his thoughts silent, these men were beer monsters and best left alone to drink in peace. The trip to Scarborough had been planned for months now; ever since the fixture list had first been published way back in June. The leading lights of the hooligan gangs thought that Christmas had arrived in August. Wolves had finished the previous season positively. Even though they'd lost in the final of the play offs, fueling optimism, within the towns football fans, that this season would provide them with the success their loyalty demanded. Scarborough had been newly promoted into the football league for the first time in their history, adding to the occasion. Leeds was situated only a short distance away and their supporters had been invited to join in the 'off field celebrations'.

Wolves' fans had been involved in several serious disturbances both home and away last season, resulting in a full scale riot when they lost to Aldershot at Molineux, a riot ensued, which left ten police officers in hospital. Walker recalled the chaotic scenes, the feeling of power as the police front line broke under the relentless barrage of missiles, they'd turned and ran away from the advancing hordes. Wolves fans had controlled the streets around Molineux for half an hour. Viva la Revolution!

The violence distracted the fans anger away from the defeat, which ensured their dreams of promotion had been dashed for yet another summer. The leading figures in Wolves numerous hooligan firms waited for the police to request the kick off time be changed and the fixture re-arranged for safety reasons. When it was confirmed the match would take place as scheduled; they sat back, rubbed their hands in glee and thumbed through the yellow pages until they found the heading: Coach Hire. Smiling broadly as they made numerous phone calls to the committed.

The door clicked and dead locked as Walker left his flat with a jaunty step in his stride. He'd moved out of his parent's home a few months ago, things were not going well with his dad and he remembered the old adage: *Two bulls cannot live in the same field,'* he nodded his head in agreement along with the sentiment. Walker wasn't sure he was a bull, but he'd been born in April, under the star sign of the bull, so the rule must apply to him then.

Walker was relieved when he had been given the keys to his independence. His dad was a head fuck: always moaning about this, that and the other. Walker's father was constantly exasperated by his son's behaviour and the frequent attention he received from the local police for a variety of drunken offences. Subsequently he called in a favour from a mate and found him a job, working in a warehouse in West Bromwich which helped to speed up the process of manhood. Walker was proud of his little home. He viewed it with pride, when he finished work he would walk around and survey his empire, satisfied at what he had achieved. He would then take his seat, open his newspaper, listen to the news and crack open a cold can. It was his coming of age ritual.

The flat was smart and modern, with a fully fitted kitchen and two large bedrooms. He'd painstakingly removed the woodchip from the walls, swearing under his breath as he did so. Walker was no DIY merchant and thought a screwdriver was best left in the hands of someone that knew what they were doing with it.

His flat was located on the local housing estate which had just been renovated. All the flats had enjoyed a makeover and the building work had improved the ambiance and feel of the area. The estate experienced few serious social problems; overzealous drunks on the weekend, and a few domestics downstairs that disturbed his concentration whilst watching television on an evening, which ruined his concentration for brief, disquieting periods. However, when Walker analysed the pros and cons over a quiet can or two of his favourite tipple, he realised that it was a quiet place to relax after a hard day with his nose locked to the grindstone.

Walker threw his sports bag into the boot of his old Ford Escort. It landed with a resounding thump, as he slammed the boot shut. His eyes were drawn to the rear window as he looked at the stickers that where displayed in the rear window with silent regret. Two stickers that some previous clown had thought were witty were firmly affixed, they proclaimed loudly that; *his other car was a Porsche,* and, to *stay back there was a baby on board*.

Walker wondered if people made a habit of rear ending cars? Was the problem they lacked confidence in the driving skills of others now the infant Jesus was safely secured in a McLaren car seat? He gave himself a mental bollocking for being too lazy to peel them off. "Fuck it." He said to no one in particular, happy to ignore his own idleness.

Walker pushed the key into the ignition and turned it, the engine sprang in to life first time, with a roar and a cloud of exhaust smoke. His hands punched the air in mock delight before he selected a tape from the glove compartment, carefully pushing it into the deck which was worth more than his car. He adjusted the volume and wound down the window. People who were walking slowly on the pavement, mindful of the peace and intent on shopping for their daily groceries were serenaded by The Specials as Walker roared off into the distance. His fingers drummed along to the beat as he used the steering wheel as an instrument.

He travelled the short distance to the pub, the journey only taking ten minutes, his thoughts focused on the song that was pounding out of his car stereo. Walker had a pocket full of money and a good feeling for the weekend that lay in front of him. The world was a good place to live in today. As he walked into the bar, the lads from 'death row' were already sitting down in their seats located in the corner of the bar, playing cards with serious looks set upon their aged, craggy faces. Walker turned to them and laughed out loud. "Fuck me boys, you lot shit the bed or what? Yam in earlier than me! " He always enjoyed the banter with the old men who used the pub regularly.

"Bollocks you wanker," they replied in unison. "Look at the way you're dolled up you fucking tosser! You've even brushed your hair, you poseur poofter. You pulled then Walker?" They asked sarcastically.

He 'd expected the usual polite reply and bowed to his audience with an elaborate flourish."Always lads." Walker laughed as he answered them and turned back to face the bar, checking out his reflection in the mirror. He was wearing his new Lacoste jumper and some GA jeans, supported with a pair of Rockport boots; a new American brand that had only just been released into the British market place that year. Walker liked clothes, and he liked to look good.

"Yes Roger," Walker greeted the pubs Landlord. "Give us a hand glider mate, and stick an Extra in for Harris please." Roger was a good gaffer. He would always buy you a beer and give you a small slate if you were temporarily down on your luck.

Peter Harris walked in The Woods, looking like he needed a wash. Harris was tall and wiry with bad teeth, skin that resembled sandpaper and a dress sense that matched his teeth. He loved to smoke cannabis, use working girls for his physical needs and drink beer, lots of beer. He drove a beat up car and looked like the lead singer of the Pogues.

Walker loved the bloke; he might look like a bag of shit, a man that was down on his luck, but he was shrewd, intelligent and well respected in the local community. Walker thought that Harris looked and dressed like he did, so people would underestimate him. If you did, you might come second. Harris always left himself room to manoeuvre in a tight situation. He was certainly a handful, always willing to have a brawl. Harris earned good money, but wasted a large portion of his income on Jamaican home grown and massage parlors. Walker and Harris had been mates for a long time; it was hard to pinpoint an exact date. They just knew they were mates and both accepted the fact without the need for an enquiry.

Harris liked to sell cars: cars from auctions, accident and recovery garages, and finally cars from outside people's homes. The question of why he chose to drive a Skoda when he could knock out a host of German vorche sprung technique motors bemused Walker. He used to quote running costs , high insurance premiums and the need not to bring unnecessary police attention to his mother`s door as mitigation for his poor taste. Walker thought it a spurious argument, seeing as he didn't purchase insurance as a rule and his M.O.T's were as fake as his false teeth and his shitty chat up lines.

They downed the first beers in one swallow. "Take it easy Walker," Harris laughed. "Power drinking again? We got a long weekend ahead; don't get the fever for the flavour too early mate."

"You scored, or we got to pick up?" Walker replied, ignoring the beer comment. " A bit of Billy should do the trick and keep us going."

" I'll pick it up in town mate," Harris answered." I've got something sorted out, as well as an eight ball on order, let's grab a cab and fuck off." Harris downed the dregs of his pint, pushed some coins into the pay phone and arranged a taxi for them. He turned to Walker. "Come on then kidder, let's go play." He said with a bad toothed smile.

The pub in the town centre was busy, and alive with the hum of conversation as Harris and Walker entered. Walker was carrying his Nike hold all, slung over his shoulder. Harris had fuck all with him, just the clothes he'd left his house with that morning, confirming his status as a tramp. It was early afternoon, their coach wasn't due to leave until three but it appeared that an early start was to be had by all the lads. There was at least forty of the firm in attendance, standing around in small groups, pints in their hands and smiles on their faces, top drawer bodies who exemplified the mantra of: 'no colours, no runners'.

Harris turned to Walker and said. "Get them in son, while I have a wet and check out shit."

Harris skillfully sidestepped two lads who were quickly approaching the bar before disappearing into the melee.

Walker cursed under his breath. "Fucking tight cunt never gets his round in," fully aware that Harris was off to purchase some of Wolverhampton's finest amphetamine. Harris knew people so he always got a half decent deal off the darker side of Wolves' criminal fraternity.

He rationalised his thoughts and dismissed the early signs of paranoia that had started to get up with him in the morning, keep him company in the afternoon, but failed to give him a blow job when he went to bed.

"Get a grip mate," he told himself. That was becoming his maxim, his mantra for the day. As the beers were placed down in front of him by a surly looking barmaid, the dark clouds on the horizon dissipated as quickly as they manifested. Walker turned to face the crowd and greeted a group of five men that were drinking close by. "Yes lads, how's it going?"

The rest of the group could have been clones. Wall to wall designer jumpers, coats and jeans with badges proclaiming their expense, all the trapping of the new breed of football hooligan. They nodded back at him and one particularly large man answered for them. "Hello Walker, you up for it then?" The leader of the pack walked over and shook his hand.

"Hello Paul. How are you mate? Of course, I've been looking forward to it for weeks now."

Paul Suchley was a monster of a man, a psychopath who it had been rumored had once smashed a glass into some poor blokes face because he'd not stood up for the national anthem when the scheduled programming had finished on BBC for the night. He didn't fit the public perception of mindless football thugs that permeated the Conservative press.

Civilians still expected to see skinheads, wearing Crombie overcoats and ten hole doctor Martin boots. National Front supporters who would support club colours with scarves tied to their wrists as they fought in town centers up and down England. This hadn't been the case for years. But *The Sun* did like to exploit right wing links associated with football violence. The stereotype was salient in the public mindset. Walker was sure it was a conspiracy, ensuring the middle classes could eat their prawn cocktails and slow roasted lamb and wash it down with a crisp chardonnay, safe and secure in the knowledge that their sons and husbands would never be involved with such thuggish behavior.

Suchely was tall, well built and looked respectable with neatly clipped brown hair, attended to in a hair salon, not a barbers. His face could look almost friendly at times, until his jaw line tensed up, his eyes lost their life-force and narrowed when action was inevitable. His nose dominated his face, an antecedent and biting reference to his past behaviours. He was dressed in a Burberry overcoat, Gianfranco Ferre trousers and sensible Prada loafers; expensive, but clearly sensible all the same. He didn't tell people what he did for a living. That wasn't their business, so why fucking ask him?

He drove a Mercedes, and lived in a part of Wolverhampton where trees and grass were an everyday occurrence, not just things that grew in the local park. He'd never been nicked, so he'd never served time in jail. Some people had luck on their side, or was it judgment?

Walker didn't care. Suchley lived for this life; to him football was a military operation, not a day out to be enjoyed. Walker liked the banter, the crack and comradeship with the lads, the adrenalin buzz that lingered in his nervous system after a brawl. Suchley was cold and at times distant. He didn't appear to derive any enjoyment from the 'disagreements' that punctuated the lads Saturdays afternoons. It was rare to see him relax and share funny anecdotes with the lads, which was part and parcel of the ceremony of football hooliganism, as they traveled back to Wolves from various grounds located around England on the train.

He was robotic in the beating he administered to rivals. He wasn't averse to using a 'tool'. However, it was out of order going 'tooled up'. Bottles and glasses were weapons that were used in an 'off'. The English had a code of conduct and would leave the knives for the continental based firms. The Italians were well up for carrying a 'wetter'. It was well known they were cowards who wouldn't fight the Germans in their own country in '43-'45, but would happily slice up an English lad when he was outnumbered.

Suchely turned away from Walker and walked off into the crowd. He was circulating the room, ensuring all the lads were sure of what was expected of them. Walker breathed out; he didn't feel entirely comfortable around the man. He was top notch in a bind, but his mood could switch rapidly and he had the sense of humour of a person who really didn't appreciate a good stand up routine.

Harris returned to the bar and picked up his beer. "Paul been giving you your motivational then Gaz?" Harris's asked a wry smile on his face.

"Yep, I told him death before dishonour and all that jazz, you sorted then?" Walker replied with a grin and a nod.

Harris patted his top pocket and smiled. "We got lift off rude boy." Harris didn't conform to Suchley's standards, and didn't particularly give a fuck. He liked football, he liked beer and a brawl and an excuse to fuck about. He was accepted because he was a solid lad. Never mind that he wore 'ascot' trainers and stonewashed jeans. That didn't matter when he was steaming in. He always used to say to the lads. "Fuck it, you lot going to a dance or a fight, dressed up like a fucking model?" It was true; the lads would waste hundreds of pounds on clothes and then moan when their designer labeled jacket had been ripped during an 'off'.

The coach drive up north was tedious, too many lads with the same old stories. Walker preferred the train when he was going away. But as British rail didn't do open ended tickets and they were stopping the weekend. Suchley had booked a coach to sort out the trip up north for them. With coaches you were tied in. Couldn't move, couldn't piss, shit or swing a cat. The only moment to lift the boredom came when Suchely wanted to stop off in Leeds and have a row with a gang of locals who were milling around outside a large pub. They gave the Wolves lads the wankers sign which incensed Suchely. But even he understood those actions might just bring the unwanted attention of Yorkshire's police force upon them.

They might have taken their time to catch: The Yorkshire Ripper. But their plan didn't involve stalking prostitutes through back alleys in the middle of the night and bashing their head in with a ball-pien hammer. Fifty lads running around the city centre might look conspicuous and bring the police on top in less time than the six years it had taken them to catch Britain's most notorious serial killer.

The coach finally arrived in Scarborough. Walker and Harris breathed out a sigh of relief as they stretched their legs after the long journey, they both scowled as they viewed the local scenery and breathed in the salt air. The crash of wave's always relaxed Walker. He was sure he had read that the sound was a redundant memory of childhood, when the unborn baby was truly safe, locked inside their mother's womb. Whatever the rationale behind the critique he understood he simply liked the sound. He glanced at the breaking waves and drank in the view. The sea was a murky looking colour and the sand looked like it had been used for sewage disposal.

 "Fuck me," Harris spat the words out. "What a shit hole! Makes your flat look habitable Walker."

Walker looked suspiciously over at his mate. "At least I don't live with me mother, you fucking knob," replying with more aggression than he felt. He slapped Harris on the shoulder. "Come on then mate let's find the digs." He added with a hint of concession in his tone.

The group split up into smaller numbers as not to bring too much attention to themselves. The fun and games were scheduled for Saturday, not tonight. It had been a long drive up and the night life was hardly beckoning them to take a trip to the light fantastic. It was a big day tomorrow and time to locate their hotel in the murk. Walker and Harris were pursued by two other lads, as they swaggered off to find a cab. Kerry and Simpson were good lads who also drank in The Wood's occasionally, they were tight and they were firm. They were in enemy territory now, they had to watch each other's backs and stay together in a small but solid unit.

Kerry looked good, dressed well and always had a story to tell, he was shit at cards and that showed in his depressing bank balance. His missus was always in the pub moaning about him gambling away the housekeeping money. She was a good looking girl but a head doer all the same. Simpson was a quiet lad, he liked fishing, loved football, but loved his home life and wife more. A straight going lad; who liked the pub on a Friday and a fish and chip supper on the way home. On a Saturday he was a top lad who would always get stuck in. "Where you off?" Simpson asked. He was sure they had home comforts and he was already looking to put his slippers on.

"We have booked some digs; I think the place is called Fawlty Towers." Walker replied, expecting them to laugh at his the joke. Vacant expressions greeted him in return.

"You're lost to the comedy world you Gaz." Harris was happy to break the view of tumbleweeds that were blowing vividly across Walker's horizon.

The taxi dropped them off at the hotel. The short ride did nothing to illuminate their holiday destination. The streets were quiet, eerily deserted for a Friday night. As they arrived at their destination they stepped out of the tired looking orange Vauxhall Cavalier. All the banter had stopped as they looked at the hotel that rose up in front of them. Their accommodation resembled The Bates motel that featured in Hitchcock's classic thriller, Psycho rather than Fawlty Towers.

 It was perched on the edge of a sheer cliff face and generated an ominous ambience, especially with the claustrophobic clouds which were now gathering in the distance. A neon sign blinked in the dark window, indicating there were vacancies.

"No surprise there then lads, do we care if Norman is on duty?" Walker commented on the amount of rooms that were readily available, even though Britain was supposedly at the height of the summer season. At long last Walker received a smile from the group as his efforts at humour were rewarded.

Twenty minutes later they'd booked in, avoiding the withering stare of the woman on duty at a table which passed for reception. She pointed in the direction of a dark corridor, informing the lads their rooms where located at the end of the tunnel. Two minutes later Harris had rolled a fat Jay and the weekend had finally begun. They'd landed behind enemy lines with no major police attention and no unwarranted interventions. Their mission had been successfully completed.

Walker pulled hard on the joint, drawing the smoke deep inside his lungs and holding it there for as long as he could manage, to maximize the effects of the drug. He blew the smoke slowly out, and enjoyed the blue swirls in the air it created around him. He didn't regularly use cannabis. Weed could make him edgy and didn't help his increasing paranoia, though tonight he wanted a good night's sleep, to awake and feel fresh for the day that lay ahead.

 Walker had been experimenting with drugs for some time now. Starting on solvents at fourteen, even petrol went up his nostrils at one time or another. Walker used to sneak out of the house when his dad had grounded him, edging out through his bedroom window and down onto the sloping porch roof. He would leap the last six foot drop with a flourish and a commando roll. All that was required to escape his captivity and arrive at his mates house: a ginger dick-head named George Radford. Radford lived with his elder sister, on their own in a nice house twenty minutes walk away from where Walker lived. He had shocking ginger hair and pockmarked, greasy pallid skin. His parents had moved to South Africa to find the elusive Krugerand, that all parents seemed so desperate to attain.

Most adults must have been mislead in the presumption that material wealth must equal a happy and contented childhood. They didn't want him to leave the school he was settled into during his important developmental years and were due to return back to England in a year or so when his dads' contract ran out. They must have thought that Wolverhampton was some sort of utopia and their son wasn't going to get involved in any mischief. What did they think was going to happen to a fifteen year boy and his twenty year old sister left alone in a nice house with all the bills paid and a generous allowance on top?

The boys used to sit around Radford's 50cc motorbike; drinking out of 'party sevens', taking it in turns to place their noses into the petrol tank, breathing in the fumes in to get high and 'trip out'. It had got harder to buy glue from the newsagents as the authorities realised that kids we're starting to get lean on household products. Petrol was no problem to purchase unless you were stupid enough to have a rag sticking out of a milk bottle. After all this was 1981 and they were troubled times the boys lived in.

Walker would trip for England, experiencing out of body sensations. He could be gliding through the air, over forests with beautiful trees. It was a great escape from life for him. One day his mates found him crying, huddled in the corner of the garage, hysterical. Walker had gone over to the dark side and stumbled across the bad trip. He'd seen his dad smashing though the garage doors, bright green with veins sticking out his neck and his arms, a vivid caricature of the Incredible Hulk, who'd hunted him down after he had done another impulsive moonlight flit out of his bedroom window.

Walker never forgot that moment, it was vivid in his mind and the memory never left him. From that moment on, he would be reticent in taking hallucinogenic drugs. He would leave mushrooms and LSD alone. It didn't stop his quest for a chemical high, it just limited his options. Then alcohol finally made its way into his drug portfolio. He discovered the magic, memory easing liquid, graduating to speed thereafter.

Alcohol gave him a sense of power, turned him into a man, into one of the lads. It made decision making easy, improved his assertion skills, or so it first appeared. He didn't realise that the knots in his stomach when he woke in the mornings, that were now evident on a regular basis, could be attributed to this new lifestyle. The Friday night binge and vindaloo down the local Indian restaurant were slowly being replaced by the weekend bender with speed taken to pull him through it.

Walker had accumulated a few convictions, court appearances were becoming a regular occurrence for him. He 'd never been a violent boy at school. He got into trouble like other lads did, but it was just boys stuff, being cheeky to the teachers and playing pranks in lessons. He was the class comedian and enjoyed making people laugh. However, under the influence of alcohol he became different, (or so he was told). His moods became deeper, sometimes he laughed, sometimes he would go quiet as if debating some relevant internal topic. Then there would be times when he would lash out and get involved. In those days it was all just lads stuff, nothing serious. This was before the days of the Criminal Record Bureau, so why should he worry about his future? You didn't require an enhanced disclosure to find a job in those days. He had his life in front of him.

He brushed the thoughts from his mind. This was not the time for self-analysis. "Shut the fuck up and enjoy the weekend," he whispered. The cannabis gradually entered his consciousness and his mind unhurriedly drifted into the moonlight melody.

CHAPTER TWO
RIOT

"Fuck me." Walker groaned as the world exploded into view, he opened one eye and assessed his head for residual effects from last night's smoke. He blinked rapidly, allowing his eyes to become accustomed to the morning light pouring in through the thin curtains. Curtains that were unfortunately decorated with a cheap floral design and did very little to enhance to rooms interior decoration.

 He licked his lips tentatively; his mouth tasted of iron and stale smoke, he needed to brush his teeth as a matter of urgency. His shoulders relaxed as the residual anxiety he felt in the pit of his stomach slowly slipped away. He took a quick inventory: he didn't have a headache, there wasn't a weed hangover and he felt like he'd slept. Ok, his mouth was fucked, dry and he could peel paint with his breath but he felt better than expected.

As he looked around the room his eyes focused on Stig of the dump, who was still sleeping and snoring his head off. The covers were pulled tightly around Harris and Walkers were in a knot on the floor. All you could see was a thatch of un-kept hair and a scrawny neck balancing on a emaciated pillow, animal like noises rose up and broke onto Walkers ears. You had to smoke weed when bunking with Harris to knock yourself out. Walker didn't need an excuse to get high, but that reason did hold water. The bloke made more noise when he was comatose than when he was in the land of the living. That lazy cunt would sleep all day if you let him, brain like mashed potato when he was lean! Walker decided to be proactive and shouted. "Harris get up son!"

"Fuck off man, what time is it? "Harris grunted back and pulled the pillow over his head.

Walker thought wryly to himself, pity the selfish wanker didn't do that to deaden the din that he made in the night, at least when he was grumbling he stopped bellowing like a fucking horny Wildebeest.

"Its fucking breakfast time mate, come on, I'm starving man. Must have the munchies left over from last night's draw. I'll go and get the other fuckers up." Walker zipped open his Nike hold-all and removed his shaving bag and relived it of some McLean's toothpaste and a toothbrush. He quickly attended to his breath, drank a pint of tepid water that refused to go cold, even when he ran the tap for two minutes. Sprayed some deodorant under his arms, selected a pale blue Lacoste polo shirt, dark blue Calvin Klein jeans and his favorite trainers Adidas Forest Hill, three gold stripes that proudly embellished the white leather.

Walker had a dull memory of where Kerry's and Simpson's room was located in the darkness off the Bates Motel, but full cognitive skills hadn't yet filtered through into his memory from the murk of last night. He hesitated before he knocked at the door; he wanted to make sure he had got the correct room.

The last thing he wanted was to wake some dopey Doris and her old man up and have them moan throughout breakfast, whilst their hyperactive kids ran round playing Thomas the fucking Tank Engine doing every diner's head in. Walker didn't mind kids; he used to be one once. However ,there was a time and a place for that behavior. Walker decided that discretion was the better part of valour and headed toward reception.

The severe looking woman from the night before was writing into a ledger, her grey blonde head pulled back severely into a bun.

"Excuse me; what room did you give the other two lads please," Walker enquired courteously. No harm in being polite to the matron working on reception he told himself, even if she did give the impression that he smelt of yesterdays shit. Her eyes ran up and down him, with no attempt to hide her distain. The reputation of Wolves fans must have preceded their arrival and unfortunately the accent he tendered was a little broad.

"Eating breakfast," the acidic reply was cordially issued to him and full of pertinent information.

"Thank you for your help." Walker replied, when all he really wanted to say was. Stick it up your arse you old bitch. Walker stifled a smirk as he imagined her with a hammer hanging out her head. Don't let her wind you up mate. Some things are best left unsaid, he thought to himself.

Walker made his way back down the tunnel, back to their room to summon Harris (who was rapidly turning the room into a cave), his t-shirt was creased and supported a picture of the Ramones, an old punk band who Harris listened to.

"You want to borrow a t-shirt Pete or what?" Walker asked.

"Fuck, why? So I can look like a robot solider?" Harris answered.

"Better than a reject from the fucking seventies mate and I was only offering, keep your hair on and your teeth in," Walker replied.

Harris looked at him and laughed, his shoulders rocking gently. "Do one Walks, you've got no class son, come on then let's eat, where's the restaurant?"

They walked down an off white painted corridor, glancing gingerly down at scorched green carpet which was now luminous as light had broke through. A couple of water-colour prints depicting Scarborough in all its finery were hanging at an angle on the walls.

They quickly found the 'restaurant' and spotted Kerry and Simpson examining their breakfasts, pushing tomatoes around with a distinct lack of interest.

"Thirty quid a fucking night for this shit tip," Kerry greeted them with a frown, he was obviously less than impressed with the opulent surrounding. "The plum tomatoes are fucking cold, and I bet the beans ain't even Heinz!"

"Yam kidding me ay ya?" Walker said." Fucking shit beans! Let's call the Michelin guide and get the place blacklisted eh?" Walker turned to Harris. "Show them a bed instead of a bench and this is all the thanks you get!"

Harris replied simply. "Some people are never happy, let's just grab some food and fuck off down to the front."

As if by magic or drawn by Harris's good looks, the Hawk from reception appeared at the table with a pen and order book in her hands, her knuckles were riddled with liver spots and her fingers resembled a nest of crawling worms. For a moment Walker wondered what she was doing taking their order and then thought of an article he had read when he was taking a dump at his mother's house. Women can multi-task. Walker laughed at the thought and the press's constant attention to the battle of the sexes. His philosophy was simple: do one job at a time and do it properly. Walker made the connection in his head that she was moonlighting as the waitress.

"Full breakfast?" she barked at them. It was an order not a question, she was short and to the point with no offers of lightly scrambled eggs, Eggs Benedict or any other delicious culinary delicacy.

"Please," Walker replied. He breathed in deeply, resisting the temptation to tell her to fuck off. It was too early to cause a scene, even if her attitude was starting to get on all their nerves.

"Tea of coffee with that?" she barked at them again.

"Coffee for me please," Walker was a connoisseur with a discerning palate. In his pre-Charlie days, he enjoyed a Columbian mild blend for his morning kick start .

"Tea." Harris snapped. He was as short on banter and charm in the morning as their hostess. He felt if you didn't drink tea in the morning it was un-English, and you should relocate over the channel to where the locals enjoyed eating pond life. Never trust a race that eats animals you can find in the bottom of an English garden.

"Could you make sure that the tomatoes are warm please, I have heard rumours about the food here," he added for good measure. The Hawk hovered, decided whether to strike, then turned and left the table, orders in hand with her nose pointing toward the ceiling and a superior air left in her wake. The breakfast arrived a short time later. Walker viewed the plate and glanced up at the boys with a raised eyebrow. He did like a breakfast, who didn't? Most English people, if you asked them before they were due to be executed what they wanted, for their last meal would reply, fry up. Unless they'd been on the piss, then a hot curry would be their meal of choice.

The sausage looked anemic, the bacon didn't look too crispy, the eggs did have a yolk. but that was all you could say about them. The mushrooms were out of a can, not the ground or were ever mushrooms came from. The beans were not Heinz, they were hard in the middle with a dribble of sauce that had never met a real tomato. To round it off, the plum tomatoes, though not cold, were never going to scald your mouth. The toast though was the right colour and they had bought real butter to the table which offered a small mercy. The coffee was instant, Walker knew it and it wasn't even Gold Blend. Fuck it, its food. Walker thought, as he idly chased a bean around his plate with his fork and ignored the increasing rumbling in his stomach.

The lads made their way toward the sea front, along the cliff face on a steep downward path better suited for mountain goats than humans. After they had finished their gourmet breakfast they needed a walk to burn off the calories. As they turned a corner they could see the beach and seafront laid out before them, the view made them stop and stare. Wolves' fans were playing football on the beach; gold and black colours were everywhere on public display and from their vantage point and at that distance, it was akin to viewing a Salvador Dali painting, illustrating a swarm of bees doing a surreal conga. Until you looked intently and realised the bees were made up of people.

*"WANDERERS HERE! WANDERERS THERE! WANDERERS EVERY
FUCKING WHERE!*

The forceful war cry greeted them as they finally hit the main road by
the sea front. Wolverhampton police must be having a day off back in
the Midlands. Every lad the town possessed appeared to have forsaken
their summer fortnight in Spain; deciding to choose Scarborough as
their alternative holiday destination instead.
Simpson spotted Suchley, nudged Walker and pointed. "Over there
Gaz." Walker turned and saw the rest of the firm. "Come on then boys,
let's make a move."
The lads took hold in a large pub called The Nelson. At midday there
were 200-300 Wolves lads inside, with many more drinking outside.
There were lads from the old Subway Army: a legendary firm. The
Bridge Boys had shown, Paul's crew were there, as were Gornal
Wolves and the Tipton lot; who'd left the Albion alone long enough to
make the trip north. No sign of any local resistance had manifested yet
and there were no sign of the lads from Leeds.
The beer and drugs were doing their job and distracting them from
their intention of causing trouble, it was going to be a good day
regardless, whether or not they turned Scarborough into a war zone.
The roof of the pub was raised with good old tunes: *'Those Were the
Days my Friend,'* and many other Wolves anthems. The police though
apprehensive, were certainly not on top and let the fun go ahead.
It was around two in the afternoon when the pub started to empty and
the Wolves fans started to make their move toward the ground. Five
hundred strong they spread out across the road in a solid wall of
troops. Suddenly a shout of 'come on then,' was heard, the pack
started to move as one energy, with one mind. Their movement
became an earthquake, an avalanche of running feet. Breathing hard,
Walker turned to Harris and shouted. "Local youth have been spotted
down the road."
The road was cleared of civilians by the tidal wave of savage humanity
that was sweeping through the main street. They jumped out of the
way and stared at the chaotic scenes that were unfolding before their
eyes. Cars were jumped over, off sales were looted for plunder by the
rampaging fans.

A few local youth that were stupid enough to stand and defend their town had their asre's slapped and were send back home crying to mummy with their tails between their legs. Walker watched as one lad from Dudley got away with some alcohol- free lager after one shop had been looted. The owner had tried in vain to get the lads to pay for their beer and cigarettes, but who the fuck was going to cough up pounds and pence when the place was being steamed?

"They were never the brightest lot off the Wrener." (A notorious estate in Dudley), Harris laughed, as he watched one lad crack open his can of non-alcohol lager.

It was open day in the town. All the police did was stand and watch. With no one was left to fight, the local shops took the brunt of the violence as the Wolves lads continued to loot them for plunder. It was a 'no cash & carry fire sale,' for the prowling hoards from the Black Country.

Paul et. al made it to the ground and took stock of the proceeding. The police stood and watched, inert as Wolves lads finished off can after can of 'liberated beer'. Kerry tapped Walker on the shoulder as he was drowning the last dregs of his cider, the can raised almost vertically. He pointed to the lines of blue clad officers. "Surely them lot are going to move in now and restore some sort of order?" he asked.

Walker shrugged his shoulders. "I'd have thought so Kes, but they're doing fuck all. They must be waiting for back up, probably coming in from Leeds." Walker hypothesised about the lack of interaction with the local police. He suddenly realised that his bladder was bursting, with a blasé grin he unbuttoned his flies and went to the toilet against a wall, a smile on his face as he could almost physically feel the polices frustration at the liberties that had already taken and were being committed around them.

"Fuck me this is all too easy," Walker said as he waved over to the coppers. He turned to Harris and pointed at the officers who were watching them from a safe distance away "look at the old bill. They're waiting for us to finish the beer we robbed and still letting us in the fucking ground."

Harris shrugged his shoulders. "Fuck um, they cunts, let's get in there." Walker surveyed the scene as he entered. The away end consisted of grass banks with some concrete terracing with safety fencing in the corner that separated the rival fans.

There were a few ramshackle old-brick building that claimed to serve: 'hot teas and the best meat pies in Yorkshire'. Scarborough Football club and police were obviously under prepared for this many fans from Wolverhampton and the level of hostility they'd encountered during the day.

The atmosphere was exhilarating; however there was a dark undercurrent surging through the venue. Harris sought out Walker in the crowd and pointed toward the fencing that separated the rival fans. Walker was still soaking up the intense mood that hung vividly around the small stadium. Harris caught his attention and said.

"Rumours that Leeds Service Crew have landed in the home end and are giving it the big un, let's go and have a look see."

Missiles were already starting to be exchanged between the two sides as Walker and Harris arrived for a closer look. Drain piping was being ripped from building, (which were now defiantly struggling to live up to its boast of previous dinning excellence), and thrown over the fencing towards the opposition supporters. Walker let go of his loose change in a mortar attack. Walls had started to be demolished, to be used for ammunition and he decided that bricks made for much more appropriate missile's than two pence pieces.

Suddenly the roof above the home end crashed through, debris and two Wolves fans landed onto the terracing beneath. Leeds fans rushed forward and kicks and punches rained down upon the injured and unconscious pair. The front lines were breached as incensed Wolves lads started to climb over safety fences, wanting to extract revenge for the events unfolding before their eyes. More fencing was pulled down as the pack found any avenue to get at the jeering Leeds fans. A beach head was secured and a serious offensive launched upon enemy lines. Walker breathed hard as he launched himself over the safety fencing that divided the opposing factions. Harris, Kerry and Simpson were all in close proximity. "Come on then you Leeds wankers. "The battle cry escaped from Walkers lungs like steam out of a kettle. The alcohol and amphetamine raced through his nervous system; mixing with the pumping adrenalin, surging his level of aggression. He didn't feel the punches that landed. He only felt the pride of fighting for Wolves and his mates.

A Leeds fans nose was smashed under his assault. Blood sprayed into the air as he slumped to the ground. Walker and Harris aimed kicks to the head and body, breathing heavily and grunting every time they connected with their feet. A brave police dog appeared into the mêlée as its handlers cowered like cowards in the background. The Leeds fans started to back off slowly and bodies that were left prone on the ground were kicked and beaten by both sides. A no man's land appeared between the two sides, with police officers now armed in full riot gear trying to gain control of the opposing factions.

"COME ON THEN LEEDS!"

The chant went up as Wolves fans charged again, breaking through the police lines.
Walker watched as Harris was hit by a copper wielding a truncheon like a samurai sword. The Leeds lads had disappeared; it was now Wolverhampton's finest versus the Yorkshire police. Walker jumped on the copper that was fighting with his mate, hitting him to his head, neck; back, anywhere he could hit the fucking pig! Truncheons were raining in from all sides and with help from the rest of the crew Walker and Harris fought their way back to the safety of the Wolves end.
Wolves` players and their manger appeared on the pitch, appealing for calm as Wolves` fans milled around on the pitch, the sight was as surreal as this morning's conga. Ambulances appeared at the scene and paramedics armed with stretchers moved the wounded fans out of the combat zone. Walker looked across at Harris and asked. "Fancy some more?"
As Walker waited for a reply he recognised a blonde girl he saw often from other away days out with Wolves. She was attractive and looked like Kim Wilde. Walker gave her his best smile as he attempted to re-enter the fray, his arse hanging over the safety fence as he attempted to climb onto the pitch. By now the police had numbers in the ground and had restored order. Leeds were a spent force, the locals had been turned over and didn't want to know as they backed off into the distance.
Walker turned to Harris, smiled and winked. "I expect we better watch the match now."
The blonde girl hadn't moved from her place on the terracing. Walker checked her out again; as she looked back at him a small smile played across her face. Harris stood in front of his mate and folded his arms across his chest. "This isn't the time or the place Gaz, leave her alone."
He removed a wrap from his pocket and passed it to Walker in an

effort to distract him. Walker accepted the drugs and rubbed some powder on his gums. "It tastes likes shit", he moaned; but the sourness of the taste was forgotten as the rush hit home.

Walker's body started to enjoy the clean feeling of power rushing through it as the drugs took effect. He breathed deeply, feeling the blood rush and his heart pound, when he was getting high Walker believed he could see inside his own body and view the blood pumping through his arteries. "Good fucking stuff that!" Harris was congratulated on his choice of vendor and nodded back at his mate.

The game finished 2:2, which aggravated Walker. The result was still of primary importance to him. The associated violence was a sideshow, a way to displace the anger and frustration at not winning, Walker craved the adrenalin rush and an outlet to de-stress. You needed a valve to release the pressure after being told what a cunt you were all week by some no-mark in a suit whose idea of bottle was shouting at next doors dog when the owner was out. He also experienced an almost pathological love for Wolverhampton. If his town of birth had been a woman, then Walker would probably have stalked her.

A few running battles were being fought out in the side streets; the shirt wearers and the beer monsters were having their day, fuelled by the scenes they'd just witnessed. Police cars were flying everywhere with their blues and twos on, adding to the dramatic effect. Walker turned to Harris and said. "Let's head back to The Nelson." In the running battles they'd been separated from the rest of the firm. "There's bound to be Wolves` lads in there, with more down on the front having a laugh come on." Walker added.

The pub was bubbling when they arrived back, teeming with Wolves lads who were busy exchanging their personal stories of the day's events and proudly showing off their battle scars. Walker was starting to ache from the beating the police had given him and he was dropping like a stone. He turned toward Harris and whispered in his ear. "What you got left Pete?" Walker needed a quick lift.

"What you want?" Harris replied.

 "Give us a dab, I need a boost."Harris handed over the parcel and Walker made his way to the toilet. "Fucking move lads, I'm coming through here." Walker pleaded with the hordes to get out of his way. "How do you expect a man to take a shit?" Walker questioned the throng as he finally made it to the toilets. Looking around, he was not surprised that the Luftwaffe had already paid it a visit.

"Fuck me," Walker muttered. As he looked around at the smashed urinals on the floor and viewed the destruction. "Wanton vandalism." he declared to a lad that was pissing into the sink and decided to do the whole wrap in one go, to save fucking about later.

It had turned nine o'clock in the evening, the sun was starting to slide behind the sea and the pub was dry, out of beer. Kerry had just returned from the digs to inform them with a red face, the landlady no longer required their tenancy because of the day's violent events. They could collect their bags in the morning. Walker shrugged his shoulders pragmatically. "Fuck her Kes, look around you mate, there is enough going on to entertain us. Harris can knock us out later with his wonder root. I take it she didn't find the stash?"

Kerry nodded his head. "Yeah Walks, sounds about right mate, hang around and play it by ear. If she did, I would have been lifted, to be fair. It's safely tucked away in a pair of Simpsons dirty boxers. Skid marks like a fucking test track. Forensics would have a time fucking finding it!"

Walker laughed. "Fair play, get the rest, let's make a move."

The police were in force down the whole front, truncheons drawn with riot shields sitting on their arms, they resembled Roman Legionaries. Police vans were doing sweeps and had cordoned off the whole sea-front.

The dimming daylight was punctuated by the flash of sharp blue lights. The occasional press-hack and television camera was visible as they tried to add to the drama. All the pubs were being ordered to close their doors for the rest of the night. There were outbreaks of sporadic violence around the town as the police attempted to herd Wolves fans into one area in an effort to maintain law and order.

Walker, Harris, Kerry and Simpson paused at a bus stop as they tried to lose the attentions of the police after they'd left the pub. It was covered and at least provided a dry bench which provided some shelter. The great British summer looked as if it was turning distinctly autumnal.

"What we going to do now?" Simpson asked mournfully, already yearning for his slippers, tea and toast.

"Something will turn up, let's walk and lose the Old Bill, find an off sales and do the beach thing," suggested Harris, who was ever the optimist.

At that moment, as if by fate, a gang of local girls passed by. The leader was an ugly skin head with ginger roots and homemade tattoos. She shared a close resemblance to 'Butch' the dog from 'Tom & Jerry'. Her mates hung behind her, well hidden by her girth. They stopped and surveyed the small crew. "What you up to lads?" enquired the ginger skinhead.

"Fuck all." Replied Walker. "There's no pubs left open! We've been thrown out of our digs! This place is a fucking shit hole!" The alcohol and amphetamine gave him the incentive to sum up how he felt succinctly.

"Shouldn't smash the fucking town up then, should you?" She defended the honour of Scarborough with more gusto than the local crew had managed to.

"What's it got to do with you anyway? Fuck off! The place is a fucking dump! Full of wankers and Leeds fans! It goes in at nine! Even the fucking pubs ain't got any beer left to sell!" Walker felt vindicated regarding his previous behaviour and the damage and destruction they'd wrought upon Scarborough with his short and eloquent speech. Scarborough's big day had been ruined, and Wolves were fans were already being awarded the obligatory trophy for being 'the worst animals in the zoo' from the nation's equally balanced and tolerant press.

The skinhead eyed up Walker, taking her time in responding. Was she reflective and judging her answers carefully, assessing each word for validity? Or was she just as thick as most northern monkeys and fucking intellectually challenged? Walker smiled at his soliloquy. The rest of the firm were quiet, they weren't charmed by the obvious delights of the ravishing auburn haired beauty. The rest of the girls weren't that bad looking. They looked a bit ropey, but ropey girls were game in Walkers experience, and grateful. The lads had nothing better to do at that moment in time.

"What you got in mind?" Kerry decided to get involved in the conversation.

The ginger girl turned her eyes slowly toward him, looking him up and down. "What's it got to do w'you mate?" The insolence in her voice was un-disguisable; the charisma of Kerry was obviously lost upon her. She stood her ground and stared belligerently at him.

"Fuck you," he replied. Kerry wasn't going to be intimidated by the ginger version of Porky the fucking pig!

Walker sensed the situation could be taking a turn for the worse. Ever the diplomat and aware that Kerry wasn't in the mood for a debate with this girl he decided to fall on his sword. "Let's grab a beer; you can show off your town to us." Walker hoped the hint of sarcasm wasn't to apparent in his voice and he came across as the sincere tourist, eager to be given the guided tour by the local talent.

"Ok then," the girl acquiesced to Walker's charm. She obviously didn't get a lot of offers to have a night out on the town Walker thought. The group left the sanctuary of the bus stop and began walking slowly down the road, ears cocked as they listened carefully to the girls' directions.

The beer and speed was kicking in again lifting the mood and the conversation between the girls and the lads was revving up; laughter was audible in the sea air as they exchanged irreverent chitchat.

"Where's the offy then?" Walker asked. He needed a beer. A headache was just starting to press on the back of his eyeballs, and he knew that the nightmare of the waking hangover was nearly upon him. He required liquid as he was becoming dehydrated.

"Offy?" She looked quizzically over at Walker.

"Yes, an off sales for a carry out." Walker hid his irritability as he explained what an 'Offy' was still amused by the fact he could play the game like a pro and convince this girl he was genuinely interested in her." Let's grab some beers and head back to yours for a drink eh?" They needed a place to crash and Walker had a plan.

"Party?" The girl was quick to seize on the opportunity for a free night's fun and games.

"Of course," Walker smiled back at her. "When Wolves are in town, it's always a party. Stick with us girls you'll have a good time."

The off -sales, finally appeared like an oasis in the desert. The lads rushed inside eager for a drink. "Any offers mate?" The group aimed their question at a nervous looking Indian lad who was manning the tills and hoping nervously from foot to foot. Walkers and his mates were not averse to a discount. A deal was a deal, however small it was. They weren't averse just to robbing the place, but the police were well on top now and could be felt at every corner. The night was regularly interrupted by the sound of sirens. Walker thought it prudent just to hand over some pound notes, get out of dodge and chill out round this girl's house. A few cans were bought for the ladies, the lads required sprits now for a quicker hit. "Get Smirnoff please Harris, that cheap shit is horrible man! It tastes like fucking nail varnish remover."Walker said.

Harris nodded back. Three bottles of vodka later and armed with two carrier bags full of mixed cans of beer, the party was ready to begin. Walker flipped open a strongbow and bombed it straight down needing a quick buzz. He liked a beer, but wanted vodka, submerging his desire to have a quick snifter. Even when he was off his tits he wasn't going to drink spirits straight out of the bottle walking down the street, acting like a low-life.

The lads followed suit and opened their cans, making sure the girls all had a beer too. They were gentleman after all, they had manners and girls were always more pliable when they were pissed. Drink as you walk. Keep the banter sweet. Have a laugh. Keep it on a level, then we have free bed and breakfast for the night, maybe even a full English breakfast in the morning. What's the worst that can happen? Walker rationalised the processes his mind. Believing that all the steps had been carefully planned; a triumph to this cunning intervention on his behalf.

"Where d'you live then?" Walker asked.

"Just through town love, not far now," the ginger pig replied and pointed vaguely in front of them.

The group reached the main shopping centre. Police, press and pissed up youth (mostly Wolvers) were all in abundance. The girl had linked arms with Walker and he didn't appear to notice as she moved closer; the drugs and alcohol making him unaware of her advances.

"What the fuck you got there Gaz?" The shout came from the pack and it was enough to break his mellow frame of mind.

Oh fuck, Walker thought as he returned to the here and now, they`d bumped into the main body of the Wolves firm. All the lads were eagle eyed for fun and stragglers and he'd just been observed with the ginger pig on his arm, blag it he thought hurriedly.

"Some local girl's lads, them showing us the sights. Wim having a laugh boys, when in Rome and all that." Walker said with a conviction he didn't feel inside.

The Wolves' lads were laughing to a man. Enjoying the joke, the mood in the camp was care-free and euphoric, their job had been completed. It was time for the invading Viking army to rape and pillage, taking the spoils of war for the victors. If that meant dog fucking, who cared! Various comments were perceptible as they circumnavigated their way through the carpet of bodies and broken bottles. Walker laughed it off, with a shrug, as did the others in the party. It was just banter after all and they were off to explore the glories of the local talent. They had the girls on their arms, they had a warm place to crash and they had done their job properly. If they had bitten it would have been worse; showing weakness and angst in front of that lot would mean they would rip you to pieces.

The Ginger pigs' house was a on the tired side of dirty and looked lonely and unloved. There was rubbish scattered on the pathway and outside the front door. Shopping trolleys, old furniture and a sofa with its stuffing and springs were sadly exposed for public inspection. The lawn required immediate attention and hadn't seen a mower in quite some time, it was a riot of weeds and knee length grass. The lads had seen some sights on their travels; they were not snobs but this was a shit hole all the same. On balance sleeping on the beach might have been the favorable option.

"Play it by ear for a few minutes. Have a tot and build a jay." Walker advised the lads with a whisper. "We still have some gear left," besides if all the rubbish is on the outside they might just well have cleaned the inside." Walker was still buzzing and willing to give the night a go. The girls nimble fingers, shaped like a pound of pork sausages located her keys which were in the last of her coat packets.

"Not the best bit of cloth." Walker lamented. She opened the front door with a struggle, the house was quiet and there didn't appear to be the family from the 'Hills Have Eyes' waiting to jump them. The lads just wanted to put their feet up, watch a bit of telly (Wolves must have made the national news) and do some drugs.

The walls in the entry hall were traditional council vogue, bedecked with woodchip wallpaper. The carpet was floral and uninspiring, unopened letters was pilling up on an old table, located by the stairway that lead upstairs. A dog started to bark as they entered the hallway.

"Fuck me, what dog you got then?" Simpson asked, he was not a dog lover. He'd been bitten by a Jack Russell once, when asked where? He replied. "Walsall."

"A Heinz 57, called Murphy." The pig replied. A plump, brindled hound with an excited tail, wobbled into view. Murphy looked well fed and cared for, there must be a heart to be found somewhere within the house. He stopped and surveyed the strange faces and decided to go straight back from whence he came.

"Is there any Irish in you then? " Walker queried, she was ginger after all.

"Not unless your names Paddy lover?" The girl laughed as she answered him. Her eyes disappearing into the folds of fat that had gathered around her face.

Fuck me, Walkers thought. I'm going to fuck the female version of 'humpty dumpty' here! Slap the thighs and ride the waves in. He thought of the music to Hawaii Five 0 and laughed out loud, amused at his own humour.

Walker knew he couldn't do the deed until he was good and ready; at least not until he'd drunk at least a bottle of Smirnoff and done some more speed. He told the lads, he was taking one for the team. Without him they would all be sleeping on a wet beach, he was awaiting acknowledgment for his self-less sacrifice, praise which never materialised. He should have realised then, how drugs alter one's perception.

"This way lads." The pig ushered them into the west wing of the palace. Walker sat down on a faded chintzy chair and the lads placed themselves strategically onto the sofa. They pulled a coffee table over, careful not to disturb the ashtrays that were full of nub ends. Walker opened his gold packet of Benson and Hedges and lit a cigarette, blowing the smoke upwards to add another coat of nicotine to the already stained ceiling. The ladies had gone through to what the lads assumed was the kitchen, to place the beers in the fridge to cool. They arrived back shortly afterwards with a tray full of beers, vodka and bottles of lemonade with sparkling clean glasses. Walker was impressed, they had clean glasses! Harris requested a plate from a petite blond who was wearing a Frankie Goes to Hollywood t-shirt underneath a blood-red-shell-suit-jacket. Her lipstick matched the jacket and her blue eye-shadow was the antithesis of classy. He was going to start building his funny fags and didn't want to waste any of his parcel. He would take speed, but he was a dedicated weed smoker. Kerry had liberated some of the stash from their bags, before he'd summoned up the courage to approach Simpsons boxer's when he went back to the digs.

None of the lads would carry a large amount of drugs with them when they were away on duty with the Wolves, this was a weekend away and provided an exception to the rule. It was bad enough getting a tug for violent disorder, let alone exacerbating the charge with drug offences on top.

Wraps of speed were placed upon the table. Drinks were poured and the girls started to laugh as the party got underway, they wet their fingers to dab the speed offered to them, rubbing the power against their gums.

"Fuck that for a game of soldier's girls." Walker said. "Bomb it." He asked for some toilet-paper and placed some gear into it. Making individual parcels before tossing them around the room. His job completed he sat back and took a deep pull on his vodka and lemonade.

The pig had been waiting patiently for him to finish his task. She placed her ample arse on the arm of his chair and touched his arm. Walker briefly wondered if it would take her weight and looked around the room. Harris was on the other chair, busy smoking and ignoring the petite blond. Simpson was chatting to a girl, she might have been a looker if she appreciated the delights of a haircut and some Head and Shoulders shampoo. He wouldn't do anything with her, he loved his wife and was faithful to her; Walker envied him that.

Kerry was involved with a girl with a pony tail and a loud track suit, she was a good looking girl even with her limited fashion sense. Kerry was a ponce, he would fuck her, simple as. Harris would have a go but only if it didn't involve him stopping smoking drugs for to long. He would probably end up with a blow job when he'd built his last fat un for the night and was lean. Sex was what working girls provided when you were in the mood for a rub down and not having a beer and smoke with your friends.

"Let's go upstairs lad," the pig finally made her move on Walker. "Fuck me it's early yet." Walker glanced at his wrist for confirmation and help. "Bloody hell it's only eleven." He knew his attempts at procrastination would fall on deaf ears. "So!" The pig retorted. "I'm ready for bed now come on lover." she eyed him up like a freshly cooked savaloy that was basting nicely in the chip shop.

The rest of the party had caught wind of the romance in the air. "Go on Walker, get in there my son!" Harris said as they all doubled up laughing."Your woman wants you…………NOW MATE!" He repeated for good measure.

Walker was feeling the effects of the day, the combined beer and speed was turning his mind into mush. He sat back and tried to control his racing thoughts. His overall need was to lie down, rest off and enjoy the buzz of the gear; he wanted to enjoy the serenity of the drugs. As his thoughts came into some semblance of order he felt a familiar tingle down below. A warm feeling in his stomach that meant he was loved up. He examined the pig once more and thought that he wanted a blow job.

"Chuck us a joint over H." Walker would require a fat un for later (not the bird) to help him come down. He hated the twilight hours, when the night was over and you couldn't sleep. It reminded him of being in a fever and delirious, your mind would shoot off on tangents, your concentration shot. If you had a strong joint it could help with falling off to sleep. Harris built the splif with expert dexterity and passed it over to him.

"Good luck mate," Harris had given his mate his last fag before execution. Walker looked back across the room at Harris, who had a smirk on his face which was a sure sign he was stoned and amused.

"Cheers mate you can stop taking the piss now." Walker smiled sarcastically. The pig came back into the room, supporting a lime green garment that she thought passed for sexy lingerie, Janet Reager it was not. The lad's laughter went up a notch in at the sight of her, the look was defiantly incongruous. Walker was now totally off it. Oblivious to her change in her dress sense. He glanced around the room, said his goodbyes and dragged his 'prize' upstairs.

"Ohhh fuck me." Walker was back in the land of the living. His head was banging, there were needles in his eyes, he had stomach ache, his mouth was like an elephants foots, he felt like a bag of tied up shit. A feeling like white water rapids churned over in his stomach. He was experiencing the 'horrors' the inevitable come down off speed. Anxiety and guilt both washed over him in a wave of conscience, causing him to break out in a sweat. He experienced these feeling on a regular basis now, not only when he was coming down off drugs. It reminded him of when he used to wake up on a Monday morning when he was at school and hadn't completed his scheduled homework assignments, knowing he was in for a bollocking off the teachers. Now as an adult he would cover his head with a pillow and conduct an internal debate, attempting to identify why he was so fucking worried over absolutely nothing. Even the smallest task could initiate another round of butterflies and a feeling of foreboding. The avoidance of these situations hadn't become an option for him yet. He would drag himself out of bed, his mind already calculating the negative permutations associated with the upcoming day ahead. Alcohol helped him control the anxiety reaction, it would push the fears away and make Walker feel confident and strong again. He hadn't started to reach for a can at breakfast yet, but the times for starting in the pub were getting earlier. He would get there at ten to twelve now and read the paper to kill time before he would hear the welcoming sound of the door being unbolted. This is what lads do with the life they lead, he would rationalise. Drink beer, fuck woman, take drugs and make money. Isn't that what being a 'geezer' was all about?

Last night's events were hazy, but his head quickly adjusted the to the picture. He glanced to his side. The pig was asleep, bellowing like a fairy princess. "Oh shit man, what the fuck have I done?" Walker had forgotten about anxiety reactions as the situation became concrete in his mind. The worry was real and not imagined. The pig was no oil painting on alcohol and drugs; she was definitely not a great sight to be greeted with first thing in the morning. Snippets of the night played in his head which now felt like an empty dark cavern filled with bats. He slowly moved away from her and dipped his legs carefully over the side of the bed. He felt nauseous, not just because of the hangover but because of the thoughts imbedded into his memory, about what had just happened with her. He'd asked her to sit on his face, he was sure of it!

 He'd fucked her at least twice in the night. She'd told him some lad from Pompey had fucked her twelve times in one session. Good for him, thought Walker, I'm not a competitive man. She'd been able to perform a decent blow job, which hadn't surprised Walker; she must have a talent somewhere because she would be lucky to pull any fucker with her looks and body.

He gagged and managed to keep the vomit down before finding his clothes; fuck the socks he thought as he struggled to dress himself. He had a bag full back at 'Fawlty Towers.' Walker crept slowly out of the bedroom, careful not to make a sound as he made his way gingerly downstairs. On his descent he made sure he walked down the edges of the stairs, his feet on the extreme sides. Floorboards only creaked in the middle, he'd found that out on his many journeys out of strange houses in the early hours after he'd made a drunken mistake.

He quickly located the kitchen. Murphy had shit all over the entire floor and it was like a minefield to find a way to get to the sink for a glass of water. Walker barely made it before he vomited a green, yellow and sour tasting substance into the sink. His eyes were still watering from dry retching as he entered the lounge. The lads were out for the count with no sign of the girls anywhere, the telly was still on and buzzing with white noise. The place looked a mess: empty bottles were strewn about, empty wraps were discarded, and ashtrays had been knocked over, spilling their contents over the carpet. Smelly feet and farts had melted into the surroundings.

Walker shook the lads in turn. Slowly they woke up and joined him in the hangover. They had woken up in Bedlam. They'd all probably caught crabs, and that was not first choice on their personal seafood menu. None of them had gone 'dressed for dinner' so they all had probably caught a dose as well.

"Come on, let's go." Walker motivated the troops. He had more reasons for wanting an exit strategy, the hound of the Baskervilles was snoring upstairs and could be woken at any time. Best let sleeping dogs lie in his opinion. Ten minutes later they were a safe distance away from the house with no clue as to their whereabouts. They were walking through a dingy looking council estate; that had been left out of the travel brochure that invited the public: *To come to sunny Scarborough.*

The lads knew they'd only walked about half an hour from The Nelson to get to the pigs' house. They couldn't be far away from their destination. All they had to do was find the sea and they were clear, home and free.

It was early in the morning when they found the main road back through to the sea front. Wolves' fans had obviously had a good night, despite the lack of welcoming landlords. Lads were using flags for tents, sleeping bags and shelter. The beach had at least fifty sleeping bodies on it. Glass littered the street, the debris left from a few broken windows. It wasn't that bad, certainly not as bad as expected.

The main trouble had occurred on the way to and from the ground, not at the sea front. Families were up and about, walking down the promenade talking to each other and drinking in the view. Relieved

that Saturday was now past history and merely provided
sensationalist headlines for the Sunday scandal sheets.
Now they could get back to enjoying their summer holiday and wrap
up warm from the sea breeze which was akin to a force ten from
Navarone. "Who the fuck would pay to come here for a week?" Walker
queried
The dads looked anxiously over at the Wolves fans, aware of
yesterday's events. However they were in no danger, there was no
chance of any trouble. They didn't bother families, only like for like
minded lads who knew the score. Besides, it was far too early in the
morning to have a spar.
"Morning to you." Walker greeted the families with a happy smile and
a strut in his stride. When he was with his mates and they were around
him; the tendrils that crept into his mind, causing his anxiety would
disappear with the distraction they provided him. He was back to
normal he told himself. His head was mashed because of the drugs and
not for some deeper reason and he could live with that.
They quickly located Fawlty Towers; their bags had been left for them.
Locked in the office behind reception. It was obviously meant to be a
pit stop, go in, collect your stuff, turn around and fuck off back from
where you came, the message hardly subliminal. The lads were alright
with that plan; they really didn't want to exchange anymore
pleasantries with 'Hawk the Slayer'.
They slung the straps to their bags over their shoulders and made their
way down to the nearest café to find shelter from the wind and enjoy a
hot drink. The coach picked them all up at two from the town centre; it
had been a long morning and all the lads wanted to do was to get back
home. The locals cheered and clapped as the last dregs of the invading
army left occupied ground. For some of the firm it was back to work in
the morning, back to normality. Their days of being somebody, done
and dusted for another week. They would fit back into acceptable
society and run like rats around 'Skinner Boxes' for their wages. Others
had to sign on and some had 'earners' to organise. They all came from
different backgrounds in the dim days of the working week. Come the
weekend they shared one vision: this was Wolves, this was football,
and this was life.
On the way out of town some comedian had painted a message close
to where a sign proclaimed:

Lewisham. Overly Medicated

'Welcome to Scarborough.'

Reassuring tourists and visitors they had reached their dream holiday destination. It read:

'Who put the scar in borough?'
WOLVERHAMPTON WANDERERS FC
PRIDE OF THE BLACK COUNTRY!

CHAPTER THREE
WALKER

Walker entered the pub in Wolverhampton town centre. It was Saturday and a home match versus Torquay United was next on his agenda. Scarborough was now a month down memory lane. The fallout from the disturbances had lead to an FA enquiry and Wolves fans being banned from all away grounds for a total of six games. Torquay had no lads, none that would make the trip to the West Midlands anyway, so the Wolves firms could relax and have a day off. He glanced around the bar; it was half-full considering it was still relatively early. Wolverhampton was always busy on match day. Regardless of what division Wolves found themselves to be in. He noticed a man, standing alone at the end of the bar with a short glass in his hand, clinking the ice to the sides as he swirled the liquid around. He had highlighted hair, styled in a 'Don Johnson' look, white trousers, no socks, loafers and a jumper with no shirt underneath that highlighted a gold chain that hung softly around his neck. Walker felt an immediate resentment toward the man. His presence was incongruous to the clientele that usually drank in' The Leopard' on a match day and an almost visceral anger rose up inside him." Fucking poser," he growled, suddenly feeling violated. It was akin to a feeling of intrusion, a feeling that he was being spied upon. He glanced around, aware that he was staring at the.....the fucking hairdresser and his eyes fell upon the blonde girl from Scarborough: the 'Kim Wilde' look-alike. She was sitting with another dark haired girl and a lad Walker knew. Walker raised his hand in recognition toward the lad, ordered a pint, turned and moved toward the table. "Hello Snowball, how are you mate?" The lad was that pale, he made Walker look like an Indian geezer. Walkers' legs were that white they reflected the sun when he was on his annual pilgrimage to the med.
"I'm good Gaz, you?" "Safe as mate." Walker looked around the table at the girls and offered his hand and introduced himself."Hello there ladies, I'm Gary and I'm very pleased to meet you. Can I get you both a drink?" Walker was feeling confidant on that Saturday and had an almost cocky air about him. When he acted like this, people failed to recognise his other side, the side he managed to cover effectively. The girls took his offered hand and they introduced themselves, giggling as

he kissed their knuckles. The blonde girl's name was Natalie; she was from Shrewsbury and drank half a lager. The dark haired girl was called Sarah and she drank the same, they probably went to the toilet at the same time too, Walker thought as he returned to the bar. He gave the man a quick stare, which wasn't retuned and ordered their drinks.
"Two halves and put a lager top in for Snowball please."
He returned back to the table and asked permission to sit down and thought to himself, today could be interesting after all. The blonde girl, Natalie, turned to Walker and spoke quietly. "Do you know him?" She nodded her head toward the extra from Miami Vice.
Walker shook his head. "No why?"
"The look you gave him when you first came in, that's all." Natalie said. Walker smiled back at her. "Really? I didn't think anyone was watching me."
"You always give total strangers looks like you want to kill them?" Asked Natalie.
"Only when they're dressed like that dickhead." Walker replied. He smiled at her as he inclined his head in the man's direction. He was aware that Natalie had checked him out before he had seen her, yes maybe today might be interesting after all.
Gary Walker was twenty one years old. He'd filled out since he was a kid and worked hard in a warehouse, lifting tonnes of packages every day. This was reflected in broad shoulders and good sized arms.
Walker was a stocky lad with the beginning of a slight beer belly, which was camouflaged by his thick set appearance. His hair was fashionably cut in a flicked wedge with a step at the back. It'd darkened naturally as he'd grown older.
He'd started out life with reddish if not bright ginger hair and was happy it had turned darker as he got older. His face was covered in freckles, which had thankfully also faded with age. Walker hated his freckles; they had been another target for the piss-takers back at school. Walker wasn't exactly Brad Pitt, but he wasn't ugly either. He had certain something that the ladies seemed to like.
Walker was raised in a middle class home, in a prosperous area of Wolverhampton. His dad had done well for himself and was always willing to remind him of the fact. Most children, especially Walkers mates would have loved his childhood, (on peripheral inspection), Walker though, would have swapped it immediately. His parents were

too busy making money to care about what he did, both in and out of school.

When he had made it into the school football team, ten dads attended on a Saturday morning to watch their sons sweat for the cause. His dad was safely ensconced in his leather armchair back at home, with the sports pages on his lap, as he worked out the latest form for his one vice, the horses. Raising him, and teaching him how to interact with his peers and people in general had been left to the television set.

Both his parents had been raised in tough working class areas in the Midlands. His Dad in Birmingham, his Mom in West Bromwich. He understood they wanted a better life for him and his sister, however knowing and understanding didn't make the pain of his childhood evaporate. He was brought up by his Nan and Granddad in the six week holidays and by baby sitters after school on weekdays.

His dad would attempt to purchase his affection, furnishing him with toys, especially action men, hoping the relationship he formed with the action figures would make up for the lack of bonding he enjoyed with his father. This was Walker`s problem he identified when reflecting on the mistakes he'd made later on in his life. His parents had overemphasised material love to the detriment of being emotional role models.

His mom tried her best and he was sure that she loved him, but she was soft and overcompensated for the lack of quality time spend with him. Walker was sent into the coliseum of school, defenseless and ill prepared for the nightmare that awaited him there.

His dad was always tired from work when he arrived home in the evening. Far too tired to teach young Gary how to be a man and act properly in company. His mother would take compensatory measures with unauthentic acts that did nothing to aid his development. She wasn't to know that this was not what little Gary wanted, oblivious to his real needs. She would send him to school, dressed in a 'Kojack' raincoat, with sensible shoes, his hair cut by his sister (with relish) and an attaché case.

The sharks had circled him when he arrived at his new school, smelling blood; it would not be long before they struck with relish. Walker ran the gauntlet and the bullies had their fun with him.

He learned, adapted and attempted to fit in with the other boys. He began to make friends, he learned that he could made people laugh, having a natural gift to be quick witted with a cutting one liner. He wasn't a natural fighter, but he wasn't a coward either. Walker always felt superior even when he was getting a beating. He understood that they did this to him because of some misguided jealousy. He had a few fights, but never enjoyed them. Some lads would happily fight all day. Walker didn't enjoy the act, but as it was a pre-requisite of being a lad and a way to prove your worth to your mates, he persevered with the chore. Walker observed and learned how to behave from his peers, his dad still far too busy to show him the male ropes.

Finally the bullies lost their motivation in targeting him. As he graduated through his school career he became one of the lads, one of the local crew, only rank and file, but part of the army of lads that were chosen to protect their area. He wasn't known as one of the recognised 'hard knocks' in his school year, but people had started to take liberties with him less and less.

Walker was bright, he knew it, the teachers knew it and his mates knew it. Unfortunately this was not reflected in his academic work, or his grades. He was content to fail and did not possess the assertion skills to break away from the poor influences in his life. He continued to get into trouble and took pride in the reputation he was building as an amusing heckler to his teachers. He always felt that he was on the outside, looking in on life, now he had his status it was easier to explain this role.

One afternoon, after school somebody decided to get high on glue. Gary, always open to peer pressure to fit in, accepted the bag and got stoned. More worryingly Walker liked getting high, he liked the diverse feeling that became part of him. He wasn't a scared, timid little boy when he was on his vibe, he was a man, able to deal with all the problems that life had already started to throw at him. Walker had started to drink at fifteen, he'd then actually won a fight whilst under the influence of alcohol. He'd given some twat with a reputation a beating when the banter had gone too far. The alcohol had taken away his inhibitions and the fears associated with violence. Walker made the correlation and came up with a flawed conclusion: get pissed, be a hard man, get respect, and life would become easier. In the movies, on the silver screen all the leading men were tough guys so Walker chose that way in life, aided on his quest by his thirst for alcohol.

Walker experienced dark moods when he was a child, he would become sullen. He didn't hurt animals, but he could be unkind to his mother's pet cats. They got more attention than him and even though he knew it was stupid, he resented them for it. The moods didn't go away with age; they became increasingly profound when he was unhappy. Walker would hurt 'things', himself and finally when drunk, other people. He was a tree and he'd decided to hide himself in a forest of violent drinkers, hoping that he wouldn't be discovered by lurking lumberjacks. The last few years in his life had been a tranquil period. He'd done the girlfriend thing on and off, but mainly off. Walker got bored quickly always wanting to move on and discover another island with greener gras

s. His mates just boasted about wanting to fuck as many women as possible. Walker didn't get off on it. He liked girls, but he wanted more than sex from a relationship. Walker wanted acceptance and love, he thought the medium of marriage would make an appropriate platform to serve these needs.

His last years at school were a journey through periods of social upheaval that left an indelible mark on his political outlook. There were the riots of '81, when whole communities, disenfranchised and frustrated by the conditions they lived in and hopeless position in 'Maggie's new order' erupted and violence was brought to inner city streets up and down the country.

There was the great recession of '82, when the manufacturing base of the economy was ripped to shreds and whole working class communities lost their means of income and ways to become 'socially mobile'. To climb the class ladder as the Tories professed was the way forward for the working classes. A way to shed light at the end of their personal tunnel. Wealth was promoted above having a social conscience and the poor, the weak, the vulnerable in the political spectrum were ruthlessly targeted as they supposedly accepted their subservient place at the bottom of society. What was point of achieving good grades at school? Walker would tell the careers advisers. There were no jobs; no future for the young, the outlook was bleak from where he stood. Working class communities had become a wasteland of no hope. A breeding ground for gangs, who would accept any outlet to alleviate the boredom and frustration they felt after being ostracised by polite' society.

Then there was the Falklands war of '82. Walker had watched it develop with interest, watching the news and keeping newspaper headlines in a scrapbook. He wanted the soldiers to win, wanted them to return home safely and supported them in fighting a war for the

United Kingdom. The Tories were trailing in the polls. Their government was proving to be the most unpopular in history, their time in power was running out and an election was just around the corner. Maggie was on her way out of government after a term of social discord, and economic failure. *The General Belgrano,* an Argentinean war ship was torpedoed sailing away from the exclusion zone that Britain had imposed around the distant outpost.

Diplomatic avenues that that had been initiated and explored by the United States were close to fruition, peace was close at hand. On the 2nd May 1982, 323sailors lost their lives out of a total 649 Argentinean war dead. The British lost 257 killed, 906 souls lost in all.

Walker blamed Thatcher for the loss of life on the Belgrano. He was sure it was deliberate decision she taken in a ruthless ploy to get re-elected; as she did by a landslide in 1983. She stated that the sinking of the old American cruiser; once voted 'the luckiest ship' in World War Two was politically expedient and militarily essential, she'd no choice but to take this action.

The Suns headline screamed: *"GOTCHA,"* to a country that was willing and ready to go to war. Walker wasn't concerned about the number of enemy casualties at the time; they`d invaded a sovereign nation and got what they deserved. However, that many dead to promote the self- serving interests of an unpopular government, with a political philosophy that marginalised the working classes and made the rich richer with a message that declared: who gives a fuck about the poor? Was an expensive price to pay.

Walker had left school and was working in the warehouse when the miners' strike of '84 was called. This was Maggie's chance to break the hated unions and beat the working man once and for all. If she could eradicate the working classes, then the labour vote would be broken forever and the thousand year British Reich could begin in earnest.

Walker watched the battles on the evening news. Hundreds of uniformed thugs beating the miners with truncheons; drunk on overtime. Their mandate; to inflict as much pain as they could by their masters in Whitehall, while they sat back in their leather Chesterfield sofas, drank their expensive Brandies and faced the cameras with looks of mock concern on their faces, while the coal industry was decimated and more communities bled dry by the Tories in their class war.

The unions led by Scargill held out for nearly a year. Activists were jailed, people died, and woman and children starved as their husbands fought on for their jobs and beliefs. Maggie dined well at her table. Mr. Scargill, though the flag bearer of the left, didn't go hungry either. The poor as always paid the price for the ideological struggle of their leaders.

Maggie won another war on the backs of the public, and the middle classes chaired their new leader and hailed her name. Who cared about the people on the estates? They had the opportunity to better themselves; the politicians informed the masses, as they pointed their fingers accursedly at *the* social pariahs and blamed them for the woes that had befallen the nation.

Unfortunately they weren't informed, that if the menu choice was limited, so were the options you could choose from. The public had yet to feel the bite of the Poll Tax, Black Wednesday or the myriad of scandals that lead to her downfall in 1990. Her own party now thought her unelectable as the public finally started to question her right wing philosophy and her position as Prime Minister. As the originator and architect of Thatcherism her position became untenable. She'd become a liability to the Tory cause and their mission for perpetual power. Subsequently, the Ides of March fell upon Maggie. She was pictured with tears in her eyes as she left Downing Street. Perhaps her tears would have been better served for the social schism that she'd created and left us as her right-wing legacy.

The door to the pub slammed, and Walker returned to the here and now. He hoped he hadn't been noticed, 'going away' for a while. The girls didn't mention it if they had.

Walker became embroiled in the small talk that introduced strangers to each other. The hour passed quickly with the alcohol loosening their tongues and helping the conversation develop. Harris and the others had made it into the pub and joined them at the table. The girls laughed at their jokes and the banter and camaraderie that existed between the group.

Walker liked the girl called Natalie. She looked good, her clothes were not traditional high street fashion, but she easily managed to carry her own personal look and exuded calm. She had a soft face, full lips, sparking green eyes and an impish grin which suggest a roguish alter-ego. She easily handled the lads clumsy attempts at sophisticated chat as they tried to one-up each other to gain her full attention. Her retorts were sharp and humorous and she gave as good as she got whilst talking to them. She and Walker enjoyed brief moments when they shared information and general conversation and he had a feeling she was interested in him. Walker was defiantly interested in pursuing her.

Most women didn't like traditional male activities, but she went to the match, (Walker had seen her at a few grounds). She liked to go out and have a good time, she was single (bonus), had a job (double bonus, she could get the round in). She listened to the same music as Walker, (Numan, and other bands from the early eighties). Walker was buoyed by the fact they shared common interests and his confidence in talking to her rose as he relaxed. He glanced at his watch; it was rapidly approaching three o' clock, time for kick off.

Harris and the rest of the lads that in 'The Leopard' weren't arsed about attending. It was only a small game and not worth the entrance fee to get in, they could find a better way to spend their money. Natalie wanted to go. The match was the reason to be in town, not to spend the afternoon getting drunk and she told them so.

Walker picked up on the cue and invited her to accompany him along. She accepted with a smile on her face, he smiled back and excused himself from the table. "If we're leaving in a minute I need to go to the toilet Natalie." Walker said.

"Too much information Gary, do what you have to do. I'll be ready when you get back," she replied with a casual smile.

Walker stood up and made his way through the thinning crowd to the toilet. Harris's was leaning against the urinal, a stupid look upon his face as he expelled a steady stream of piss. "What you think Pete? She's fit mate, I think I've pulled there kidder." Walker said.

"She's fit," Harris agreed. "And she likes Wolves mate, you got a first date at a football match and she is already half pissed. Does it get any fucking better?" Harris added.

"Not really." Walker laughed and left the toilet. Happy with the result of their impromptu conference . As he re-entered the scrimmage he spotted Natalie at the bar and walked over to her.

"Probably best we leave now," she nodded back at him. Walker reached for her coat and helped her to slip into it. They left the pub together and waved goodbye to the rest of the group who were left inside. Sarah had decided to leave ten minutes ago, to check out the local shops and they'd arranged to meet back in Shrewsbury later that evening. Wolverhampton had a better choice of fashionable outlets than Shrewsbury and she relied more heavily on generic fashions than Natalie did.

As they walked in the sunshine they were both slightly merry, courtesy of the alcohol and high on the atmosphere in the street, Wolverhampton always bustled on a match day. Walker's lines were flowing and she was giggling at his inane rambling and silly jokes. She slipped her arm through his as they walked through the streets up toward Molineux: the Holy Grail.

There were lads scattered around the town centre in small pockets, standing outside pub doorways. Walker greeted them as they walked past and several comments were aimed at him. She looks a bit different from that one the other week Walker. Sacked the other one then Gaz? Walker laughed them off and assured Natalie he would explain it to her later; it was a very long story.

They arrived at the South Bank, a huge roofed terrace end, where the true believers stood and prayed every other week to the footballing gods. Walker drew a twenty pound note out of his pocket as they joined the queue. "Let me pay," he offered.

Natalie declined with a smile. "I can pay for myself, I'm an independent woman. I'll let you pay next time you take me out."

"Next time?" Walker asked excitedly.

"Yes, if you behave yourself!" Nat let a playful smile slip across her face.

"Me behaving? That goes without saying" Walker said.

As they entered the ground Walker stood in line for his obligatory steak and kidney pie. "You fancy a pie or a drink?" He asked politely still determined to impress her and show his charming side, eager to prove he was a gentleman.

"No, thank you. I'm fine, I'm trying to lose a bit of weight actually," she answered. Her accent was exquisite; it reminded him of fresh berries picked straight out of a farmer's field.

"You look great, you're a beautiful girl." Walkers took the offered cue. He meant every word of it. He found it strange that he could be honest about how he felt, without feeling that he was pulling a cliché on her.

"Thank you," she replied as she looked into his eyes. Walkers sincerity wasn't lost on Natalie. She grabbed his hand, and squeezed it. "Show me where you stand then big man."

Walker had been giving it the 'big un' all day. He laughed and appreciated the joke, leading her to where he stood on the terracing each week.

Eyebrows were raised amongst the crowd on the terrace steps when they arrived. "Hello Walker, who's that?" Paul Suchely pointed his finger at Natalie's chest. His manners lost. Suchely didn't miss a thing and he didn't miss a match. It was a motivational obsession for him, to prove a point; so he could dangle it over the heads of the other lads like the sword of Damocles when he had one on him.

"This is Natalie lads, "Walker introduced her to the boys that had bothered to pay the entrance fee to watch the game. They mumbled their hellos and nodded back at her. Nat smiled and waved, oblivious to the stir she had created. Fifty or so of them where by the fencing, salivating when they looked across the no man's land at the few supporters that had made the trip up north to Wolverhampton.

"*WE ARE WOLVES, WE ARE WOLVES, WE ARE WOLVES!*

The battle chant roared out from the massed ranks as both teams were lead out to music. The Liquidator rang out across the stadium.

"*FUCK OFF WEST BROM, THE WOLVES.*

The crowd sang along, introducing their own lyrics to the song.

Lads were hurling themselves at the fences, fists pumping, group hypnosis well underway as the teams warmed up on the hallowed Molineux pitch.

Walker steered Natalie away from the main body of the firm. This wasn't the time or the place to for her to view his extracurricular activities, even if she had mentioned that she'd noticed him trying to climb onto the pitch at Scarborough. They headed a short distance away to where a few of the less committed lads were standing; lads that could hold a conversation, without throwing a sharpened coin at the heads of opposition fans.

They continued to enjoy each other's company throughout the match and the game went well for them despite Wolves poor performance on the pitch. She seemed to enjoy his company, she laughed at his jokes even when they were not funny. Walker was convinced he was making a lasting impression as his latest ditty resulted in a laugh and a playful slap on the arm.

They bumped into Rob Carter. Who was a good mate of Walkers. Carter was a top lad with a brain and respect for others. They bounced off each throughout the game, and their banter made up for Walkers poor taste in one-liners. They made sure the only dull moments for Natalie were on the pitch. Wolves finally lost 1: 2.Walker needed cheering up and food generally did the trick for him if there were no opposition supporters to attack. "Are you hungry yet Natalie?" Walker asked." We could go and grab a bite to eat." Walker wanted an opportunity, an excuse to prolong the date.

"I've got to catch my train back soon." She replied, thinking she detected a hint of rejection in his eyes. "But it's not for half an hour or so, I'd like to come with you if that's ok?"

Walker beamed back at her. "Of course it is." Natalie was reading from the same hymn sheet and Walkers heart beat some more.

Carter heard the exchange and added. "Yes Walker, lets head off and get a kebab then mate." He might usually have been quick on the uptake but today he didn't consider the premise that two was company and three was a crowd. Walker liked a kebab. They were a reasonably new fast food phenomena that were springing up in Turkish takeaways located in big town centers. He would never look back from the moment he had first tasted one with extra chill sauce after a night out in Birmingham.

Natalie confirmed she was fine with the arrangements and would happily go with the flow.

Carter walked off in front of them as they left the ground. The streets around Molineux were busy but clearing quickly, the sun was out and the result hadn't seemed to have affected the supporters. Most still had a smile on their faces. Carter was on the mooch, and dived down an old Victorian alley in the town center that headed toward 'The Leopard,' he'd finally given the loving couple some space.

Walker followed with Natalie on his arm, he looked slightly confused with the route that Carter had decided upon and shouted. "Where the fuck you going Rob?" Carter turned to reply to Walker and at that moment, several police officers, happy at the opportunity presented to them grabbed Walkers arms, and shouted the obligatory line. "You're nicked mate!" It was a line straight out of The Sweeny.

"What?"Walker said. He was confused and wanted an explanation. "What the fuck for? I ain't done shit?" Walker struggled briefly, going through the motions but he knew it wasn't worth the calories exerted.

He was angry at their behaviour and still slightly drunk. Dark clouds had started to roll in and were beginning to rain on his parade. "Do me a favour? Are you being serious lads?" Walker attempted to appeal to their better nature and entered into negotiations to secure his release. Instead the police officers thrust his arms up his back and frog marched him up to the waiting white van that was marked, *'West Midlands Police.'*

They knocked on the back door and Walker was thrown inside like an old bag of rubbish when it finally opened. He blinked as hit the floor, wide eyed with surprise at the treatment he was receiving. He sat up and eyed the interior of the van; they had three captives, the brave old bill.

"Fuck me lads, what's going on," he asked. Walker was talking to his fellow prisoners, the coppers that were in the back ignored him, sitting down with self-satisfied grins on the faces. Walker wanted an answer off anybody who could offer him a reasonable explanation for his current tight spot. He still couldn't believe how fucking puerile they were being. "Has it kicked off in town or what?" He asked again.

Walker still required a reason to the unwarranted attention he was receiving. The other lads looked as pissed off as he felt. Fuck knows, was the general consensus of opinion amongst the gloomy faces that sat dejectedly with him inside the van. The police officer sitting with them had a patronising smile on his face. Walker looked into his fat porcine face and laughed. "You fat fucking cunt, I bet you take it up the arse, you fucking nonce!"

"Not as badly as you will, when we get back to the cells boy, we'll beat you and make it look like you have fallen, you gobby little shit." The copper answered with the smile unmoved off his face.

Walker sulked in the corner of the van and rationalised his current position. The old bill were bored and looking to inconvenience people, it was that simple. Walker did the sums in his head and came up with the right answer. To add insult to injury, this was the first decent girl he'd pulled in years and now he had been arrested for doing nothing. The feeling of anger and sadness melted together in his mind and he abused the police some more for their petulance. "Bet your mother made your fucking sandwiches this morning eh mommy's boy?"Walker added for good measure.

"Carry on son." said the smiling policeman.

"Why? You going to try and fuck me in the cells? I've already told you, you're a fucking nonce!"

The van drove slowly around the streets in the town centre looking for more victims. Walker saw Natalie through the windows, making her way slowly to the train station. He started to bang on the shatterproof glass to get her attention.

One officer looked at him. "That your girl then lad? "Was this copper decent? Walker hadn't met many coppers with a heart.

"Yes," came Walkers reply. "I just met her today," he added, hoping for added sympathy.

"Slow the van down Norris let this one off, his missus is out there and he has just met her."

Walker could not believe his luck. There was a God, he was omnipotent, and he was gazing down on Gary Anthony Walker right this minute. Walker stood up to leave as the van slowed down.

"Sit the fuck down you stupid little prick, the only place you're going is to the cells, calling me a fucking homo." They pushed him back down into his seat with a little too much relish and Walker knew he was on thin ice with them. The Old Bill pissed themselves at their practical joke, they were still laughing amongst themselves as they pushed Walker firmly back down on his seat for the second time as he struggled with them.

 "These football twats are as thick as shit, all they can do is sign on and get pissed at the match, fucking bunch of wasters and wankers." This was a cutting- edge social commentary from the Sergeant, who had obviously researched the subject of sub-cultures thoroughly.

They arrived at the station and were led out of the 'Paddy wagon' in handcuffs and were booked in by the duty sergeant. Walker was shown to his cell and waited patiently to be processed. He didn't like being locked up and even though he now had a few convictions related to football, being in a cell drove him mad. His convictions ranged from: drunk and disorderly, violent disorder, to entering a designated sporting event whilst under the influence of alcohol, assault and all the other charges the government could invent to ruin Saturday afternoons for the masses. God he fucking hated Margaret Thatcher! He was also piling up the convictions away from football: criminal damage, theft, assault occasioning actual bodily harm. He'd been charged with a section 18 wounding with intent and causing grievously bodily harm during a scuffle with some beer monsters in his local area.

They were pissed and underestimated the local youth. Their mistake. They ended up on the wrong side of a serious beating. Walker had been found not guilty of the wounding at Crown Court, his first step into the serious arena. He was found guilty of a lesser charge, and ordered to complete 100 hours community service and pay victim compensation as a deterrent and subsequent punishment.

Walker smiled as he was released from custody, he'd been in the cells for five hours. He clasped his charge sheet in his hands as he stepped back out onto the street, notification that he had been bailed to appear before Wolverhampton's magistrates courts in four weeks time on a charge of 'Threatening words and behaviour'. Walker walked the short distance to the taxi rank and jumped into a cab, instructing the taxi driver to take him to the Dog and Partridge.

The Dog and Partridge was a nice pub, where the beautiful people choose to drink on a Saturday night. The lads from The Woods would be down there, on the mooch for a pretty girl to spend some quality time with. The taxi arrived at the pub twenty minutes later; there were a few couples outside enjoying the warm September evening.

Walker paid the driver with a five pound note. "Keep the change mate." He was happy and relieved to be back on the street. They could easily have kept him in overnight. He was pissed off and frustrated about getting arrested again, it was happening far too often now. His criminal record was growing and he hadn't made a penny out of it.

"Isn't like I'm a fucking villain." Walker muttered in disgust at his latest brush with the law as he entered the pub.

The music was loud and the girls were in abundance, he looked around and saw Harris and Carter at the bar. Great timing he thought I can finally get a beer out of Harris.

"Alright Gaz how's' your day been?" Harris asked with a smirk. They turned to face Walker, Carter and Harris appeared to be enjoying a joke at his mate`s expense. Walker looked into his eyes, he wasn't pinned up, he was simply having a wind up. Walker accepted the banter and ignored the bait that would lead to a heated debate; when he just wanted to relax with a beer and forget about being a cunt.

"Heard you had some bad luck Gaz," the look had gone from Harris's face. He accepted this wasn't the appropriate junction to get off and have a joke at his best mate's expense. "Fancy a beer then Walks, cheer yourself up?"

"Diamond White 'H' please mate."Walker answered gratefully.
Diamond White was a shocking drink that caused a man to have fits
and lose his memory when he'd fucked up big style the night before.
"Two bottles of Diamond White please mate." Harris said to a harried
looking barman in a white T-shirt who was trying to serve three drinks
at once. He turned toward Walker. "I guess you could do with a pint of
that shit to get your head together."Harris patted him on the shoulder,
which passed for affection in these circles.
"Cheers buddy." Walker accepted the bottles and glass from the
barman and poured in the alcohol and drank it gratefully.
The story of the day was handed over to the group; with a different
tinge on it became a funny anecdote. Walker finally managed to regain
his sense of humour. It was a stupid charge, a few pounds fine and a
day off work to attend court. Not exactly crime of the century and it
didn't come with a custodial, it was no big deal. He was far more
disappointed that he hadn't had chance to exchange details with
Natalie.
Walker told himself to, get a grip and stop worrying over nothing.
Again he wrestled with his own inner monologue ,she attended Wolves
matches regularly. She knew where he drank; he'd seen her about lots
of times, so he was bound to bump into her again in the near future.
The sooner the better in his eyes. The consolation prize was that he 'd
made a good impression and this brightened his mood.
The night took its usual course, banter and a good time in the pub. A
few dabs in the toilets and a carry out of cans and bottles to take back
to a local yard where they could build a few 'j's', chill and relax.
It was the weekend after all. There was no specter of the early morning
dash to work with a blinding hangover to ruin the humour.
Sunday wasn't a bad day either nowadays, not the depressing day it
had been when he was a kid. Fucking bath-night and school in the
morning! Now he could enjoy his moms roast after two hours in the
pub with the boys. An afternoon nap gave him time to get his head
together for the shit week at work that lay ahead.
Walker would have to find a career that was worthy of his brains, a
career that would pull him out of this routine existence.

CHAPTER FOUR
NATALIE

Wednesday quickly came around and the arrest Walker received the proceeding Saturday dulled in his memory. His thoughts turned to Natalie, and a subtle excitement began to rise in the pit of his stomach. He grabbed his Nike bag off the settee, flicked the switch and the telly clicked onto stand-by. The news was boring anyway; some evangelist had just announced his candidacy for the Republican nomination; he wanted to be President in the U.S for his sins. The BBC were covering the trial of a German lad, which was ongoing in Moscow. He'd landed his plane in Red Square. It didn't impress Walker, he thought the bloke was a tit, what did he hope to achieve with his antics? The television preacher was a hypocrite. Those who were overt in sermonising to the public, generally had a covert agenda.

Walker bent down and re-tied his steel toe-capped boots, slung the bag over his shoulder and jumped down the stairs two at a time. His bag contained his clothes for later. Walker had freshly laundered them the previous night; he wanted to look and feel the part. Inside were a new pair of Versace jeans, a round necked Lacoste T-shirt, and a light summer Ralph Lauren jacket , all purchased on his last trip to Spain. They had it sorted over there, good weather, cheap designer labels, beer and fags. God he hated fucking Maggie Thatcher!

Whistling happily he jumped into the car, turned on the radio and pulled out onto the road. Walker enjoyed the peacefulness of the morning, away from the noise and necessary gossip that had to take place in the daylight hours. He liked silence when he was thinking. He didn't understand the need to fill a gentle silence with the harsh noise of an internal monologue. It was different from normal banter and having a dairy with your mates, and the olds from work. It promised to be a good day. He only had to suffer work until two, and then he was free for the day. Walker had swapped shifts with a mate, so he could finish early and grab an afternoon beer in Wolverhampton town centre before the match. Wolves had drawn Man city In a Milk cup tie so he was up for a big day.

 Walker bought the local paper to catch up on local gossip, and found himself a quiet seat away from the crowd. He'd chosen a pub that wasn't on the lads radar. He wanted a few pints in peace, sometimes you just needed your own company. The paper had few stories that took Walkers interest, so he turned to the back pages to check out the latest team news for tonight's game.

His thoughts slowly drifted toward Natalie for the twentieth time that day, he was starting to get on his own nerves. Would she be down for tonight's game? Shrewsbury was only 30 miles down the road and this was a big game. Surely she would make the short trip? But she did have a job, and it was an evening kick off.

Walker stopped the debate dead in his mind. Leave it alone, he ordered himself, if she comes down, then she comes down; it's as simple as that. He walked to the bar, ordered another beer to distract himself and looked at his watch. It was half past four. He would knock this pint back and head off down to The Leopard.

The streets were busy in the town centre, workers were winning the battle to get home. Early evening drinkers were starting the race for drunkenness. Fans in Wolves replica shirts were heading off to their favorite locations to debate the merits of the manager, and tonight's important game.

Walker stopped outside The Leopard and paused before he entered. The pub was discreet and if you didn't know it was there, you might pass by without a second glance in its direction, oblivious to its existence. The pub had been trading for as long as Walker could remember, it had a small frontage and a large bay window that dominated its facade. It overlooked The Dragon. A large pub that was used by several other Wolves hooligan firms. The Leopard's interior was like the TARDIS, featured in Dr. Who; It was long and slender, with a small bar area and a larger niche in the back that had a dart board and a fire exit. Outside the back door, there were several tables scattered haphazardly in a medium sized cobbled yard. It had the look and feel of a Victorian terraced house.

The gaffer was christened Fat-neck, by his regular patrons and the football followers that drank there.

He was a top man, who would provide crates of beer on match days for the lads, to save them having to wait at the bar like the rest of the minions. There were secluded nooks and crannies where you could enjoy a private conversation if the mood took you that way. It was a decent pub all round.

Walker entered the bar, it was quiet with a few lads playing on the gambler and a few more in the back. Some suits were reading their papers at the end of the bar sipping on their real ale as they viewed the headlines after a hard day talking on the phone and playing at being captains of industry. The Leopard had a reputation for keeping a good pint and was only used in force by the lads on match days. It didn't enjoy a poor reputation like The Dragon, whose status for trouble was legendary. The lads knew that you do not shit on your own doorstep and didn't want to drink in a shit hole. Walker pulled up a stool and sat at the bar, making small talk with Fat -neck and sipping at his cider.

He'd drunk a few pints; wasn't pissed yet, but not exactly stone cold sober either. It had hit five in the afternoon and the lads were due in soon. They might have some gear on them to bring him back on a level if he got too carried away.

The door to the bar opened and Natalie walked in. Walkers' heart quickened two hundreds beats a minute without the need for drugs. She looked good he thought: she was wearing a denim jacket with a matching mid length skirt with black legging on underneath and black ankle boots. She looked wonderful, wearing blood red lipstick without it making her look cheap. Her look was fifties style icon and she had managed to pull it off easily. Walker stopped staring and tried to act cool, after a second or two he regained his composure and hoped she didn't notice his heart hammering against the walls of his chest.

"Hello you, what happened last Saturday then," she said and dipped her head to one side inquisitively, a smile on her face.

"Occupational hazard of being a dick head. "Walker replied, there was little point in blagging it.

"You a dick head all the time then?" Natalie asked.

Walker smiled back at her. "No, but I do have my moments, my timing Saturday couldn't have been any better eh? I never even got my Kebab." He paused, found his manners and asked her what she was drinking.

 "Lager please, a half. I had a good time on Saturday and was going home anyway when you decided to run off with your mates from the police, so nothings lost, it was quite funny actually," Natalie said.

"I'm glad my predicament amused you then." Walker was aware this was the first time they'd been really alone together. He suggested that they seek refuge in one of the nooks and crannies.

Placing their drinks at a table they sat down facing each other, enjoying their conversation as it flowed naturally. Every now and then they would raise their heads and glance up, as the door opened and more lads walked in. It wasn't long before Harris, Kerry, Carter and Simpson entered, laughing and talking loudly. Suchley was in the back of the pub, holding court with the serious souls.

Harris walked up and greeted Walker. "Alright are you, tucked away in there?" Walker was just fine. Harris turned to Natalie. "Come down for some more then have you?" They both nodded and Harris winked at Walker. "You pair look sound as, I'm going to do the rounds see what's occurring."

Natalie and Walker continued sitting at their table as people came and went. Walker enjoyed snippets of people's conversations when he went to fetch their drinks from the bar and interjected some of his own words of wisdom. Walker checked the time on his watch and suggested that they leave and make their way down to the ground, Natalie agreed and they left the pub together for the second time in a week.

Walker decided to splash the cash and pay for tickets to sit in the stands. He wanted to watch the game away from the firm and without the risk of getting involved in any potential bad behaviour, not wanting a repeat of Saturday's performance. There were plenty of Man City fans in Wolverhampton, who'd made their way into town to watch the match. Most were shirts and football fans who'd come to watch their team play football and not to have a pitched battle in the streets. However, they were sure to have a few game lads in tow, who were looking for a row, to keep Suchley and company amused.

As they left The Leopard, arm in arm they were accompanied by wolf whistles from the lads who were remaining in the pub. Walker looked back, gave them the finger and held the door open for Nat, as they hit the street he turned to her and grinned. "I could get used to this." They both laughed at the attention were receiving, ignoring the looks it brought from several old people, waiting by the bus stop, who thought young people were all hooligans and wasters.

There was a buzz of anticipation around Molineux as they queued to get into the ground. Wolves had suffered in the past few years, being relegated more times than Walker would care to admit. They had nearly gone out of business, now it seemed the good times were just around the corner. Walker missed the big match feeling.

Natalie allowed him to pay this time and there was a good crowd already inside the stadium when they took their seats. The two sets of supporters were baiting each other across the terracing, adding to an electric atmosphere. Wolves lost again 2:1. Walker didn't let the result dampen his mood, he was enjoying Natalie's company as he marched proudly through Wolverhampton with her arm once more linked in his. Walker was not a naturally tactile man, this arm holding was not common place for him, but he enjoyed feeling her close to his side, it felt natural. They made their way onto the platform to wait for her train and sat down on a bench . Walker slid his arm around her. Natalie didn't resist and moved closer to him her head leaning on his shoulder. He turned her face to his and they enjoyed their first kiss.

In the coming weeks and months Nat and Gary became inseparable. They would go to the match together, go out on the town together and sit on the sofa and watch films together. Walker frowned at the thought of her bringing cushions into the flat; you had to draw the line somewhere he told himself.

His mother made her customary fuss when she first met Nat and they soon chatted like old friends. His dad looked on, his eyes peeking out over his paper as he looked over at his son and nodded approvingly. The puzzle which was Walkers mind was becoming solved. He told her he loved her and Nat replied she loved him right back.

There had been downs in their relationship. Nat presented him with a quandary, when she drank too much (which was very rare). She possessed a rare talent to let all-comers know exactly what she thought of them. Those, who were on the receiving end of her displeasure were unsure of where her motives lay as she appeared inconsistent with her choice of victim. Walker smiled and pushed away any doubts that permeated his thought process as a night out turned violent after Nat had provoked a fight in The Partridge. Telling himself that Nat was being assertive and she took no prisoners.

Christmas Eve was a big day out for the lads, they looked forward to it for months in advance. Nat had been nagging him for weeks regarding his plans, telling Walker it was important and they should spend it together. He finally succumbed to her harassment and despite his reservations about her head when she was drunk, he finally agreed that she could come along and join in the party.

They started drinking early on Christmas Eve in Wolverhampton, it had become a tradition in the firm for years. Start in Wolverhampton town centre and then head back to their local area for the evening entertainment. The pub near the market was open from ten in the morning, and the lads were in from opening time. They planned to drink enough beer, take enough speed and enjoy the festive season with a smile on their faces.

Walker had advised Nat to take it easy, pace herself and inject soft drinks into the routine so she didn't peek too soon, it was going to be a long day. Storm clouds appeared on the distant horizon when she downed a treble vodka and fresh orange in one-go at approximately twelve o'clock. The lads liked Nat; they just wanted her to have fun, they didn't mean any harm, it was Christmas after all. She told Walker not to worry as he looked across at her, doubts etched on his face. She walked across and laughed as she kissed him gently on the lips and whispered in his ear. "I'm fine, I'm enjoying myself. Take that worried look off your face."

Walker nodded back at her, but the smile on his face was forced, he had a bad feeling about her freedom in kissing him. Nat was a private girl. Generally, she didn't show her emotions in public. Nat could be funny when she was merry. Small amounts of alcohol did improve her mood, so he faked happiness and kissed her back telling her. "I trust you." She was dancing to Slade, not with her normal fluency but she could still strut her funky stuff. Her arms were a bit wild and he did think that she had got the wrong tune and was having a bop to the 'Funky Chicken', a tremendous tune released by The 'Goodies'.

They both wished it could be Christmas every day as they sang along with the crowd. Walker slowly relaxed, he thought his earlier misgiving were symptoms of his paranoia. Natalie tried to climb on a table, sure that the pub goers wanted to see her perform live in concert, but thought better of it when it started to wobble precariously, spilling the drinks that were on it.

Like most people when she became pissed, her moods could turn ambivalent. Her sense of humour lost in the suspicion and the self loathing that alcohol could induce. She could jump off the cliff of pissed-up and land head-first on the beach of self-pity down below. Natalie could switch from cheerleader to hooligan in a micro-second. During a night in front of the telly she told Walker that she had a few problems from her past that hadn't helped her head in adulthood and caused her a few conflicted moments. (Didn't everyone have a story to tell Walker wondered?) Children were fucked before they were born at the hands of selfish parents. Her dad had left home when she was seven. She blamed herself that her dad had abandoned her mother and brother. Her mother was still young had wanted a 'life', so she enjoyed a healthy social adventure.

Natalie was left to look after her four year old brother and baked beans on toast became their standard diet. When she related this fact to Walker, she was matter of fact and monotone in her delivery. It didn't affect her anymore, she would tell him. Her body language suggested otherwise, life moved on, she added. Walker could discern a change in her when she talked about her dad, her shoulders would stiffen and she would sit forward as she became tense. Her lips would become terse and her complexion would pale, minute droplets of perspiration would ooze out onto her forehead and it didn't matter how quickly she wiped them away, Walker noticed. Her knees would cross and her hands would clasp the outside of her thighs and pull her legs together.

Walker knew these memories caused her pain, but he wanted to help her find peace and some semblance of closure. He was proud that she had trusted him enough to talk about this time in her past life. He wanted to be a facet of every part of her; including earlier periods of stress. He tried to be sensitive and understanding toward Nat, he loved her, so it came easily for him. She would resent him, for a short period, after these sessions and become cold and unresponsive toward him, the resentment tangible in the air. Walker left it, he didn't want her upset. When she was ready she would seek him out he told himself. Walker's pages were easier to turn; he didn't see the point of locking pain away and repressing it. It would always find a way of making its unwanted presence felt, and he had experienced his fair share of childhood angst. He understood, that if you trusted people, selected people, you could disclose without feeling naked and vulnerable. It was better out than in.

Around two in the afternoon the pubs were packed in Wolverhampton town centre, it was a struggle to move and a battle to get to get served at the bar. Some lad bumped into Nat and he knocked her drink, spilling it over her. Words were exchanged between the two, a glass was smashed. Pushes and punches were exchanged between the two sides. Screams came from girls as the fight escalated.

Walker heard the lad try to apologise to Natalie. He heard Nat tell him to. "Go fuck himself." He'd watched as she pushed him, watched as she chucked a glass, closely missing him and banging harmlessly off some other punter who hardly noticed it in the scrum. Only then did he step in and attempt to calm the situation. Nat was out of order and he knew right from wrong. Walker would protect her with his dying breath, lay down in front of her if she had been wronged, but this was Christmas and the lad was just after a good time. He wasn't to blame for the way things turned out. She was pissed out of her face and being fucking obnoxious.

The start of the trouble was over in a matter of seconds. However the lad's mates had taken offence to the abuse Nat had poured over him and turned their interest on Walker and his crew. They quickly became the focus of the pubs attention as angry words were hurled between the groups and the inevitable fight broke out. Walker got Nat out the pub; acting like a shield to protect her as he pushed his way through to the exit. Some bloke had been glassed and the lad's side were second best in the brawl. They backed off after a blood stained bloke held his hands to his head and the blood ran readily through them, the contradiction in the colour of his face and that of the man in the Santa's outfit clear to see. Peace on earth, let it be.

Walker's mates were used to violence, how to take it and how to dish it out. These lads were pissed and ready for a row, but didn't understand that to some lads a fight was a way of life, a statement of intention for them. The pub was a ruin and Nat was sobbing hysterically, her chest pumping up and down, snot was blowing bubbles out of her nose, her stained mascara adding to her distressed look making her look like a drug addict. Drunken depression had hit, she had landed on the beach below. Walker was angry with her, he'd trusted her and she had let him down. He stomped furiously away into the town centre not sure he could control his temper and she followed him closely. "Fuck off and leave me alone," he shouted at her as the eccentric game of tick weaved its way through the shops. Natalie didn't; she stuck to him like glue. He conceded defeat after twenty minutes, his anger burnt out, he stopped, put his arms around her, kissed her forehead and they headed home in a black cab, it was just four in the afternoon. A wonderful Wolverhampton Christmas was being had by all except Walker.

He stayed up with her through the night as she was sick into a bowl. He made sure she had plenty of water, and she drank regularly to help keep hydrated. As she lay groaning on the settee, he stroked her hair as she fell asleep, whispering gently, as she slept that he loved her and he would look after her. She was his girl after all.

There were other arguments, but having a straighter was normal in Walkers view, it cleared the air and kept things fresh. Walker required reassurance; he needed to know he was the most important person in Nat's life. Walker would purposely seek out conflict, start an argument, blow it up out of proportion, just so he could end the relationship. He'd always done this to girls he'd liked in the past; it was his modus operandi. Walker could assess how much he liked a girl from the pain he felt at their split. He could read the signals and see the pain in their eyes, and assess how much they liked him. It was fucked up, and he knew it, which didn't help his head. These episodes happened when he was drunk, (mostly), and he regretted them (mostly) when the alcohol had worn off. He didn't give a flying fuck if he had no feeling toward them, girls could tell him they loved him, and he would discard them like a chip wrapper without a second glance and they would never enter his thoughts again.

 It was different when they provoked deep feeling within him. He felt he needed to be out of control to feel the pain of love. There weren't many girls that made him feel that way. Only once in his life had he developed a strong feeling for a girl. He liked to make her cry before he would hold her in his arms and wipe away the tears. It made him feel superior, like her protector, like her god. He'd tried the tactic once with Nat, they'd split up over some nonsense and he over reacted intentionally. She tracked him down at work to apologise after he twisted and manipulated the situation. Walker accepted her apology magnanimously. It was normal behaviour, he spuriously rationalised, as he sought reassurance from his inner voice. It was the alcohol that made him that way; he was a nice bloke really, not manipulative, he cared. He would believe that until the day he finally stopped breathing. Still when he sobered up, he did remember the feeling of power it gave him and he liked it. Walker was certainly a paradox.

These were happy times in Walkers life. He still drank more than he should, but he was young and he didn't see it as a problem. It was just a part of enjoying life. Nat didn't approve of drugs so he lowered his intake and kept that part of his life quiet. You had to compromise Walker told himself, he was an adult now and he would act like one. He had a job, a nice home, a beautiful girl friend, all the things he had once begged God for.

Walker still went to the match, but he was now on the periphery of the violence, he would get involved if required. Football was becoming a day out, a laugh, not an excuse to beat the shit out of people. As the arrests reduced, the anxiety and resulting guilt reduced. Walker was a bright lad, but he didn't appear to notice how his life was changing for the better, due to the reduction of the substances he pushed through his body. He simply attributed the change in mood to contentment in his personal situation, he hadn't been happy for a long time now.
So why should he rock the boat with a ridiculous hypothesis about his mental health?

CHAPTER FIVE:
PREGNANCY

"Jo the waiter worked for me, serving wine in basement bars. Only mad men ever say, got no time. If you're mindless please take mine. Jo the waiter held me close, behind the door marked gentlemen, and just for now that's all I need, won't someone call me friend. Long gone I recall good times, I must confess I cried. "

Gary Numan's eerily metallic voice echoed around Walker's flat. Walker had been a fan of Gary Numan for some time; his music and lyrics appeared to capture his individual moods and thoughts. He had once dumped a girl to the words of M.E (we were so sure, we so wrong, now it's over….) with Numan accompanying him in the background. Walker respected the fact it was an over melodramatic moment and it didn't make him look profound, it made him look like a prick.

Walker considered Numan's lyrics defined his emotions and his pathway of adolescence insecurity, and creeping paranoia. He felt attached to the music; he'd never felt attached to much. He understood and appreciated that it was disquieting to invest so much of his soul into music; to most people music was easy listening and fun to be had. For Walker it was a portal into his current state of mind. Most people didn't understand Numan: thinking him cold and impersonal. He sang about robots and a dystopian society; he sang about insecurities, paranoia and being unable to conform and accept society's norms and values. Walker understood his lyrics all too well. Natalie was a Numan fan too, dating back to when he was big from '79-81'. She didn't take him as seriously as Walker, but then most people didn't.

The red wine bottle was half empty, kept company by various other cans and bottles sitting on his glass coffee table in his front room. Walker and Nat had decided to spend New Year's Eve at his flat to welcome in the New Year. Walker thought it a prudent move after the shambolic events of Christmas Eve; he didn't want a repeat of the drama. The thought of a six o'clock knock from plain clothes over the festive period had exacerbated recently dormant anxiety symptoms and the brain wave that he was getting too old for battling in the town centre resonated long and loud in his head.

 Walker reflected, he wanted an easy life with no further complications. Natalie had turned the town centre into a battle ground a week ago, over a childish situation because she was pissed and out of her head, he didn't want to find out what she could achieve with a couple bottles of fizz inside her.

Historically New Year's Eve had never been a moment of celebration for him; for Walker it just signified another year of his life that had passed away and pushed him closer to death. The public would boast about their New Year's resolutions on a Monday and would have broken them by next Tuesday; it was all bollocks in Walker`s view, when he listened to excited chatter about people's promises to give up smoking and then listened to a variety of spurious excuses when they lit up again a month later. Driven by a blinding flash of inspiration, Walker had decided to relieve his dad of his left over 'Christmas spirit' and had liberated enough alcohol to smooth out the fault lines in his thinking. It was their first New Year`s Eve together and Nat wanted to mark the occasion with a romantic night in, away from his ubiquitous mates.

 Walker relaxed on the settee with his remote control, thinking there was a discrepancy between his opinion and the BBC's on what passed for light entertainment. "Shall I open another bottle of wine?" Walker asked.

"Yes why not. "Nat answered." You do look funny when you're singing along to Numan you know."Nat spoke beautifully and Walker liked to listen to her talk, enjoying the sound of the countryside in her accent. He laughed, as his face turned as red as the wine they were drinking, embarrassed at being caught doing his Gary Numan impression.

 He poured them both a drink, enjoying the sound of the wine hitting the glass with a resounding glug. Walker put the bottle down carefully and handed the glass to Nat. "You're quality you know Nat, I love you and love spending time with you."

Walker words were full of sincerity; the wine making him talk freely. Alcohol had always been a catalyst for his feeling and tonight he was defiantly 'loved up'. His thoughts turned to a halcyon future. He looked into her eyes as he spoke. "We should have a baby; I bet we would make great parents. Can you imagine me taking him over the field to a kick a ball and teach him to play football; he would end up playing for

Wolves and England." Walker was living vicariously as he continued to paint a blissful domestic portrait. "You would play with him in the park, pushing him on the swing, chasing him around the house because he had come home dirty from school. His school trousers ripped after having a kick about with the lads! Me having to hide him to save him from a beating!" Walker smiled at the thought.

"It would be a boy then?" Nat asked laughing. The mood between them was intimate, similar to the ambience of an old French restaurant. Nat continued. "We're not having a girl then? I could take her shopping and teach her to avoid boys like you." They both started to giggle.

Walker continued. "Yep, I am just the type of man I would forbid her from seeing!"

"Absolutely! You're no catch! Swaggering around town with your mates." Nat said, her smile radiated by the soft lighting.

Their laughter grew as Walker wrestled her to the ground, tickling her stomach until she begged him for mercy. They both took in deep breaths and looked at each other; their eyes locked, their minds made up.

"If we had a girl she would be so beautiful, you're sweet to look at and I'm a handsome bloke. Walker said. His voice heavy with irony as he glanced at his reflection in the window. Nat looked across at him and pulled a face. Walker continued with his review of their future. "You could teach her all that girlie nonsense and I will kill all her boyfriends." Walker liked the idea of him being the lord protector. If they had a baby he would love her or him and be a proper father. Paternal love would never be replaced by material possessions.

As the night wore on, stories of a perfect future continued; happiness and contentment shone brightly in both their eyes. They saw in the New Year with their Scottish neighbours from Edinburgh castle who were dancing around swords, dressed in kilts, holding hands and singing *Auld Langs Syne:* a song written by Robbie Burns back in 1788. It must be an anti-English tune Walker thought in a drunken moment. All the Scottish hated the English back then (and a fair amount still did today after watching Braveheart). Yet the public still chose to spend their New Year's Eve with the lads and lassies from across the border. When Walker and Natalie connected, their worries were pushed next door and the conversation was easy on the ear. It flowed gently and they inherently understood and knew each another. They enjoyed talking about the future; it was pleasant to dream about the rose garden, the white picket fence and the house in the country. It was a beautiful fantasy and locked the harsh reality of life outside their front door for a little while longer

Walker felt the sweat running down his back as he handled another parcel. He was at work on the back of forty foot trailer. He'd worked on this trailer before as he had christened it; scrawled on the walls was some Wolves graffiti and a simple message:

'Never mind Superman.
Mind Walker, the Walkerman: the most powerful force in the universe'.

He was trying to be profound; you had time to be reflective when you were loading shrink wrapped parcels of heavy steel shelving.

The packs were three feet by two and had to be loaded by hand. The stacker truck would drop a pallet on the back of the trailer; Walker would then unload the contents. Pallet after pallet until the trailer was full with two tiers of shelving, fifty pounds in weight per pack.

These trailers could hold forty tons of stock and he could load one on his own, in a little over two hours. He worked hard and he worked quickly. The more they shipped out, the bigger the weekly bonus. It was simple arithmetic, and he became frustrated when others who worked with him couldn't work out a simple equation. He needed the cash: he wanted to go out on the town, he needed to pay his bills and he wanted a new Armani jacket. There were too many things he wanted and too little money to pay for them all. Walker would find a way, he always had a plan.

The older men that worked with Walker had christened him *'Yampy'*. Yampy was a Black Country term for: barmy, mad, not quite right in the head, but in a puppy like manner. He tried to have a laugh at work and talked bollocks to the older heads so they had christened him accordingly. He had once (or twice), given a bloke some lip, the man was a bruised old boxer from Darlo (a tough area in Walsall); they got on well and it was just banter.

They had shadow boxed for a moment before he picked Walker up and deposited him in large black bin that was located outside the warehouse office. The workers laughed as they milled past slowly after leaving work; amused at the sight of Walker as he acted like a turtle on its shell, legs in the air, struggling to turn over. Walker could take a joke. He could see the funny side; you had to have a laugh at work. It was prison from the minute you clocked in, until the moment you clocked out. Watching the clock and counting the hours down until you were free again. That's why Walker liked to work hard and be busy; time moved seamlessly in that universe. It was Walker's theory of relativity.

"Yampy!" The man in the dirty overalls shouted at him from the office door. "Come here, you deaf wanker, your missies is on the phone." Walker motioned with his hand that he was on his way; he slid around the pallet that was perched on the back of the trailer and jumped off. Swaggering toward the office giving it the big un with a broad smile on his face purposely winding the old cunts up! The lads at work had seen Nat when she had landed on him and now they looked at Walker with grudging respect. She was a looker, so maybe all those bullshit tales he told them around the canteen table on a Monday morning had some truth in them after all? They originally thought he was just a young cocky bastard from Wolverhampton and full of bullshit.

According to the locals they were all dickheads from that that part of the world anyway. Slowly their attitude changed and they would laugh, as he informed them that West Bromwich was not exactly the centre of the universe, full of dog shit eating, over-tattooed idiots, whose idea of a good nights' entertainment was watching the missus open them another can of Banks Mild Ale.

Walker walked into the office, wiped his hands on his already dirty jeans and picked up the telephone. "Hello Nat, you there?" He asked, as he examined his fingernails.

"Hello Gary how are you?" She replied. There was a strange tone in her voice. Walker detected it immediately; she appeared hesitant and nervous. Walker felt there was a hint of trepidation in her words which wasn't like Nat at all.

"I'm fine Nat. But I'm sure you ain't called me at work to ask me about my health?" It was after five; the lads from the warehouse were the only ones that worked shifts, so they had the run of the whole factory in the evening. The warehouse office was theirs, if and when they needed it. This was before the days of big brother and digital readouts that told the bill payer: who had made the call, when they had dialled the number, what they were wearing as they held their conversation and the menu for their supper as they arrived home from work and sat in front of the telly.

"I've missed my period Gary. I'm two weeks late, I... .I could be pregnant!" She blurted it out and waited for his reply. Walker sat down at the desk and rubbed his head, he tutted as realised he was spreading dirt all over his face."I'm not tutting at you Nat, I'm camouflaging myself, ignore me."

Back in Shrewsbury, Nat pulled an annoyed face as she held the phone away from her ear, looking suspiciously at the receiver, what the hell was he going on about? Maybe he'd lost the plot, or what she said hadn't registered, or even worse he was simply ignoring her.

"Best get a test then eh Nat? Then we will know for certain. You ok? You sound worried about it".

"What do you think?"Nat asked. Relieved he had been paying attention."If you're pregnant then wim going to have a baby, if you ain't we're not," Walker replied with a flippancy he didn't feel.

Walker tried to turn situations into jokes if he could feel tension in the air; it was a coping mechanism for him to remain in control of circumstances.

"If I'm pregnant!" She hissed down the phone. Walker imaged her rolling her eyes in exasperation. "You are a dickhead at times Gary, be serious please." She was looking for answers, not his stand-up comedian routine. Walker attempted to add some gravitas to the conversation in an attempt to quell her unease.

"If you're having my baby Nat, then I'm the happiest man on earth. We've talked about this. I love you, I'm happy Nat, truthfully I am."

"Good. So am I. I just wanted to make sure you felt the same," Nat said.

Walker could hear the relief flood out in her voice. "Best find out for definite though Nat eh? Before we go to Mother Care and blow all my inheritance!"

Walkers strut was not quite as profound, as he made his way back to the wagon. He was pleased that she was having his baby but the realisation he might be responsible for another life, had just started to dawn on him. He would have to find more money. Things were tight as it was. Nat wouldn't be able to work anymore. They could get married. Should he ask her? At least they should move in together. He would have to change dirty nappies. He didn't do shit! It made him spew up when his parent's dog had an accident. How would he cope with a nappy full of the brown stuff? His days of being a gad around town, as Nat liked to call him would be over! Would he get to see his mates? The Special's song resonated in his ear: 'Too much, too young'. Calm down and grow up he told himself; you wanted this, you have asked for this all your fucking life. Walker told the other voice in his head to shut the fuck up. His adult side was kicking in an attempt to stop his growing anxiety reaction: the debate in his head raged on. Nat is the same age as you for fucks sake, think how she is feeling. Things would turn out well; life always had a way of working out.

They both had decent families that would support them. Walker's mom would be the doting Granny, but he wouldn't let her soften his kid up as she had done to him. He weighed up the pros and cons in his head and reflected on the things you did after a beer." Fuck me," he whispered. "Don't say fuck all to anyone yet, it might be a false alarm." "She dumped you then Yampy?" Walker returned to the land of the living and looked up at the faces on the back of the lorry.

"Don't be so fucking stupid! I'm God to that girl." For the first time in his life Walker thought he may just be right.

Walker laid the drinks down on the table and sat on the sofa next to Nat. It had been two days since they'd spoken on the phone. The weekend had arrived and Nat had landed at the flat; it was their normal routine if not quite a normal situation. Nat had the pregnancy test clasped tightly in her hand; her knuckles were white, the blood struggling to circulate.

They'd talked on the phone for sometime in the intervening two days; since she had broken the news that she may be carrying his baby. Nat's mom was getting pissed off with their constant dialogue, unaware that she may be close to achieving her life's ambition of becoming a granny! Walker could hear her moaning in the background and he started to lose his cool; fucking eavesdropping into a private conversation, the fucking nosey bitch, mind your own and keep your neck out! Walker wanted to shout out loud but managed, with a massive effort in diplomacy and decorum to preserve his integrity as he kept his thoughts to himself.

"Put the phone down Nat, I'll call you right fucking back, if she is worried about the bill."

"There is no need to curse Gary, I'll talk to her." Nat was not over keen on Walker`s foul mouth at the best of times and especially when it involved her mother.

Walker did like her mum (most of the time), and they hadn't yet started the negative mother-in-law dynamic relationship that Les Dawson made famous in his humorous standup routine.

Natalie's mom was bright, young and enjoyed a laugh on a night out in the pub. She was attractive, dressed fashionably and enjoyed a drink so it was an excellent night out when he ended up over 'Sheepbury' as Walker liked to refer to Shrewsbury. They were all sheep shaggers over that end, in his opinion. When he went for a piss in the first pub he ever drank in, in the town centre, he saw scrawled on the toilet wall:

'Shrewsbury young farmers inter-harvest boot boys!'

and nearly wet himself with laughter! For fucks sake! What was that about? Shrewsbury did have a few game lads who called themselves' *The E.B.F,'* or English Border Front. The lovers of a sheep's arse lived that close to the Welsh; they had to name their firm accordingly. They were a small tight squad and could bang it about if they had to, but they were strictly small time and Walker hated them with a passion, after they broke all the rules and tried to start with him when he was out with his woman. That highlighted their small town mentality and distinct lack of class.

Nat came down to Wolverhampton every Friday, jumping on the first train out of Shrewsbury, her bag packed with feminine supplies that would be lighter when she made the trip home. Walker would laugh silently and speculate that if she intended to move in by stealth, it could take her some time as he viewed his bedroom and bathroom being invaded by: curling tongues, eyebrow tweesers, body lotions, bubble baths, scented candles and all the paraphernalia that women required. After a weekend spent doing their thing, she would head back off into the countryside either late on Sunday evening or Monday morning dependent on their relative shift patterns.

Walker would wait excitedly at the local train station and dutifully pick her up and drop her off; always looking forward to seeing her. Their weekends would be relaxed, leisurely affairs that mirrored there feeling toward each other. Sometimes they would step out and go to the pub with Walkers` mates on a Friday night, sometimes they would spent time in with each other, lying on the settee watching television and listening to music. On a Saturday Walker would buy them a curry or whatever she fancied from the local take away. Nat was funny about her food; she would only eat chicken if he would cut it up into small pieces for her. Nat was *a* 'spurious' vegetarian'! She would eat chicken because it was an 'ugly animal'. She didn't like chewing big pieces of meat because the thought of it in her mouth made her feel sick (leave it alone!). She wouldn't eat beef, because cows were cute or lamb, (she was from Shrewsbury so maybe she thought they could be family members!) She would have an occasional nibble on a bacon sandwich or a bite on a sausage in the morning (leave it alone part 2!) But she didn't like a pork joint,(or any other type of joint), only Hippies smoked weed Nat would say , and she fucking hated Hippies!

On a Sunday they would go over to Walker's Mums for a roast lunch. She could hold her own in the kitchen could Walker's mum. Her Sunday lunches were excellent; she should market her gravy Walker would tell her with a full belly and a contented gaze. It didn't come out a packet; she made it properly using the fat off the meat, deglazed the roasting tin with red wine, mixing in corn flour and adding gravy browning before pouring in the water from the vegetables and slowly bringing it all to the boil, reducing it to concentrate the flavour. Nat would only eat the vegetables that were set on the table.

Walker told his Mom about her idiosyncrasies regarding food, so she rotated the meat accordingly, ensuring Nat could enjoy poultry at least once a month. Christmas dinner wasn't a problem. Nat hated Turkeys, the fucking ugly animal deserved to die! She could make her point, could Natalie when she needed to. Natalie also worked in a factory, a clean one though, without the gnarled, rough working class types that plagued Walker's working hours. Modern factories were popping up all over the country, in new enterprise zones, to manufacture personal computers to the techno hungry public. She constructed the circuit boards that went inside them.

Britain was entering a period of rapid expansion in technology; soon a generation would huddle around their lap tops and interface online. In their day, they had to struggle with a BBC Acorn, Sinclair ZX or an Amstrad and play games that took three days to load on a tape! Still at least, they got to meet people face to face and not on the medium of MySpace or Facebook. The television stayed on later too, the public now had another channel (four) to watch, augmenting the BBC and ITV. At times there would be late night boxing to watch if you could be bothered to stay up until three in the morning, to watch Mike Tyson knock another *'contender'* out in the first round, without having to pay to view for the privilege.

The public even had breakfast telly and had done since 1983. Walker would wake up and switch on to Frank Bough and marvel at his jumpers, amused by the fact that the middle aged balding gentleman liked to use the services of escorts and snort *'Charles'* as he partied with them! If you tell today's kids that the telly used to shut down at eleven and they played the national anthem, they would look at you as if you had gone mad. Tell them that you had to wait at least another thirteen hours for another adult programme, they would laugh themselves into a coma. The masses didn't even have Sky TV yet, they had to wait until the 5th of February 1989 to reach the MTV age and get their 24 hour fix of flashing lights and trashy American imports.

"Come on Nat, this is killing me here, just go and piss on the dammed thing for fucks sake."

 "Be a bit tactful Gary please," when she called him Gary, she was not in the mood for a debate. She'd taken lessons from his mum in how to put him down with just the tone of voice and the focus on the two syllables that constituted his name.

"Just get it done will you," Walker rapped back. He was losing patience. He'd been sensitive all along and couldn't understand what all the drama was about? She left the front room and headed off into the bathroom. Walker could hear running water and laughed. Natalie knew that Walker knew she was having a piss so she'd turned on the tap to camouflage the sound. Little moments like that made him realise what a good girl she was and how lucky he'd been to go out with her. Well not all luck, he gave himself an imaginary pat on the back. Walker managed to submerge his impatience, wiling away the time with a can of Strongbow, a cigarette and some generic shit that was on the telly on a Friday night. Walker recognised the dulcet tones of Terry Wogan as he blew smoke out of the window.

Nat entered the front room, his concentration focused upon her; he had curious feeling in his stomach that he couldn't explain. He looked up at her, trying to read her expression.

"Well?" He asked.

"Put that cigarette out, it's not healthy for the baby." Nat answered.

Walker ejected from his seat with a vertical takeoff, a harrier jump jet would have been proud of, he just about remembered to jettison his cigarette out of the window before he rushed over and hugged her; his arms like an octopuses. He relaxed his grip, as he thought, he didn't want to hurt the baby (could they still have sex?). There was a lot he had to learn.

"We need to celebrate." Walker said, his heart was pounding, his throat and lips and were dry and he needed a drink.

"Sit down you idiot." Nat ordered him, with a smile on his face. She loved him when he was excited and acted like a wide eyed child, playing happily on Christmas morning, tearing the paper off all their presents and trying to play with all the new toys at once; their faces flushed with excitement. Walker didn't exactly have a poker face; she wanted him to calm down, he had energy to burn when he was assaulted with good news and it could be draining to the soul.

"We need to talk, we are going to have to sit down and plan."

"What's to plan, we are going to have a baby, it's simple" Walker said. He was lost in the moment, he and his mates could plan a visit to Sandwell town under the old bill's noses to have a bash with the Albion, but they did find it hard to think past the next pint.

"Where we're going to live? Telling my mum, your mum, what we are going to live on, simple stuff like that". Natalie told him and hoped Walker accepted the change in their circumstances.

"You can move in here, let's get in the car now and spread the news. I've got a job to pay for things. I'll earn extra money if we need it. The olds will have to like it, hey presto all the problems have disappeared." Walker opened his arms in a grand gesture.

Natalie did love the fact he had answers, Walker had a knack of simplifying life. He thought it was complicated enough, without people spending precious time worrying over scenarios that had an easy solution. In some quiet, philosophical moments, as Walker progressed through life, he contemplated that maybe it would have been wiser to take a step back and reflect on the situation. *'Act in haste, repent at leisure'* was a solid pearl of wisdom and an appropriate mantra. Walker was to hand it out many times in the future to both friends and clients. If he had taken his own counsel, maybe his life might have taken a different course.

Nat finally managed to calm the excited daddy down; it didn't prove difficult, adrenalin can only buzz the brain for so long. She left him fidgeting on the settee and went into the kitchen to boil the kettle, pouring boiling water over her Typhoo and Walker's Gold Blend. This was the perfect time for the great British Intervention *the hot cup of tea*! She carried them back into the front room and handed the Wolves mug over to Walker. He blew on the contents with the steam rising up out the cup. He wanted to reassure her; he wanted to ensure her happiness. He thought he must sit down and act like a responsible adult and talk it out with her, if that's what she wanted. Walker reached for his Bensons packet and quickly rejected the idea of lighting up a cigarette as she looked at him with patronising sternness. Sheepishly he took a drink of his coffee and waited for her to fill the silent void. Walker was good at talking, however he understood that he needed to develop his listening skills.

"I'm obviously going to have to give up work." (Tell me something I don't already know Walker thought). "I'll continue to live at my mum's until the baby is born and then for couple of months afterwards, for her help and support, I've never been a mum before." (Tell me something I don't already know the sequel to), thought Walker. Nat paused and waited for Walker to respond.

"Marry me," Walker said. That was not quite what she expected him to say.

 "What, what did you say, excuse me?" Nat replied. She was surprised and ill prepared for Walkers proposal.

"Marry me," he repeated his proposal.

"Why?" She asked.

"That's lovely Nat! I love you that's why. I want to marry you; we're having a baby, let's do things properly for a change." Walker waited and looked at her. He wanted this, he really did and he continued to market his proposal. "You can move in here, I agree with you about the work thing, we need to save up a few quid and you need to save some money for yourself. I can always earn some extra money. I'll provide for us, you ain't got to worry about that shit Nat. I want the baby born in Wolves though. I want you to live here with me, when our baby`s born. Not at your mothers. I will help and support you with the baby. That's our job, not your mothers (he could already envisage the interfering scenario) my mothers or any other mothers. She can drive over here, she's only a phone call away, she can be here in half an hour if you need her. My mother is fucking ten minutes away as well." Walker jerked his thumb at the window." You got all the help you need close at hand. We live as a family, now that's the end of it. The baby will be ours, it will be our family. I love you, I will love our baby, and I want you to be my wife, is that ok with you?" It was a challenge, a statement of intent more than a proposal. Walker knew it wasn't a romantic proposal; he understood that girls wanted this to be a special moment in their lives. Walker wished he was on one of the Seven Hills of Rome overlooking the distant lights of the eternal city. Smelling the delicate fragrance in the air; sitting outside a quaint Italian restaurant, dressed up to the nines. Holding hands across the table; looking lovingly into each other's eyes, a white gold ring with a single diamond at the ready. Separated by a crystal glass full of red wine accompanied by seafood ravioli with a fresh herb salad, enjoying the ballad sung by an old Italian crooner who resembled an extra from the Godfather; a single violin in the background for accompaniment. The Italians and the French had this shit covered. The English lagged some way back, when it came to sweeping a lady of their feet. Mediterranean fellows could bamboozle a naïve English Rose them with their romantic smooth talk:*"Heya baby you looka beautiful tonight, come ona and beya my wife, with you're a beautiful eyes and your beautiful hair.* Walker mimicked the accent in his head. "Fucking cunts" he whispered inaudibly, not wanting to ruin the moment.

"Would you have asked me, if I wasn't pregnant?" It was a fair question.

Walker answered instantly. "Yes, maybe, not this week, but soon. I love you Nat, it's that simple. Fuck me, you're killing me here. Do you want to marry me or what?" He held his arms out open dramatically. He thought the situation needed an added sense of drama!

"Yes I will," Nat said with a broad smile spreading all over her face. The couple, (that's what they were now Walker thought, a proper fucking couple), spent their last few moments of peace laughing as they had done so many times previously. It was just them at that moment. Their lives were about to transform, it was a simple equation: this was life, it was never static and if you didn't keep the fuck up, you would end up overtaken and in be in the slow lane with the pensioners.

CHAPTER SIX
CEREMONY

Walker and Nat planned to tell their parents at the same time on Monday so chins couldn't wag. Walker wasn't concerned whether Jimmy Hill's chin was involved or not. But Nat wanted the situation addressed in an *'appropriate'* manner, so after *'the look'*, had been passed his way, he conceded defeat and watched as a smirk broke out on her face. He felt a temporary misgiving, was she trying to manipulate him? He sucked in his paranoia and gave himself a mental dressing down for behaving like a child.

They'd decided to spent Sunday at Walker's flat, relaxing on the settee. Walker hit the shop, bought a beef joint and a bottle or two and got to work in the kitchen. Domestic bliss and adulthood consisted of Sundays with the family, not the lads. He'd never revised for a fucking exam at school, he'd decided to put some work into studying for his 'groom' finals.

He called his mum and fabricated some excuse about going to his mates for a beer and got the requisite nagging. "Don't have too much to drink, you have work in the morning you know, you don't want to turn up with a hangover and Gary, behave yourself."

"Yes mom, I will mum, three bags full mum, of course I won't mum." Walker pulled a face and pointed to his head.

Nat got the message and smiled at him sympathetically. Walkers mum picked up on the tone in his voice and tutted down the line at him.

"There is no need to patronise me Gary."

Fuck me Walker thought, I'm twenty two next birthday and she still treats me like a kid. He had to reinforce this point to her more than he needed to or wanted to, but she would simply reply. "You'll always be my baby." Fucking mothers! You had to love them, he told himself with more than a hint of cynicism: not sure of what he would do without his. She tried hard enough, she just thought he was a different person, that was all. Nat had good reason for not wanting to go to his mother's house; she didn't trust him to keep a lid on the fact she was pregnant. He would defiantly boil up, bubble over and fess up. He was still running around the flat like a puppy on speed. She had to pull him away from the phone when she found him dialing Harris's and the others` numbers to arrange a monumental piss up down The Woods.

She wanted them to spend some time together, to let the news resonate, sink in, before they put an announcement in *The Times*. Walker finally agreed, after she had smacked him on the nose with a newspaper; he needed house training, she thought. His flat, though nice, was tidy not clean. Walker didn't understand the concept of moving ornaments to dust, he didn't understand the concept of cleaning at all.

He would hang up his clothes in the wardrobe, which was fair enough, instead of dropping them all over the floor. He didn't leave that much washing up, because he lived off take away food. However, he did need to realise that dust had to be dusted, floors had to be mopped properly, and not in some half arsed attempt to move the stains about. Natalie would ensure they had a nice home, a respectable home to raise their child in. Walker would get the message, she would see to that.

Walker called in sick for work on Monday morning. He rarely took a sick day and he thought that this was defiantly a moment to have one. He put on his depressed and pity-me voice, as he croaked down the phone, smiling as he got the sympathy he required from the concerned administer named Joan, who had the unenviable job of sitting next to the warehouse manager: George. George Parker wouldn't show you sympathy if you had lost your legs while on active service. He would send a car and arrange a fucking wheelchair, old school was the best way to describe his point of view.

He decided (after a motivational from Nat), to drive to his mother's office and inform her of his news. It was a co-ordinated attack. Nat was dropping her mom the news later. Walker couldn't wait any longer the excitement and apprehension was driving him to distraction, he rationalised that if he told her in front of people it would defiantly limit the inevitable lecture he was going to receive, about responsibility, the future, the state of the country, schools, the weather, he shuddered at the thought.

Walker had already called Harris to arrange a little tete-a tete and a pint later, nothing too heavy, it was Monday after all.

The drive to his mum's office dragged. The traffic was heavy, the clouds were low, and the rain was depressing; he had reservations and knots in his stomach. What would she say? He just wished it was all over and he was at the bar, sipping on his beer and telling Harris what a master of the universe he was, Walker hated the anxiety he felt. He pulled onto the office car park and parked his car next to his mum's Mini. Walker's mother loved Minis, she always had. When he was 17 she had taught him drive in a purple Mini 850, and he'd then duly written it off a year later, after he had passed his test, when he'd been pissed. He 'd done a runner and for once hadn't been caught for a crime he'd committed. The bollards got the brunt of the collision when he'd tried to take a corner too quickly and he safely embedded the bonnet into them. Walker had suffered a broken nose, and a bang on the head. Two minutes before the crash he'd clicked his seat belt into place, if he hadn't...........

He sat quietly for a moment plucking up the courage to break the news to her, running his hands over his jeans before he took a deep breath and whispered. "Fuck it, be a man," a few times to reinforce his case. After another brief moment of hesitation he left the sanctuary of his car and walked over to the entrance into the office block and jerked open the door to the building. He acknowledged the girl on the switchboard and waved over to her with a smile which masked his true feeling.

The girls in the office liked Walker. He was bright, brash and cocky and always had a story to tell them. His mum was the manager of the quotations section, in a building supplies company that was located in the Bilston area of Wolverhampton. She was good at her job and had six girls working under her. If his mom did have a night away from his old man it was with the girls from work.

"Is she in her office Trish?" Walker asked as he smiled lopsidedly at her. She looked up at him from the maze of wires that were stacked in front of her face and smiled back at him as she plugged a red cable into a suitable hole.

 "Hello Gary. Yes she is upstairs in her office. You want me to let her know you're here mate?"

"No thanks, Trish. I want to surprise her." Wasn't that just the truth he reflected. Walker walked slowly up the stairs, turned left and entered the office. It was his Crucible and he'd just crossed the Rubicon.

He quickly opened the door to his mother's office and marched straight up to her desk. The smell of cigarettes assaulted his nostrils along with the sound of frantic typewriters. Mrs. Walker had her head down, scribbling into a blue ledger; she had not seen him enter the room as she was concentrating intently on working out a competitive price for a potential customer. The other girls were looking up from the desks, curiously, as Walker tiptoed down the plank. They were used to seeing Walker in his mum's office on a Friday, but first thing on a Monday morning was a rarity. He stopped abruptly in front of her desk. "Hello mum, how are you this morning?" He'd interrupted her concentration.

She looked up hurriedly. "Gary, what are you doing here? To what do I owe the privilege?" His mum's look was quizzical, and then turned into worry, her eyes shaded over briefly. Was he in trouble again? She knew that he had trouble with the police. She'd been down the police station with him more than once when he was a juvenile.

His dad had gone to court with him the first time he appeared before the bench for theft and quickly got bored with the situation. "If he got into trouble let him get on with it and sort it out himself," he would tell Walker's mother. He was always too busy to bother with anything other than his own life.

Walker swallowed deeply. "Morning mum, are you alright? If you`re sitting comfortably then I will begin." His mom looked back, her confusion rising. Before she had chance to say another word, Walker continued spreading his news." Just thought you'd like to know that you're going to be a Gran!" With the bomb dropped and right on target, with his head held up high, he turned around and exited the office, without looking back, he would catch the fallout from the explosion later.

The Woods was populated with the usual crowd. Harris sipped his Tenant's Extra leaning casually against then bar and looked sideways at Walker. "So you're going to be a dad then?" Harris was as ever razor sharp.

"Yep, yam up to speck on the situation speedy!" Walker smiled at his mate as they took picked up their pints from the bar and sat down at a scarred wooded table that was located in the corner of the bar, hidden by the juke box. Walker brushed the remnants of an old pack of ready salted peanuts onto the floor. They'd exchanged pleasantries with Roger and the lads from death row, which thankfully hadn't lost any of its number in the last few months. Walker was happy to see that Harris was pleased for him. Nat was lovely girl, Harris agreed that Walker had done well for himself; other lads in the firm that used The Woods had kids and they were a similar age to Walker so it was no big deal in Harris's eyes. Walker raised the subject of money and explained that things were going to be tight.

"You could always earn a bit extra, you don't just have to rely on your weekly wages you know Gaz," Harris said. Walker knew how to spend money; he wasn't too bright on how to make it without a wage packet in his hand at the end of the week.

"What you saying Pete?" Walker asked.

"You work in a warehouse mate, there is no security and people buy the stuff legally, yes?"

"Yes." Walker agreed.

"So knock some out through the back door, you don't need to be greedy, just a nice little touch every now and then to improve you bank balance, be selective and don't tell fucking Nat, show some discretion eh mate."

"I don't tell her everything you know," said Walker

Harris raised his eyebrows, "Sure you doh Gaz, yam a rock mate!"

Natalie was a legal eagle, she knew that Walker got into trouble at the match and when he was pissed up, out on the town, but she did not see that as criminal. He wasn't a scumbag that sold drugs and robbed old people. He just had a few beers and got involved in silliness.

"Sell to who?" Walker asked.

"Use your fucking imagination Gaz. I can hook you up with a few lads that are after shelving and racking, but I want a piece of it. You can build it from there mate."

They sat down and discussed business options, how the warehouse worked; what were the best times to get a van in and out of the premises without arousing suspicion. Who were the nosey bastards and who could be trusted. Measure twice, cut once, don't jump in like a cunt and don't make silly mistakes. It was silly mistakes that got you caught. Harris would come into Walkers work, have a look see on the pretence that he was picking him up for another pub mission. It was always busy at one o'clock on a Friday lunch time. It was pay day, when you queued up to get your brown envelope full of beer tokens.

The lads from The Woods bought him a few beers by way of congratulations, his back was getting sore and bruised from all the pats he'd received, he felt like a spaniel.

Roger had dipped into his pocket to buy him a pint, the lads from death row had laughed with derision when he shook his empty glass at them. "You want a reward for getting your missus pregnant? Fucking kids today!"

Some of the worries that had been nagging at him, like the start of toothache had been addressed. Walker was in a contented frame of mind when he arrived back home, he threw himself on the sofa, opened his pie and chips and switched on the TV to see what nasty Nick Cotton had been up to on the square. He would phone Nat tomorrow, she didn't want to be disturbed tonight, mother and daughter stuff.

The next few months went like a blur for the happy couple; it reminded Walker of a holiday video. They informed their respective parents about the marriage and gained approval and consent. Fuck it Walker thought, they didn't require approval but it was always good to get on and keep people happy. Their parents met with each other and plans for the wedding were discussed and a formal structure formulated. Walker didn't get involved with it. That was up to his mum, Mrs. Crawford (Nat's mother), and of course Nat. Nat liked to organise things so she wasn't concerned that Walker took a back seat in the preparations; it was her day after all. Walker was fine with that. He was more than happy to keep a smile on her face. His dad, (under duress) had agreed to pay for most of the wedding with Nat's mum adding some funds into the communal pot ensuring Shropshire was home to the wedding of the year.

Walker and Harris managed to move some shelving out the back of the warehouse and were making extra money. Walker's mate from work had become involved watching his back, things were progressing. They were making some extra dollars and they could afford to involve another hand, without feeling the pinch. It was always better to be safe than sorry.

The wedding date had been arranged for May 7th 1988. It was the last day of the football season and Wolves were away at Leyton Orient in London`s East End. Walker had visited Brisbane Road once before, when Wolves had left their mark on the locals, they'd used a hot dog van as a battering ram, ending one mouthy cockney`s interest in the fast food market.

Nat didn't look too impressed when Walker raised the point. "A few of the lads want me to go down with them, is the date set in stone Nat?" She gave him 'the look', her hands placed firmly on his hips. "Set in stone then? What your tombstone?" She replied without humour.

Walker smiled sheepishly at her as he exited the kitchen; the date was confirmed. They would get married in Shrewsbury and have the reception at a restaurant near to the church, before adjourning to a pub located a mile outside the town centre for the evening festivities. Coaches were booked to transport Walker's mates to and from the evening party. Harris agreed to be Walker's best man. He scowled when Walker asked him if he understood what it involved. Yes, he did know that he had to wear, a suit, and make a speech. Walker would help him through the ordeal. They were both in the twilight zone. Walker had never been a groom before and Harris had never been a best man.

Walker woke up in a flat, his head was pressed against a purple dralon settee and he felt a crick in neck. He groaned as he twisted his neck like a pendulum to regain parity. He blinked and looked around, he didn't recognise anybody in the photographs that were hung on the beige stained walls, that had originally been brilliant white. He shook his head as the memory of last night slowly came into focus. It was his fucking wedding day! He assessed his surrounding, and took a quick inventory on how he felt. His head was slightly the worse for wear, but his eyes were still in his head, which was a bonus. His mouth tasted of vindaloo. He was due at the church in Shrewsbury in less than three hours time. He checked his watch and relaxed, smiled and shouted at his sleeping companions, who were pressed like sardines into the rose colored carpet, their faces aimed at the small electric fire.
 "Come on boys, let's make a move then, wakey, wakey, rise and shine." Walker motivated the troops and groans started to emanate from the floors at they sluggishly started to move. Walker felt excited; he was happy and eager for the day to get started. "Come on lads" he repeated, and then with more urgency. "LADS!" Now there was discernible movement from the floor.
 The night hadn't gone according to plan, they bumped into some lads they knew while on their way to an Indian restaurant to have a sit down meal and keep out of trouble. These lads boasted they had the best bush in Wolves and did they want to try it? It was a stupid question! Free drugs! Of cause they wanted a sample and a burn on the old peace pipe. After a brief period of discussion they decided to do the next decent thing; they piled in to the take away and ordered half of India, before they went back to the lad's yard. They'd smoked

purple haze until they passed out at three in the morning. Walker had enough about him, to make sure he set the house`s only alarm clock; he would have had to emigrate to South America with the Nazis if he'd missed the wedding.

They arrived at Mrs. Walker's house at half past nine, his parents were happy to see him and relieved that he'd made it. The house was busy and bustling with endeavor. His sister was moaning about the bridesmaid dress, which apparently was standard operating procedure for a woman, Walker was informed as he started to lose patience with her constant bitching.

 Walker's mom was wearing an elegant tailored blue suit, a wide brimmed white hat which she modeled regally, waiting for her guests to pass positive comments upon it. His dad stood quietly sipping tea, flicking through the paper and wearing his obligatory lounge suit, he looked the part of the successful business man.

Their suits were hanging up in reverence safely tucked away in the spare room, covered and protected by his mother with greater security and diligence than the crown jewels. Walker's mum had covered all the bases. Walker felt pride rise up in his throat, and he choked back the emotion, shocked, he had nearly started fucking crying. He regained his composure, before anybody noticed that he'd felt the moment. In all the chaos of coffee and toast it had been missed, he felt relieved and suddenly strangely vacant that he'd shared the moment alone. All the years of feeling that he was on the outside, looking in on the Christmas feast like Tiny Tim were nearly over, the feeling slowly dissipating as his wedding date drew closer.

They'd all been provided with co-ordinated slate grey Ascot suits, white shirts and blue cravats accompanied with top hats. Babbling excitedly, they quickly got washed, dressed and presented in a line ready for inspection. Mrs. Walker walked slowly up and down the line and pronounced she was satisfied with their efforts, as she arranged red roses in their lapels. Red roses, blue cravats, white shirts, they were making a national statement. Walker felt like it was the first day at school all over again.

 More of his friends arrived at the house and the kettle was struggling to keep up with the constant demand for hot drinks. The lads hadn't let him down; they looked smart and when he blinked twice even normal. Their girlfriends had done their best to brush up, looking spectacular in their assorted garments. They'd taken the opportunity to go shopping with their men's hard earned cash to compete in the fashion stakes. Friends and family took photos of them ensuring a pictorial record of the day was recorded contemporaneously.

Walker had been sure that when the day arrived his nerves would take over and the butterflies would be having a rave in his stomach. He was pleasantly surprised by how calm he felt, even tranquil. The excitement he was experiencing was simply associated with expectation of the day ahead of him.

Carter, Harris and Walker decided to walk over to the local shops after they'd inspected each other. "Look the fucking part doh we eh?" Harris said with a big grin on his face. This was going to be one of the few occasions in their lives when they could get to dress up and look like aristocrats.

The sky was a hazy blue as they made their journey over the small patch of grass, which passed as a make-shift football pitch; when Walker was young, the locals had called it, Walkerly, after the national stadium. They stopped to let a car pass; it slowed down as the occupants threw them a stare out of the window and Walker waved back happily, a spring in his step and a song in his heart.

The shop was crowded when they arrived, couples were choosing cereal off the shelves, old men were picking newspapers to take home and read. Their day as domesticated as the weather.

Harris steeped forward. "Sixty Bensons please and a half a bottle of Hennessey." He asked the white haired old woman who stood behind the counter.

She smiled back at him. "Who is the lucky one then?" Harris pointed at Walker, whose neck reddened above the starch of his collar. "You all look very smart," she said cheerfully.

"Thank you my darling," Walker laughed back. He glanced across at his mate and Harris felt the stare.

"It's only half a bottle mate, a last drink together as single men; it's not the start of a mission." Harris had read his mind as good mates can and should.

Walker patted him on the shoulder. "I didn't think anything else mate."

When they arrived back at Walkers parent's house, his mom was busy organising guests, into cars, she was pointing and talking and nobody was moving. The street was awash with vehicles but people were milling around like cattle. It was nearly time to leave for the church and she was trying to make sure that everybody had a lift. Walker was starting to bounce with anticipation. Harris could tell his mate would rather be on his way there, than hanging round the house and assisted Mrs. Walker in getting the cups of tea drunk and people out of the kitchen. They had to lead the convoy as Walker was the only person that knew the way to the church.

Walker found his Nan in the garden, with a cup in her hand. She was looking up at the blue sky with a distant expression on her face. He walked up and kissed her on the cheek. His Nan was salt of the earth, working class stock. She'd worked as a press brake operator at a factory in Darlaston for most of her life and had looked after his granddad for the other half.

"You ok Nan?" Walker wondered if she would start talking posh and do her impersonation of the Queen delivering her annual speech on Christmas day. On family occasions (when under the influence), she would adopt her Queens English accent instead of the Black Country brogue that Walker loved so much. He knew she would be missing his Granddad, a lovely old man, who'd worked all his life as a tool setter and had died three years previously, suffering with dementia. She was wearing a hat that would have won ladies day at Ascot; it had more feathers on it than an ostrich's arse! His mom had bought her a suit to mark the occasion. His Nan would have been happy with a second from a charity shop. The dry cleaners would have sorted it out for her. She knew the value of money and didn't want to wear Chanel or Prada. She loved people not things.

"Nan, you look bloody beautiful."

"I prayed for good weather Gary," she replied looking toward the sky.

"I knew you would ask for good weather from the big man upstairs Nan. That's why I haven't checked the forecast, it's a beautiful day, thank you. Make sure you see me when you need a vodka and lime, or a glass of sherry, I'll make sure you get decent drink."

"You are a naughty lad Gary, you'll get me drunk," she said merrily.

"That's the idea Nan." They both laughed together. Walker was happy he'd got to spend a quiet moment alone with her, away from all the well wishers. Walker's Nan had found religion as she got older. Walker would tease her around the table on a Sunday lunch time. Informing her he would believe in God too, if he prayed on a Sunday night to win the pools and the cheque turned up in the post the next day. He would laugh as she cussed him. Walker would fill up her schooner with sherry when his mom wasn't looking to add to the fun.

She was a good old lady his Nan, and hilarious when she'd a couple of glasses of sherry inside her. She would take a different slant on world events as they competed for intellectual honors around the dining table. Walker's mother would become exasperated with her and that would make Walker's grin become all the broader. His sister who had turned into a liberal left wing Champagne socialist would get involved and Walker would have to remind her to respect her elders. Walkers' sister had turned into a confirmed Guardian reader and bristled with the values that the paper professed to promote.

The cars finally left in convoy and headed toward off to Shrewsbury, the neighbours lined the streets to wave them off, curious as to what was going on next door with no net curtains to twitch. Walker's Ford Escort proudly led the way; his dad had insisted that he take the car in for a service and MOT at his personal expense and checked that he had valid road tax. He'd even removed the philosophical stickers from the rear windscreen. Walker knew his mum had a hand in his dad's generosity; it would have put a dampener on the day if they'd broken down or he got stopped and arrested, his mum wouldn't have been able to live down the embarrassment.

Forty minutes later and without drama they arrived at the church, it was midday and the schedule that had been set was being adhered to with military precision. Nat was expected to make her entrance at half past: Gary Walker had thirty minutes left as a single man. As he walked into the church yard he viewed the throngs of people milling around, laughing, modeling their hats and making polite conversation. He found it hard to recognise a friendly face. He must have been pissed when he met these people; a few greeted him by name and shook his hand and he didn't know who the hell they were. Aunties and Uncles he'd met once at a long forgotten Christmas party, he imagined. He played the game for a while and circulated for ten minutes, shaking more hands and kissing more cheeks, hoping he didn't stink of last night's curry.

Finally he became bored playing the politician and wanted to spend some time with his mates, his real people. Looking around the church yard, he couldn't spot them and guessed they'd found a place to hide away from the peripheral friendship being offered. He walked to the back of the church, into the graveyard and found them standing under a large oak tree. Walking over to them he stood beside Harris.

"You alright mate, finished kissing babies have you?" Harris knew Walker and knew the nerves would start to take effect soon.

"Ay that`s the truth Pete, I doh recognise half them fuckers, me one uncle looks like Peter Sutcliffe for fucks sake."

Harris laughed and opened his jacket, producing the bottle of brandy he'd bought earlier, along with a packet of cigarettes, he removed one from the box, flicked his lighter and sparked Walker a cigarette before passing it over to him. Walker deep a deep pull and blew out the smoke out in a steady stream. "Cheers mate," he said.

Harris opened the brandy and turning toward Walker made a toast and raised the bottle skyward. "Good journey mate, all the best." He took a pull, before passing the bottle over. Walker did the same; the brandy was passed round the group until it was empty. They all repeated the toast as they drank.

"This is like going before the beaks Pete." Walker smiled nervously.

"No jail at the end of this though Gaz and you wake up with a bird in your bed, not a fucking con." Harris answered.

"Aint that the truth mate, I could do without that in the morning!" Walker meant it.

They both giggled as Walker's mom rounded the corner breaking the moment, she was hunting them down. "Come on you lot." She pointed at Carter. "Robert, you need to start giving out programmes at the entrance now please. Gary, Peter, come on you need to be in church now." She adjusted their flowers as they walked past and gave out one final inspection."You'll all do." That was high praise indeed Walker thought sarcastically, but he smiled sweetly anyway.

The time had come; Walker and Harris looked at each other and followed her across the lawn. The church suddenly seemed oppressive, their footsteps became measured, their laughter had ceased it was now time to take care of business. They paused at the entrance and removed their hats placing them under their arms, they turned, taking one last look up at the cloudless sky. Next time Walker would see the outside world, he would be a married man. He turned to Harris. "Let's fucking do this." Walker said. They both breathed deeply and entered the church.

They were facing the altar, their eyes fixed on the vicar, concentrating and trying to remember their parts when the wedding march started.

Walker knew, from rehearsals, it meant Nat had entered the church. He wanted to turn round and sneak a peek; he knew that it was taboo after their many rehearsals and many more motivation speeches from both Nat and his mum. Walker was now aware of the etiquette involved and remained patient. They took their cue stood up and moved forward toward the vicar and took their places in front of him. Walker was reminded of his many trips to see the headmaster; his school days seemed a long way behind him now. Harris moved to Walkers right side seamlessly, as Nat glided up the aisle and finally reached them. Walker turned as he felt her arrive by his side. The term breathtaking is overused but he had to admit that Natalie looked stunning. He looked into her eyes and mouthed the words. "You're beautiful." Walker was a proud man.

She took his hand in hers and squeezed gently. She looked nervous and he thought she wanted to feel him and be reassured. She smiled tenderly and they both turned to face the vicar .The ceremony sped by rapidly, Walker was surprised he didn't feel self-conscious or nervous. The church seemed empty; there was only him and his bride inside. Natalie stumbled slightly over the vows, her voice nearly cracking. He held her eyes and they were soon pronounced man and wife. Walker kissed the bride and Harris remembered the ring. Natalie wasn't sure he would, making her reservations well known to Walker prior to the ceremony. Walker laughed it off, Nat liked Pete, she just thought he was irresponsible. She even accepted the fact he smoked weed and wasn't a Hippy. He would brush off her question and change the subject to cover up his own nagging doubts.

They finally walked out of the church and down the aisle. Walker surveyed the faces as they left; the lads greeted him with a sea of smiles and an honour guard of thumbs up. They were greeted with laughter, photos and confetti as they made it outside and stood in the church grounds viewing the world as Mr and Mrs. Walker. He glanced across at his bride and smiled. She was a beautiful vision in her wedding dress. They posed for the official photos smiling, and said. 'Cheese' when they were requested to, when all Walker wanted to say was." A pint of cider and a large vodka please."

Finally the crowds quietened down and they were informed to make their way to the restaurant for the start of the reception. Walker tossed Harris the keys to his car; he was travelling in style now he was a married man and had secured a place in the wedding car. A polished

white jaguar limousine was waiting to whisk them away together, as
man and wife.
Walker liked Jags, and had promised himself he would buy one when
he was successful and had made it in life. He waved through the
windows to the crowd, feeling like royalty as they left the church and
headed toward the reception, which had been booked in a restaurant
next to Shrewsbury Cattle Market. The lads laughed riotously when
Walker had told them were the meal was being held, commenting,
"We really are going to the country then? Better hope that we don't
tread on old McDonald`s toes.
 "At least the meat would be fresh," Walker fired back at them.

The guests were all lined up for inspection when Nat and Walker
entered. Walker wasn't sure of the protocol involved, unaware that he
had to shake every guest's hands in the line-up before he could sit
down and have a beer. He was reminded by the Maitr'd, as he nearly
made his escape to the bar that he had duties to perform and he
returned with a lopsided grin and another red face. He walked passed
his mates with the air of a man who knew what he was doing as they
pushed cash into his pockets by way of a present, as he shook their
hands vigorously and thanked them all for coming with a pronounced
serious expression on his face. He could feel the bundles of cash
swelling his pocket, knowing he had done well financially.
The guests cheered and clapped loudly as Mr. and Mrs. Walker were
formally introduced. Walker raised his hands in acceptance of his
plaudits before he remembered to order two pints of cider, as his
minder pulled back the chair for him as he prepared to sit down,
looking out at the sea of white tablecloths, floral centerpieces, and
smiling faces in front of him. He was enjoying being the centre of
attention and silently toasted the audience with his pint of Strongbow
firmly secured in his hand, downing his first drink in one go to the
cheers of the spectators, happily wiping his mouth with the back of his
hand. Nat leaned across and whispered. "Behave please."
 Walker smiled back at her, "Of course I will, I'm a married man aren't
I."
They'd tried not to over complicate the menu and had chosen
traditional fayre. A choice of starter between: tomato and basil soup
served with herb butter and freshly baked rolls, or a prawn cocktail

with Marie Rose sauce. Roast beef and seasonal vegetables were being served for the main course, or a vegetarian option. Walker didn't know what the vegetarian option was, he didn't care. If you fancied a nut cutlet instead of a joint of prime British beef, good luck to you in his. If you liked a pudding you could indulge with a chocolate mousse served with strawberry compote or a selection of fine French cheeses. The wine was flowing, a fruity little number available in either red or white, to be followed by a modest champagne for the official toasts.

Walker thought they'd created the perfect balance, the etiquette not so stifling the guests couldn't relax and enjoy themselves, comfortable in the knowledge that if they got a gravy stain down their ties they wouldn't be asked to leave by the protocol police. Just formal enough that the reception fitted the wedding criteria laid down in law by the *olds'*. Walker visited Harris at his table. Harris hadn`t wanted to sit at the top table, so Walker insisted they break tradition and allow him to have a table that was close to the front, but allowed him some freedom away from the confines of people he didn't know. Walker's mum, had been persuaded and like Solomon, agreed to the break in tradition. Walker was surprised to see that the gravy stains were minimal, but not shocked that the red wine stains were increasing. He wanted to make sure that they all had enough wine and food; It didn't look like he was needed. So he trotted off back to his throne. Walker managed to give Nat the slip briefly and sneak away for a crafty fag, and a couple of tots with his guests, before her laser eyes located his whereabouts and dragged him back to the table. Soon after, and with his trousers starting to pop under the strain. The Maitr'd banged a spoon on a glass and called for order. It was time for the speeches, and the room fell silent. Walker took a deep pull of his pint, and crossed his fingers. Harris had told him he was not looking forward to this part of the proceeding, neither was Walker.

The best man stood up with a flourish, raising his arms and the room waited for his speech to start, hushed in anticipation, their full attention focused upon him. He thanked everybody for coming and he thanked Natalie for looking beautiful and the bridesmaids for looking, "just as sweet as can be." The truth was simple; Nat did look beautiful, she illuminated the room, the bridesmaids looked like rejects from an episode of' *Dynasty'*.

Harris's speech continued without effort; the beer must have loosened his tonsils and installed confidence in his ability to tell a story. Walker did wonder whether he had dropped some speed in the toilet to aid him in his seamless delivery, either way he was grateful that he wasn't fucking up the speech. The crowd laughed when they were meant to and listened when they were expected to. Someone from the crowd shouted. "Tell us how they met." This part of their courtship was never mentioned in polite conversation. Harris now full of and self- assurance decided to disclose the full story of their first meeting……….

"Their eyes met across a pub, crowded with football hooligans eager for trouble and drunk…..."

Walker remembered his mothers head snapping toward him as the story hit the part when he was trussed up and thrown into the back of a police van, he thought it was well past the point for a timely intervention and shouted across. "Thanks Pete, enough of my glorious past thank you very much."
The crowd laughed and applauded at full volume. Walker loosened his shirt encouraged by their response and made a mental note never to get arrested again, it wasn't the court appearances that bothered him, it was the look on his mum's face when she found out he'd let her down again.
His turn arrived to say a little something to the crowd, heavy with beef and beer he raised himself slowly from his chair and looked at the wrapped presents that had been placed on the table in front of him. For a brief moment he looked confused, until Nat whispered in his ear, with a grin he handed the bridesmaids their gifts. He wasn't aware that they received presents and he asked Nat where his was. The crowd thought it was part of his act and laughed loudly.
Walker's speech was short but sweet: "Thank you all for coming, thank you to the bridesmaids for looking so lovely. Thank you to Pete, even though you have dropped me in it with my parents. Thanks most of all to Nat." he turned toward her. Raised a glass of champagne he took her hand in his, before looking into her eyes. "For being silly enough to agree to be my wife, now that's enough from me the bars are open, I'm sure you would rather have a tot than listen to me go on."

The speech ended, Walker sat down received his applause and that was that. They were both relieved that all the formalities had been conducted and they could now relax. They enjoyed drinks at the bar with their guests; Nat and Walker played their parts beautifully.

Taxis and cars had been organised to convey their guest across Shrewsbury for the evening jamboree as the restaurant started to empty. Walker's mates had found out there was a hospital nearby to the pub holding the evening party and had decided to investigate. One ingenious soul amongst them decided they should invite some of the nurses to the party, to add a little glamour, full of hopeful anticipation that, 'Nicola the naughty night nurse,' might agree to their lecherous advances.

They paid an impromptu visit to the facility to issue out invites. Walker thought they should have attended to their homework more diligently; they'd just presented at Shelton: the local mental hospital. R.M.N,'s (Registered Mental Health Nurses), had to deal with mad and complex individuals as a matter of course These lads were lucky to get away without being held under a section of the Mental Health Act! They were escorted off site by security and told firmly, but politely, never to darken the doorstep again. The guards swallowed laughs as they turned to go back into the reception. Harris grumbled to no one In particular. "So that's what a nut-house fucking looks like then? Not a friendly bunch am they?"

As they told the story at the bar even Nat laughed as she saw the funny side. The bar in the event`s room was crowded. The room was split into two halves, one area containing the bar, the other the dance floor. Long tables with silver-foil salvers full of food were in view and already one or two peckish piss-heads were circling the offerings . The dance area was a ghost town, the cellophane wrapping still waiting to be ripped open from plates of sandwiches, chicken drumsticks, sausage rolls, and all the other accompaniments that would find their way onto the ever-present papers plates that were stacked like casino chips at both ends. Tables had been moved to the perimeter of the room and the lights had been turned down low, to fuel the atmosphere. A few children were dancing to a, 'Walkers Brother's song:

The sun ain't going to shine anymore........

monopolising the dance floor until the adults had imbibed enough alcohol to let their inhibitions run wild. Walker watched as they waltzed over the shiny wooden tiles and smiled for a moment and thought of his child, sleeping warmly in his wife's belly. He breathed out, suddenly tired and decided he needed a moment and sat down. He glanced around and reviewed the scene and blew air slowly out of his cheeks.

He hadn't had time to reflect on the day's events, it had been a blur. His world was filling with responsibilities and he pondered over the question was he responsible enough for his part in life's play? He looked at his mates standing at the bar, fucking about, laughing and joking, chatting up Nat's mates and being politely shown the proverbial door by the bride. He wondered if this was it? Was his life really complete? For a brief moment he felt flat, as numerous other questions flashed through his mind. Was his life now over? Was he condemned to domestic drudgery? Was this the goal he had always sought? Was it true, you always only ever wanted what you didn't have? Now he had it, did he really want it? Was he ever going to enjoy the pub again, chatting up new skirt? Flirting with the barmaid? He was married now; Nat was the only woman that he could sleep with and be with from this moment onward, without risking a divorce. He suddenly felt trapped in a cage going round on an exercise wheel and not getting anywhere.

Walker loosened his shirt collar and took a healthy pull on his pint. Harris had noticed his mate, 'had gone away', and ambled over to him. Harris was aware that Walker did this at times, he could be in a room without being there at all. Harris knew Walker had thoughts that would raise his blood pressure. He didn't pursue the matter, accepting that was part of his mate's innate character. If Walker did have an outburst and go over the top, Harris simply attributed it to the alcohol. "Alright mate?" He asked. Walker looked up.

"Yeah, I'm fine Pete, just having ten, been a busy day eh kidder, what you think about it?" Walker replied with a tried looking grin.

"Quality day Gaz, a good day out mate, apart from the mental hospital bollocks. You would have thought that if they dealt with nutters all day, they would have fitted in well here!"

They both burst out laughing. "Bunch of cunts!" Walker exclaimed. He was back in the room and back in the moment.

Lewisham. Overly Medicated

There had been rumours that some lads from Wolves were in town and were having a function at the pub. Some local youths, around ten of them who'd been drinking in the bar decided to investigate and began to sit on picnic benches located nearby to the entry into the function room and weighed up their options. The leader was a blond haired lad, wearing a Goi, Goi, T-shirt, baggy dark-blue jeans with badges plastered all over them. It was a new fashion trend that had started to hit the streets. Walker fucking hated it, and the lad with his half arsed attempt to grow a goatee beard, face full of fucking pimples. "Can I help you mate?" Walker made sure his accent was broader than usual.

 "Not really, you from around here then mate?" The lad answered, trying to sound assertive.

"It's a private party kidder. You fucking know I ain't from round here. You fucking know where I'm from. I don't sound like a cunt now do I?" Walker hissed back, his finger pointing at the lad's chest.

"What did you say mate?" He replied, the bravado quavering in his voice.

"Don't make a cunt of me, you fucking heard. If I wasn't getting married you would have been fucked off by now. So be a good little lamb and fucking trot on."

The rest of the goatee's firm, had closed ranks, the situation was becoming claustrophobic. Harris and two others had made it outside now and stood firm behind Walker. "What's the rent-a -farmer after then Gaz?" Harris pointed at the lad, with an amused look on his face.

"An alternative venue to while away this beautiful evening." Walker replied, his eyes never left the face of the Shrewsbury lad.

Voices were getting raised as the coach from Wolverhampton pulled in, the air brakes signifying reinforcements from Wolverhampton had arrived. The locals made a quick sweep of the bodies moving off the coach, and decided to heed Walker`s words of wisdom. They walked off; shoulders swaying in the breeze. They turned as they left the car park and the leader looked back. Walker motioned with his hand that they should keep moving, they did quietly. He turned to Pete and the other two and burst out laughing, "What a fucking bunch of cunts," Walker said, as he threw cigarettes at his mates. He lit his own and enjoyed the taste of the smoke, looking up the sky; it was a deep azure and he enjoyed the feeling of warmth on his face. The sun was slowly slipping in the sky, becoming impaled on the tress. The others lads were happily slapping hands with the guests who were now exiting the bus and making their way into the bar.

"Everything alright boys?" One lad queried.

"Some rustlers, that's all boys, get a drink, and enjoy yourselves. The first ones on the house." Walker said with a smile.

After ten minutes, Walkers mum came out to see what was happening, her nostrils twitching as she detected an unfamiliar ordure.

"What's that funny smell Gary?" She asked.

"Horseshit mom, remember you're in the country now." Walker answered, covering up for Harris who'd just sparked up a joint. Nat had come outside to investigate the goings on and knew the smells of the country and cannabis was defiantly not one of them. Harris was, 'politely,' requested to put it out before she put him out. This was her wedding day. Harris complied and no more was said about the matter. Walker managed to navigate Natalie away from the crowd; it'd been an emotional day for him and he wanted some downtime alone with his new wife. "Let's fuck off Nat and go to the hotel." Nat's mum and step -dad had paid for them to spend the night at Shrewsbury's finest hotel as a wedding present. Natalie quickly agreed, she was tired and the baby was having a little party of its own in her belly. Walker went over to the DJ and whispered in his ear, he stopped the music to make an announcement that the happy couple were leaving.

Before they could make it to the door, Harris stepped in and gripped the microphone. Walker blew out air of his cheeks. He was nervous about making a speech, now he was grapping the bloody microphone without the, bloody need to! Walker looked up to the heavens and asked for divine intervention. Harris held his arms aloft. His fingers outstretched, his palms facing the crowd. Fuck me, he thinks he is the bloody messiah, Walker thought and half-expected him to start his new speech with. "Friends, Romans, Countrymen, lend me your ear." He was no Laurence Olivier, this wasn't Shakespeare's Julius Caesar and this was not the Old Vic.

"Hold on! " Harris bellowed into the microphone, he was high Walker knew it. They both watched him nervously, hand in hand, fixed smiles on their faces, hoping he wouldn't fuck up to badly. They were in the country, but this was no time for 'foot in mouth disease'.

"Let's put our hands together and wish the happy couple a right royal night and a great life together. Great bash, Gary my man; let's hope not as well as your bash goes tonight eh my son!" He winked at

Walker, as the crowd roared with laughter. Walker smiled hesitantly as he felt Natalie's grip on his hand tighten. Harris took his top hat off, and ran his fingers through his dirty brown hair in an attempt to brush it. His hat had become a permanent fixture on his head since one girl had made a comment that it made him look handsome and distinguished.

 Harris continued with his impromptu speech. "I'm going to pass my hat round, make sure I get it back please. Mrs. Walker has already reminded me, any damage to it and I'm up for the deposit." (More laughter). "Pass it round and throw some money in, so the happy couple can have a bottle of champagne, and a breakfast from room service please." The hat was duly passed round and people's hands went into their pockets.

 "Here you go mate," Harris passed over the hat when it was returned to him, full of money. He hugged Walker and whispered. "Love you mate," before they exchanged head gear.

The driver pulled the car around to the front door and Gary and Natalie made their way outside to the cheers of the crowd and started married life together.

Nat continued to live with her mum after they got married and worked up until her maternity leave started. Walker continued to spent time with his mates, getting pissed and doing what he shouldn't be doing, reassuring himself that when the baby was born he would embrace adulthood. He tried to leave the match alone, football was on top, prison sentences were being handed out to lads involved in violence like parking tickets. If you slapped a bloke in the town centre on a Friday night; you might get a short lie down with a fine being the likely outcome. You gave a twat a slap on a Saturday afternoon, who had come into Wolverhampton with the sole intention of having a fight you get a prison sentence. The government had set up a task force to combat football hooliganism, labeling it as organised crime. Walker could see the misnomer: How could they be mindless thugs if they were organised. Independent studies were initiated to take place: at Liverpool and Leicester Universities in an attempt to explain the phenomena. The establishment didn't care about studies, they just saw it as organised criminality and banned people from attending football matches. Walker knew it was a quick fix to appease the voters and it didn't address the fundamental issues involved. It would take understanding and commitment to understand other people's views and origins of behaviour, an ingredient not found readily in Thatcher's England.

Finally the authorities tired of the exploits of Wolves hooligans. An undercover operation to break the gang was named and initiated; Operation G.R.O.W.T.H. (Get Rid Of Wolverhampton's Troublesome Hooligans), ground into operation. Dawn raids were carried out at addresses across the West Midlands. Over sixty men were arrested and taken off the street.

The 'Bridge boys', a firm that had grown out of the remnants of the old Subway Army had been identified as the core element of the problem and were subsequently targeted. It was the biggest undercover operation ever seen in England to combat organised football violence. The chant went up from the terraces:

"WE'VE GOT MORE THAN SIXTY HOOLIGANS."

 A lot of the lads became tired of the scene without the need for a major police operation. The sentences handed out were disproportionate to the crimes committed. They were getting older and wanted to generate an income, correct in their thinking, If you were going to jail it was better to earn a pound note out of it.

 The summer of love dawned in 1988. Parties were being organised in units and warehouses up and down the land. Ecstasy came into the market place, a drug that made you want to love thy neighbour ,not beat the shit out of him.

It was a climate that warranted exploitation. Walker was aware of the change in mood and accepted the fact. The government with its short sighted agenda had created a culture of organised crime, as rivals fought to supply the clubbers. Gangs armed themselves with guns, not pride for the town they lived in. The law makers and politicians saw drugs as evil and a stain on civilised society; while they happily got drunk on subsidised twenty five year old single malt whisky, debating the old school network as they sat in their clubs and bars located in Westminster, their hypocrisy knowing no bounds.

Walker was experiencing financial problems; his scam at the warehouse had to be down sided due to the greed of some idiot. An employee, independent of Walker was caught red handed trying to fill up a seven and a half ton lorry with shelving packs in one load! Greed always got the better of them in the end, Walker lamented. If he got a custodial, it was his own fault for being fucking stupid. Computerised stock taking was introduced to ensure there wasn't a massive discrepancy in the stock levels carried in the warehouse. Walker applied and was promoted to stock administrator. This allowed him to knock out some moody stock, as he was the one that entered the figures into the computer and filled in the scrap returns. The role was a promotion and carried extra responsibility. Walker had begun to feel unrewarded with his career choice; his attendance at work had started to dip and was no longer one hundred percent. He hoped this new role would re-motivate him and the pay rise would help him in paying the bills. He had to find money for rent, fines, food, rates, petrol, and all the other expenses associated with running a home. He wanted to go out: buy clothes, he had a bank loan for a nice car parked outside, a Triumph TR7, he smiled ruefully as Nat told him that it would have to go. It wasn't practical anymore.

CHAPTER 7
VICTORIA

Nat finally made the move to Wolverhampton in the early autumn of 1988. She moved in with a flourish, three suitcases and a heavily distended belly. She'd finished work, as she was nearly full term in her pregnancy.

Walker was about to take the giant leap into fatherhood. He had ambivalent feeling about the transition. He was excited about becoming a dad; the feelings bubbled constantly in his stomach as he waited for the call and the mad dash to hospital. He also reflected that it was a difficult job being a parent. Being totally responsible for another life; a life that was created in your image.

The old men in the factory informed him, it was easy to make a baby, it was a lot harder to be a father. He listened to their wise counsel across the canteen tables, crossed his fingers and hoped he was man enough for the job. Walker had promised to look after Natalie; but he didn't think that would include rubbing her swollen ankles on a daily basis and she didn't believe him anymore when he told her she was beautiful. Her moods polarised, as she overdosed on hormones. To reinforce his commitment to her, Walker took time off work to escort her to the countless appointments which pregnant women have to attend, as he read endless magazines as over-emotional women, held their bellies and discussed topics he didn't understand. The stresses of life continued unabated and he took more time off from work than was necessary to massage his thoughts and look in the mirror for an answer. His line manager was aware that Nat was nearly ready to burst and granted him some leeway with a smile and words of understanding for his new role in life.

"Gary! Gary!" the shout burst out from the office and sounded important. Walker looked over his shoulder at Joan, and dragged himself away from the interesting job of counting shelving for his latest round of stock taking.

He made a mental note to deduct, the 200 or so He'd just moved out the back door the other week and popped his head into the warehouse office.

"Yes, what's up George?" A phone was thrust quickly into his hand.

"Hello is there anyone there?" Walker inquired

"Gary," it was Nat's voice on the other end of the line

"Nat you OK?" He asked again.

"Gary I'm having the baby!"

Walker broke a few laws on his way to New Cross Hospital, it was around eight miles from where he worked, straight through the heart of the industrial West Midlands and it took him nearly half-an-hour to arrive. He was swearing vigorously to himself as he struggled to find a parking place. Finally he located the maternity unit and presented at reception, red faced and out of breath, his chest pumping in and out.

"My wife's having a baby." He panted to the receptionist.

"Name please." The receptionist asked.

"Gary Walker." Walker answered.

The receptionist raised an eyebrow at him. "Your wife's name please."

"Oh, of cause, I'm sorry, Natalie, Natalie Walker." Walker felt conspicuous with his stupidity.

"Don't worry love, calm down, we will look after her, there's no need to worry." She thumbed through the admissions book and confirmed that Nat was indeed in the building and pointed Walker toward the delivery suite.

Walker exploded into the unit, his eyes rolling first one way and then the another. He didn't have a clue what to do; a passing nurse spotted the lost look on his face and rescued him.

"Can I help you Sir?" She asked.

"My wife's having a baby." Walker answered again.

The nurse offered the same response. "Well you're in the right place then love, can you give me a little bit more information to go on please?" She was used to hysterical men running about the ward like lemming and causing a ruckus. She ushered him to a chair asked him to take a deep breath before she clicked her pen and took some details from him. Walker happily handed the relevant information over, calmed and reassured by her professionalism. The nurse called an auxiliary over and instructed her to take Walker to see Natalie.

"It's your first baby then dear?" She could tell, it wasn't hard to read the signs.

"Yes, is it that easy to tell?" Walker panted like an exhausted dog oblivious to what he looked like.

"Calm down dear, it will be alright, your wife will want you to be calm, she is probably twice as nervous as you."

Walker nodded his head, understanding and grateful for the common sense that was being imparted to him. "Thank you, you're right, I'll try." He smiled at the lady, his heart beat starting to return to normal.

"Would you like a cup of tea?" Without tea there would not have been a British Empire. Walker was certain of the fact.

"Coffee?" He asked hopefully.

"Sugar?"

"Two please." The auxiliary showed Walker to a cubicle that had the curtains drawn around it, she pulled them back so they could both enter. Nat was on her back, legs akimbo, with the midwifes head in-between them examining Natalie closely.

"Hello there, are you two alright?" Walker was slightly taken aback from the strange sight in front of him. The nurse stopped what she was doing, and looked up at Walker. "Mr. Walker I presume."

"No Dr Livingstone, it is a hospital!" Walker said, though His humour was lost on her and a stony face greeted him by way of reply.

Natalie looked how he felt and peered sheepishly up at him from the bed. Walker realised this was not the time or the place for jokes and decided to try and act like an adult. He nodded toward the nurse and said. "Sorry."

"Your wife is only dilated a few centimeters, the baby's not coming for a while yet." The nurse tried to explain the rudiments of labour to Walker.

Dilated? He thought, isn't that what happened to orange squash? What the hell was she on about?

"Relax please Mr. Walker, it will take a while yet, we'll come back and check on you and Natalie shortly. There's a television room just down the corridor, if you want a change of scenery." She turned and left the cubicle, just as Walker's coffee was being delivered. Nat turned over and threw up into a cardboard receptacle to mark the occasion.

They decided to have a walk around the ward to find the television lounge. Walker walked; Nat wobbled and held her stomach with both hands wrapped tightly around it; protecting the precious cargo it held. She was nervous and scared about the pain, whispering to Walker that she wanted it all to be over soon. Walkers was attempting to be calm, his head nearly together now in attempt to reassure his wife. He spoke quietly, held her hand and asked what she needed him to do, could he

fetch her anything? She held his hand, her grip cutting off his blood supply as she was hit by another minor contraction. She glared at him aggressively and said. "No, it's painful and it's entirely your fault."
The clock hands were on a go slow as they refused to move around it's face. Walker was impatient; he would query the time scale with the nurses, who would simply explain that the baby would make an arrival when it was good and ready. Walker made calls to both their parents and advised them as to the non- state-of- play. He'd been at the hospital for hours now and was getting tired, giving birth moved as fast as a Test Match. He looked over at Nat, who was snoring softly on her bed; he smiled as he brushed her hair. Walker left her bedside and found a nurse; he was tired. "Where do I sleep please?" He asked.
She looked at him and replied. "How far away do you live darling?"
"Ten minutes down the road in a fast car," he replied.
"Go home and wait by the phone, when the labour starts in earnest, we will call you straight away, you have left your contact number, yes?" The nurse asked.
"Yes, it's on the forms, and written on a pad by the side of Natalie's bed," he stopped and looked back confused. "I thought she was in bloody labour?" Walker didn't understand this process at all and shook his head as he walked toward the door marked exit. Walker thanked a nurse, he recognised as she walked past. She smiled back at him and gave him a thumbs up. They were being patient with his constant questioning and he was sure they had more important jobs to attend to, than listen to his moronic rambling. After careful consideration of the situation he decided to head to his mother's house for a hot drink and further reassurance.
His mum was calm when he arrived on her doorstep and made him a cheese sandwich; He didn't notice was what in it, he chewed mechanically without taste. Walker appreciated the company and required the comfort that family provided in times of pressure. She brought him a coffee and placed it by his feet. He looked up at her; Walker looked tired and very young.
"Thanks Ma." Walker thanked her.
"You're welcome Gary; don't speak with your mouth full please. I'll listen for the phone so you don't have to worry about missing the call."
He shook his head, as if he would oversleep.

" I've plugged the spare phone in next to our bed." She added for extra encouragement. Walker nodded his mouth full of lettuce and tomato." If you want to sleep down here to hear the phone, I'll make you up a bed on the sofa, is that OK with you?"

Walker nodded again, his mouth full of salt and vinegar crisps, his appetite returning, he didn't realise how hungry he 'd been. As he lay on the sofa he looked up at the ceiling; totally alone with his thoughts. His parents were a lot calmer than he`d expected and this helped in soothing his initial fears. He smiled quietly, thinking this time tomorrow he'd be a daddy. He pulled the quilt up around his ears and attempted to watch an old black and white movie that was scheduled to send insomniacs to sleep and waited for the phone to ring.

Walker was woken by a shard of light that hovered over his eyes. He looked up, blinked and thought momentarily about shutting the curtains fully. He suddenly remembered where he was, and checked his watch, it was just after six. He 'd only slept for three hours, but felt refreshed. Morning had broken with no fresh news from the hospital. Walker paced the kitchen and made a coffee; he wasn't hungry but managed to force some toast down. After yesterday he understood that today could be a long one. He looked at the phone, and frowned, looking at it, isn't going to make it ring is it? He soon became bored with the lack of activity and the anxiety of inertia, deciding to drive back to the maternity ward.

There was only the occasional milk float as company and Walker enjoyed the quiet roads and the peace of the early morning. The tranquility and bird song helped him in mentally prepare for the events that lay ahead. It wasn't every day that one became a father.

The nurses greeted him back on the ward with smiles and offers of hot drinks, which he happily accepted. When he turned the corner with his coffee in hand, he saw Nat sitting up in bed looking like she hadn't slept for weeks, her eyes were dark and she was pale. "You look beautiful in the morning," he said quietly. She attempted to smile, grateful he was trying in his own inimitable fashion to reassure and comfort her. She was glad he was back without the need for a phone call to summon him.

Holding his hand she turned to him and said. "This child is too lazy to be born; I'm going to ground it when it finally makes an appearance!"

The day continued to drag on with no sign of the baby. Nat groans deepened and the time between visits from the nurses shortened.

Finally Nat was moved to another room: which was white and full of medical gadgetry. Natalie was fighting with a tube to get more gas and air into her system in a futile attempt to alleviate the pain. Her hair was matted with sweat and her skin glistened. Her chest heaved with the exertions and in-between being told to. "PUSH," she would slump back down on the bed, tears of pain running down her face.

There was blood on Walkers hands, where her fingernails had ripped into the flesh on his palms as she fought the agony of child birth. Walker remained quiet in the pauses between the screams, he'd tried to reassure her with wise words of comfort. "Come on Nat, nearly there now."

Nat looked across and snapped. "Shut up, you caused this, just let me get on with in!"

People that knew Walker well, understood that he couldn't remain quiet for long and he was soon exclaiming loudly." I can see the baby's head Nat, not much longer now, come on girl!"

The nurse told her to push; one last push and the baby would soon be with them. Walker left her side and walked around the gurney to get a better view; he could start to see, his baby! Her baby! Their baby, and shouted further encouragement.

It was a continued struggle for Nat who lay back and panted clearly exhausted by her efforts. The baby had reached the goal but was not over the line yet. The midwife left the room and a doctor quickly entered. What the fuck was going on, thought Walker as the doctor quickly put on a mask, donned some gloves and picked up some surgical scissors from a nearby table before striding confidently over toward the bed. After a brief examination, he started his work and there was soon blood everywhere as he completed his procedure, within seconds a baby appeared in the nurse's arms

Walker peered intently at the 'birth 'and after a pause identified the sex, it was a girl. "It's a girl Nat! It's a girl!" He celebrated like it was 1966 and jumped around the room. Waving his arms hysterically into the air and attempting to dance with the assembled staff, who smiled back at him warily.

The baby was carried to a nearby table and some more procedures were undertaken with rapid efficiency by the nursing staff. Walker heard the baby cry. Nat was lying on her back her face ashen, her chest still heaving from her exertions. The doctor was still employed between her legs, tying up loose ends.

The nurse brought the baby over to Walker, who'd now managed to
calm down. She was wrapped in hospital blankets and placed gently
into his arms. She was beautiful with red hair, just like his Nans. Walker
smiled down at his daughter. Big blue eyes looked back up at her dad,
she was covered in slimly green mucus which didn't detract from her
beauty, she was simply a masterpiece of nature. She blinked up at him
oblivious to all the fuss she'd created. Walker blinked back and said.
"Hello." It was all he could think of to say. Victoria Louise Walker had
entered the world. It was Wednesday October 26th 1988.
He called their respective parents and advised them that their status
had changed; they were now grandparents. He waited at the entrance
of maternity, leaned against the wall and lit a cigarette and waited for
the inexorable deluge of family that would kiss him, offer him advice,
patronise Nat, and generally do his head in. His mum was the first to
arrive. Don't fucking kiss me, he sent out the mental message and his
mother received it loud and clear.
"The baby is in there somewhere mom." Walker gestured vaguely
toward the big building that was supporting him with his hands. "I
don't exactly know where. The nurses have taken her. Don't worry
though it's all good, she is healthy and around the seven pound mark."
Walker had been in the maternity unit for a day now. He'd picked up
on the chit-chat and knew woman needed those snippets of
information for future gossip related references.
"I'll sort out where she is Gary don't worry," she replied.
Walker wasn't worried: he was happy, exhilarated, tired and close to
tears. It had been a moving experience for him. He wasn't worried,
because the nursing staff had done such a dam fine job in putting up
with him as well as assisting Nat in the delivery suite. There were few
doubts in his mind and they were able to watch baby Victoria for an
hour or two. Nat had to stay in hospital for a few days before they
would discharge her. She'd needed stitches to assist in the birth and
had lost blood and was weak as a result. Walker went in to see his
wife. Natalie was sleeping soundly and his mum had Victoria cocooned
in her arms. "She is beautiful Gary."
"Naturally mom, she takes after the parents," he replied.
 Victoria was beautiful; she didn't look like Winston Churchill, like other
peoples new born babies . She was perfect in every way. Nat woke up;
Gary looked at her and took Victoria off his mum, holding her with
delicate precision.

"Say hello to our daughter Nat." Mum and daughter eyed each other up for a moment before Nat held her close, their initial introductions performed.

Walker left soon after; other people were arriving and the blue rinse brigade were in full battle order. Thinking defensively, Walker decided to get the fuck out of dodge, grab some sleep and have a beer with the lads. He was a man, he had a child. He was a father! He would shout it from the rooftops, to all who wanted to listen.

Walker visited Nat twice a day, happy to play the dutiful daddy. She wasn't overly impressed when on Saturday afternoon he arrived with Harris, Carter, Simpson, Kerry and a couple of others lads who were all drunk. They'd been to the match and were in the process of wetting the baby's head for the umpteenth time. She tried to smile but her eyes rolled at Walker, when a camera was produced and photos were taken of her (she wasn't looking her best, but they still remain in the album to this day).

Alerted by the noise and in a hurry to investigate the commotion, several nurses descended on the lads and halted their impromptu party, quickly ushering them off the ward, explaining that. "This was a maternity ward, not a football match!" They managed to separate Walker from the pack to speak to him. "Natalie is due to be discharged tomorrow, can you fetch her in the morning at around nine please?" The ward sister asked.

"Of course it's not a problem. I'll be here on the dot and thank you." Walker replied. He was a man now; he had a wife, a child and was learning to be a responsible adult. All the problems associated with money and the stress of their life leading up to Victoria's birth had been forgotten and banished from his memory. It had all been worth it.

Life continued as they both expected it would do, with a young couple and a new born baby; dirty nappies, sleepless nights, and endless bills. Walker managed to fund a ten day holiday to Benidorm to celebrate their wedding and finally take Natalie on a long overdue honeymoon. Both of them enjoyed the break away, they returned to the days when they'd first met and they recaptured their youth. Nat's mum had agreed to look after little Victoria for them whilst they away. She didn't work and had spare times on her hands, preferring to be supported by her comfortably well off third husband

The majority of Walker`s income went on keeping their heads above water. It was a struggle, life was a struggle, but then he looked at Victoria as she started to giggle, smile and display emotions other than crying. The times when he bounced her up and down off his knee, as he looked out of the window, explaining the vagrancies of the modern world made him realise that all the scrimping and the meals consisting entirely of mined beef were worthwhile. She gave him a better high than any substance he'd ever dropped.

Victoria was mostly her mother's girl for the first period of her life. Walker didn't really get a real look in until she could hobble round and start to talk. Nat had secured herself a part time job at the local pub to help out with the family finances and pay her little slice into the pot, to help them afford other luxuries such as fruit and heating. With her first wage packet she went to the butchers and bought Walker a steak the size of a coffee table. As he savored the taste, with a cold class of cider in his hand, he felt like the richest man in the world.

Natalie would enjoy getting ready for work, humming as she listened to radio one, applying her lipstick and checking her hair in the mirror for the umpteen time. Nat enjoyed the break from the confines of the flat and a day of cleaning nappies.

Walker dismissed disposal nappies as a waste of their already stretched budget. Walker would watch with dread as the hands on the clock ticked round, like a funeral procession, signaling it was time for her leave and start her shift.

From the moment she left to the moment she returned Victoria would scream and cry the house down. He would pick her up, rock her, sing to her, tell her stories and finally shout with frustration, but she would not relent. The only thing that would induce a period of tranquility was a nocturnal drive, when he put her in the back seat of his car. (The sports car had been jettisoned for a Vauxhall Cavalier). Then she would finally rest, close her eyes and peace would rein on the western front; when Walker stopped the car and attempted to carry her upstairs to place her in her cot, hostilities would resume unabated.

Nat would walk back in from work several hours later and a smile would spread across Victoria's face, she would gurgle and laugh. Nat would look at Walker and ask. "What was all the fuss about?"

Italia 1990 arrived: The World Cup descended upon an expectant nation. Walker would rush home from work to watch the games, still in love with football. His car had gone, the police had stopped him one night after he and Nat were on their way home after another rare excursion into town. She'd thrown a bottle at a bouncer after one too many shandies. Walker had managed to get them out the situation quickly. The bouncer was not a man to be trifled with, he was the elder brother of some well known lad that was top of the food chain in Wolves.

When he told Walker to stop being a tit, Walker stopped. Nat didn't give a fuck and she hurled a bottle at him, which luckily smashed at his feet. Her aim was as bad as her ability to handle her beer, otherwise they could have been in a mountain of trouble.

They'd originally decided to get a cab back home but events overtook them. Walker jumped into the seat of their car and wheel spun it off the car park. The old bill stopped him on their way home as his brake light wasn't working and they smiled as they breathalysed him. In court he received a three year ban as it was his second conviction for driving whilst drunk.

Walker bought a pedal bike to get him to work and back and found a silver lining in the situation by focusing on all the costs that he would save on motoring expenses.

He'd pedal home furiously on his twenty geared mountain bike (wondering which one would get him up the hill as he hyperventilated and sweated) to watch the matches. Making the eleven or so miles back home in about forty five minutes, arriving through the door with a bright. "Hello." Before he plonked himself in front of the television and escaped the drudgery of work in the blessed relief of football. Sometimes Victoria would sit on his knee as he tried to explain the offside rule to her. Walker believed in subliminal learning techniques, it was a good start in life for the young lady.

Money was scarce, so he didn't go to the pub to watch the England games. He lived three miles away from The Wood's and even if he had the money for a beer he wasn't about to pedal there and then get pissed and have to pedal back. He would probably kill himself on the ride home, crashing into oncoming traffic. He would grab a few beers from the local shop and watch the games in front of his own television set, he'd invested in a new 26 inch screen and it took pride of place on his video unit.

The world cup started slowly for England, they played poorly at first. A 1:1 draw against the Irish, 0:0 against the Dutch. Finally they managed a victory over Egypt with a Mark Wright headed goal; they were through to play Belgium in the last sixteen. The press wanted Bobby Robson to *'Release the Bull'.* Steve Bull was the God of Wolverhampton. He'd been called up into the England squad and taken to Italy. He'd scored on his debut against the Scots and Victoria had nearly died of shock, her old man ran round the house like a demented hamster in a ball. Screaming madly. "YESSS, GOAL!" At the top of his voice. He was a top player was Bully and would get a deserved chance to show the skills he possessed in a World Cup Finals match.

England won the game 1:0 with a David Platt goal, the last kick off the game. Walker repeated the hamster on acid scenes and then some more on top.

Victoria had gotten used to her dad being loud. She simply blinked and took it all in her stride.

The nation grew behind the team and the excitement mounted. Walker needed some stimulus during these nail biting times so he agreed to watch the games at his dads and brought Victoria along with him. Walker and his dad had called a truce since he had grown up and become a father and it gave his mum a chance to spoil Victoria and dote over her granddaughter.

The quarter final was the next match. England versus The Cameroon, Walker expected a walk in the park. He had to spend the last minutes walking around the garden, unable to watch the last moments of the game, the tension unbearable as England hung onto a slender 3:2 lead, deciding he would need more than just a few beers to watch the game against West Germany. On his way to his Dad`s to support England against the dreaded Germans he stopped at the shop and bought a dozen bottles of Diamond White. He got louder as the cider and patriotic fever kicked in as the match progressed.

His dad wasn't overawed with his drunken behaviour. Walker`s Granddad on his dads' side had been an alcoholic, His dad had felt his drunken moods physically, subsequently he didn't approve of alcohol. It worried him when Walker drank, as he could see his own father alive and well in his son. Lineker equalised for England and Walker lifted the roof off the house, he was drunk and needed a crowd, the old football adrenalin pumping through his veins.

The pub Nat worked in was within walking distance ,so he decided to pay her a visit. Her eyes narrowed as he entered, she knew he was volatile over football and she knew he'd been drinking. The game went into extra time and the tension mounted. It was end to end stuff, in the two periods of extra time with both sides coming close to a winner, finally the ref blew his whistle, it had come down to penalties.

Penalties! England were just a shoot out away from World Cup glory! From the World Cup final! They were that close! They scored the first three penalties without drama.

Walker needed a piss, and fought his way through the throng to the gents. He stuck his head around the door and shouted. "Who's taking the next penalty?"

"Pearce, " the reply came back.

"He won't fucking miss, he's got a shot like a tracer bullet." Walker told the crowd.

The crowd held it's breath as he ran up to take it. The ball cannoned off the Goal Keeper's legs. The lucky German twat! They converted their next penalty easily. Waddle looked like he was going in front of a firing squad as he strode up to take his. It was no surprise when he missed. The pub went deathly quiet. Walker could not believe it, they had been so fucking close to glory. He went to the lounge to see Nat and bend her ear about the injustice of it all. She was serving a customer at the bar; the prick was wearing a fucking stupid straw cowboy hat. He had blond hair, blue eyes and looked Germanic. To make matters worse he was laughing and having a good time. He ordered a large scotch with a smile on his face. Fuck me, England had just lost in a penalty shoot out to the hated enemy and this little cunt thought it was a fucking joke. Walkers temper began to rise.

"What you got to fucking celebrate mate?" Walker spat the words out, saliva landed on the blokes face.

"Nothing," the blokes' eyes widened. He didn't like football and didn't know what affect his behaviour was causing. The bloke was naïve, he should have known better.

"Gary...... NO!" Nat knew what was coming. His fist connected and the bloke went down. Nat was already on her way around the bar to stop her husband. She grabbed hold of him as he aimed kicks at the bloke who was prostrate on the floor.

"Get out!" She ordered, adding "and never come back into the pub." His wife had just barred him from the pub! Walker couldn't believe the situation; he arrived back at his parents' house and cried in his mother's arms. Fucking Germans!

Walker added another addition to the family, a beautiful Rottweiler puppy he christened Baskerville. Baskerville was a bundle of black and tan fluff with a little pink tongue. Victoria fell in love with her immediately. She would point and laugh excitedly as the little puppy would wobble around the furniture, her paws moving in time to a silent military beat. Baskerville had internal rhythm. Their little family unit was now complete.

Life got more perfect for him when Mrs. Thatcher was disposed by her own party in November 1990 after a leadership contest. Her arbitrary actions taken against the British populace was over. Her reign of terror over the poor and vulnerable finished. Her own party knew that she was unelectable. The Tories as ever, eager to serve their quest for power toppled her. The coup was completed and the nation rejoiced. In her place a man that was as grey as a summer day in Blackpool became Prime Minister. His appointment was an appeasement, to keep warring factions of the party at bay, stopping the Tories from imploding and going into meltdown.

A general election was just around the corner and they would do anything to cling onto government. It was a great day for the country in Walker's opinion when the woman he loathed left Downing Street. John Major stepped forward into the political spotlight. His first major action was to take the country back to war. What was it with Conservative Prime Ministers that they had to take the country to war, a year before a general election? Walker pondered the question. This war was just, however. The pacifist brigade shouted out. 'It was an American war. A war for oil'. The fact remains the Saddam Hussein invaded a sovereign nation in an attempt to gain land and secure ports to export his oil, to promote and fund his struggle against dissident factions in his own country. On August 2nd 1990 his armies rolled over the border and invaded Kuwait. The man, who was responsible for genocide against his own people, now turned his attention toward his neighbour. He slaughtered anybody that did not agree with his 'word'. No one else had invaded Kuwait so blame him, not the Americans. It was a simple equation for Walker. Thirty four nations formed an alliance, while the peace brigade debated the merits of an 'American war'. 956,600 troops had been gathered to restore order to a troubled region. The British sent 43,000 fighting men, 2,500 fighting vehicles. It was their largest deployment since the Berlin wall had come down.

Arab nations had been included in the coalition, another kick up the arses for the Anti-Western campaigners.

On the 16th of January 1991 the world got its taste of the first video game war. A war that you could follow twenty four hours a day on CNN, as Desert Storm was unleashed. Viewers could ride the laser bombs straight onto their targets. It reminded Walker of Kubrick's cold war classic *'Dr Strangelove'*. When *Major T.J "King" Kong* rode the nuclear weapon down like a man in a rodeo, whooping and waving his cowboy hat excitedly. Walker agreed whole heartedly with the war, not the methods employed to report it.

On February 23rd 1991 Operation Saber was launched: the ground assault was underway. In one hundred hours, the Allied Blitzkrieg rolled over the Arab deserts and swamped the ill equipped armies of Saddam. 26,000 Iraqi soldiers died serving their tyrannical master, to an allied loss of just 379. The allied armies nearly managed to kill as many of their own soldiers as Hussein's troops did. What did the old men used to say at work? "When the British bomb the Germans duck, when the Germans bomb the British duck, When the Americans bomb every fucker ducks. It did appear true.

The years rolled forward; they had not been able to secure their own house. These were the days of the property boom. Walker would make an offer on a house and get out-bidden. Houses would rise in price expediently to their real value. One house they viewed, in an inner city area of Wolverhampton, price went up from £15,000 to £32,000 in three weeks. It was madness.

Maggie had turned the country into a heaving mass of greed and a stamp on others to get to the top philosophy. It was the 'I've got more than you', culture mutated. Idiots would walk round with phones the size of call boxes clamped to their ears. Shouting loudly down the handset so everybody could hear their business. No wonder Sony took the opportunity to release The, *'Walkman,'* to drown out the sound of bankers and estate agents professing that their worth was entirely financial. They served no other purpose to society.

The economy began to take a downturn; factories were again being shut by the Tory's mismanagement of the economy. It was the 9th of April 1992, the day Walker was made redundant, the day that the county went to the polls, the irony was not lost on him. Surely the people would not vote for a Tory party that had ruined the economy again?

The Sun newspaper declared on polling day: '*Would the last person to leave Britain turn out the Light*'.

If Labour, under Neil Kinnock won the election.

The turnout was 77.7% one of the highest recorded. The Tories were returned with a small majority of twenty one seats.

 Walker woke up on the tenth of April; unemployed with a hangover and another Tory government.

Part Two:
THROUGH THE LOOKING GLASS
CHAPTER 8
DOMESTICTY.

George Coleman walked into The Woods. He was loud, brash and arrogant with a ruthless air about him. Instinctively Alpha male. His gold teeth flashed when he smiled, he was as black as the ace of spades, with close cropped hair, which sat on top of his head, shaved at the back and at the edges. He walked like a man who'd seen the inside of a gym; his poise wasn't elegant, but he had a certain animalistic grace, like a hungry lion patrolling the grassland of the savannah.

"Who's that?" Walker enquired, inclining his head toward the bar, his curiosity fully engaged regarding the new edition to the pub's décor. Walker felt his nose pop out of joint. Previously he and Harris had been the unruly element in The Woods, Walker had the distinct feeling they were about to be usurped.

"A geezer, calls himself Silks." Harris replied.

"Silks? What kind of fucking name is Silks!"Walker queried.

 Harris shrugged."Yeah, apparently he was like silk around the pool table when he was in jail." Harris enlightened Walker, who shrugged his shoulders dubiously.

 "What the fuck is he doing in here, giving it the big un?"

"He's just done a ten stretch for armed robbery Gaz, in tough nicks too, by all accounts. Best leave him well alone for now mate." Walker saw the wisdom in Harris's words. He sipped his pint and greeted the lads that were out with Silks. He knew them, but not well. Harris and Walker continued their night out and nothing else was said about Silk`s arrival.

Things were unsteady at home as Walkers ship ploughed through stormy waters. Nat was on his case and nagging him to get another job; he was under her feet and she wasn't used to having him around the house all day. He was always in her way when she vacuumed, dusted and he created merry hell in the kitchen when he prepared the evening meal. Nat couldn't cook and considered it a chore. She'd once managed to burn ice cream. They'd wanted to snack on some raspberry ripple while they were enjoying an evening in front of the television and it was frozen solid and impossible to spoon into bowels, without upsetting the cutlery. Nat was a clever girl; she could problem solve and was aware of the premise of lateral thinking. Subsequently, the tub was placed with due diligence into the microwave and Nat pressed cook, wandering back into the lounge to check out what was happening in Eastenders. She'd pushed the ten minute button by mistake and got carried away with the dramatic events unfolding in Albert Square. When she returned to the kitchen to collect their supper, it was liquidised and the tub had melted. From that moment on Walker took responsibility for ensuring that Victoria was spared her mother's culinary acumen. Walker loved it in the kitchen. He loved to rattle the pots and pans and had become quite the accomplished chef. He would prepare gourmet food that looked and tasted surprisingly good. They invited Nat's mum and step- dad to the flat to sample his cuisine and they'd gone home impressed by his gastronomic skills. Walker had learned the basics from watching countless daytime TV cookery shows as he relaxed on the sofa oblivious to the sound of the omnipotent vacuum cleaner.

The adaption process from spending his life in a factory, to living without the phantom of regular work haunting him, hadn't presented Walker with an insurmountable obstacle. They had money in their building society account due to the generous redundancy package he'd received along with his final wage packet. This ensured they weren't destitute and had savings for the first time in his memory. Walker had stopped enjoying his job years ago. It'd started to become a head fuck for him. Days off had started to become a regular occurrence with all sorts of bullshit excuses tendered to explain his now regular absences. It was a wonder the World Health Organisation didn't park a tent outside their flat there were so many pathogens contained in his bedroom.

 When Nat asked him if was intending on searching for a new job any time soon, Walker would answer arrogantly, there were better jobs out there for a man of his talent and intellect. Oblivious to the looks being passed in his direction, he would settle down on the sofa with his remote control and plan his afternoon`s viewing. If Natalie's moaning became too grating, Walker would simple state the fact, he had worked hard for the last eight years and maybe he deserved a month or two off.

Walker made sure his bank balance was under the level required to receive his giro and they started to receive housing benefit and a small touch off the dole every two weeks. His redundancy provided for the little luxuries that made life bearable and there was no discernible lowering in their standard of living. Walker didn't understand what her nagging was all about. He'd worked all his life and paid his fair share of taxes into the exchequer; let the Tories take care of him for a while he had paid far more into the pot than he was about to take out and their policies had plagued him all his life.

His contempt for their voting demographic was reinforced when he remembered the time he'd enjoyed a political debate with Nat and she moaned about the poll tax. She'd gone on about the unfairness of the charge for days at an end when she received her own bill in the post. Walker went into a political tirade about the imbalance in society and was stopped mid-speech when she dropped out the gem that she had voted Tory!

"You voted for Maggie Thatcher?" Walker was confused.

"Yes," she replied.

"And you're moaning about the poll tax?" Walker queried, requiring clarification.

"Yes, why? What's that got to do with it? This poll tax, it's unfair." She placed her hands on her hips and made her point. Her gaze was stern, unaware of the flow of the political tide. It was no point falling on the rock of empathy the Tories felt for the working classes. Death would be a certain result.

"How can you moan about the policy when you voted for it?" Walker said.

"I didn't know they were going to bring it in, I just voted conservative that's all."

That just about summed up a typical Conservative voter in Walkers' opinion. Mention manifesto and they thought it was a late night Italian detective show!

Nat wasn't stupid; she could hold her own on selected topics. When it came to the academic world or the understanding of current affairs and the state of the planet she wasn't the quickest off the mark.

Walker had more time on his hands now to consider relevant topics and attempt a discussion regarding the ways of the world with his wife and a conversion in her political stance. She just thought it a stupid theme for a conversation and asked him. 'If he was going out any time soon?'

Natalie sipped at her tea and sat on the sofa and let out a sigh of comfort, she'd taken a rare opportunity to put her feet up. Walker was in Victoria's bedroom getting involved in some nonsense involving Lego and she enjoyed the temporary peace and quiet their absence afforded her. She flicked with casual disinterest through the pages of the evening paper until her eyes rested upon an advertisement for Care Assistants. She thought for a moment and weighed up the pros and cons, her concentration broken as the circus arrived back into the front room. "I'm going to apply for a job at Country Meadows old folks home, working nights for three days or rather nights a week."

Walker stopped tickling Victoria, looked up and nodded. "Go for it Nat," he said. His thoughts were pragmatic. the more she earned the less he would have to stump up every Friday. When Walker thought he had dealt with one round of bills, another letter would drop through the letter box demanding another slice of his pie. Walker was all for female emancipation and admired Germaine Greer's feminist stance. A man that stopped at home and played with his child was called a 'bum'. Walker laughed ironically, women who did it, and then told their friends they'd sacrificed their own career and personal growth to raise a man's child were called wonderful mother's and afforded all the parental accolades. Walker could see a double standard when it walked up to him and kicked his arse.

Natalie applied for and got her job, he admired her work ethic as she tried on her new uniform and pinned her name tag on proudly, as she got ready for her first night at the home. As he listened to her excited chatter about becoming a wage earner; strange pangs of guilt rumbled in his stomach and feelings of emasculation filtered into his mind: should he not be the one getting ready to go to work to provide for his family?

Walker debated the merits in the feminist stance and found a job within two weeks. His dad`s mate was looking for some hands to work on a big job he'd tendered for and been duly awarded; erecting the shelving and storage systems he'd once used to load on an assortment of wagons. He thought it would be interesting to see how the product went together and the technicality of how it was built. The bloke would pay him £30 a day on top of his dole cheque, bonus thought

Walker. He didn't have to get up to go to work every day and face the grey drudgery of the rat race.

The added incentive for his new lifestyle was that he got to spend more time with Victoria, whom he'd now christened Shorts. She was short, had shorter legs than him, would always have shorter legs than him hence the fact she was shorts. The name would stick with Victoria but only Walker ever used it to refer to her.

As Victoria's grasp of the English language improved, so did her relationship with her dad. Walker would sit and listen, captivated by her fledging ability to construct simple sentences as they discussed, Thomas the Tank Engine's lifestyle. Walker motivated to teach her all the activities he'd missed out as a child, bought a ball and he would spend hours over the local park in an attempt to teach her the vagaries of football, quietly encouraging her when she fell over, after being tackled by the ball for the umpteenth time. Victoria was beautiful, eloquent and intelligent but she was poor at football there was no doubt about it. Walker looked forward to their time in the park together, he would pack a little bag with a fruit loop drink, an apple and a bag of crisps, happily pushing her madly on the swings enjoying the sound of her hysterical laughter. Walker simply enjoyed doing all the daddy and daughter stuff, she would listen intently to the stories he would read to her at bedtime, sometimes from a book or sometimes from his own imagination. Galvanised by his renewed interest in family life and in an attempt to pacify Nat and her now endless nagging about when he was going to land a 9-5, five day a week job, he took her to allied carpets to invest some money in a new carpet. It cost him £300 with fitting included. It was well worth the cost for the grief on the ears it saved him.

His dad and mom joined in the assault on his ear drums, worried about his future as he'd taken to the dole far too well.

Mr. Butcher, his casual employer was able to give him one week's work in four. Walker was happy with that arrangement, his parents thought he needed to knuckle down and move forward, so did Nat. He was sure at times that they and Nat got their little heads together and were conspiring against him. His former paranoia sitting quietly in the background.

Walker would argue back at them and explain, that he was learning a trade, that a big job was coming up that would last three months and he was on it, let up on his head and give him a fucking break! During

Sunday lunch they'd turned on him on mass, the cacophony of advice built up in is head until his mum's best glasses had been smashed against the wall. They all sat and watched as he kicked off, only then did doubts cross his mum and dad's mind that, maybe their son wasn't quite right in the head.

Walker paid a visit to the pub to cool off, finding solace at the bottom of a bottle and a stay on his mate's sofa for the night. Walker finally relented to the pressure and told Nat that he had found a way to make money and appease her right wing outlook. He would start his own business. Keith Butcher would pay a small fortune to have shelving and other materials delivered to site. He was always complaining that he needed a van, why he didn't invest in one, Walker never understood. Mr. Butcher's loss was his gain. He found a niche in the market and a way to exploit it to his own ends. He sat down after making peace with his parents to discuss his plan. They still worked in the trade, and love him or hate him, his dad had built a big business from nothing and was well informed about this new world that Walker was about to step into to. They listened to his plan and agreed about his initial premise and offered support in setting up the business. Walker went to the building society drew out a large chunk of his redundancy money and purchased a white van. G.A. Walker business services came into existence.

Walker contacted various printers and negotiated a competitive price before he placed his order for a thousand cards and letter heads. He purchased a mobile phone on contract, the terms and tariff was expensive, but he was a business man and needed a gadget to keep his finger on the pulse and keep ahead of his competitors. Nat smiled and kissed her husband as he typed invoices on his new word processor as she glanced at the cost of his labour. At last her husband was looking toward the same future as she was. For Walker it was his ticket to freedom, the days of 9-5 drudgery were consigned to the past.

He could work the hours he chose to, and he could quote his own price. His dad had promised to invest in the business if he did it legally and signed off the dole. Walker agreed with him whole heartedly, they were too nosey anyway at the job centre always asking him this, that and the other. They made him feel like he was a beggar when he went to sign on. On his last trip there he took great pleasure in telling them to 'Fuck off,' as they asked one stupid question to many. He told the balding bureaucrat, with the sad, fleshy face, who was obviously drunk on the power he held over the jobless, and probably beat his wife and kids in his spare time; that the term job centre was a misnomer, that the only people that went there had no jobs. The civil servants who sat behind their desks were not concerned with attempting to empathise with the people who'd fallen on hard times or how to find them gainful employment. Their brief, their employment criteria, was to ensure that the already oppressed masses fulfilled petty conditions which meant that they could be issued with their weekly pittance that the government stated they could live on per week. Again the Tory press spread right wing propaganda, suggesting the 'great unwashed' lived a cushy number on benefits, arguing that most people would rather live on social security than work for a living. Walker accepted that there were people that were happy to live that way and some that didn't. He was also aware that most jobs paid low wages and the poor needed a safety net to survive. The rich evaded taxes and exploited loopholes in the system, able to pay cooperate lawyers a small fortune to reduce their tax burden. It cost the exchequer millions in unpaid revenue but the Express and Mail didn't print daily headlines professing they were the lowest of the low. Why couldn't the low paid have their piece of the pie too?

The Middle-Classes, safe behind their neatly mowed lawns and double glazed windows gobbled up the propaganda, reading the daily diatribes against the poor, patting themselves on the back for being productive members of society. They should walk in the steps of the unemployed who were honestly looking for work and were not content with their poverty ridden existence.

 Walker and his Tory bride accepted the help offered to them from the state. With no fixed income, they had a percentage of their rent paid, and a portion of their poll tax contributed to. It was fuck all compared to the lump in taxes he'd paid over the years. Walker would eat at the top table and he would not forget his journey to get there. He knew his parents were financially well off and he hadn't experienced a deprived childhood. However, since he'd left school, he'd worked in a factory, on the shop floor and had made his bones with the lads from West Bromwich and gained their respect with his attitude and hard work. He knew he'd been presented with and wasted his early opportunities. He also knew that he hadn't been born with a silver spoon up his arse when it came to his work ethic and outlook.

CHAPTER 9
SILKS.

Harris and Walker were seated in The Woods, it was Friday night and Walker was spending some of his newly hard earned cash. The pub was filling up nicely. The lads from death row had the dominos out and were arguing and knocking amongst themselves. Some beer monsters were playing darts, money had appeared on the table where a group of lads had started to shuffle a deck of cards. A group of girls with high heels and low skirts, faces painted like clowns with language like builders had just ordered their drinks. They were dressed up and laughing, excited in the vivid anticipation of losing their pants to Mr. Right, or whoever bought them their last vodka for the night. The sun was dipping in the sky and the slightest aroma of Buda hung in the air, the fire exit was open and the car park was crowded with the local youth. Bottles and glasses in their hands, wearing more track suits than the start of the London Marathon They were talking loudly, all of them were white, but sounding as if they were trying to talk Patois. Black is a colour Walker thought, not a fashion statement. He was starting to feel the effects of the alcohol and wanted a lift to his night out. He hadn't done speed for as long as he could remember and he missed the clean feeling of power amphetamines offered
 him.
 Walker still liked a drink, getting drunk regularly, even when times were hard he could find money to visit the off sales, when he couldn't afford the pub. This would irritate Nat and she didn't bite her tongue in her forceful attempts to make him abstinent. She had to suffer him when he was drunk, and slurring in front of the telly thinking that everybody in the room was on the same train ride as him. He thought he was intelligent and topical when he was drunk. She thought he was an over-opinionated dick head! On some occasions, the day after one of his little bouts could be tense. They would conspicuously ignore one another. On others they recaptured those halcyon moments of 1987. George Coleman A.KA. Silks was in the pub drinking a short at the bar, laughing with a group of lads. Walker was seeing him around the local pub and area on regular occasions; he was becoming a local fixture. Coleman was the brother in law of a well respected lad, called Darren Langley. This relationship had provided him with a beachhead into

unfamiliar territory, he was now advancing on all fronts. Coleman hailed from the other side of Wolverhampton, a menagerie of council estates and ruffians. Walker didn't have much to do with him at first, unsure of the thin ice that surrounded them. They hadn't spoken at length, simply nodded politely to each other in the pub which was the extent of their relationship to date.

 The bubble of conversation provided a raucous backdrop, almost drowning out the jukebox, Adamski's Killers was playing: It reminded Walker of that hot July night back in 1990 when they'd lost to the Germans on penalties. The evening was starting to show some promise. Walker wanted some speed as the alcohol was no longer providing the buzz he required. "Got any gear on you Pete?" Walker asked.

"No mate, go and get some off Silks he knocks a wrap out now and again." Harris answered him.

"Why, is he carrying?"

"Most of the time, he will be tonight its fucking Friday ay it mate. Come on." Harris said.

Walker looked at him. "Ha-fucking-ha. Alright Pete, alright mate go to the top of the fucking class. I'm sorry I'm fucking boring you with mundane things like facts." Walkers sarcasm was not lost on Harris.

" Sensitive tonight aren't we Gary? Pull you pants up and stop being a girl, you might even get a date if you smile sweetly enough."

Walker smiled back without humor, got up from the table and wandered over toward Silks. "Can I have a quick word?" He indicated with his head that he wanted a chat.

Silks looked him up and down, and then straight into his eyes. "What can I do for you?" He asked, the tone suggesting boredom.

"It's a bit public here mate." Walker answered.

"The names Silks, I'm not your mate. "Silks replied, his look non-committal.

Fucking hell Walker thought. This was becoming stressful and he only wanted a wrap to buzz his night out. Most people would go through the preamble of being polite when they were starting to generate a dialogue with someone they'd just met. This bloke was breaking all the fucking rules. What had happened to manners? Walker had never met a man, who genuinely didn't give a fuck what people thought about him. Most people would say that in conversation, to appear assertive, and confident, but in his experience everybody wanted to be liked.

That was human nature. His self-confidence must be up in orbit, either that or he was fucking arrogant. From the look of him he was blessed with both those characteristics. Walker looked around at Harris who had that dim-witted look on his face, that punctuated his life when he wanted to act nonchalantly. Harris had suspected that Silks might lead him a merry dance at first.

Walker had previously got Harris to supply most of his drugs via his own contacts. Harris didn't do speed, he would take it if it was on offer but he liked the drift that cannabis provided and was still well into his bush. If Walker wanted to speed, he had to cover his own back and sort out his own deals, it was that simple. Walker persevered with his negotiations with Silks. "You carrying?" He kept his voice low he didn't want to bring unneeded attention toward them, as this bloke was obviously fucking nuts. Best tread carefully around him he thought to himself. This was a different world from getting pissed in the boozer and giving some tit a dig and fucking off home to the wife. This bloke was a bank robber and had served proper time in proper nicks. Harris had been up town with Silks, with the rest of the lads from The Woods on a football team night out. Walker had been at home living the domestic dream. Silks moved with Wolverhampton's finest. He was mates with men that were folk-law in hooligan circles.

"You carrying?" He asked again. Unsure if Silks had ignored him, or just hadn't heard him. This man was making him feel like a fucking child.

"Might be, what you looking for?"

"Billy."

"Tenner a wrap," Silks said.

"A Fucking tenner!" Walker forgot his previous misgiving in dealing with the bloke.

"If you want it pay, if you don't fuck off, it's all the same to me."

That was how their first conversation went. Walker paid the man, took his gear and went to the toilet, locked himself in a cubicle and dropped it in one go, it tasted like shit and he wished he'd taken his pint along with him to wash the bitter taste out of his mouth. He still couldn't understand why he'd felt like a beginner, he shook his head to rid his mind of any negative thoughts and went back to the bar.

Harris still had a dumb look on his face. "Any good?" He asked.

"I'll let you know in a bit, when it kicks in." Walker answered him with a wink.

The speed was rocket fuel. It took half an hour to kick in, nearly knocking him out, as the drug entered his system. He'd felt tired, even lethargic before the rush stared. "Fuck me." Walker whispered as his eyes popped, he started to breathe deeply to cope with the feeling that were now rampaging through his mind. He couldn't keep still, his feet were tapping to an internal beat. His hands brushed imaginary specks from his t-shirt and jeans. White froth flecked the corners of his mouth.

Silks looked over toward the table and saw the change in him. He put his empty glass on the bar and sauntered over to the table, he nodded at Pete." You alright Harris?"

Harris nodded back. Silks rested his hands on the table and looked at Walker. Walker noticed he had massive hands, fingers as thick as frankfurters.

"Happy?" He asked.

Walker didn't know if was a question or an order. His brain was turning to paste, as his synapse's attempted to halt the rush charging through his CNS.

"Very." He just managed to say, his mouth had turned to sand.

Silks smiled. "Have a drink mate," he empashised the word 'mate', or did he? Walker was confused, happy and then energised. He felt like Popeye after spinach.

"Told you it was worth it. See me in future if you want to get sorted OK." Silks said. Turning, he nodded to the lads at the bar and left the pub, his mobile phone clasped to his ear.

Nat wasn't impressed when Walker arrived home. He was 'loved up' and wanting some action. She was trying to catch up on her sleep having just completed her allotted night shifts. She pushed him away, and pulled the pillow over head, irritated with his fumbling hands. "Go away Gary, sleep on the sofa. It's 'three in the morning what the hell are you playing at?" Walker sighed, he knew there was no need carrying on with his seduction technique and decided to pick a video to keep him company. In the twilight hours his thoughts shot off in different directions, he closed his eyes to try to put them in some semblance of order. They hardly socialised with each other anymore. When he went out with the lads, she would stay in and look after Victoria. It was a fair trade off, but he missed her at times. He'd got married because he wanted to be with somebody, not fucking single. Nat had turned old, and she'd begun to nag him. When the morning broke and he looked like shit she would ask him. "What time did you get in last night? I suppose you were drunk again? How much of OUR money have you spent again?"

Walker would reply with ever-increasing frustration. "Fuck knows but you're about to tell me. Yes off me head. The last time I checked the dollar was out of MY account" and march off with Baskerville into the distance. His head or conscience didn't need the Spanish inquisition. He didn't want to argue and as his anger blew away he would convince himself that It was merely banter between man and wife, surely they had not started on the slippery downhill road that signified the start of a decline in their relationship? This was how life turned out, blagging the wife when you were out and about with the lads. Making up stupid excuses, it was all part of the game. It was an integral part of the married dynamic. When he had worked in the warehouse and was tied to that fuckwit existence, she never patted him on the back and praised him when he handed over his weekly wage packet. Walker hadn't gone out for months at a time, in order to provide for them and ensure there was food on the table and a roof over their heads. Now he was earning and showing ambition she should shut the fuck up and not start on him. The clouds weren't black yet, but they had slowly started to cross the blue skies and their relationship was becoming overcast. He put the cushion over his head and attempted to relax, his sweat staining the cover. Another bollocking in the morning he thought ruefully.

Walker had started to get more bites with the business. He did deliveries for Butcher on a regular basis and his mom used her leads to get him some information regarding installation work with contractors she knew. Armed with insider information he would phone up and give them a quote, hand over his number and use his new fax machine to send over a list of costs loving prepared by his mother. She patiently led him through the minefield so he didn't undercharge, but didn't take the piss either. When he was on site with Butcher, he learned the basics on how to erect storage systems and started to become proficient in his new role. Walker wasn't a handy man; he wasn't what you would call a practical bloke. But he could read a drawing and as the shelving was steel it wasn't that difficult to build, resembling big boys 'Meccano.'

The business was progressing and the lifestyle it provided suited him. The money he charged for a delivery was nearly as much as he got (net) weekly when he worked in the warehouse. Some weeks he did well ,others he didn't. It averaged out. When he started to build storage systems independently the money he charged increased. Walker didn't have to work every day now to make a good living, he averaged around 2-3 every week. Butcher, good to his word booked his services for three months, both as an erector and a delivery agent when he was awarded a big contract to build a sizable storage system for the main branch of Lloyds bank, located in Birmingham city centre. Three months solid work, with a few extra jobs thrown in. Both his bank balance and his profile within the business community was raised. With an account full of money, money that Walker couldn't waste, Nat appeared contented, even happy at times.

One fine day, they took a trip to MFS to choose a new three piece suite. Walker enjoyed looking at the suites on offer, jumping on the brand new leather with the feel of a thousand in cash in his pocket. The decided on a dark grey three piece and suite and moved on to the section marked coffee tables. Further drunk on domesticity Walker paid a trip to 'Do It All' and invested in some paint. Apparently it was 'eggshell' it looked beige to Walker. It was only when they made It back home he realised that Nat expected him to start there and then, and have all the decorating done in a week. Fully completed so that the new sofa could sit in the new front room. He sighed with a resignation, got the rollers out and splashed the walls with designer paint, commented on the blandness of the colour and was duly informed by his wife that new pictures would add colour, more money Walker thought!

She wanted a bright room, to add to the illusion of space. She paid another small fortune for a mirror, a heavy dam thing that weighed as much as it cost. Nat placed studiously above the fire place. When she had positioned it perfectly she stood back and admired her handy-work. Walker nodded, applauded and smiled to keep the peace, bored at this new exploration into unwanted territory.

He'd fought the urge to kick the fuck out of the television set and the poseurs that appeared on the screen in the myriad of new television programmes that were now popping up on the small screen. They were all smiles as they wielded paint brushes. It was like a fucking party when they got together, helped by about a thousand handy men off camera. The woman that presented it was always happy, all tits and teeth. Walker couldn't remember her name, but he knew the programme was called 'Changing Rooms'. It`s theme tune struck a note of dread into his heart as Nat would place her magazine neatly on the floor, and pay intense concentration for the next half-an-hour. Soaking up the latest in innovative design. He smiled and played the contented husband. Hoping that his week's exertions would buy him a pass for the weekend and maybe a blow job on Sunday morning. Walker was pacing around the flat muttering threatening words to the walls. He'd slammed down the phone and tutted. Nat had ignored him peaking at the telly from behind her magazine. Baskerville raised her head from her curled feet and looked to see what all the fuss was about.

He had to sort out some business, and he had to sort it quickly. He brushed his hair with his hands and looked over at his wife. "Where's the cash polnt card Nɑt?"Walker asked.

Nat placed her magazine down and looked up. "Why?"

"I fancy a pint with the lads. I need some help with a job that I've got coming up. It will save taking an advertisement out in the Express and star I need another hand, some twat has just let me down The pubs the best place to find one." He answered, trying to hide his frustration. He didn't understand why they had to go through this stand- up routine every time he wanted a pint. He did need a hand, otherwise he was going to lose a job, a good earner and look like a prick to a new project manager who had the key to the safe.

"I suppose you will get drunk and come home talking stupid."

Walker grinned back at her, hoping his stand-up routine and boyish charm still had some mileage left in the tank. "Do I need a beer to talk stupid eh Nat? Come on, how long have you known me eh?"

She frowned, but the creases weren't too deep in her forehead, signing she answered. "To bloody long, get a taxi please Gary. I don't want you crashing the van." She went into her bag and fished out her purse, opened it, peered inside and pushed around bits of paper before she passed the card over. Its silvers numbers glinted in the light, the cash point key to a happy evening.

"While you're at the shops get some pig out food please, I fancy something nice," she paused and shouted. "Victoria."

A round face with a red haired bob appeared round the door. "Yes mommy?"

"Your dads going down the shop, you want some sweeties?"

"Yes please," she answered sweetly. Walker loved her politeness.

"What you want Shorty? What can I get for you"

"I'm not sure Daddy, chocolate?"

"Chocolate it is. What sort Shorts? Come on, give me a clue."She placed her head to one side so it was resting on her shoulder, her face scrunched up with concentration.

"I'll tell you what, get your shoes on and come with me and choose, OK." He looked across at Nat. "The pub shuts in five hours you know." She raised her hands in mock defeat, knowing she had got her pound of flesh out of him. "Don't take too much," she shouted. "The electric bill needs sorting," the door slamming shut answered her. Nat settled back and put her feet up. Bliss, a night of peace and quiet in front of her. She would be safely asleep by the time he came home.

She knew Walker wasn't a bad man, he was a good dad, he cared for her, but his cash flow projections weren't great and he was worryingly irresponsible most of the time; a good trait for a boyfriend, but it needed to be ironed out for a husband. If he had money in the bank he would always find a way to spend it. Walker wasn't great with money full stop. He didn't seem to appreciate its true value. Nat knew when the cheques were coming in. She managed to get to him before the bills needed paying. She didn't mind that he spent more and more on alcohol and his nights out, just as long as the bills were covered and there was some money in the bank account for her and Victoria. She still wanted a house, but it was hard to get a mortgage when you were self employed, that's what Walker told her. With the recent recession, cash was hard enough to get out of the banks, even if you had a steady income. Nat didn't like politics or economics; she thought that all politicians from all parties were self-serving hypocrites after her poll tax fiasco. She'd been to the bank, and talked to an advisor just to be sure she was up on the Walker family`s fiscal policy. She did understand about money and she now knew that they would not lend to the newly self employed, as it was considered too risky an enterprise. They were young; she could wait a few years for her house. The flat was looking nice and he'd invested heavily in it.

Walker didn't see the point in pushing the situation with the banks anyway. When she started searching estate agents windows, he would tut and sigh and make a song and dance. Nat knew when he was becoming annoyed and would back off. She had learnt which battles to fight and which to 'lose'. The estate they lived on was in a nice area with good schools nearby. She had time, she settled down with the remote with a steaming cup of hot chocolate and 'Take a Break magazine.

Walker ordered his pint, relived he'd finally made it for a drink. He 'd taken an extra twenty out of the bank, and pounded Nat with kindness bringing two shopping bags home, packed with goodies. As they walked home from the shops he called a taxi as Shorts swung on his arm. She laughed when her daddy talked to the invisible people on his new plastic toy. He sat down, sighed and decided whether to enter the conversation that was being bandied around the table. It was pertinent; it was about fucking women and their fucking nagging!

He now saw less and less of Harris, who was working away with a local builder for weeks at a time. Life was hard; making a day to day living was tough and stressful. As you got older you needed that extra security that a proper job provided, Harris would comment wisely over a pint. The latest recession was fresh in the public memory, the record number of repossessions, bankruptcies and the spiraling unemployment was daily news. Every man needed a steady and honest income to keep the Police and the Bailiffs away from his front door.

Walker placed his drink on the table turned and spoke to a lad sitting next to him. A good looking lad with long hair, he was well dressed with his own style. Leaving the high-street fashion names alone. He was respected and had earned a good reputation over the years, he was one of the top lads in the area. He'd made his bones from when he was a young man and didn't force his status onto other people: Mark Gibson was comfortable in his own head and body.

Walker patted him on the shoulder." Safe Gibs, I need a bloke to work with me for a couple of days, you know anyone who might be interested?" Gibson reflected briefly on the question. He'd met Gibson, when he having a brawl with some Leeds fans (again) on Wolverhampton ring road. They'd known each other well enough for a peripheral greeting when they were hunting opposition fans in the streets around Molineux, after that little incident they'd become friends.

"Ask Silks, he wants to work. He is after a job."

"You sure?" Walker was non-committal. "I thought he did OK without the need to get his hands dirty?" Walker was sceptical about employing him; his head awash with reservations after their first meeting.

" I don't know about that Walker, but I do know that he has been asking about some casual work, he asked me for some a few weeks ago."

"You think he is reliable?" Walker asked.

"He says he wants to work, if I had some spare, I would have taken him on. He is a good enough bloke. This fucking recession`s making it hard for everyone, ask him. What you got to lose? You need a bloke, he needs some work." Gibson stated Silks case.

Walker had bumped into Silks a few times since they had originally met. They nodded to each other and said. 'Hello'. Walker would buy a wrap off him when he fancied a dab. Walker looked up and saw Silks, he was sitting at the bar eating. Walker noticed that about this bloke, he always seemed to be eating in the pub. In fact he was always in the fucking pub. Walker left his seat and carried his beer over to where Silks was sitting.

"Hello Silks, you alright mate? Have you got ten?" Silks was mopping up a Chicken Madras with a naan bread.

"I'm good Walker, you? What can I do for you?" He looked up and nodded a curt greeting.

"It's all good mate. Gibs says you're looking for some casual work, a few days here and there, is that right?"

"Could be, depends on what it is."

 Walker thought it was like pulling teeth to get information out of this bloke, a simple yes would have sufficed, he was verbally constipated. You had to spoon feed the fucker to ask him what time it was, when he had a fucking wrist watch on. Walker knew he`d been in jail for years, but surely he could trust him, into at least, not thinking he was a fucking narc!

"I need a bloke to help me load some shelving, deliver it to Chester and build it. It isn't hard, you can watch me for a bit, you will pick it up as we go along. It's only a small job a couple of day's work, but it could lead to more. You interested?"

 Silks nodded again. "Yeah I am, when and how much?" Straight to the pound note.

"I'll pay you thirty a day. Cash in hand, you get paid when I drop you off at home on a daily basis, not before. We start the day after next, you in?"

Silks contemplated the offer, wiped his mouth with a napkin before tossing it onto the bar. "Yeah I am, cheers Walker." Silks smiled. It changed his face. He didn't look that hard and angry now. The bloke always looked like he had lost a ten pound note and found a ten pence piece to replace it.

"You want a beer Walker?" He asked

Walker smiled and nodded. "Yeah, go on why the fuck not."

They spend the next hour talking about the job, dropping a few social titbits, slowly building a rapport, the alcohol loosening their tongues.

"I'll be at yours at seven Thursday morning, what was the address again?" Walker said.

"You got some paper Pam?" The barmaid handed him a sheet from beside the till."Thank you beautiful." She smiled and laughed, pleased with the complement. Silks jotted down an address and a telephone number and slid it toward Walker, who glanced down, before he folded it neatly and placed into his wallet. They shook hands and Walker left the pub, winking at Gibson and raising his thumb as he opened the door to leave. His cab was already on the car park waiting, he wanted to surprise Nat and arrive home early, not plastered for once. He had ideas.

Thursday morning arrived and Walker landed at the address that Silks had provided him with. He checked the road and house number against the piece of paper, satisfied he'd got the right address he opened the door to the van. Before he put his feet on the pavement, the door to a little house opened and Silks stepped out onto the path. He was dressed for work, he was wearing some old hob-nailed boots, a pair of baggy jeans, two sizes too big, not a fashion statement and a thick jumper. He blew into his hands. There was the beginning of a slight frost in the air, even if real winter was still months away. He patted his jeans and checked his pockets and scowled, waved at Walker and went back into the house. A couple of minutes later he was sitting next to Walker in the van. "I forgot my fags, "he explained. Walker was impressed, not with the fact he had bought his own smokes, but that he was early. Walker was always early, it was pathological trait for him; part of his psychopathology. He hated lateness. To be late was rude and tardy and showed no respect. There was no excuse for it, always leave early to give yourself self plenty of time to get where you going and meet whoever you were meeting. He wanted to shoot lorry drivers who would use the middle lane to overtake other lorries who were travelling a whole one mile an hour slower than them and taking ten miles to finally pass each other. He hated drivers that would go 0-30 in two seconds to cut you up when there was fuck all behind you and then sit at thirty miles an hour in front of you for the duration of the trip. He hated idiots that would sit in the middle lane of the motorway for no apparent reason. He hated miles and miles of road works with no fucking work being done and no workmen in sight. He fucking hated the Conservatives. But more than anything, he hated lateness.

"Morning Silks you alright?" He got a grunt of recognition in return. Silks turned the heater up without asking and sat hunched against the door, his head leaning on the window. Some people just didn't start the day well. He put the van into first gear and drove off, only the radio breaking the silence.

When they arrived at the warehouse Silks jumped out of the van, he was eager to start. He worked quickly, lifting the packages off the pallet that the stacker truck and dropped at the back of the van. He didn't abuse the shelving by chucking it around. It was placed in sensible order, and it was placed so it wouldn't move around when they took corners and hit bumps. Silks had done a good job, Walker dotted another mental note down in his cerebral diary. He spotted a drinks vending machine next to the office, stuck his paperwork in his back pocket and walked over. He checked the prices, stuck in fifty pence and pushed a button and waited. He picked up a steaming Styrofoam cup took a drink and pressed a sequence of buttons, another cup dropped into the tray and filled with hot brown liquid. He picked it up, walked to the van and handed it to Silks. "Hot drink Silks, keep the cold out and start the day."

"Thanks Walker." He said, taking a sip. Enjoying the warmth in his hands.

There are sandwiches and shit in that bag Silks, help yourself when you're hungry." Walker offered him half his lunch. It wasn't a big deal, he always went on a job well prepared.

Silks nodded. "Cheers, I don't eat in the morning, but I'll put a dent in them later. Your wife sorts out the eats then?"

"No fucking way." Walker laughed. "Nat's a lot of things Silks. All mostly good, but a fucking cook she ain't."

"What, you made them yourself?"

"Yes, I like to cook." Walker answered as he jumped in the van and started the engine up. Checking the traffic in his rear view mirror before he signaled and pulled out into the traffic stream.

"You like to cook?" Silks repeated the question.

Walker looked across the cab. "Yes why?"

"You a poof then?"

Walker looked again, Silks had a smile on his face, he was having a laugh.

The way to Chester is a picturesque, relaxing drive up the A41.The route is filled with beautiful scenery. The glorious country-side laid out exposed for townies to marvel at. The road is not built for speed though, especially when you get stuck behind some pensioners who are towing a caravan on their way to Rhyl. Walker's shouts at the ignorant driver in front woke Silks up. He'd dropped off to sleep, when they hit the rabbit run. He wiped his eyes and joined in the foul mouthed harangue as Walker tried to overtake them. They spend the next hour shouting at other road users who dared to drive at less than seventy miles an hour around hairpin and blind bends. They laughed at each other's tales of their colourful past. Silks found Walker amusing as he dropped witty anecdotes about football, drugs, Harris and Scarborough. Walker could paint a picture when he added his personal spin to them.

They arrived on site nearly two hours after they loaded up. Two hours to complete seventy miles. Silks was eager to start work when they finally arrived at the neat little office block, that was located on a new enterprise estate that were now popping up around the countryside. He didn't do exactly as instructed in the beginning, but he was polite to the customers, only glanced briefly at the assortment of pretty girls in office wear and was a quick learner. He was good with his hands; his strength and talent lay in building, he used to help his dad in the garden and round the house, where he picked up the rudiments of DIY as a result of his dads tutelage. He actually volunteered that information to Walker who nearly passed out in surprise, as he watched him handle a cordless drill with some dexterity.

They started doing a few jobs together as Walkers work load increased and he wasn't reliant on Butcher to give him a majority of his installation work. Silks was a reliable worker, always on time and at the place where he said he would be. Walker was happy with the relationship; the bloke was capable with his hands and a good addition to the squad. Some jobs that Walker tendered for, and was subsequently awarded required more skill than just tightening up a nut and bolt and using a torque wrench. Silks was good with those jobs and they became an effective partnership. They saw each other down the pub and would now sit at the same table to share a joke and tell a story.

Walker hadn't yet been given a free wrap, but the time when he would be offered one was now not far away.

The pair had just finished a job in the East Midlands, it was foggy on the drive home and the traffic on the roads was at a crawl. Walker had stopped at an off sale to purchase a few cans and some food to shorten the journey back home to Wolverhampton. He placed the Doritos and dip on the dashboard and the cans on the floor. Silks downed a bottle of coke and filled the empty bottle up with cider and passed it over to Walker. He'd once watched Walker drink straight from the can and had shuddered in agitation. Was the idiot asking for a tug?

"What you up to tomorrow Walker?"

"Fuck all mate, sleeping" Walker planned to do just that, he and his settee had suffered a temporary separation. Walker loved his settee.

"You free then in the morning?" Silks was polite he was after something.

"I am yes why?" He looked across at Silks and added suspiciously. "What you after?"

"I need a lift with something, pick me up at ten from this address." He wrote down a street name on a ripped up fag packet.

"Go on then, why not. I'll give up my day off up to help you." Walker added for effect.

"You have every fucking day off mate, you only leave the house to work and drink, you're a fucking couch potato." Silks wasn't lying. Walker was loath to move off his settee unless it was an emergency. Silks couldn't sit still unless he was in a pub with a lager and a short in front of him.

"Yeah, fucking yeah. I got a family you know, I`ve got to spread the love around!" Walker said.

Most of his spare time when he wasn't in the pub was spent with Victoria. His evenings were dedicated to teaching her how to read and write, spreading flash cards around the floor. He hoped the mental stimulus would knock her out for the night and stop the bickering between him and his wife. He would get frustrated with Nat, she would make Victoria go to bed at a certain time, even when she wasn't tired. 'What was the fucking point?' Walker would say? She was barely out of nappies. Let her stay up and chill with them. They would row over it, and sometimes Nat would let it go, sometimes she wouldn't. She insisted that Victoria had to learn a routine. Walker could see her point (tentatively), but she didn't try to see his.

Walker decided to take Baskerville out for a run in the car to pick Silks up. Nat had moaned at him as he was buttering his toast and making the morning drinks. "If you're having a day off work and gadding about with your new friend take Baskerville. I have work tonight and don't want to be bothered with having to walk the dog." It was all white noise to Walker.

 He rolled his eyes at her. "OK, Ok, you've made your point" and left the flat with Baskerville in tow, trotting happily with her new chain jingling around her neck.

They arrived on an estate, not far away from where Walker lived. He parked the car and locked the door behind him, checking the house numbers to find the right address. A small window above opened and Silks face peered out with a wide grin on it. "Yes Slim, you made it then?" He shouted down.

"Of course I did, who you fucking calling Slim anyway?"

Walker had put on weight since his days of working in the warehouse. He walked up the path to a modern little house and knocked on the front door and heard footsteps banging as Silks ran down the stairs to open it. "Come in mate." Walker was invited over the threshold. Silks was effervescing and obviously excited. He followed him through an entry hall to the second door on the left which lead into the kitchen. "Put the kettle on then, we've got a guest." A blonde girl, who looked to be in her early thirties, raised her head from the newspaper it was buried in and stubbed out her cigarette, sighed, stood up and moved toward the work surface. She was ruddily attractive, even though her hair hadn't been brushed and she was still in her pajamas.

"Jules, this is slim, otherwise known as Walker."

"Hello Julie, you alright then? I'm very pleased to meet you." Walker introduced himself.

"You alright Bab, you want tea?" She acknowledged his presence with a slight smile.

"Coffee please."

Julie put the coffee into mugs for him and Silks and waited for the kettle to boil. She handed him his cup, Walker sipped it and thanked her. As he drank his coffee he looked around the room interested to view the house that Silks called home. The kitchen was neat and tidy, furnished with brand name appliances. You could detect a lot about a man by the state of the place he resided in. He appeared to have his shit nailed down judging by the quality of the goods on display in the house.

When they finished their drinks Silks made a move and Walker followed him down the path toward the car before he stopped abruptly and Walker rear ended him.

"What the fucks that?" Silks pointed toward the car. Baskerville head was in the gap that Walker had left in the window for fresh air to circulate.

"A dog". Well it wasn't a fucking cat was it!

"I ain't getting in the car with that man, it's a fucking killer devil dog thing." Silks looked sideways at Walker, his eyes were wide. Was he really worried about Baskerville?

"It's Baskerville Silks." Walker introduced her. "And she is soft as shit. She will more likely lick you to death than bite you."

"If she bites me, you're getting it," he looked at Walker. The bloke was genuinely worried.

"Get in the fucking car, you're safe, fuck me what a palaver. I guarantee your safety alright!"

Baskerville met Silks with no teeth and all tongue, he soon realised that the only danger was that the dog might get dehydrated from the amount of liquid she was smearing all over him. He fussed her and made his introductions, safe from harm under Walkers guidance; they were now ready to make a move.

"Where to Silks?"

"Stafford Road, pick up some fireworks."

"You having a bonfire then mate?"

"Yep, tomorrow night, you're coming aren't you?" Silks asked.

"I am now I'm ferrying you round to get the stuff," Walker was happy he'd got the nod to attend.

"Bring your misses and your kid it's a family thing." Walker nodded back impressed. It was a show of respect and it showed consideration that he'd invited his family to come along.

"Thank you, I will, cheers Silks, nice one buddy."

They drove around Wolverhampton for hours visiting various shops until Silks was satisfied he'd bought what he wanted for his big display. It turned out that he was a pyrotechnic freak, hence the excitement when Walker had picked him up. Silks loved things that went BANG! It had taken them hours to locate a specialist rocket, which was nearly as tall as Walker and cost as much as a whole box from a supermarket. Silks was adamant that he would put on a show that would be remembered. They collected firewood so the bonfire would go with a crackle and a pop and burn Guy Fawkes effectively. A small gang of helpers were busy in the house when they returned armed with boxes of fireworks. Silks delegated some help and with the accompaniment of excited chatter they all helped to carry the wood into the back garden. Silks baited the children as they worked, smiling he turned to Walker. "I'm cooking up some yard food tomorrow, so come with an appetite Slim."

"As if I wouldn't." Walker patted his belly for affect.

Walker briefly helped to build the bonfire, carefully placing small pieces of kindling at the bottom, careful not to usurp Silks position as king of the hunter gatherers. After ten minutes he became bored and headed off home to inform Nat that they had been invited out to play. Nat quickly agreed it would be a nice evening out for them. She and Victoria both liked fireworks. Walker went to bed with a sense of contentment and a clear head, he thought it would be nice for them to go out as a family for a change.

Walker parked the van, as he jumped outside he could smell the gunpowder and excitement in the air. Bonfire night had a certain smell about it that always made his stomach tingle. He walked to the passenger door, opened it and swept Victoria up into his arms. "Wim going to see some fireworks Shorty, you excited?"

" Are we seeing them here Daddy?" She asked quietly.

"Just in there Shorts." Walker pointed toward Silks front door.

"Come on mommy." Victoria looked at Natalie. "We don't want to be late do we?"

Victoria held both their hands as Walker escorted them down the tidy path and knocked on the front door. Julie opened it with a flourish. She recognised Walker, smiled and said hello before inviting them in. Walker introduced Victoria and Nat to her and they were led into the kitchen and given a drink. Walker looked out of the kitchen window into the garden, to where the extravaganza was slowly unfolding. Silks was surrounded by children who were following his instructions with a sense of seriousness that belied the laughter that rose up around him. Walker grabbed a can of Strongbow off the kitchen table and made his way outside.

Walker pointed at children and laughed. "They all yours mate?"

Silks looked up and smiled."Yes Slim, how are you?" He was on his knees sticking matches and lighting white blocks of firelighters, smoke was starting to rise from the bottom of the bonfire. Silks placed some small pieces of kindling and gently blew on them.

"I'm good Silks, looking forward to the show, whose are all those?" Walker repeated the question

"Off the estate, they're every bodies mate." Silks answered.

Walker found out that Silks liked kids and he liked to entertain the public. He wanted them to have a good time, some of the children that lived nearby had dead heads as parents and at least this way they had some fun in their lives. The house slowly filled up with lads from The Woods, and more locals off the estate where Silks lived. It was quite an audience for the show he was preparing.

Walker pulled Silks away from his admiring audience to introduce him to Nat and Victoria. He beamed at them as he introduced himself, his smile wider that the Grand Canyon. The man was infectious when he was in a good mood. He kissed Nat on the cheek, she smiled back and said hello politely. Silks then bent down and made a fuss of Victoria before plucking her up into arms to be given a VIP tour of the garden. She clapped as she was handed a sparkler and introduced to the other children, immediately comfortable in their presence she quickly joined in enthusiastically with the fun and games. Silks proudly recited his lines and the children listened intently, engrossed in the itinerary of the night that lay ahead. The party went with a bang and a great deal of laughter. It was cloudy and cold but the fire and hospitality kept people warm. The beers and food flowed; the kitchen was loaded with rice, salads and meats. Silks had prepared chicken, goat and mutton, it was good food and in plentiful supply, there was alcohol in abundance of good quality: Smirnoff, Jack Daniels, Hennessey, and Bushmills. He had taken the extra touch and gone that extra mile. Nat wouldn't touch the meat but under encouragement did pick at her salad and enjoyed a few glasses of white wine, the alcohol and bonfire finally thawing her out. The grand finale arrived; it was time to let the rocket off. There were gasps and cries from the kids as the huge 'projectile' was carried into view. Walker hadn't seen a rocket like this in his lifetime so he was positive that the surprise would impress the spectators.

"Stand back." Silks ordered. The crowd hushed and drew back. He looked around his audience, a sense of theatre enveloping him. He made sure that everybody was quiet to mark the occasion and that launch control had set the trajectory for the missile that was about to light up half of Wolverhampton.

Fizz…………….the fuse started to burn, the ignition process underway. Walker looked across and laughed. "We don't require the launch codes from NASA do we Silks?"

The rocket exploded into the night sky, it was certainly travelling at some velocity, the vapour trail looked impressive. The cloud base was low that night and the rocket disappeared inside the cloud bank. The crowd turned and looked at each other lost for words. This was not the 'big bang' they'd expected to end the night's entertainment.

Laughter rippled like a wave and reached Silks. Walker tapped him on the back. "Bad luck mate, they will remember that for years my son."

Walkers business continued to prosper. Silks worked for him on every job he could pick up. Silks liked money and wanted more of it. He was good at the job, so Walker increased his daily rate to £50 and watched as the cash flowed in. He once earned over £1000 for a job in Knightsbridge for two hours toil. It was a simple job that some other contractor had messed up. The company responsible needed a body to go down there and deliver some parts and fit them ASAP. The bank was putting them under pressure and penalty clauses were about to be implemented. He invoiced them £600 for delivery and £500 for labour. His mom had told him the price was in line with what other teams would have charged for that notice period. Silks got paid £200 for a few hours work. It was a better earner than crime and legal.

They got to enter bank vaults and look at the cash without masks on. No jail, no doors coming through in the morning, it was a perfect career choice. Silks could see the potential and didn't understand why they couldn't work seven day a week. Walker was patient and told him about market forces, tenders and such. To Silks it was an easy equation; if you had a van you should make it pay every day instead of having it parked up outside doing fuck all. Silks asked Walker. "If I find a way to use it are you going to be interested and get off your arse?" Walker nodded "Of cause I would, I like money man." Walker had always admired Arthur Daily and Del Boy Trotter, the days of making some 'easy' money were upon him.

To halt the decline in his relationship with Nat, Walker decided to spend some cash and take the family on holiday. There could be tense atmosphere around the Walker household, Natalie was becoming middle aged at the age of 28 and fussed like old maid forgetting she was still young. If he did help with the chores and made the mistake of not evenly dividing the curtain folds, Nat would tut, glare and finish the job with military precision. When the toilet seat was left up the atmosphere in the flat could become hostile. Walker didn't understand, arguing. 'What was the point in having a domestic over such trivial bollocks?'

Nat would retaliate. "If you cared, you would just do it for me." There was an impasse between the couple when it came to cleaning. Nat had OCD and Walker though not exactly a slob was simply more relaxed with the whole household scene, and he didn't give a fuck if the seat was on the toilet let alone up or down.

The holiday was pure joy for him; blue skies and still waters without any of the rows that punctuated their life back at home. When he was drunk on their first night Walker managed to lose all the travellers cheques. Not trusting hotel security he'd put them all in his wallet deciding no local was going to 'rob him'. After a few cocktails he lost his wallet and launched an attack on the bar man because he thought he was responsible for the theft.

Walker expected Nat to play her face when he broke the news he'd lost all their holiday cash. Natalie ignored his drunken rambling and walked to the police station calmly wishing the drunken prick behind her would shut the fuck up! She reported them stolen and was given a crime reference number to take to American Express and get them replaced. She'd sensibly got them insured when she purchased them knowing her husband's preclusion for irresponsible behaviour. Walker was intent on telling the police that they were all thieving cunts and would pay for robbing from him, not realising they would be fully reimbursed. They didn't understand a word he was saying which wasn't a surprise. Walker's mates found it hard at times to, he would talk quickly with a thick Black Country accent, so the local police from Malta had no chance of a translation. They nodded and smiled back at him unaware he was questioning their parentage. Nat acted as the diplomat and thanked them for their help before dragging him away into the distance. This was not the moment to pick a fight with him. When they got back to the hotel she put down a deposit on a safe and frisked him for valuables, which she placed away securely. She would use this opportunity wisely and not waste it on him when he was too drunk to remember. Walker was being repentant anyway. On the journey back to the apartments he apologised to Nat with the same ferocity as he was abusing the locals.

Walker loved the break. He would spent time in the pool with Victoria, helping her to swim, and pushing her around in her inflatable dingy, making sure that they both had their sun factor 50 on. Nat went brown; Walker went a dirty sort of colour before he peeled. Victoria was an English Rose and required regular creaming. On their way back to the apartment, Walker would buy some refreshments from the local supermarket. He would drink wine, the girl's fruit juice or pop. He'd found out you could get a local red or white for half the price you paid for Strongbow. Walker would pour himself a glass of wine and hold court on the balcony. He would place a tape in the deck and various artists would entertain him as he happily sang along. The words in these songs were just words and didn't have some darker undercurrent. The song didn't have to be dissected for some subliminal meaning that was directly aimed at him. He placed black and green olives in dishes to snack on and brought them out to the table. Walker loved these moments, watching the world go by from his vantage point. It was two hours of bliss, looking at the ocean, watching the cars, watching people come and go. He enjoyed the serenity of it all. Nat would spend her time getting herself and Victoria ready. They both looked resplendent when they stepped out with him. Walker would put on his shorts and Lacoste shirts, his beautiful wife and stunning daughter holding onto his arms as they strolled down the sun kissed boulevards.

Victoria was perfect in Walkers eyes; she had deep blue eyes, dark
auburn hair and a creamy complexion. Nat always chose clothes that
suited her. Clothes that looked good but were inexpensive, she wasn't
stupid enough to spend a fortune on ridiculous designer clothes for
her child. Walker would reflect upon this when celebrity culture was
firmly etched in the public's mind. Idiot women, high with stupidity
would deck out everything in Burberry check. Their hats, coats and
even the baby's buggy were not left out of the equation. They looked
ridiculous, with not an ounce of style. Nat had taste, it was easy for her
to go in to any number of high street stores and come out with bargain
after bargain.

Walker remembered when his mom and dad had taken Victoria for a
small get away in Cornwall. When the photos were developed it looked
like Victoria had been attacked by a mad designer from Laura Ashley.
Nat was not a happy camper! The icing on the cake was when Victoria
was paraded in a sailors outfit, even Walker was pissed off with that
photo and backed Nat. Together they stopped his mom's assault on
their daughters dress sense.

As they wandered through the winding streets, Walker would find a
nice restaurant where the waiters would make a fuss of Victoria and
give her free ice-cream for desert. Victoria had developed a passion for
pizza and together they found a restaurant that overlooked the bay
that served a wonderful margarita, it was a spectacular view and it was
a beautiful holiday.

Walker arrived home and called Silks. He'd bought some cigarettes and
a bottle of Jack Daniels back for him. The duty free was a nice touch as
Silks now offered Walker his wraps for free; he knew it was time to
spread the wealth. On a Friday they would travel around
Wolverhampton so that Silks could pick up his gear. When they arrived
back at his flat, Silks would stick on his do-rag and string vest before
wrapping the drugs out. He looked the part of the Jamaican crime
warlord, as he sat down and counted out the wraps in his bright yellow
vest.

Walker told Silks that he would have to something about his dress
sense! Silks had appeared on television. A guest on a Sunday current
affairs programme dealing with the problem of juvenile offending. He
had dressed in his 'urban commando shirt' as he liked to call a piece of
cloth that was an explosion of green and brown patterns on cheap
material.

Walker shuddered as he saw it. What the fuck had he turned up in to represent the firm? He'd taken his son with him or 'Man Cub,' as Silks lovingly referred to him. He looked like a food fight, but talked good sense, he knew his subject and was confident when facing questions. Walker had to admit he cut an eloquent and impressive figure. As their relationship and friendship continued to develop, they discussed doing a 'bit of business, with each other. Silks could always get hold of some goods, but transport had always been a problem for him.
 Walker loved this existence; he could wake up in the morning with his pockets empty and then get a call from Silks. They would spend the morning driving around Wolves, before whiling away the afternoon in the pub with the money they'd made from fresh air. Walker would come home drunk, more often than not and push twenty pound notes into Nat's hand. Sure that would appease her need for him to secure a proper job. It didn't make any difference how much he earned because Walker would haemorrhage money and the books never balanced.
 More and more they had to rely on Nat's income for mundane things like the bills.

CHAPTER 10
ECSTASY

Christmas was always a happy period for Gary Walker, he loved the festive feel and the crisp expectation that hung in the winter's air. The sound of carol singers, the vision of the tree, merged into Walker's mind to provide the perfect picture of family orientated enjoyment. His mum would issue invites to the family and they would descend from Liverpool and the Black Country to spend the festive season with her.

Walker's parents lived in an 18th century cottage, when it was decorated with boughs of holly and sprigs of mistletoe it could mistaken for a gateway into the past and take its place in a Dickensian novel. His sister dressed the tree which added to the magical feel of the house, and turned its wise walls into a vivid depiction of the perfect Christmas card. Increasing the heavy anticipation that Santa Claus was indeed coming to town.

The family would attempt to arrive early on Christmas Eve to complete the preparations for the big day together. Now that Victoria understood what Christmas was all about It Increased his thriving enchantment for the period. Walker enjoyed preparing the food, using his newly found culinary skills to make a varity of homemade stuffing which filled the kitchen with an exotic ambience. He would take centre stage in the kitchen with his ever-present can of cider, roll up his sleeves, don his apron and get to work on the task in hand. His dad though teetotal, always provided a fine supply of alcohol ensuring the festive sprit stayed with them throughout the holiday period.

This year was going to be a bigger occasion than usual; his sister had started seeing a scouser a year ago and had finally managed to get Christmas off from her nursing post, to spend three days back in Wolverhampton. She had moved to Liverpool to specialise in working with children, becoming a top paediatric nurse and subsequently being voted nurse of the year. When she was working in Wolverhampton she had been promoted to ward sister at twenty four, the youngest in Wolverhampton's nursing history. Walker didn't give a fuck when his mom would read out her achievements. He'd made the local press more than once and managed to get nicked in front of the whole family on Easter Sunday for a serious assault charge. His achievements were equally as splendid. It was just they'd decided on differing career paths, that was all. Walker's mother didn't grasp the dichotomy involved.

Walker wasn't impressed with his sister's choice of potential husband. He was loud, ignorant, a misogynist and rude; he simply didn't posses good manners. The only time he would smile was when he pissed. Walker came close to kicking his head in a few times and would talk to his mum and Nat about him. They would calm him down and his mom, sister and especially Nat forbade any direct physical intervention. It was her choice who she went out with they told him, she had to live her own life, and she was an adult.

Walker had always defended his sister's honour against men in the past. He remembered one time; a long time ago it seemed to him now. Christmas Eve had gone well, Walker was pissed. He had enjoyed a quality night down the local with some mates, it had gotten raucous, but their antics were good spirited. When he had arrived home he was hungry, found a bag of KP ready salted nuts and slumped onto the sofa, turned on the telly and started watching some choir perform from some church or other. He enjoyed carols particularly, 'Oh Come All Ye Faithfull', they added to the Christmas ambience.

His eyes were becoming heavy and he was covered with the nuts that he'd opened, they'd been stashed behind the bar. Hardly hidden at all. He heard the door in the kitchen open and recognised his sister's voice. He was about to get up, when he heard a second voice, a deeper voice. They were both giggling like naughty school children He shut his eyes, listened and waited.

"Who's that?" The man asked.

I'll let you know in a bit Walker thought. Cunt. He breathed in deeply.

"It's my little brother, don't mind him, he's drunk and passed out don't mind him," she repeated.

Course I am, Walker thought, carry on.

He heard nothing for a few moments, then there was the sound of leather squelching, and a slight moan.

"Wake him up and tell him to go to bed, I can't do this while he is down here."

Walkers eyed opened. "Cant fucking do what mate?" Walker sat up and looked at the bloke, curly hair, shirt opened, fresh out of fucking university."Can't do what?" He repeated."I'm all fucking ears here son."

"Gary." His sister interrupted. "It's not what you think."

"What the fuck am I thinking eh Jackie? That dick-head, sitting there is trying it on with you, while I'm fucking lying here and mom and dad are upstairs. It's fucking Christmas day!" He looked at the man, his eyes narrowed, the man looked down. Walker knew he had him beaten. "Well mate, what you got to say?"

" I,.......I like your sister........err...........Gary. " He stuttered like a prick.

"Cause you do mate, now fuck off!"

Walker left the comfort of the sofa, put his hands on the man's shirt and pulled him to his feet, dragging him towards the door.

"Leave him alone, I like him Gary........ no!" Jackie shouted out in vain.

"Spent the night round his gaff then." Walker threw them both out and shut the door, made sure all the lights were out before he made his way up the stairs to the carnal warmth of his bed; conscientious even then about his carbon footprint.

His mum heard the banging on the door at around six in the morning, the woodpecker beats rousing her from her comfortable sleep. Dazed she went to explore the root of the noise and found her daughter on the doorstep, shivering in the morning frost. Walker was wrapped up warm in his bed, dreaming of the presents he would soon be opening as he enjoyed his bacon, eggs and freshly ground coffee.

"It was his sister's mess." He explained to his mother. "Ask her what she had intended to get up to on the day of Jesus`s birthday under her roof?" With a superior air, he sang deeper into his eider-down and went back to sleep.

Nat's mum had split up with her step dad and found romance with an alternative vendor (not for the first time in her life). His wife not overly enamoured with the situation had thrown him out of his mock Tudor house and Christmas looked like a 'Bleak Mid-Winter's Tale' for both of them. Walker listened to Nat's pleas and presented their case for inclusion to his mum. Ever the willing entertainer; she agreed immediately and extra places were laid at the table. Nat's brother and sister were put on the guest list and invited to a good old fashioned Christmas in Wolverhampton, they readily accepted the kind invitation. Nat's sister was a whining spoilt rat who got constantly on his nerves. Her brother was a member of the E.B.F, but Walker liked the lad all the same. He was good to his sister and Nat loved him to pieces.

Walker had spent a small fortune on Victoria. He hid her presents with a thrilled cunningness. When she searched under the tree for packages with her name written on them, and couldn't find any, a small frown would appear on her face. "Where's my presents Daddy?" She would ask with a sorry look written upon her expression.

"In the North Pole I presume, with the elves and Santa, that's if you've been a good girl," he would answer with a smile as he continued to build the myth and excitement of the season. The nativity play, (banned now in case we offend other religious denominations), was always a good show and highlighted the real story of Christmas and not just its materialistic aspect. Walker would record it on his old man's video camera, which was heavy and about the size of Santa's sleigh, (the practise banned now, in case you are either a paedophile or looking to stream the video on the internet). The schools had woken up to the market potential, motivated by the Tory`s plans for good state education, despite cuts that meant that children had to use out-of date text books. Their views tempered by an out-dated concept, that children whose parents couldn't afford to pay thousands per month for private tuition, might actually have a valid opinion and important role to play in the countries future when they grew up. Victoria would make cards at school, (no charge) and excitedly bring them home, to show off to Walker and Nat. Pictures of glittery Santa`s, Rudolf the red nosed reindeer and perfectly shaped Christmas trees where all over the walls of the Walker household. Victoria would chatter excitedly about their next project at school and what decorations they were making tomorrow. Walker would listen intently with a wide smile on his face. He would explain who Father Christmas was, the story of St. Nicholas, recount the story of Mary and Joseph making their way to Bethlehem. The three wise men: Gasper, Balthasar and Melchior and their trek to the stable where Jesus was born. Victoria would become serious and ask what frankincense and myrrh were. Walker had expected this, he had completed his research conscientiously. If he wanted his daughter to understand the meaning of Christmas, then he should too. He wanted her to be a child, to feel the thrill and to savour the moment and expectation.

It was four in the morning when Walker woke on Christmas. He had put Victoria to bed at ten; she was getting tired of waiting for Father Christmas and had started to yawn repeatedly. He checked upon her soon afterwards, making sure she was sleeping soundly before he

played the part of Father Christmas with Nat, they silently laid her presents out by the foot of the bed and hung a Santa sack over the chair in the corner. He thought that she would have been up by now, too excited thinking about Rudolph and all the presents, to sleep long into the morning. Nudging her gently he whispered. "Father Christmas has been." Baby snores gently rose from her nose and her eyes remained shut. He nudged her again, a little harder this time. "Santa`s been, baby girl." Still no response from her." Santa's been!" Nat opened her eye like a sleeping giant and glared at him. "Leave her alone Gary she will be awake soon enough."
"She needs to be awake now Nat!"He answered.
Nat remembered the day when she had loved it when he had been an excited puppy, relishing his drive and energy, now she wished he would roll over go back to sleep. He tried again and achieved success in waking her. Victoria finally entered the land of the living, with a yawn and bored eyes, she looked around the room and promptly closed her eyes and went back to sleep.
Walker had to laugh silently, how cool was she? Nothing fazed her. He couldn't fall back to sleep. The anticipation heavy in his stomach, the excitement of Christmas singing through his thoughts; sighing he tiptoed down the stairs to make a start on the vegetables for lunch. He did enjoy the peacefulness of the night and the unique atmosphere of Christmas. The pine needles and the aroma of slowly roasting turkey were special for him. He would taste it and memorise the scent. It made him feel strangely secure and strangely tranquil. Victoria finally woke up, ripped open her presents and displayed the obligatory excitement. Nat and her family sang along with the karaoke that his mom had invested heavily in. It was a day full of laughs and full bellies, Walker could not have received a better Christmas present.
The lads had arranged a night out to celebrate Yule tide. Walker was about to bite the buzz and experience the feeling of group consciousness that clubbing brought to the boardroom. The pub was alive when they arrived. All the lads were all dressed up for the occasion. Walker felt self-conscious at first, having to ditch his usual uniform of jeans and trainers. This was dress up time for the Friday night 'soft shoe shuffle'. Walker had been motivated by Silks to go into town and buy some black trousers (Armani) a shirt (Armani) and some boots (Base). Silks preferred Nicholas Deacons for footwear. Walker wasn't about to take fashion advice from a man that dressed like he

did from day to day, however Walker had to admit that Silks did look good in his club gear.

After a few beers and a wrap Walker started to like the way he looked, the confidence flushing through his system. He and Silks had done their tour of Wolverhampton earlier in the week and got some premium gear for the firm. Silks had wrapped out some good parcels for the lads and some not so good ones for the club goers who would be happy to part with a few quid to keep their buzz going. When they walked into local pubs and bars in Wolverhampton, they were known men and got plenty of looks off the numerous pretty girls who were out celebrating on the town.

Along with Silks were; Gibson, Langley, Gibson's brother Durant had also made an appearance along with Cooper and Chamberlin. Chamberlin was a wise crack merchant, with a quick wit, readymade wise cracks that he didn't have to stop to think about. Cooper was Langley's mate and part of a large family of brothers that were well known in the area. John Durant, Gibson's brother had a touch of the Irish in him, looked Italian and thought he was Robert De Niro. Alternatively he also thought he was Jake La Motta (Raging Bull) 'Tommy', (Joe Pescis character in Goodfellas), or any other poor role model from the Italian American population. Durant could be an arrogant man at times, on other occasions he was intelligent and sharp with a sensitive plane that belied his egotism. Walker sensed the same paradoxes that existed within his head, were alive in Durant's. His brother had all the lads` respect. Walker felt his pedantic and overly aggressive behaviour was an attempt to come into the sunshine from behind the large shadow his elder brother created. Durant would endeavor to start a fight with man or beast on their many trips to the pubs and clubs in Wolverhampton. He could fight, but his mind was his superior asset. Walker thought he should have used it more.

Later on in life, Walker found out that Durant had settled down with a sensible girl (aptly named Joy), who'd nearly had as many degrees as the pop group. Lived in a nice house, drove a Mercedes, and loved his children, as only a loving parent can. Walker was happy, that he had found peace. Even if it had taken a journey out of Wolverhampton to achieve it.

Walker always felt a grudging respect for the bloke, even when he was pissed and shouting: *'You talkin' to me? You talkin' to me? You talkin' to me? Then who the hell else are you talkin to. You talkin to me? Well*

I'm the only one here. Who the fuck do you think you think you're talking to?'
Walker understood the resonance in his choice of speech. John Durant, Travis Bickle: separated at birth.
Gibson was a top man, he could fight, looked good, dressed well, talked sense and had done well for himself. He'd moved to a house in a decent part of Wolverhampton which was his, not the councils.
He had married a well- spoken wife with academic qualifications behind her and career in front of her. Gibson had been to jail for various violent offences, one being football. He liked a fight down the match. The jail time had not held him back in life and he had started his own small business which had flourished. Walker would ask him for snippets of advice on tax, cash flow and Gibson was happy to help him. Durant was accepted at first, Walker suspected, because of Gibs, a few of the firm nodded in agreement. Others simply enjoyed his erratic behaviour because, like a good record he grew on you. It was no surprise to Walker that it was Durant who gave him his first pill.
"What they like then John?" Walker asked.
 Durant replied simply. "It's fucking ecstasy mate." Walker believed him. He took the man's word on face value. Durant was delegated to locate the missing link in Walker`s club development. At the end of the month a well known club in Wolverhampton would have a big party. A top trance DJ would be booked to play in a big venue in the town centre. Silks knew the lads that organised them and the night out was duly planned.
Gibson parked the car up and the lads climbed out. They could hear the music in the night, a loud guttural raucous beat. The town centre was populated with well dressed groups of lads and girls making their way to various locations. Walker sniffed in the atmosphere. He drunk in the centre on match days, but he enjoyed the comfort of the local for nights out. The whole atmosphere was like a carnival and you could taste the expectation in the air. They walked to their destination, there was a long queue winding around the corner and out of sight. Silks walked straight past it and up to the front, laughed and shook hands with the three large black men on the door. Walker knew that he knew people and after he had a word in the doorman's ear they were let in. Feeling like kings, they climbed two staircases and entered the fray.
 Walker soaked in the view: It was dark and it was exciting. There were flashing lights and gyrating bodies, moving to the beat of the music.

The atmosphere was heaven. It wasn't like the clubs of old. Men hugging the bar and eyeing up the talent. Girls dancing to disco tunes, using their handbags for partners with beer monsters lurching around, looking to kick some blokes head in at the end of the evening. These people were all on one wavelength. On one mission to feel the music and dance. The words in the songs were all about highs and love. There was no aggression and the music even started to make Walkers feet move. He wanted to join the party; he wanted an *'E'*.

"You can get a pill then John?"

"Probably." He shrugged his shoulders, all De Niro.

"How much mate?" Walker didn't care he would have paid the price quoted.

"Ten quid Walker, get the boys round. If we buy in bulk they might throw extra in." It was plausible; he seemed to know the ropes.

After a quick conference at the bar; Durant counted out ten pound notes and headed off into the void to spend the cash wisely. The lads were dotted around the bar. Their legs had started to move to the drum beat. Durant returned to the group. He'd done the business and had a cocky edge to him. He handed over their pills and grabbed Walkers hand. "It's your first pill Walker, do half mate, trust me." Durant was giving it the big un, preaching like he was Jesus on the Mount of Olives. Walker had been doing drugs for years. He would drop the lot in one bounce and fuck the side effects. After ten minutes, Walker was feeling a little aggrieved. He felt fuck all.

Langley saw Walker heading his way, knowing he wanted an answer.

"It takes time to kick in," he explained to Walker; trying to talk and bop at the same time, an insane smile on his face. He was obviously buzzing his balls off.

Walker was impatient, he expected the feeling now! He was like that with most things. Walker had to have everything NOW! He would nail the first five pints when he first entered the pub to get pissed quickly. He would bomb the speed to get mashed as quickly as possible. Walker needed the high that drugs offered and he needed it soon. Suddenly he felt a tingle and a lightness in his head. The beat from the music matched his movements.

"Fuck me I can dance," he shouted over to Silks, who was too much in the moment to answer him. The sensation grew in intensity and he felt energy coursing through his body. When he breathed the air it felt like it had been purified. He could feel it enter his lungs. He felt love, he felt confident. He felt fucking great! The pill had hit home; his central nervous system poured out sublime messages to his head. He was free, he was flying. Josh Wink told him: *'It Was a Higher State of Consciousnesses'* and he believed.

The lights and the music became one. He raised his arms and the crowd raised theirs. It was a fantastic feeling of unity. All you could see was a river of good emotion flowing in the same direction. He looked around at the lads. Silks was off it, shirt open dancing like a maniac. Gibson was bopping till he was dropping. Langley was dancing round, his enthusiasm infectious. Chamberlain and Cooper were red Indians, dancing round some girls. Durant still had a serious look on his face. He was still trying to be De Niro. Don't fight against the tide, go with flow and let the lord Ecstasy set you free. God said let there be light and the strobe lighting burst into action. The crowd was illuminated, their movement enhanced by the light show. It was a pseudo -religious experience for Walker. He would hug lads he knew from his match days. All they wanted to do was hug him right back and laugh. No talk of any future battles. He would hug strangers and shake their hands. They understood and they would smile and shake his hand right back. Girls dressed like models would move on past. They would smile at him because he could dance and he was having a good time. It was a magic kingdom for adults.

He had to open his shirt; the sweat was starting to pour down him. Cooper thrust a bottle of water into his hands. "Keep drinking star, take on board some water man." Cooper smiled and winked.

Walker was buzzing like a hive of bees. He didn't want the journey to end, it was a feeling he'd never experienced before. He would never look back. He had found the power of the pill. Ecstasy was in his soul. Nat passed him on her way to the kitchen to do her morning cuppa and Victoria's breakfast.

He was starting to come down and felt like shit. The panic attack was not far away. He felt tired, irritable and anxious. Walker was in no mood for a stand up with the wife over his night out. He knew she would start, he could see it in her face as she glared over at him. Her looks had spoken a book; her mouth was quiet, firmly shut in a thin line. He already knew there would be no offer of a cup of tea. God, he felt terrible. He might even do the ASDA mission, if it would keep her quiet and off his back. He checked his pockets and counted a few ten pound notes and loads of shrapnel, all that was left to do the weekly

shop. He focused hard, had he got any left money in the bank? Did he visit the cash point last night? The anxiety welled up again. He about fifty quid on him, that should do her if she started. When he was single he never had this fucking pressure on his head. Fucking married life was bollocks, on a Saturday morning, when you was low as a plaster on a snakes stomach and your misses was about to give it you for blowing a week's money in six hours. The thoughts raced through his head as she returned into the front room, a cup in her hand standing in the doorway."I suppose you think you're clever?" she broke the silence. "What?" Walker was bubbling up nicely; please don't let me boil over he prayed to God.
"Going out with your mates all the time and taking your rubbish."
"Fuck off Nat! I mean it. I am not in the mood for your bollocks this early in the morning."
"You're a disgrace, spending all your money on drugs and clothes."
"How the fuck do I spend all my money on clothes and drugs? Go and have a look in the fucking cupboards! Look around you! Who bought all this stuff? You're a silly cunt. You knew all this when you fucking met me! Now fuck off and leave me alone." Walker was up off the sofa now. He moved toward her and was close to invading her personal space. Nat didn't let up.
"Think you're a big man do you? Go and hide behind your mates and your beer and your drugs. I had to pay the electric bill yesterday when you were out spending twice that amount on new clothes."
 Walker thrust his hands in his pocket and pulled out some ten pound notes. "Here you cunt!" He grabbed her round the throat and pushed the money into her mouth. "All you ever care about is fucking money, so fucking eat it!" Walker was angry, hurt and it was fueling his anger. He did provide for them, but he also knew that he was spending more than he earned and he had to damp down the lifestyle. Nat was all housewife these days and it bored him. They were still in their twenties, but she acted like a seventy year old. She never thanked him when he had a nice touch and when he did help out; but she would be the first to cast a stone when he fucked up."You fucking like that do you?" His eyes were glazed and bloodshot. Tiny red veins extended away from his iris: resembling a road map of narcotics. Veins stood out on his neck. He smelt like last night: sweat, smoke and beer. He was spitting in her face such was the venom in his words."You fuck off with my mum today." He pointed directly into her face, his finger nearly

stabbing her eyes. Nat was white, her eyes wide open."Here is the cash point card! Fucking have it all! You fucking bitch!"
Victoria started to cry. Walker stopped; he didn't realise that he was shouting. He took his hands off her neck. His anger departed as quickly as it erupted and he moved back away from Nat, shocked at his own aggression. She held his eyes for a second before she turned and walked out of the room. He would never forget that look in her eye. He was becoming a stranger to her.
 It was the beginning of the end.

CHAPTER 11
DRUDGERY

The weeks went by and that morning was never mentioned again. Walker felt shamed; it was written all over his face for a month. It lay inside for longer. He asked questions he couldn't provide an answer too. Was he now a bloody wife-beater? He hadn't hit her, she didn't have any physical marks, but Walker knew there was more to domestic abuse than hitting. Emotional scars sometimes never healed. Walker ignored the warning to his own future and kept plodding on with life and tried to be a better husband, attempting manfully to accept Natalie's point of view. He made sure that Nat had money when he had money. Sometimes when he was short, he would ask her for some change and she would moan at him. He could never understand why? They were man and wife, for richer and poorer, in sickness and in health.

Walker told Silks about the trouble he was having at home. He shrugged his shoulders and told Walker that it was, 'man and wife' stuff and none of his business how Walker behaved in his own house. His only advice was to drop a surprise on her, take her and the family out, make a fuss of them occasionally. Keep it fresh. Walker nodded and listened; he knew they were stuck in a world of shopping, telly and magazines: domestic quicksand. Silks could be hard on his women; he was hard on most people that didn't see his point of view, or he thought were stupid. He didn't have gender bias. He would freely admit it. However, he would always make sure that he provided regular entertainment to the people in his life keeping them all sweet. They called another ceasefire. Their household was becoming like fucking Beirut. Walker sat down and explained his thoughts and actions, they weren't excuses, they were reasons. He had learned it was healthy to talk, had he read it? Or seen it on *This Morning?* He didn't remember, but he knew experts reckoned it was better to talk through problems to find a solution. So Walker talked, talked about her, about their marriage and about their life. He opened up his soul to her. Nat, as usual, kept her cards close to her chest with no major statements volunteered in return. Walker told himself he would find a way, he always did, he always had a plan.

Walkers charm, like his jobs were lost. His quips only hit home occasionally now and instead of laughing, she would just smile. He thought and modified his strategy; he would give her more money, if that's what she wanted, if that was her goal. He found regular work with a respected sub-contractor. The job was now on a daily basis and Walker hated it. He felt like he was back on a treadmill: going nowhere. The bloke he worked with was a nit-picking, pedantic type, boring and him had got married and lived happily ever after in drab city with 2.4 children. They shared nothing in common. If Walker stopped at the café for a sandwich he would ask Mr. Charisma if he wanted anything. "No thanks," he would reply. "It's a waste of money, my wife had made me a packed lunch.

Walker would reply. "Live a little and have a fucking bacon and egg on crusty, it's on me!

Mr. Boring would talk with that slow Brummie twang that did nothing to alleviate the veil of grey fog that hung around him. Walker had never met the woman he called wife. God what a night out that would be? He told Nat. Drinking Darjeeling out of china tea cups with scones and fucking cucumber sandwiches for company, talking about the anomalies of daffodils coming out and flowering early this year. When all Walker wanted was to bomb a can of Strongbow and drop a wrap in the toilet. The thought of spending time with this man made him shudder.

He resented Nat for making him do this, he didn't want to conform and play happily. He wanted a wife, he wanted freedom. Couldn't she see that? Walker felt trapped, guilty and frustrated at the lack of control he had in his own life. She'd started to smile occasionally, Walker hadn't. Their ying and yang were not in balance.

He continued to go out on a Friday night and get mashed like a potato, needing to feel like a man again. The pills and wraps in abundance. He loved to dance, the feeling ecstasy gave him was an unrivalled high. The music set him free, like the football violence of the past. He would try and smile on a Saturday, the come downs were bad and anxiety would seep out of every pore. She would smile back occasionally, knowing that he was making an effort. If he felt like it was coming on top it, he would tell her to shut up and leave him alone.

Baskerville would be leased up and taken on a long walk. Baskerville loved Saturday morning! Walker would walk her over to the church and talk softly about how the wife needed to die violently. They'd called another truce. Kissinger was in town on a visit, with the ceasefire barely holding. The conflict he was experiencing bubbled over into all walks of their life together, not just when the horrors were about.

Walkers mind was made up for him concerning the rat race. The 'honest' sub-contractor tried to pull one over on him. He'd used Walkers van for a job, and charged for its usage, but only paid Walker him day rate for that job. Walker found out via a second source that the Brummie had charged a small fortune for taking the goods on site with them. This prick had told him that delivery was included in the price to secure the job. Walker's anger grew as he reflected on the situation and questioned him when they were arranging another job. 'Why he hadn't tried to work in the cost of delivery into the job?' The Brummie would become evasive and change the subject quickly. Walker was no mug and smelled a rat and he sought out a second opinion and had his suspicious confirmed. When Walker finally established the fact that he had been blagged, he wasn't pleased, and considered various courses of action, most of them violent. He talked the situation over with Nat and she agreed that he should be paid for the use of his van. She helped him type up the invoice and faxed over the extra charge. Their phone rang five minutes later and Walker heard his wearisome tone on the other end of the line, attempting to justify his actions. Walker stopped him in mid sentence. "Are you going to fucking pay me you blue nosed prick, or what?" Forgotten memories of his childhood screamed at him, feelings that he was trapped, scared and vulnerable crept into his stomach, an anxious dog Is more likely to bite you than a confident one. His anger started to boil as he dismissed them furiously with a shake of his head.

" What did you say? No, that job is done now, we move on." Clipped nasal tones of boredom washed into Walkers ears.

"Fuck you and your move on bollocks, you robbing fucking cunt! Stick your fucking job up your arse! You'll fucking pay or I'll kick the fucking shit out of you!" Walker shouted as he smashed the handset against the wall and watched it splinter.

Nat flinched as it shattered into pieces and looked witheringly at Walker. "What you done that for. You'll have to replace it now," she said with resigned annoyance.

Walker grabbed his keys off the small desk that was hidden in the corner of the living room and slammed the door, on his way out. Small pieces of plaster floated in his wake. Nat sighed and followed him with a tired stride. When she got outside Walker was already sitting in his

van, head down looking for the ignition. She stood in front and placed her hands on the bonnet. She must have thought her body weight would stop a 2.0 litre van that weighed around a metric tonne.
 Walker wound the window down, looking surprised and shouted. "What the fuck you doing Nat?"
"Stop shouting and don't curse at me, you drive over there and cause trouble, and get arrested then I will leave and take Victoria with me." Her eyes weren't lying."Calm down, and come back in, stop making a public exhibition of yourself," she snapped back.
Walker noticed a few nets were starting to twitch. He sighed and turned the engine off, before he leapt out of the cab. "He's a twat Nat," his voice lowered and he prepared to accept the inevitable.
 "I know, but being an idiot isn't going to help is it?" She asked him. Walker looked sheepishly down at his feet, his temper evaporating into the evening sky. "I suppose yam right," he said and crept back indoors.
 Walker had other plans on how to pay the bills. He'd spent a couple of long nights formulating his next strategy, sitting, thinking pondering."I'm going to take out some advertising in the Express and Star."
The beers were on the table it was time to talk tactics with his mate and P.I.C (Partner In Crime)."Saying what?" Silks asked, if it involved making a pound note then Silks was all ears. The money was running as low as the work. Rumour had spread through the trade that Walker had threatened his previous sub- contractor. He still received delivery jobs, but the installation work dried up to a trickle. Installations were the bread and butter of his business, deliveries the bacon that went in the bread.
 "I've got a van, we can do all sorts. Removals, house clearances all sorts. I'll sit down with my old man and develop some brochures and some adverts. He is good at all the bollocks, he was involved in marketing or some shit when he was at work." Walker's dad was now semi-retired but still did some independent advertising and marketing for people he knew within the business. He had an office in his house that resembled a studio with banks of TV screens and videos. He'd started producing his own videos. Silks liked this fact; he could always get his hands on electronic equipment from independently liberated sources and Mr. Walker liked a deal and would pay cash on delivery.

The Express and Star ran the ad, asking if people; *'Needed a man with a Van?* The flyers that his old man helped with were printed, hundreds and hundreds of them in all colours, no prejudice when it came to money. The kids on the local estate posted them and handed them out for a few quid: they were now back in the game. People in the pub had little jobs for them to do, which kept the cash flow ticking over. Silk`s charm and megalomania, managed to secure them a big job doing some refurbishment work on a house, which included rendering a large garage. Silks proudly stuck out his chest and professed he could mix cement and put it on the wall, it wasn't a problem.

He could certainly mix it. He could put it on the wall, however putting in on the wall and having it stay there were two different things. Walkers face grew redder and redder as yet another attempt failed. Silks face turned blacker and blacker which was never a good sign. It meant his temper was frayed and he could be about to explode. With more confidence than they felt, they told the owner they had to pick up some more sand and ran off to seek advice on how to do the job properly .

Greg was Julie's dad. He'd been a builder before he retired; not a builder like the dynamic duo, he was a registered with the builder's guild and fully certified. They dropped round to his house and begged him to come out of retirement to help them out with the job. He refused their offer and started to laugh when they explained what they were doing. "You pair should be called *'Botch it and Scarper'* or *'Wreck It and Run Rubbish Removals."* Walker listened while Greg and Silks bantered back and forth, sorting out the method for completing the job.

He liked the names; they were original and they would raise a smile, curiosity value at least. Other ideas had started to peculate in Walkers mind. If he couldn't earn a legal pound, there were other alternatives. Tools cost a fortune, so did the materials that they had to buy to complete a job. He could cut down their overheads by a massive margin if he could 'liberate' them. Walker had stolen things in the past; he was not averse to committing a crime. He and Harris had performed a couple of street robberies when they'd been pissed off and in need of money to fulfill their needs. Walker used to carry a blade in case he got jumped. He'd cut a couple of people in the wars that were common place in Wolverhampton, between lads from opposing areas. He'd received his fair share of beating too. Walker had been slashed

and glassed. It didn't arse him. You would get a beer and attention
from the ladies in the pub next day as you recounted your war stories.
Attending accident and emergency was an occupational hazard.
Everybody carried a blade in those days; just in case you needed a
weapon to get yourself out of a tough spot. Walker would hold it at the
victims' throat and Harris would relieve them of their valuables. They
didn't do it often, just when they needed to, a bit like Robin Hood; take
from the rich and give to the poor.
Silks was not into theft, he was a kiter by trade and passed dodgy
cheques and cards. His conviction for armed robbery was a set up and
he was in the process of litigation. That was his story and he stuck to it.
Silks would come alive when he spoke about his days in prison. He
would retell the story of how Reggie Kray had given him his tea bags
on his first day on the wing. How Reggie had told him, a nonce was
undercover on the spur and said to him. *"They didn't like that, did
they?"* The child rapist was battered so badly, that when Silks went in
front of the governor he was asked the question. "What did you use
on him then George?"
Silks replied. "I didn't hit him, he fell over." There was no charge and
no loss of remission. Silks didn't give a fuck about remission anyway.
He was intending to serve his full sentence. Why ask for remission and
admit your guilt when you were innocent?
When Labi Siffe sang; *'There's Something Inside So Strong'*. It would
move Walker when Silks told him that was his anthem and that he
used to sing it to himself when he was scared, or lonely doing another
two weeks in solitary, down the block on segregation. He also
dedicated, *'My Way'* as a song that told the story of his life. When he
sang these songs in the pub, or on Karaoke evenings, there would not
be a dry eye in the house. He could hold an audience in the palm of his
hand when he was on form. Silks was a category 'A' prisoner. Tough
jails had been his home for seven years. Jails like Gartree and Long
Lartin to name a few. Britain's toughest criminals were imprisoned
inside them. Langley would tell the story about when he had received
a VO. He had sat down at the tabled after getting the coffees and
chocolate bars and said to Silks. "I recognise that bloke, who the hell is
he?"
Silks looked across the room and replied. "I'm not surprised mate,
that's fucking Reggie Kray!" The man moved in violent circles. It was no
wonder he wasn't too fussed when Walker went on about scuffles that

erupted on a Friday night or Saturday lunch time. The people that Silks had lived with were 'life men' who would maim and kill without the need for back up. They would hurt you with no drink and no drugs inside them. They would harm you because you were in the way. They would harm you for money. They would harm you because it was their job and their business to. They were hard men; there was no need to argue.

Walker decided to run three separate adverts when he did the rounds of the local post offices and shops to market the business and put up the flyers. The official advert would have Walker's mobile on it. Botch it and Scarper would have Silks mobile. Wreck it and Run Removals would have Walkers landline printed on it. This advertising campaign even brought a smile to Natalie's tense face; not much did these days. To underpin Walkers blossoming carer as an entrepreneur Silks christened him *Bruce*. Silks had just watched a film called, *'Brewsters Millions'*, a tale about a man who had to waste a fortune over a calendar month and have nothing to show for it in order to earn a larger, vast inheritance. Walker's nickname duly became Bruce, and the name stuck with him, but only Silks ever used it on a regular basis. To most people he remained Walks. After a month; Botch it and Scarper won the battle of the businesses; the great British public had spoken.

Desperate to earn some money, Walker decided to drum up his own business. He placed cards around different areas, offering picnic tables for sale at a competitive price with free delivery included. He would receive a phone call; the lads would pop to a pub, liberate a table and clean it up before they delivered it to the happy new owners. They would target different pubs as not to attract police attention. The last thing he wanted was to turn up at the local nick to the amusement of the local constabulary. The pubs wouldn't bother to report them stolen because of their limited value and the paperwork involved in the process. Walker would charge £50 a pop for them. If he could move six a week it was a decent little enterprise. He and Silks would split it, £150 each which was on top of their other little earners.

Walker started to relax and repeated the mantra; from little acorns do large oak trees grow. Nat was oblivious to his latest fuckwit behaviour. She accepted the money he gave her for housekeeping and she knew that some days were better than others. Walker managed to hand over £100 a week to keep her satisfied. She knew he and Silks must be up to no good, but if the money kept coming in she was prepared to turn a blind eye to their activities. Walker had bigger and better ideas. If landlords didn't report their belonging stolen, would other people? He pondered the question over a pint and ran scenarios through his head. SOCO wouldn't turn up to an outside theft and even if the victims bothered to report the crime, would the police bother to turn up to investigate it with a conviction unlikely? They would, usually, prefer to issue a crime number for insurance purposes only. Walker decided to do some research into the matter and got the dog lead out to walk Baskerville around the local garden centre.

His mind boggled when he checked out the prices for tools and furniture, they were outrageous and people just left them lying around in their gardens and sheds with no real security. Walker's latest plan was fully formulated and ready to be implemented.

Walker looked at the clock, it was half two and dark outside. Nat would be sound asleep by now, Victoria also. Baskerville was snoring, wedged under his feet. There was nothing left to watch on the television. It was time to go out and about and earn some money. He checked his dress sense; he was all in black and looked like Raffles.

After initial successes, easy targets were running out. Walker had to spread his wings and move his operation to a wider area. To identify potential sources for income he would take Baskerville and Victoria out for long afternoon walks in the summer sun scanning gardens as they walked passed. Nat was happy (for once). She could have some peace and quiet when they were out; she thought it was a nice touch on his behalf, oblivious to the real rationale behind his new love affair with nature. Walker would sit in the pub on a Friday and take orders from people who were eager to accept a bargain when they saw one. Business was booming. When his orders had been taken and business conducted he would happily make his way to the toilet to take more drugs and wonder how many pills to have tonight.

 On weekdays, Walker would always take Victoria over the local park to push her on the swings. He had never noticed before that the place was surrounded by countless homes whose gardens backed straight onto it providing perfect cover. He could case the place and then remove goods without any suspicions being raised. The money continued to flow in from his sale of stolen goods, his legal business was placed firmly on the back burner.

BUSTED
CHAPTER 12

Darren Langley was diminutive in stature, wringing wet and in socks he stood five feet six inches tall and weighed no more than 160 pounds. The lads christened him *'Wee-Man'*, a take on both his size and his love of all things English. The man's heart was decorated by the cross of St, George, he bled patriotism.

Langley dressed in smart clothes, lovingly bought for him by Sarah. She avoided the brand name cattle market. However, Langley was always a smartly turned out lad, who had the look of the 'clean liver' about him. His hair was razor cut and mousey blonde; his face carried a generous look, even if his eyes could turn to stone when the mood took him that way. His wife and child-hood sweetheart Sarah was an attractive blond, with a warm smile, and a backbone made of high-tensile steel, together they earned the nick-name 'Posh &Becks'.

The couple lived in a three bed roomed flat, housed in a block built in the sixties, three storey's high, located in a semi-affluent area of Wolverhampton; an area without daily shooting and live in drug dealers. If you wanted a weed, a delivery could be arranged in under ten minutes; you were never very far from a ten bag of green in Wolverhampton. He lived there with Sarah and their three children. Good kids who were raised properly and knew the difference between right and wrong and the importance of having a good work ethic. He was a solid dependable member of the firm, a man who had worked all his adult life. He didn't break the law, didn't have a criminal record and was a good husband and father.

He would take class 'A' narcotics but only when out clubbing and he utilised the ten minute rule to order a weed. Langley liked to settle down after the kids were in bed and chill out with a joint; he wasn't a big drinker and would avoid getting drunk if he had work the next day. He was the sensible side of the bunch and was well thought of by his peers. Langley was a straight up bloke. If you were being a prick he would pull you up and tell you.

He was assertive and not scared to make his point. His wife Sarah was built from the same mould, she liked to have a party, but always put their children first. The entire firm respected Langley's morals and his value system. They were closest of all to the perfect social ideal portrayed in the press. He was a good amateur footballer and played for a local pub side. That's how he and Walker first became friends. Walker had found an outlet to satiate his thirst to be abusive at football matches.

On a Sunday he would turn up at the local park with a bag of beers and watch the match with Victoria by his side. Most Sundays were family time for the firm. Their children would stand on the side lines and cheer as their dads sweated for the cause. Couples would chat as they watched the ball disappear into the grey skies above. Even grandparents would make an occasional appearance to join in the family orientated fun. Nat would chose to spend this time to relax and read on her own. She worked hard; she just wanted to chill out. She didn't want to be bothered with standing on a windswept field watching men drink and swear at each other.

Walker would watch the other couples with an empty feeling as they shared quality time with each other; he would then shake his head at his own stupidly. He had the best of both worlds; free time to drink with the lads, without the brooding presence, of the missus looking over his shoulder and a wife back at home who looked the part. He couldn't understand the erratic misguided thoughts that interrupted his happy mind-set, and left him with the impression that maybe he had forgotten to turn the gas off when he had left home in the morning. After the match they would adjourn to the local pub for three hours of heavy drinking and loud singing, before he would land at his mums to eat his lunch. Walker would fight off the urge to sleep as he watched contentedly as his mom made a fuss of Victoria. After an hour he would search the kitchen for Natalie's lunch, which was always safely wrapped up in tin foil, with his moms gravy in a separate bowl. Walker would hold Victoria's hand and together they would escort it back home and present it to her on a tray before he fell asleep on the sofa and snored loudly.

The evening telly was boring, Nat was reading, Victoria was gazing intently at some basic arithmetic her dad had given her to complete and Baskerville stood with her head out of the window, searching avidly for cats. Walker's phone beeped to alert him that he had an incoming message; he flicked on the menu and opened it. Silks had got them on the guest list for a forthcoming party to mark the end of the month and Graham Parks was playing a set. It had all the potential for a good night out. He turned to Nat, "You want to come to this party at

Decadent? Silks reckons he can get us in for free." The question hung in the air.

"Go on then, why not, I haven't been out for ages." Nat answered.

"You sure?" Walker was surprised, Nat never wanted to go out any more.

"Yes I am, it will do me good. I'm getting bored with doing nothing but working all the time. let's see what all the fuss is about."

Walker felt the guilt rise in his throat and wondered briefly if she was having a pop at him. "Okey dokey, I'll sort it then," he started to tap on the buttons of his phone to return the message, marveling at the miracle of modern text messaging.

Silks and Walker were at a loose end and were momentarily bored with the inside of the pub. Walker didn't want to go home; he was sure of the frosty reception he was going to receive off Nat after they had indulged in another round of guerilla warfare. They discussed their options and decided it was time to drop on the Langley's. They hadn't seen Darren for a week and were always assured of a warm welcome when they descended with beers and treats for the kids. Armed with two crates of beer and cider, they buzzed his door and the lock clicked allowing them entry into the building. Darren met them at the door as they hurdled the final flight of stairs. He looked suspiciously at them as they arrived with a gasp at his front door.

"Are you pair being chased by the police?" Langley questioned the pair with a hint of a smile breaking onto his face.

Silks raised his eye brows and did a good impression of Roger Moore. "Don't be daft wee man, I've come to see me nieces and nephews, is that's alright with you?"

"Them nearly ready for bed, so don't wind them up, I mean it Silks don't start fucking around." He turned and looked at Walker and greeted him with a firm hand shake. "Safe Walks?"

"Yes Dazer, cool mate." Walker smiled back."Here mate stick these in the fridge then. Walker" handed Langley the crates of beer. Darren led them through to the front room, flicked open a can and sat down in his chair sipping on a Carling. Walker liked Langley's home; it was well furnished with all the trapping of modern living, a nice telly, good sofas, DVD and CD players. Sarah had managed to create a balanced atmosphere keeping the feel of a family home and adding modern chic to it. The Langley's home always had a sense of happiness and contentment about it. After a few beers and time spent winding the kids up, Sarah tucked her three children safely into bed before she left to pay a visit to her friend who lived nearby, leaving the lads to their own devices. It wasn't long before Langley steered the conversation around to his favourite subject; when were Silks and Walker were going to grow up and get proper jobs. Langley never understood 'the life' he needed the security a weekly wage provided.

"How are things at home Walks?" Langley had met Nat and got the impression she wasn't happy with his current career path and sensed her dissatisfaction with her husband's lifestyle.

"So so, she always fucking nagging me man, doesn't matter what the fuck I do."

"Get a job then you fucking numpty." Langley said. Walker tutted. He got nagged at home, now his mates were having a go, there was no escape for him! Perhaps Langley was correct, perhaps it was time to get a proper job, admit his failure and become a rat and enter the race. He sat quietly drinking his Strongbow listening to what Langley had to say. Langley stopped his motivational and looked at Silks. "What you got too say then eh!"

Silks contemplated the situation and looked back at his brother in law, and said. "I don't care how a man makes his money. That up to him and God, Walkers a grown-up he can make his own decisions."

Walker jumped in."Give it a rest now Daz, I know, I know all about it, about how Nat feels. She's OK man, because we got money we live well. If that dries up then I'll consider getting a 9-5. Anyway what the fuck am I meant to do? Go back to working in a factory? That'll be a head fuck, I don't want to do it OK." The thought of returning to that life filled him with dread, dark memories and a sense of foreboding. He remembered the feeling of anxiety that had risen with him, as he had brushed his teeth in the morning. Walker made a mental note to increase his motivation to succeed in the legal world. It was too late today. He would start the business back up and do it legally if he had to. Getting a proper job was the last item on his list. A jail term looked a cosier proposition. He didn't want to lose Nat, but he wasn't exactly prepared to walk over hot coals to keep her either.

"What you going to do if you get nicked Walker?" Langley prepared the case for the prosecution and mounted his cross examination.

"I won't get nicked Daz, I don't go out when I'm pissed, and I'm fucking careful. I pick the spot a couple of days before. I'm careful Daz I fucking am mate." Walker reinforced his point. He was meticulous in his preparation when he was out on a job. He didn't make mistakes, measure twice cut once. Walker continued to prepare the case for the defence. "Your best mate, Chamberlain has given me an order, he wants a patio set. Have a word with him instead of me. If there was no market I wouldn't steal would I?"

"Here, here fucking tell him Bruce." Silks decided to enter the debate. Langley looked across at him. "What you got to say then?" This was how they enjoyed spending their time, debating current issues, threatening each other with a good hiding and insulting each other. Comfortable in each other's company and secure in their roles as mates. It was paradoxical in Walker's opinion; you greeted your mate with, 'how you going Silks you old bastard! But if you were going to have a word with a stranger, your eyes would narrow and your speech would lower as you asked the question 'what you looking at mate?' Walker couldn't get his head round the simple semantics involved.

"I won't get nicked Daz, simple as." Walker put a lid on the conversation. Silks was good at most things, however when it came to drunken banter he could take things the wrong way. His paranoia was as far gone as Walkers, his temper and ability to commit violent acts worse. The rest of the evening passed off with talk of pills, wraps and clubs. Silks and Walker would sort out the gear Thursday, ready for the Friday night jamboree.

Walker dropped Silks off at Julies and prepared to go home. He looked at his watch, It was already the early hours of the morning. Nat would be asleep and he would have to explain why he had been out and about at all hours again. As he was driving home, he spotted an expensive patio set, sitting in an open garden with a sign on it saying. 'Steal me'. It matched exactly the specification of a set he had written down in his order book .The alcohol took effect and all previous caution and planning was lost in the greed of the moment. He stopped the van, got out and started to load it up. "Five minutes work, £70 in my pocket. Not bad that," he told himself.

"OI! " The shout broke Walkers train of thought; as he arrived back in the here and now. He had been spotted doing his thing. He assessed the situation, dropped the chair and got on his toes. He heard footsteps behind him. Fucking hell the bloke was only chasing him! He couldn't believe it! Walker was unfit, carrying an extra three stone in weight and pissed up into the bargain. He hoped the adrenaline now frantically pumping around his system would be enough carry him through to the winning line; he carried on running hoping the fucking vigilante was as unprepared for the race as he was. Walker eventually lost him as the sweat ran down his face and his lungs cried out for air. He tried to get his breath and thought. 'Fuck me' Langley was correct, I'm too old for all this. If I get away I'm going back to promoting the business and living an easy life. He made those promises far too often for them to be taken seriously. He turned and made his way stealthy back to the van, like a fucking marine commando. As he turned the corner and peered cautiously around it, blue lights were illuminating the scene with a strobe-like effect.

Swearing under his breath and with his heart pounding and a rising feeling of doom and anxiety, he listened carefully to the police talking into their radios. They had run his registration through the PNC. His name and address had come up and they were about to go and knock on his front door, the knowledge he had been bubbled sank in and his stomach dipped. He quickly weighed up the situation and made a decision to try and limit the fallout. Walker walked forward into the light with his hands in the air and a grin on his face. "Lads, it's me you're after. I'm not resisting arrest."

 The police turned toward him, smiles on their faces and said. "Hello wanker."

They pushed him to the ground, snapping the handcuffs tight onto his wrists; he was on his way back to the cells again.

"Can I make a phone call please?" Walker looked around the custody suite, posters informing him of his rights were on the walls. The benches were empty, and the white-board behind the desk was barren. They were having a quiet night. He knew his rights, he still had a plan. The phone was pushed over the counter toward him. He picked up the phone and dialled in number, praying under his breath that Silks had not gone to sleep. A sleepy voice answered and didn't sound especially impressed at being disturbed. Walker got in first he didn't have time for a debate. "I've been nicked mate, come and pick me up tomorrow would you?"

"Yeah, yeah, where are you?"Silks asked with no element of surprise in his tone.

"Wombourne." Walker answered.

"What the fuck are you doing over there?" Silks asked, surprised.

"I was in Staffordshire when I got lifted, just come and get me in the morning please mate." Walker replied. The two police officers were running out of patience with Walker.

"Put the phone down you prick. The call is to let someone know where you are, not to tell them your fucking life story."

"Ok, fuck me, calm down lads; you ain't paying for the call are you?" Walker was pissed off, tired and had the beginning of a hangover pressing against his forehead. The alcohol had dulled the effects of the arrest and sobriety was initiating a new round of angst. They had ruined his night; cost him £70 in earners and a head fuck off the wife when he finally surfaced tomorrow. The least they could do was show a bit of empathy, the fucking tossers! He hoped momentarily that the police had the power of telepathy. He smiled insincerely as they ran through his details. Wishing he was at home tucked up in bed. Ten minutes later Walker was processed into the system, swabbed for DNA, his genetic code was now locked in. He looked surprised as they placed a cotton bud into a test tube and sealed it. With a frown Walker was led to his cell, he sat on the bed and looked at the drab walls as the heavy door slammed shut behind him, he heard the keys and footsteps of the copper reducing into the distance. His inner gloom matched the warmth of the new surrounding, he visited the well of optimism once more as his brain repeated the message there was still a way to get out of his predicament. They would let him go early in the morning, it wasn't a serious charge. Silks would drop him off to get the van. He could tell Nat that he'd slept round Darren's. Daz was law abiding and took the keys off him because he was pissed blah, blah. It sounded plausible, it could work. He closed his eyes, and tried to sleep. The police had wanted to pin all sorts of crimes upon him. 'Apparently' in the area he lived, there had been a spate of thefts of tools, furniture and other collectables running into tens of thousands of pounds. The crime wave had been serious enough that it had made the front page of the local press. Walker told the police 'He wasn't aware of any crime spree, he was simply unemployed, had a stupid idea and decided to act upon it. He wasn't a criminal, despite what his record suggested. His wife was pissed off with the lack of money, so he had decided to earn a bit. It was a desperate act, but did he look like he was a thief and did this for a business?' Walker hadn't planned to go out and earn that night; hence his dress sense was not congruent to their profile of Raffles.

They kept him into the early afternoon of the next day before he was charged and bailed to appear before the local magistrates. Silks was waiting for him in the foyer as he was released from custody. Walker heard him before he saw him and couldn't understand why he sounded so cheerful. Turning the corner back into the daylight he stopped and frowned, his mate was draped over some cheep looking girl with too much make up on and a bad taste in clothes; was he really after some skank when he'd just spent hours in custody? Walker stopped himself from creating a scene and reflected, Silks didn't deal in hours, weeks or months. He dealt in years. Silks looked up, feeling his mate's eyes upon him. "What the fuck." Silks looked at Walker, a laugh creeping out of the corner of his mouth. "You went out on the rob dressed like that?" His incredulity was obvious.

"Shut up man." said Walker, he was embarrassed and could feel his face burning with the blush.

Silks got up from his seat and led the way out the police station; he stopped and opened the door for his mate. "Sailors First."

"Yam a fucking riot of laughs, when I've just spend the last fifteen hours in the fucking cells!.

Silks carried on regardless. "I told that bird that my mate had been lifted for robbery and you were a top man, and you come out dressed like that!" He couldn't hide his amusement.

Walker hadn't gone home to get changed; he was still wearing his checked Lacoste shirt, blue shorts and sailor's pumps. He didn't look like a blagger, he looked like he was about to go into a bar in Benidorm to have a cold beer.

"The police have searched your yard as well, they ain't found shit and you're dressed like that!" Silks pointed at him." It's no wonder they let you go, you fucking dickhead!"

A worried look settled on Walkers brow. "Searched me yard? How the fuck do you know they turned over my yard? Fuck me Nat will go fucking ballistic." He'd brought trouble to the door. Was Victoria in when they'd turned him over? The day was getting worse.

"I heard the police talking mate."Silks said.

"Oh fuck man, she's going to kill me Silks." Walker could feel his anxiety levels rise. His throat went dry and his heart started to beat.

"Be a man, what can she do? Take your bollocking and stop being a pussy." Silks said dismissively. Silks was not in the sympathy business. Get a grip, sort it out and be a man, was all you could expect out of him. You might get a pint and ten minutes of his time if it was serious shit that you were in. If you were blowing the situation up out of all proportion then you would get fuck all but a slap. Deal with it or be a pussy was Silks philosophy.

Walker entered the flat gingerly, his footsteps light. He had half expected to find Nat on the pavement, weapon in hand, black bin-bags in both her hands. "Hello." Walker said gently announcing his return home , expecting a pot, pan or some other object to come whistling toward his head.

 Nat was sitting down on the sofa with a steaming cup of tea in her hand reading her obligatory magazine , with a plate of sandwiches cut neatly in triangles perched on the arm of the chair. Where was her tray? He would have copped it for fucking up the carpet with his crumbs. Baskerville was sleeping soundly and Victoria was still at school.

 "Sorry Nat," he eyed the hot tea in her hand apprehensively. Nat looked up at him and put her magazine down, she didn't appear angry. She appeared very calm. His worry deepened. What the fuck did she have in store for him?

"Why are you saying sorry? You're always out with your mates now. I always come second, what's changed today?" Walker knew that they had problems, but now she didn't even give a fuck where he was or where he spent the night now. Walker lowered his head, as if he was praying for absolution. "For the police Nat."

 "The police?" Her tone was questioning." What do you mean the police?" Nat looked at him and her brow became furrowed.

"They've searched the flat haven't they?" Walker still hadn't entered the front room. He thought that standing in the doorway might offer him some protection from the hot drink in her hand, and give him a head start should he needed to get on his toes.

"What police? When did they search the flat? What the hell have you been up to again?" the furrows on her brow deepened as she barked questions at him.

"I don't fucking know, I was banged up in the cells." He knew he was making a mess of this and should end the conversation while he was still in one piece.

"Banged up?" there were deep lines scaring her forehead now, she was up off the sofa, stepping from foot to foot tensely. Walker had held off a police interrogation and dodged the bullets aimed at him by

CID. Nat had him confessing in minutes. Her expression and the colour of her face was changing rapidly. "Banged up for what?" She was slowly edging toward him and he was happy to see that the tea was not making the journey over with her.

"Fuck all really Nat." Walker answered with more confidence than he was feeling.

"The police have arrested you……AGAIN! You thought they had searched MY home, and you have done NOTHING! Don't lie to me! You're a disgrace, you can't work, and you're always out with your new mate. You're always drunk. I have two jobs to make sure that we have money for bills and you think you're clever?"

Walker listened meekly and then countered in an attempt to stop the one way traffic heading in his direction. "You get plenty of money off me each week, we live Ok. You know where the money comes from, so don't act like a fucking martyr." Walker was in the wrong. But he was not going down without a fight. He had spent the night in the cells, he was tired and he'd got away with a clean pair of heels, compared to the charges they could have laid at his door. When he sold the set he would have stuck £30 in her purse and she wouldn't have asked any questions as to the origin of his wealth. His own anger started to build. If she wanted to give him some home truths then she was getting some back. "I've looked after this family for years. I always come through with money; I didn't go out for months at a time."

"Poor you, having to stop in with your wife and baby daughter." Nat said.

Walker stopped arguing. This was going round in circles, and not getting them anywhere. It would only end in tears. He walked to the kitchen to get Baskervilles lead. The dog would again feel the benefit of their row; Walker thought he must have been the fittest dog in Wolverhampton. He placed the chain round Baskerville's neck and made sure the door nearly left its hinges as he left the flat. "Fucking bitch!" He yelled at her as a parting shot, he heard her shout a reply but he wasn't interested in what she had to say.

As he walked Baskerville across the field toward the church he knew she had a point. Perhaps he should sort his life out. He was a pain in the arse when he was on a come down, he remembered her face when he had shoved the money into her mouth and he knew that had been a watershed in their relationship. Things had never quite got back on a level with them after that. They tolerated each other more than they enjoyed each other's company. In seven days, they would get on for four, wouldn't speak for two and would be openly hostile for one. He had to make amends. He dialled Silks number into his mobile and explained the situation and was awarded a loan for his efforts. Silks knew he'd been nicked, faced up to it, so he would receive his reward. He pulled up at the pub car park and fussed Baskerville before passing him over five twenty pound notes."That will do you, yeah?" Silks asked.

"Yeah mate, I got enough for a week or so, but I got to keep it on a low for a bit. The old bills are on top and I've got shit at home to deal with before I can earn again. They serious with this garden theft bollocks Silks. I didn't know I'd got away with so much."

"Fuck it mate, give it me back when you earning, you got the van. Something will turn up. Look Bruce, I've got to trap, be good yeah and be nice to Nat." Silks nodded toward Walker. He knew there were problems in the camp; he also knew how Walker felt about her.

Walker had calmed down when he arrived home, he smiled apologised and passed her £60. She pushed the notes into her purse ignoring him. Another truce was declared and Nat agreed to buy a new frock for Friday night. He breathed a sigh of relief as he crept into bed, at least he wasn't on the sofa tonight.

CHAPTER 13
BETRAYAL

"Hurry up then Nat the taxis here." She was late, always fucking late.
Walker hid the irritability in his voice. Let's start the night out with a
smile before it turns into *'Platoon'* he reflected wisely.
"Be nice", he whispered as he checked his appearance in the mirror
and used his fingers to add the final touches to his hair. Nat appeared
out of the bedroom. Walker turned and gazed at his wife, his
tetchiness lost. She looked beautiful: good dress, black, halter neck,
showing off her tanned lean arms, chiffon, knee length, black stocking,
black ankle boots, hair sorted, face a picture. She'd spent his money
wisely. He nodded his head in acknowledgement as old feelings
rumbled through his head as he took a trip down memory lane.
"Stunning Nat, you look beautiful." Walker said honestly.
Nat smiled confidently back at him. "Come on then Gary, show me
what all the fuss is about with these nights out and why you can't bear
to stay in on a Friday night."
As they arrived at the pub, it was a cacophony of colour and sound.
Walker struggled to make it to the bar, surfing his way through the
crowd with a, thousand excuse me's and cheers mate as he brushed
past the hordes of drinkers that were blocking his pathway. As he
arrived at the bar he placed one elbow on the counter and waved a
twenty pound note in the air with his free hand. Harry the barman
sauntered over to him. Walker smiled and ordered the drinks, large
vodka, a pint, half for the lady, and one for your-self. He turned around
to view the scene as he waited for Harry to finish pouring their order.
The bar was crowded with the beautiful people, all prepared for a
nights clubbing. Walker didn't enjoy lavish entertainment when he was
straight headed, he'd dropped some speed while Nat was getting
ready and its familiar presence had introduced itself. He started to tap
his feet and feel the buzz. There were Ladies in designer dresses and
lads supporting the latest in Italian fashion, smiling and talking,
comfortable in their environment. Walker turbo'd his vodka, took the
head off his pint and attacked the distance between him and Nat.
Silks was already mooching, a leery grin on his face as Walker handed
Nat her half-a-lager. Nat excused herself to go to the toilet; she had
just spent three fucking hours in one. Walker didn't understand how

her make up or hair could possibly have altered in the ten minute taxi ride there. Silks smiled and waved a little bag in front of Walker face. He nodded and they dropped some powder into Nat's drink. Walker swilled the glass until all the powder had dissolved. It wasn't exactly rohypnol, only half-a-wrap of Billy. It should liven her up and make her smile, induce a dance, maybe stop her from getting pissed out of her face and turning into a fucking werewolf. Walker had been relieved she had started with half and not a large vodka.

"Nat looks cool Bruce, sweet as a pancake."

"A fucking pancake? What the fuck you on?" Walker said laughing.

"Life." Silks answered philosophically.

Walker shook his head and laughed again. "Wrap it up, and sell it my man, you'll make a fortune."

"Already have Brucie boy, already have." Silks patted his pockets." Langley's over there." Silks nodded toward a large, corner booth filled with smiling faces, married with three smaller round tables that were surrounded with people. The tables were filled with glasses and overflowing ashtrays. Smoke hung in the air, creating blue clouds around the heads of the punters who were gathered.

"Wee-man is with the girls come on man, let's go and mingle." Silks said.

"Go on, I'll grab Nat when she has stopped with the make-up and hair malarkey." Walker replied. He had to raise his voice against the bubble of sound that was now surrounding his ears. Silks smiled as he raised his hand and pointed.

Nat eased to Walkers side, and relieved him of her drink. She downed half of it in one swallow. Silks smiled at her. "Another drink Natalie?" She smiled back. "Please Silks, if you don't mind."

"For the wife of Bruce, anything." He quipped back.

Walker showed her over to the table and a sea of manicured faces without a hair out of place looked up and smiled, making a space for Nat to sit down beside them. Nat smiled, sat down and entered seamlessly into the conversation. Walker felt the relief wash over him, he had been tense about Nat coming out. She could have hit the doldrums early and put him on a para for the rest of the night. She appeared relaxed and in an easy going mood. If Nat was a Red Indian they would have called her *Rain-cloud* but tonight maybe she was her alter-ego *Sunny-shine.* It was going better than expected. Walker swallowed the rest of his pint, took another off the table that Silks had placed there and lost himself in the frantic banter of the pub. Nat danced herself dizzily into the firm, laughed and enjoyed her night out on the town.

Later on in the week, when Nat was making a point to sharpen her claws in another ambush on his life style Walker told her, with a some relish she'd taken some powder on her *'mega, mega-night out'* and it hadn't harmed her. In fact it'd added to her night out, no harm done then and better than being pissed. Nat paused and relented her attacks, the realisation that the term pot, kettle and black now applied to her arguments.

Walker's anxiety regarding her previous resistance at living the life wavered at her new found love of going out. He'd shown her the blue horizon and she sailed there with gay abandon. Nat became one of the girls, they would take her out on their weekly night outs and made Walker agree that she would have new clothes and money to mark these occasions. Her moods gradually brightened, the sullen middle-aged woman was replaced by the girl that had turned up in Wolverhampton, to watch the match, drink, laugh and have a good time. Reservations began to mount in his head, and he remembered those dark days of paranoia as the power of rationalistion became a focal point in his head as she headed over to Shrewsbury; armed with an over-night bag every month or so. Sometimes she would take Victoria, sometimes not, explaining that she needed to have her own friends away from Walker and the firm. Walker could see the logic and swallowed his gut instincts, things were better. He wasn't going to rock the boat.

Nat tried a pill once, her anti-drugs policy now fully disposed off. He had dropped her one when they decided to head away from Wolverhampton for a nights clubbing. Walker talked her through it, when he noticed her wide eyes, dilated pupils and the tell-tale beads of sweat that had just started to bristle on her forehead. She looked confused, her mind obviously attempting to come to terms with the new feeling that were exploding in her synapses and the change in perception that drugs offered. Walker held her hand and sat her down, gently whispering what was happening to her body. "It's nothing to be afraid of. Embrace the feeling, breath in and let the chemicals marry with your body, feel the vibe and use the drug, don't let the drug use you. Use the energy, enjoy the buzz." After twenty minutes her mind resolved the conflict and the religious experience began for her, she kissed Walker and laughed as she danced without the inhibitions of the straight headed. In the darkness and intimacy of the club they shared a lost moment in time.

Walker stopped stealing to make a living after his latest court appearance in an effort to appease her and the poverty hit home. There were no jobs available, none that he was qualified to do and the realisation of his predicament hit home hard. The police liked to knock on his door every now and then make sure he was being a good boy and maintaining his new law-abiding outlook. Nat wasn't impressed when the neighbours twitched their curtains as the police made a show of leaving. She was different now and took it all in her stride. She became increasingly confident in herself. Walker noticed a 'power shift 'in their relationship. For the first time in their marriage Walker felt that he needed her more than she needed him.

He now spent all his spare time with Victoria as he retreated to the safety of the home to escape the world that didn't offer him a job and a future. She was the most important thing in his life now and they became inseparable. His days of living in the pub became a dull memory. Walker didn't have the motivation or the money to live the scene anymore. Friday night was still the lads night but he had things on his mind, internal debates, creeping paranoia and anxiety lead to an increase in his drinking. Churlish moods were now in evidence as Walker tried to stop his personal slide in their power struggle. He started to drink more to combat the feeling of weakness and emasculation that coursed through his veins.

One afternoon they drove over to Shrewsbury to visit her brother and his girlfriend to pay their respects to the happy couple on the arrival of their new baby. Walker had agreed to go, stay in to look after the new edition to the family; smiling ruefully as he played the dutiful uncle and waited for the brownie points his efforts were worth. He made a bottle of milk, changed a nappy and settled down in front of the telly. Finally falling asleep with the baby Jeremy cradled in his arms. The banging door and the sound of laughter woke him, he checked the clock it was three in the morning. Jeremy was still sleeping soundly next to him on the sofa, a small smile on his face. The drunken parents fell into the lounge.

Walker yawned and looked up. "You had a good night then? Where's Nat?" Walker hadn't heard her voice; the twilight that separated the senses between being awake and asleep had lifted and he was now fully alert. Frown lines began to scar his forehead.

"She gone on somewhere Gaz, don't worry mate she won't be long," her brothers eyes were red rimmed. He was high, drunk and they dropped to the floor avoiding Walkers stare.

"Gone on where?" Walker asked. The sound of his voice quiet and assertive.

"Back to my mates house with some people, she`s safe Gaz," the assurance was weak. "They wanted to carry on, we came back for Jeremy. He`s been good yeah?""Safe as mate, right then I'm off to bed." Walker stamped on the misgiving that started to rise in his thoughts. There was no real need to create a scene with a sleeping baby in the room and Victoria in bed upstairs. Walker didn't sleep; the clock kept him company as the first beads of the sun's rays penetrated the curtains. At eight in the morning she'd still h
ad not returned. Walker bit his lip and kept his anger in check as he got Victoria ready for the trip home. He could feel the rage bubbling up as his attempts at humour were lost on his daughter. Children are hyper-sensitive alarms for tension, and waves of it were pouring of her dad. She ignored his roughness when he pulled a jumper over her head, she was quiet and deep in thought, this wasn't like her daddy. "I'm sorry Shorts, bit rough today. Ignore me. Jeremy kept me up all night along with the sheep." Walker tired to joke. His smile didn't make it to his eyes as he ruffled her hair.

"Daddy! You've just brushed it don't make it messy please." She glared up at him, her blue eyes defiant." It hurts when you brush it."

"Sorry S." Walker held up his hands in surrender and tried to laugh. The anxiety, doubts and anger melting into one. He looked at his watch it was now nine and still no sign of Nat. She was ripping the fucking piss.

Walker hurriedly packed up the rest of Victoria's toys, clothes and all the assembled paraphernalia. Shoving then roughly into his bag, with a grunt. He found his keys, took his daughters hand and led her out to the car. Victoria shielded her eyes from the glare of the morning sun and asked. "Where's mommy Daddy?"

Walker lied." She's visiting Nana Shorts, we going home to chill out and eat pizza is that ok?"

"Of course daddy, you know I like pizza, watch a film too?"

Walker nodded with a tight lipped grin. "Of course," he packed the car, turned on the radio and headed home.

Natalie finally arrived home at 9pm. She looked tired, but not guilty. He heard the door shut and breathed deeply, trying to sort out his feeling that were on a rollercoaster, into some semblance of order. Walker had been drinking all day, he was pissed, hurt and angry and the voices in his head had raged unabated, the alcohol adding to his paranoia. The power of rationalising events working against him this time, instead of addressing the problem and reducing the anxiety, they merely made it worse.

As he looked at the clock countless times and she still hadn't returned his mood turned darker. He talked to Victoria and went through the motions but his head was elsewhere. It was not with postman Pat and his black and white cat, nor was it with *Simba* and *The Lion King,* it was in Shrewsbury, it was with her.

 Nat tried to play it cool and brushed off his peripheral questions. She knew he was drunk, her own anxiety sharpening at the tell-tale signs of the hiss in his slightly slurred speech. Walker wanted to show no emotion, show no reaction to her obvious attempt to provoke him. He understood the rules of the game, unfortunately he was unable to play nicely for long. The sensible side of his brain was fighting a losing battle against the demons that nested there and were being fuelled by the cider. He asked pertinent questions and she avoided them. His temper broke as she evaded one simple question and he took scissors to her clothes, watching triumphantly as her defiance crumbled.

Walker was angry, very angry. The confusion in his brain acting as a catalyst to emotions he couldn't control. The feeling that he was powerless and lost keeping the fire burning brightly. The shreds of her clothes were flung through the window when she couldn't answer the questions that were barked at her in rapid succession. She was lying, he knew it, her story changed and his gut instinct told him she had been with a man. Bored with the argument, safe in the knowledge she now knew who was boss, he fell into a troubled sleep on the sofa, white noise from the telly to keep him as company through the night. In the morning Nat woke him up, with a shake. Walker was in the twilight zone and blinked twice as his eyes focused on his wife."I want a divorce." She said her tone was matter of fact, as if the last nine years had been swept away by the tide.

"What?" He listened for a moment, the taste of last night's alcohol and cigarettes a fresh reminder of another fuck up in his life. He shook his head, and ignored the headache and rising nausea. "Who are you seeing then?"

"No one, I promise you. I'm fed up Gary, it isn't working anymore with us is it? We want different things from life."

" Fair enough," he thought she was bluffing. He could play the game when he was sober.

She wanted revenge for him making her look like a cunt last night. He nodded back at her as he got dressed ready for the day in the pub, he needed breathing space, room to maneuver.

He didn't want to feel numb; he couldn't understand why he felt so disassociated from events. His wife had asked him for a divorce, like she had asked him to fetch her a drink, a hanky, a paper. He wanted a release, he needed to feel. If she had fallen out of love with him he could accept that. It would be hard, but it was better than the alternative scenario of her leaving him for another man. Nat was married, she had a daughter, she was not free skirt to be pulled on a whim. This was not fun or games; this was his life they were affecting. Walker made a vow that they would be made to pay the price for his pain if she was lying.

His mum made him a hot drink as he drunkenly relayed the story. Walker was slurring, incoherently. His eyes were blood-shot, the stubble on his chin glistened. He looked a mess. She listened to what her son had to say, and offered him a bed for the night. When he was sober, he would be rational. He was talking inane rubbish at the moment. Going off on tangents and spilling his coffee. She raised an eyebrow when he kicked the cup over onto her deep green pile. She didn't say a word. Now was not the time.

The split lasted a week. In that week Walker was hardly ever sober, he went to the pub in the morning, took drugs, any drugs he could get his hands on with his head in pieces. The numbness had been replaced by a pain he never imagined he could have felt. So this was heart break then. He would return home, red eyed and rambling to his mother after he had completed another mission in the pub. His mother could see the change in her son. Silks could see the change in his mate. He was an angry, mean drunk. Sitting at the bar, picking fights with no one in particular. The venom and malevolence clear in his eyes. With no target for his dark mood he became a machine gun, everybody would feel the bullet of pains that Nat had caused him. Walker bombed speed in massive quantities. He wanted the drug to clean his mind of emotions he could not cope with. He could understand speed, it was women who were the problem.

 Silks and his mom, concerned with the rapid downturn in his mood and behaviour got their heads together and tried to fix a plan that would arrest his slide. Walker was deteriorating rapidly, he would be dead, in jail, or in the nut-house very soon. They dropped by the flat and had a word with Nat. She promised she was not having an affair and that it was all in his head. Silks was not sure of the veracity in her answers and could smell a rat. Walker's mom just wanted to see what she wanted to see. Her boy was hurting and she wanted him to be happy.

Nat agreed that she would give it another go and he moved back in but things did not improve. The bond and intimacy they had once had in abundance was lost, gone forever. He found money and booked them a holiday to Malta to try and save the relationship; it was his last throw of the dice. Walker went into the past to find answers for the present and find the spark they once had. He'd always gambled, not on luck but on himself. His mates wished him the best of British at trying to rebuild his marriage. The doubts that it would work clear to be seen on their faces.

 As they boarded the flight he knew he was on a loser, her body language wasn't that of a woman that wanted to be there. She told him after another stand up row she was leaving him for another man. Walkers head imploded. They had another eleven days to go on the holiday, a holiday that he'd booked to save their marriage. Another eleven days stuck in a room with her, three thousand miles from home. Away from his mates, away from his family, he was on his own with no support network.

How fucking cruel was she? Walker blinked through the haze and heart break. Had she picked this moment for optimum effect to wound him, had she made plans with her new boyfriend to break him? He tried to appear normal for Victoria; he would laugh away the tears and tell her that he was having a good time, his true feeling drowned in a pool of alcohol and non belief to his situation. He would take her to the pool and play with her. Through his headphones, *The Doors* would profess *'People Are Strange'* every word hitting his heart. When the evening came round and he was getting ready to go out, he would start to

drink heavily while sitting on the balcony playing cards with Victoria remembering the days from their previous visit to Malta, hoping Victoria's laughter would bring Nat around from the course of madness she had decided to take.
Walker had to drink, the alcohol would make the nightmare go away for a short moment and afford him brief moments of peace. For the for the first time in his life, he considered suicide.

CHAPTER 14
RECKONING.

Walkers mobile came to life and broke his train of thought, breathing deeply he answered. "Hello mate" the small screen on Walkers new mobile had identified Silk`s number, he'd been back in England for twelve hours and he realised that the lads were interested on the outcome of Walkers attempt to save his marriage.

"How did it go over there mate?" Silks asked.

"I'll tell you over a pint." Walker replied.

Walker left the flat without telling Nat, she was busy unpacking and sorting out her holiday clothes. He was off to the pub for some advice, his head had been battered and he was relieved to be home. Walker walked the short distance to the pub and ordered a cider. The third was on the table when Silks and Bamford walked in five minutes later. They looked around the empty pub and spotted Walker. Silks motioned to him and another pint was brought to the table and placed in front of him.

"So?" Silks could tell by Walkers persona and the lack of incoming phone calls that he had been unsuccessful in achieving his ambition.

"She's fucking out on me." Walker was eager to talk, having spent nearly two weeks trying to hold it together, he needed an outlet.

"Told you Walker, sorry mate." Bamford entered the conversation. Josh Bamford was a local legend; he had a violent past selling most things to earn a penny or two. His ability to hurt people was without doubt, so the locals were always edgy around him in case his mood was not conducive to their presence. His reputation defiantly preceded him. He was nicknamed *'the Bear'*; he was as big as a fucking grizzly, as hairy and at the wrong time as capable of ripping off your face off. Silks and Bamford had become friends through some nefarious business going down in Wolverhampton. Walker got to know him well via Silks, but had known of him for years.

They didn't speak as mates; they would nod and have the occasional chat, it was nothing to write home and tell your mom about. The stories that people told of him, suggested a man that would kill you on sight if he heard you had bad mouthed him, owed him money or simply didn't agree with him. He had a thirst for beer and a hunger for drugs. Walker liked him and found he talked common sense. Perhaps the press he'd received was unwarranted?

Walker described the holiday and Nat's revelation that she was apparently seeing another man. How she'd broke the news, how he had dealt with it. They were quiet as he disclosed, not shocked but finding it difficult to accept she had waited until she had seen the sun shine before she'd decided to cause thunder and lightning. They stopped him occasionally to ask a question and to clear up a point when Walkers tale became convoluted. "So, what are you going to do now?" Silks enquired.

Walker rubbed his head and relayed his next plan. Victoria would stay with him that was a cert. Nat was moving out when she had enough money to set up home with her boyfriend.

Bamford and Silks looked at each other. "You alright with her doing that then mate?"

"She is my daughter she stays with me."

"Not that, you divvy, her living with you while she is fucking another geezer?" Bamford shook his head and downed his pint, went to the bar and fetched refills.

Walker didn't know what day off the week it was. His ability to make rational decisions was severely compromised, not focusing on any logical train of thought. A small part of his brain told him that if she stayed, she would stay forever. He hadn't wanted to digest the rest. It was simply easier to get lost in the wilderness of alcohol and drugs until he was strong enough to land back on planet Earth and deal with his problems.

Three months ago he had been married. Two weeks ago his wife was going on holiday with him. Now she was seeing another man, and was about to set sail on her new life without him in it. Give him a break and time for it to sink in for fucks sake, Walker thought. He listened quietly as they spoke, their words resonating with the truth of the situation. The alcohol was not fulfilling its job description as *'harsh reality radar'*. Alien concepts, concepts he didn't want to accept were hitting home in his head. Walker experienced his moment of clarity. He knew what he must do. He sunk his pint, thanked the lads for their time and input, turned and left the pub.

Nat was in the kitchen when he arrived home. Victoria was in front of the television watching a cartoon. He looked at his watch. She needed to go to bed as there was school in the morning. He turned the set off

and kissed his daughter. "Time for bed Shorty." Walker whispered
gently. She looked at him and went without argument, noticing the
strange tone in his voice. Walker followed behind her to make sure she
brushed her teeth. His mind was clear for the first time in months.
Kissing her goodnight he promised to read her a bedtime story
tomorrow night, telling her he loved her before closing the door
behind him. Making sure the night light was left on to keep the
monsters in the dark away.

Walker shut the kitchen door behind him blocking any exit. Nat heard
him enter and looked up from the washing machine. She didn't see the
punch; she felt the thud as his fist connected with the top of her head
and she went down. Walker smiled as he kicked her in the stomach
talking quietly to himself in his own personal monologue. He wasn't
red faced and raging, he was calm and in control of his emotions.

"Who is he?" Walker asked quietly.

"Nobody," she gasped, struggling for breath.

The punch hit her in the stomach, just hard enough to elicit pain. He
didn't want her knocked out, he wanted her awake throughout the
entire experience. Pulling her head back Walker looked into her eyes
and repeated the question. "Who is he?"

"Nobody I'm not seeing anybody else."

"Fucking liar! Not giving it the big un any more are you? You cheating
fucking slut!"His fist crashed into her forehead and Nat went down
again. Her head hitting the wall with a dull thud, her brain scrambled
with the force of the punch. He let her drop to the floor and kicked her
hard in the stomach. She groaned as the wind escaped her body in a
wheeze.

"Who is he? Where does the cunt live?"

"I don't know what you're on about, I only said those things to make
you realise that it was over."

Walker dragged Natalie back to her feet before smashing her head
against the wall. She dropped again. Walker spat down on her as she
lay quivering on the floor. The sputum clear on her face. Her hands
made an attempt to wipe it off. Walker stepped on her stomach to
refocus her attention. Nat gagged, tears in her eyes.

"Crying for the cunt are you? Get the fuck up!"He grabbed her hair and
pulled her onto her feet. All those long nights of seeing them together
in his mind's eye, all the humiliation spewed forth. He had been
powerless in Malta. He would readdress the balance tonight in

Wolverhampton. She'd laughed at him and she'd taunted him, now it was her time to suffer.

"Tell me his name and address and I will let you go it's that simple." Walker waited for an answer.

"No, I don't know what you're on about." The fist and feet connected again. His eyes were cold. He felt no sympathy.

She had deliberately hurt him. She had picked the optimum time to stick the knife in his back. Tried to break him as a man, tried to break his spirit and his heart. Deliberately tried to push him over the edge. It all made sense to him in now. She would break Victoria's heart when she left. She would hurt his girl. His baby.

Bang! His fist hit the target again. He had wanted better for his baby girl.

Bang! She was now a government statistic.

Bang! Some fucking farmer could not keep it in his pants and she was too much of a dog to resist the scarecrow's fumbling.

Bang! His lips were centimeters from her face; spit launching toward her as he hissed. "Tell me his fucking name!"

The phone rang breaking the moment. Walker shook he head to clear his thoughts, to identify another tactic. "Call the wanker, tell him I'm beating you up, make him come and save you! Let's see what the cunts made off!"

Nat wasn't stupid she knew if the man with no name showed in Wolverhampton he would not be going back to Shrewsbury in one piece. He might make it alive, but he would be found in the local supermarket with the other fucking vegetables. The beating and the interrogation continued until Nat began to sob. Walker looked her in the eyes and stepped aside. "Get your fucking clothes, call your fucking mom and get the fuck out of my yard. Do not wake Shorts up, get the fuck out!"

He heard her talking on the phone as he sat down and opened a can of cider, dispassionate to the situation. Walker lit a cigarette watching intently as the smoke curled into the air. "Keep your fucking voice down please, wait outside and DON'T wake Victoria!"

Her case made it downstairs in record time. She followed with a kick up her arse for good measure. Shutting the door behind her Walker sat down and checked the television listing in a glossy magazine. He was sure there was a good film on later. Checking on Shorts, he was thankful to see that she was sound asleep, unaware of the drama that had just unfolded. He kissed her on the forehead, apologised, turned and left the room.

The television set woke Walker. It was early and the sun hadn't yet risen; his eyes throbbed and a brute of hangover was making its way to his forehead. Last night's events filtered into his consciousness and his hands comforted his head. He was single, a single dad. Nat, his wife, partner and friend for nine years had gone. It was over. His stomach hit the dip and he rushed to the toilet to throw up. When he'd finished he glanced at the time. It was seven in the morning, he had to get Victoria up and get her ready for school, coffee first and fix yourself up he thought, you look like a bag of shit.

 Walker made his coffee and wondered about the future. He had no fixed income; Nat had sorted all the finances and bills out. His safety net had been pulled out from under him. He had to grow up and look after his daughter. A list of jobs that had to be taken care of came into view. He would contact the benefits agency and discuss his options. Call the council regarding rent and getting the tenancy changed over. He pictured Nat and reminisced about their past. Baskerville licked his hand and he came back to the here and now shaking his head to rid himself of the memories. The dog had to be taken out for a shit. Where was Nat when you needed her? In bed with some other man, having breakfast! Pull yourself together he told himself. You have only got to get your daughter ready and walk the fucking dog. Make a few calls. Get a grip. You have to be strong for Shorts now. You are responsible. He quickly let Baskerville out into the community garden and crossed his fingers she didn't shit or he would have to clean it up. The thought induced another gagging reflex.

He shook her shoulders gently. "Shorts, Shorts." She moaned and turned over. "SHORTS SHORTS!" She was back with him in the land of the living. "Your clothes are out ready; get your teeth brushed and I'll do your breakfast." She yawned by way of reply. "Shorts I mean it …….bathroom now…….. get it sorted NOW!"

"OK OK," she looked up at him quizzically. "Where's mommy, she usually gets me ready?"

"Working, I'll sort it today, now come on move it."

Victoria left the warmth and comfort of her bed and staggered toward the bathroom.

Walker checked the clock again, there was still plenty of time; she only had to put on six items of clothing, how long could it take? He poured her some orange juice, fixed a bowl of cereal and buttered two pieces of toast and placed it on a tray before making the journey back into the west wing.

Victoria had managed to attend to her underwear. One item in ten minutes, she looked half baked and ready to go back to sleep. Walker blew out his cheeks and tried to make a point. "Get ready Victoria, NOW!" She yawned again and moved like a snail, testing his patience. "If you carry on like this yam getting up at six every morning and see how you like that," he told her, as she continued to move like a sloth. Walker looked around the room for her hairbrush.

"Where's your brush Shorts?"She looked back with a blank expression. She was dim in the morning; there was no doubt about it in Walkers opinion."Hairbrush?" He repeated, rolling his eyes, how hard could this be? He looked down at his watch he had five minutes to achieve his mission feeling like James Bond as he saved the world. Rushing to the kitchen he picked up a fork, before making his way back to her bedroom. She had managed to put on the other four items and was standing up ready for inspection when he returned.

"Have you brushed your teeth?"

"Yes."

"Washed?

"Yes."

Walker brushed her hair with the fork; it was a genius moment of improvisation. He pushed her out the room and grabbed her school bag. The breakfast left uneaten on the floor. They closed the door and hit the street. "Where's my packed lunch Daddy?"

"What? You have a packed lunch? I thought you had hot dinners?"

"I prefer a packed lunch now."

"You're having a hot dinner today."

Bloody hell this was a complicated process, Walker thought. He was full of praise for the mothers that had to do this on a daily basis. Thrusting his hands into his pocket he located a single five pound note, all he had left in the world. "Here." He handed it over to her. "Get your dinner and some tuck." He would worry about money, lunches and all that bollocks later.

They made the short trip to school in time, he waved goodbye to her as she made her way onto the play ground to find her friends. His mood turning south as he thought about ways to break the news that Mommy and Daddy didn't live with each other anymore. He stuck his head in his dad's house on the way home. His old man lived close to the school. "Hello dad, you alright mate?"

"Morning Gary, to what do I owe the privilege?"

"Nat's gone mate, I kicked her out last night. Just thought you needed to know, call mom please and tell her to come round tonight and I'll explain the situation."

"OK, you alright Gary?" His dad asked.

Walker shrugged his shoulders, turned and left to start single life.

The phone rang, and Walker pulled himself off the sofa, he had just got in from walking Baskerville, fighting back the tears as they walked around the field, coming to terms with his new situation. The initial shock had shielded him briefly from the trauma, slowly sadness punctuated his thoughts. "Hello." His tone was flat, the call was sure to bring added stress.

"Gary, it's your dad, Nat and her mum has been down, they are on their way round to you. Her mother's on the war path so be warned." His dad was always succinct and to the point.

"Thanks dad, I'll sort it out." Walker sighed, knowing the visit was expected. He wanted to procrastinate and pretend the outside world was warm and welcoming just for a brief moment longer. Looking out of the window, Walker saw a car pulling in across the road. The door opened and Natalie and her mom got out. Nat appearing stiff as she walked across the road toward the communal entrance to the block. His hands rubbed his face again; he really didn't need an autopsy into last night. It was a bad memory and he wanted it to go away.

The door slammed shut as they entered the flat without knocking. Walker was sitting in his chair attempting to look nonchalant. He looked up as they walked into the front room and turned to greet his visitors. "You don't live here anymore," he pointed at her. "I would appreciate it if you would knock in future."

 His attention was focused fully upon Natalie; he didn't acknowledge the mother- in-laws presence. She avoided his stare, looking down at the floor as she walked straight into the bedroom to fetch the rest of her clothes. Her mom circled. Come on then thought Walker. I'm fucking ready for you.

"Hung-over are you? Proud of yourself?" She started the verbal assault.

"Not really, and if your daughter is big enough to have an affair and leave her daughter, then she is big enough to accept the fucking consequences. Do you understand what I'm saying to you?" His words found their target. Walker was bubbling up again. He got up off his chair and moved toward her with his finger aimed at her head. He didn't need a lecture off her mother, when he was picking up the pieces of his life.

"Think you're big don't you with all your mates and your beer and drugs?"

"You pathetic cunt, you know fuck all about what's gone on! The only time we ever saw you was when you were hungry and wanted a hot meal. The last time you took Victoria out the fucking mini skirt was in fashion!" He laughed to himself. "I'm not fucking interested in what you got to say, she is having an affair, just like her dog of a fucking mother!"

"No she's not," her former bravado dissipated as she backed off. Walker laughed and waved his hands in the air, dismissing her. "Family of fuckwit liars, just get out and fucking leave me and MY daughter alone." The woman had made no mention about Victoria. "If I'm such a cunt why would Nat leave Victoria with me? I'm a drunk and a drug addict aren't I? But you're going to leave her with me? With logic like that it's a good job you never sat on a jury you fucking knob!" Walker waited for a reply but obviously she didn't want to ruin the argument with logic.

 Nat came back in the room and told them to stop it. Her mum picked up her daughters case and left. Nat walked to the door, turned and looked at Walker, he saw the girl from Scarborough all those years ago as the tears welled up in his eyes.

"All I wanted you to do was get a job Gary, a proper job, I'm sorry." With the final statement of their marriage, she turned and left, closing the door behind her. He knew that he 'd neglected the thing he valued most. As the door shut, so did a part of Walkers soul, he would never be the same man again.

CHAPTER 15
SINGLE

Walker was left feeling exhausted by the morning events. He couldn't fathom out his life, and had the distinct impression he was sinking in quick sand. As he closed his eyes and tried to find some peace on the sofa he heard the front door bang. Walker's mum arrived at the flat, fussing and bristling. Looking more like Peggy Mitchell than ever, her brow furrowed, her eyes ablaze with mock anger and her venom aimed at Nat. She viewed the wreckage of his existence; shooting questions at him in quick succession: How are you going to manage? How are you going to look after a girl? What are you going to do for money? Are you getting a divorce? Walker sat back down on the sofa, blew air of his cheeks, a breeze of discontent and let the questions wash over him hoping she would burn out sometime soon. He wanted to shake her and shout back. Shut the fuck up mum! My wife had just left me to move in with another man! My heads in bits trying to come to terms with it all! I'm now a single parent! I will fucking cope! I haven't got all the answers! Please ask me one on fucking sport! After ten minutes of listening to her go on unabated, he stood up and raised his hand to hush her. "Mum be quiet and sit down will you please. I will make it work because I have to and make sure you don't say a word about this to Shorts please. I mean it Mum, not a word!" He aimed his finger at her chest to reinforce the point he was making. "You understand, yes?" She nodded her assent. Walker knew she would be over sympathetic and try to hide the reality of life from Victoria, thinking that she would actually be doing her a favour. Walker knew to his cost that method didn't work. He had lived that unique dream.

Walker wanted his daughter to be strong and ready for the trials and tribulations that life would serve up to her on a plate. He was her dad and he would raise her his way. Victoria would be shown love, but she would also be shown the ropes and taught to beat the struggles that life tossed up regularly. She would not be cushioned, he would teach her the premise of respect, and life would be a lesson she'd be adept at taking.

His mum finally left him alone, her curiosity satisfied, leaving him with £200 after a quick jaunt to the cash point and a cheque for two months rent. Walker thanked her, it was a nice gesture and he politely refused a lift to his dad's house, preferring to take Baskerville for a run out over the park. He needed to clear his head and think after the latest inquisition into his life.

He arrived at his Dads and found Victoria in the back garden with her Granddad planting flowers. Walker had to admit he made a far better grandparent then he had a father. He always made time for Victoria; he was patient and kind making sure she wasn't spoiled, respecting his son's philosophy on parenting. Walker liked the bond they'd discovered. His dad looked up from the flower bed as Baskerville made her usual grand entrance, all paws and slobber. Victoria started laughing as her granddad fought off the licks and paws coming his way. Walker laughed too , relived that pain was not the only emotion he could feel and admitted that Baskerville did have some funky moves. Walker said hello to his dad and his eyes shouted out that he didn't need another interrogation before he strolled over to Victoria and took her hand in his. "Do you want some chips for tea Shorts?"

Always partial to a fried potato, she nodded her head and answered. "Yes please."

Turning to his father he asked. "You want anything fetching Dad?"

His dad shook his head and watched silently as they headed off, hand in hand toward the chip shop with their shadows lengthening behind them; Baskerville in tow jumping up and down excitedly, to spend their first night as a single parent family.

Silks arrived just as they'd opened their chips, typical Walker thought. That bloke could smell free food from ten miles away. Victoria happily let her Uncle Silks steal the odd chip when Walker wasn't looking, they both laughed as they pulled the wool over her dads eyes, happy with their game. Walker watched from a distance, before he entered the room. He would need support from all his friends and family to pull this off. Silks looked up as his mate sat down, Walker fumbled in his pockets, he needed a drink.

"Stop nicking her tea man, and go to the shop mate, get some beers eh, do something useful." Walker passed him over a twenty pound note. "Get some sandwich stuff too please."

Silks accepted the cash."Sandwich stuff?" He looked blankly back at Walker as he munched on a chip. "What's ya old man mean, sandwich stuff eh Vic?" Victoria laughed at Silks expression of mock stupidity. Walker sighed, Silks didn't do shopping. He turned to Victoria. "Go and get changed out of your school stuff when you've eaten enough, we're off to the shops, to fetch some supplies."

While she was out the room getting changed, Silks asked."What's gone on mate?"

Walker nodded toward Victoria's room."Details later. I listened to what you and Bamford said and took steps."

Victoria came back into the front room dressed in her jeans and trainers, marvelous Walker thought, it took her less than two minutes to take off the uniform, how come it took her half an hour to put it on! She held both of their hands as they left the flat, laughing as she was swung high into the air. As they sat in the car she looked across at Walker. "Where's mommy daddy? I thought she was at work, she still hasn't come home."

Walker paused."Visiting her mom Shorty my girl, you want a yogurt for tomorrow's lunch?" Walker didn't want another 'episode' he had experienced more than enough bollocks in the last twenty four hours to last him a life-time. He would tell her the truth soon enough. They waited for her to settle down in bed before they explored the situation further.

"Where is she then?" Silks asked. His stare fixed on Walker.

"Fuck knows!" Walker met his eyes. "I don't care Silks, probably with her cunt of a boyfriend!" Walker described the events of the previous night, the beating and her leaving.

Silks was unmoved, the girl had deserved it. She had played away, got caught, been convicted and punished. Such was life. "What's going on with Shorts then?"

Walker went through the same story; that he would raise her, she was his, no other man would bring her up.

"Fair play to you mate." Silks nodded, he was happy with Walker's attitude. He was impressed that his mate was going to stand up and do the right thing. Silks, always one to find the silver lining told Walker, he could use the situation to his advantage."Think of all the pussy you will able to pull mate. The girls will love the fact you're a single Dad, they will want to mother you and all that."

They agreed to meet up in a couple of days and *'sort things'*. A man in Shrewsbury needed to watch his back. Silks downed his beer and left. Walker sat Victoria down on the sofa after he had collected her from school the following day and told her he needed to explain something. She settled herself as if she was listening to a story her teachers read on an afternoon. A look of intense concentration on her face. Walker wanted to be sensitive; he wanted to explain what had gone on without hurting her. He chose his words carefully. "Daddy and Mommy both love you very much; unfortunately your mommy doesn't love me anymore so she has gone to live somewhere else. She still loves you very much and she will see you whenever she can. You're going to live here with me because it's close to your school, your mates and nanny and granddad."

He waited for the inevitable questions. Victoria blinked a couple of times, digesting the information before weighing up her reply. "It's for the best daddy, I didn't like it when I heard you and mommy shout at each other, I wanted you to laugh, and you didn't."

Walker felt proud of her, she called him silly as he wiped his eyes. "Yeah, I know. I've always been a bit tapped eh Shorty?" He pulled a face and pointed his finger at his head and she burst out laughing. "You want to stay up and watch a film with your old man?" Victoria nodded and they settled down on the sofa to watch the evening's entertainment on BBC. Life must go on.

Life did go on, Walker got into the swing of the morning routine and always had Victoria at school before the bell, he would blow her kisses and wave goodbye to her as she trotted off onto the playground to find her friends. The other mothers would try to mask their curiosity but he knew he was the centre of local gossip. His social life, though compromised, continued. After he dropped Victoria off, Silks would come and pick him up and they and Bamford would go about their daily business. This didn't involve crime for Walker anymore. That was too risky with his domestic situation. He could always get a top up of his resources via the benefits agency, Silks gave him a tutorial on how to play the system and Walker exploited the loopholes. There were such things as *'community care grants'*, *'the social fund'* and other top up benefits. Walker successfully applied for income support and was awarded £80 per week, added to his child benefit that topped it off to a £100 a week net. It was a steady income and a safety net for him and Victoria was now in place. He supplemented his income by stocking his dads business with video and audio cassettes that he came across in his day to day travels.

Silks was suffering from post traumatic stress syndrome (apparently) from his forced incarceration at the hands of the justice system and did very nicely financially. The psychiatrist that he visited was happy to confirm this *'disability'* after Silks tried to throttle him. He didn't like to be analysed and reacted violently to the perceived invasion. He just wanted the documentation to provide evidence for benefit reasons to get his rent and council tax paid.

Bamford liked to gamble and could get most things he wanted from most people. It was an easier option to keep him sweet, so he got away with murder. They were decent men with a code of conduct; it just involved drinking and taking drugs.

Walker's mom and dad had provided much appreciated support for him. His dads bond with Victoria continued to grow and she would love to spend hours with her Granddad in his garden helping him to plant and weed. His mom would take her out shopping over the weekend to buy her clothes and take her for *'lunch'* as girls do when out in town. Victoria could twist his mom round her little finger and had mastered Walkers art of manipulation.

Walker kept her grounded and made sure she wasn't spoiled by his mother. Silks and Bamford would make a fuss of her when they all arrived to pick her up from school and one day a week and they would all sit down for a meal at a local carvary. The other children from the firm would now show and it became a social occasion. Victoria's life had improved in Walkers opinion, he knew that she missed her mom but he made sure she was too busy to dwell on it. Walker made sure her school work was given priority and reinforced the credence of a good education. Victoria was starting to get rave reviews from her teachers, and her first school report contained 13 A's and one B. Walker framed it and cried with pride, careful to do it in the privacy of his front room when he was alone. He could just imagine Silks face if he caught his mate teary eyed over nothing.

Nat didn't see her regularly, too busy with the invisible man to make regular trips to Wolverhampton, using the excuse that she was scared to bring her new boyfriend down in case Walker and the firm would turn him into diced cabbage. When he told her she could always use a train, come alone and that maybe, she could talk to her daughter and be a parent. Explain the situation before she introduced her to the *'step dad'*, she merely glared and stonewalled the advice.

Enquires had been made in that direction, his knee caps could go when the time was right and make a wheel chair his permanent residence. Silks knew some bad news boys from Birmingham who would be happy to finish his athletics career for a few quid. The hit was arranged, he only had to put his head above the trench for a moment and say *'boo'*. On her few visits down when she did pick Victoria up, he would watch them walk down the road out his window and his heart would go with them. He missed Nat terribly. He fought these feeling every day, he felt alone, he felt despair and he felt desolate. The emptiness of the flat when he was alone was filled with the sound of cans opening, feelings would come to the surface and he would reflect on the mistakes he had made, the tears rolling down his face. He would sit in front of a silent television and play Gary Numan records, the alcohol talking to him. Numan would sing to him, songs full of lyrics that summed up his situation perfectly. *"We were so sure, we were so wrong, now it's over and there's no one left to see and there no one left to cry. Now there's only ME"*.

The words would hit home and Walker would cry some more and reach for another beer becoming frustrated with his weakness and then angry at himself. He had started on rare occasions to cut his arms with a knife in an attempt to regain control of the pain. He had reached for the pill bottle once but he always saw Victoria's face and brought himself round, telling himself: he was alive, he had Victoria and things would get better. Walker made the right noises in his head and waited patiently for the pain to go away. He talked to Natalie on the phone to sort out the divorce, enjoying the sound of her voice and trying to sound reasonable and behave like an adult. He knew he was grasping at straws, but he wanted her to see through the looking glass and realise that she should come home. She never did. He was too proud to tell her how he felt, scared of further rejection and humiliation.

Silks couldn't handle Walker's self pity when he got drunk and started to reminisce about the past. Walker was having a *'moment'* on a Saturday afternoon in the pub and he asked the table. "What's he got that I haven't?"

"Nat." Silks replied simply. He wanted his mate back, not the self pitying moron Walker became when he was pissed. It hurt him to see his best friend going through the mill and Silks didn't like to be hurt. Walker had to be a man and men deal with their emotions accordingly. After a night out to cheer Walker up, Silks was driving him home. Walker was talking about Nat and had started to cry. Silks stopped the car and told him to get out, to get a grip, worried about his mate`s head. Silks knew he needed tough love to break him out of his self destructive cycle. Walker carved a trail of destruction on his way back to the flat as his frustrations boiling over. Cars and shops were vandalised, he needed an outlet, any medium to show his hurt, he couldn't find a person who was about at that late hour to share his pain. His moods were polarising, but through it all he kept it together for Victoria. She hardly noticed a thing.

 Walkers use of amphetamines increased to five days a week. When he drank he would feel sad and depressed, his melancholy barely disguised. With speed he would talk more; it could lift his mood when the alcohol would drop him to the point of no return. He had energy on speed and motivation to play with Victoria and at times he appeared animated, even happy. She didn't like it when he drank and became miserable.

Bamford would stay over at Walkers flat occasionally, when they were 'whizzing'. He surprised Walker, Bamford would empathise about how he felt; he would talk and explore Walkers feeling. Walker would watch the wedding video over and over again, sitting in front of the television and remembering the day. Bamford made him smash it up. It was not healthy and Bamford knew it. The routine and obsession had to be broken. Walker would get through this crisis with his mate`s help. Walker tried to keep Nat's relationship with Victoria on a level. Walker would borrow his mom's car to drop Victoria off in Shrewsbury if Nat played her face about train fares. Walker would look into his daughter's eyes and see the disappointment and he would try to make her pain go away.

 Natalie gave him a location, where to meet her, scared that if her ex-husband found out where she lived her new man would feel the ramifications of his actions. One night Walker and Bamford had driven to Shrewsbury, so Josh could see his estranged girlfriend. Bamford would later tell Walker that he had seen Nat and her new boyfriend in a pub they visited when he'd gone to the toilet. Nat had begged

Bamford to get Walker out the pub before he saw them together.
Bamford did.

He didn't want Walker to go to jail and lose Victoria because of a pub
fight and hand Natalie a sense of satisfaction. Walker would have hurt
him; his head was not in a good place at the time. They could get the
bloke when they were ready, when they all had alibis; he knew they
had time on their side.

His parents took Victoria to Orlando in Florida for a holiday; Walker
agreed it was a good idea. Victoria was going to America to the land of
the free, away to Disney Land to explore the magic kingdom and have
a childhood. Walker and Bamford went on a mission while she was
away. It was a ten day bender with no food and less sleep. They would
have a parcel ready for the morning, one for lunch and another for tea
time. The pubs knew they were in business. During one session,
Walker decided to shave his head completely bald. When he was out
and about in the local pubs he got a few looks from people that knew
him. Silks inspected it and declared he looked like a thug and that was
the general consensus of opinion. Walker looked in the mirror and an
extra from 'romper stomper' stared back. He looked mad and it wasn't
far from the truth.

On the tenth day he found himself in a club in Wolverhampton. While
the strobe lightening and beat was pulsing Langley danced round, high
as high, singing to Walker. "I can't get no sleep." Walker knew it was
time to stop and go home to rest.

Langley was correct. Walker hadn't been to bed since Nat had moved
out. He couldn't sleep in the dark with no sound to distract him from
his thoughts. He would focus on Nat and visions would haunt him long
into the night. He slept on the sofa, concentrating on the television to
block out these intrusive thoughts. Sometimes in his dreams, the world
would be normal and Nat would be in soon with a cup of tea to wake
him. When reality broke through the clouds, despondency would
follow soon after.

CHAPTER 16
JUNKIE

The pub was tired and empty. There was never any sport to be had in Wolverhampton on a Wednesday evening. Victoria was enjoying a home cooked meal and a night of video entertainment at his mums, with the promise she would drop her off at school the next morning. Walker had seized the opportunity to trip the light fantastic. Bamford had made a call and an eighth of Charles and a gram of speed was working its way toward them.

Walker sipped at his pint; the effects of the drugs were wearing off, he swallowed the growing anxiety as he looked at his watch. Drug dealers were akin to taxi drivers; they simply lied when they said they were only ,*'ten minutes away'*. Bamford looked into the flashing lights of the gambler and hit a button, the machine exploded and twenty pounds dropped into the tray. "Keep us going for an hour." He laughed.

"Yes Josh, nice one buddy. Has G-Spot been in touch yet?"

"Over there Walker." Bamfords eyes pointed to the doorway where a tall black man was hovering by the entrance, Prada cap pulled down over his face, wearing a baggy black Adiddas track suit, Nike air Jordan's and a gold watch. He could not have looked any more conspicuous than if he'd arrived with a placard that proclaimed: DRUG DEALER. His eyes swept the pub ,checking out the dribs and drabs who were dotted around the sparse tables. He spotted the pair standing at the gambler, raised his hand in a lazy greeting and meandered over to them. "Alright boys, on another mission are you then? You pair never know when to stop." He laughed as he felt in his pockets.

" You on fucking Jamaican time Dalton? And what the fuck have you come as? You're trying to be undercover? You look like a fucking pimp mate." Bamford had an amused grin on his face. He pushed the collect button and some more cash popped into the tray.

Walker looked on, he wanted a beer and a hit. Dalton kissed his teeth. "You're always on my case you know Bam, you need to quit you know man. Might forget I'm a fucking gent. You white boys calling me up and expect me to shoot right over. The days of slavery gone y'know Ay you seen *'Roots'*?" Dalton and Bamford had been mates for time, this was foreplay."You got me dollar for the ting?" Dalton turned Jamaican. He had been born in Wolverhampton, twenty five years ago. His accent was pure patois with a Black Country slant.

"Fucking Yardie now am you? We got a £150." Bamford was examining the nudge reel. He had six, but needed ten for another jackpot. He tutted and slapped the side of the machine as the reels spun, and the sign,*' lose'* flashed up.

"It's a £180 Bam, you know the price." He returned to talking English. "Just hand it over. Wim you're best customers and we always pay. You know yam going to anyway. So stop being a girl and give it us."

Bamfords eyes made the slow journey from the gambler to Daltons face. He stared at him for a second, his mouth set firm.

"You want a beer Dalton?" Walker interjected before Bamford brought the eyes of what few patrons there were drinking there straight onto them. He didn't want a protracted negotiation, he liked Dalton but wanted him gone. He wanted peace to chop a line and get mashed.

 The big black man turned to Walker. "Coke please Walk."

"Are you taking the piss Dalt or what mate?" Walker said.

They all started to laugh as they saw the irony in the request, the tension broken. Still laughing Walker sauntered over to the bar and ordered the round. Three girls were standing there, chatting excitedly. The leader turned round and her eyes fell upon Walker who smiled back at the pretty blond, with the shinning hair cut in a longish bob, tight jeans and knee length black leather boots with a heel to die for. She was wearing a little too much blusher that might be disguising less than perfect skin, but the rest of her makeup was subtle and didn't make her look like a doll. Her white t-shirt had glittery gold letters emblazoned upon it proclaiming: Junkie. Walker smiled inside, did she know the score? Was he transparent? How many drugs did she do?

"Hello Alison, how the hell are you?"

"Gary, It's been a long time mate. I've heard on the grapevine that you had some bad news. How are you getting on mate?"

"Coping."Walker shrugged his shoulders in a blasé gesture. "You have to, don't you really?"

 Alison nodded back and smiled. "Fair play, at least you ain't whining like a pussy. Who's with you? Or do drink alone now in these troubled times?" A slight smile played across her lips. If only she knew the truth. The endless nights when he had a can for company, his phone turned off as the self-pity became his friend for the night.

"Bamford." Walker jerked his thumb in the direction of the gambler. He scratched his forehead and sipped at his pint.

"Josh, I ain't seen him in ages, is he still mad?" She said.

Walker hadn't done a Psych evaluation on his mate and ignored the question. "Join us for a drink, say hello. Bring your mates." Walker sensed an opportunity to liven up the proceeding.

"Ok then. Why not." She turned to her mates, who hadn't stopped talking long enough to notice Walker as they continued their hushed conversation, with whispers that were punctuated with dramatic gasps and laughter. Their conversation must be have been about sex or make up. It appeared they liked both, judging by the blood red lip-stick that scared their faces, and their t-shirts that donated the facts they were 'whores and tramps.' Empowerment for the modern generation of assertive women.

They stopped gassing long enough to look at Walker and nod their heads, their eyes running him up and down, innocent shy smiles on their painted faces that were best saved for mug punters. Walker smiled back as he introduced himself with a smile and an outstretched hand. The night had taken an unexpected turn for the better.

Alison and Walker started to see each other. She was the first girl in a long time that put a real smile on his face. She was attractive, dressed well and held down a good job. On some intimate moments they connected and discussed his current behaviour. After another round of dissecting his lifestyle Alison simply told him, he looked like a junkie with dark eyes and ill fitting clothes. He had lost five stones in five months. Walker would explain it wasn't that long ago he was fat and could do with losing a few pounds. She knew the ropes and did the party rounds on a weekend and knew his drug use went deeper than a social outlet, she told him she was worried about him. Alison would make trips to his flat with bags of fish and chips and nutrient drinks in an effort to improve his health.

This girl liked him, when he was lucid she understood him and where he was coming from and his old charm would shine through. Nat had taunted him over his weight. So he'd lost it all in another futile attempt to gain respect from a woman that clearly didn't know he existed anymore. Once he was round hers and she made the mistake of telling him she had some speed in the house and Walker started craving. She gave him the choice; her or the speed. No contest, the speed won. No woman was going to tell him shit again. They would all pay for Nat's sins. He was on a mission.

The day started as every other. He got Victoria to school well on time and popped around his dads with Baskerville for a cup of coffee and to see if he needed any tapes or other electronic gadgetry for his business. As he arrived home he called Silks to see what was on the agenda for the day. Silks told him he had to go over to Stourbridge to pick up a part for his new sports car. An orange red MGB GT, a classic car. Walker wondered if he was going to don, driver's gloves, a scarf and call himself, 'Biggles', he would eluogise at some length about the overdrive gear. He'd look like fucking,' Alan Partridge,' in his Sunday drivers outfit .Walker smothered the laughter as he listened to Silks telling him he would be over to pick him up in ten minutes.

Walker sat down and sipped at his coffee, checked tele-text for the latest sports and current affairs news and wondered why Silks just didn't pick up the fucking phone and ask if they had the part and save his petrol. Silks would cuss him out for being lazy and just wanting to go in the pub, trying to motivate Walker to follow a different direction. Silks knew that the split had hit him hard and Walker was using drugs heavily to cope. Silks was no junkie, substance abuse was for the weak minded. Drugs should be used to enhance the dance mission on the weekend not to strangle emotions in the week. Walker had been granted a pass for his recent behaviour, but it was time for him to start living again. He knew that you could only function for a limited amount of time if you were depended on drugs and Walkers time was up.

They enjoyed their normal banter as they drove around the West Midlands. Walker was broke; Silks and Bamford were holding so he played it right and tight, he wanted a beer and a wrap. Silks may have thought his time was up; Walker didn't want to feel too much emotion right about now, his party still had time to run on in his head. They finished their tour of duty and headed for Bamfords house. They had one more chore to do, they went to the bookies to put on his bet and then to the pub. Walker checked his watch. It was already one. He had to be back to collect Victoria from school soon, knowing he would have to bomb some beer to get on a level.

Bamford made a call to score some gear and they were waiting for the man with the goods to arrive. Silks was pissed off and giving them a lecture about using speed in the week. Bamford didn't give a fuck when he took gear. Walker kept out the argument. Silks turned to

Walker. "Come on I've got some business to attend to, if you want a lift we got to chip now."

Walker needed the lift to get him home and was placed in a quandary; his speed hadn't been delivered yet. Bamford told him to stay in the pub and he would sort him out a taxi. Silks looked at Walker and shook his head sadly as he left the pub. The man with drugs was late the taxi on time. When the deal was finally concluded he had five minutes to make it to the school. Plenty of time, he reassured himself, Victoria was always last out anyway. He bombed some gear and started to feel the confidence running through his veins, sure that the plan would come together. He looked impatiently through the taxi window at the stragglers as were making their way slowly home. Harassed looking mums, kids dragging their bags on the floor, shirts out their trousers, they looked like a retreating army. He was ten minutes late when he finally arrived at the school.

The playground was quiet with no sign of life, let alone Victoria. He felt some misgiving when he walked over to the reception but he knew that Victoria was a sensible girl, she knew her Dad would arrive and would simply wait at reception for him. When he arrived at reception the chairs were empty and there was still no sign of her. Feeling guilty and trying to mask the tight jaw and the grinding teeth, a sure sign of an amphetamine use he hoped the middle aged lady in the patterned cheap shirt didn't notice the signs he was as high as kite.

He asked the receptionist to check for her and it was confirmed that Victoria was not on school grounds. The seeds of doubt started to sprout in his mind. She must be at my dads, he thought. His dad's house was less than a hundred yards from the school gate. She would have gone there. Walker required a lid to cap the mounting panic. Sprinting the short distance, he was positive he would see her with her trowel in hand sitting in the back garden weeding with his dad as normal, a smile radiating across her face. His dad's car was not in the garage when he arrived, the back door to the house was locked. Blind panic hit Walker, like a shovel straight in the face. Where the fuck was she? The thought that she had been kidnapped hit home and his world collapsed around him.

He ran to the police station and informed them of the situation; the officer on the desk took down a brief statement, trying to calm Walker. Walkers flushed face and rapid speech could be attributed to the panic not speed. "Take a seat Sir, I'll put a description over the radio on a

general alert, she will be round her mates, over the park. Think of her
friends names and we will contact them for you."
Walker nodded and tried to focus his mind, which was racing, leaping
over fences and hurtling into the distance as if it was a horse that had
thrown off its rider and was enjoying the feelings of freedom. The duty
sergeant advised Walker to go home and wait; they would keep him
informed of any further developments. When he arrived back at the
flat, he phoned Bamford and Silks panting as he tried to explain the
situation to them. The cavalry duly arrived at the flat twenty minutes
later.
 They listened to Walker, frowned, told him to shut up, before they put
photos of Victoria in their pockets. A smiling picture which had
recently been taken at school. Walker had ragged her out of bed early
to make sure she looked the part. She looked beautiful in the picture,
her face full of joyful innocence. Silks looked back at Walker. "Be calm
mate, we will find her." They turned and hit the streets to help in the
search.
Walker, as the police instructed remained at home in case any further
information was required or she returned. He sat on the sofa, walked
round the flat, looked in the mirror, looked at the phone, checked his
messages, talked to Baskerville, who licked his hand oblivious to the
drama erupting around him. The gear was pumping through his veins,
surging like a torrent. He listened to the silence echoing around him.
This could not be happening, she was there this morning, he clasped
that picture in his mind. What had he done! What had he and Nat
done to this girl! He hated himself more than ever. He was a fucking
disgrace! He was a fucking junkie! He deserved to die! The police
knocked on his door breaking his internal diatribe. It was plainclothes
officers and they needed a statement from him. Walker blew air out
of his cheeks that had been swollen like a balloon, and tried to fill them
in on the sequence of events. In his alternative reality he had been up
town, shopping. They looked gravely around the flat, their eyes resting
on a can of strongbow left over from the night before.
Quietly they reassured him and told to stay where he was in the event
she returned. There was no warmth in their tone their persona was:
cold, polite, business like and cordial; assuring him that in nearly all
cases the child came home in under two hours when they were
hungry. Walker checked his watch; they were at ninety minutes now.
The clock was ticking.

Langley arrived at the flat after Silks had called him, he didn't know
what to do. He was more panicked than Walker. He sat down with a
long sigh and muttered to Walker comforting him and checking the flat
for things the police didn't need to see. His mom arrived; adding to the
fog of Walkers mind. The police arrived back, and avoided Mrs. Walker,
who was just adding to the general feeling of chaos. They'd arrived at
her house to ascertain if Victoria had made her way there, she hadn't.
The room was filling up with concerned relatives, friends and police
officers. Walker was sitting on the floor in the corner by the television,
huddled and rocking, his head in his hands, trying to make sense of the
situation and praying he was in a bad dream, praying for salvation to a
God that was deaf. Bamford and Silks returned back at his flat shaking
their head sadly, explaining there had been no sign of her. Nat and her
mom arrived to add a silver topping to the cake he had created. Nat
had a look about her, caged tiger, spitting cobra. A wild animal that
need a release, her mascara made her eyes look like they peering out
of a dark alley. She took a minute to take stock of the situation before
her eyes fixed on Walkers shape in the corner. Without hesitation she
walked straight up to Walker and started to attack him. Walker let the
kicks and punches hammer down on him, the blows did nothing to
unblock the shit that was revolving in his head. He deserved his
chastisement, he thought that maybe God wasn't deaf and that Nat
was the Angel of Death send to drag him away. He was deserving of
the kicking he was getting, he was a loser, a prick, he'd lost their
daughter!
 Silks pulled her off his mate and held her tightly in his arms. She
stopped struggling, his arms were locked around her. Silks had muscles
on top of muscles. He relaxed his grip and whispered gently in her ears.
"It will be alright," over and over until she believed him.
The police advised Nat to come down to the station and wait there in
attempt to diffuse the tense situation that was now evident in the
room. Natalie was not popular with Walkers mates and they were
taking offence at the treatment handed out to him. They formed
together, natural instinct turning them into a pack. She verbally abused
him again for good measure on the way out of her former home before
being ushered out the flat by two burley uniformed officers, three
minutes later she would have probably needed police protection. The
police asked Walker if Victoria kept a diary and if so they could see it?
They asked him more seemingly inappropriate and absurd questions.

He looked up at them and shouted. "Am I a fucking suspect?" His anger boiling over.

Langley patted his shoulders in an attempt to calm him down, trying to prevent the situation deteriorating even further. Even his cool persona shattered when they asked to look in the freezer and the shed. "Do you think that we're nonces! Fucking child killers! "He challenged them before more CID arrived just in time to save the situation from turning into a war zone.

They assessed the situation quickly; it wasn't hard, the scent of confrontation hung like a veil in the room. Silks was scowling, his glare fixed on uniform. Bamford was rubbing his arms; he always did as a prelude to attack. The Wee-man was jumping from foot to foot. He was the one in the room with the most explosive temper. Walker managed to look red faced and ashen at the same time. His lips were drawn pack in a prime-evil snarl. With relief in their voices they informed the crowd that Victoria had been found safe and well. She had been with her granddad all along.

Relief flooded the room; it had the effect of turning on a fan in a heat wave. They informed Walker that, she had gone to her granddad`s house as Walker was not at the school to pick her up as usual. Walker's dad was due to visit a friend so he had taken her with him. He had left a note, had they not read it?' Walker nearly blew another gasket! "Read it!" he shouted aloud. The door was fucking locked! What was the point of leaving him a fucking note and locking the fucking door when he didn't have a fucking key to let himself in? He had to be physically restrained from confronting his dad, unburdened feeling flowing like many inflamed tributaries converging on an already flooded reservoir.

The police slipped away. It was a good result for all the DC said. These things did happen and it was natural that it worried parents. For Walker it had been the worst moment of his life and he'd experienced many. He had thought in those few hours that his daughter had been taken and that she was dead. The tears and anguish he had felt in those few hours would never leave his memory. If she had gone, he would not have survived her, he would have taken his own life that night.

Silks stayed with him long after the others left, feeding him beers to reduce the shock and trauma of the afternoon, until he passed out and started to snore. He left quietly; he would have a word, a proper word with his best mate, in the clean and sober light of the morning.

Victoria spent the night at her Granddads, oblivious to the drama her excursion had caused; unaware that she had made the front page of the local paper the next day. Dogs and helicopters had been called out in the search for her. The police had taken it seriously, that much was certain.

Nat had returned home to, 'Sheepbury', when she was informed that Victoria had returned home safe and unharmed. She was comforted with the words, 'that these things happened' and Walker had done the right thing in raising the alarm immediately. When he woke up after a few hours sleep, Anger and resentment burnt deep inside him. Natalie had blamed him and beaten him in front of all those people! Where the fuck was she? Out and about with her boyfriend enjoying life while he was trying the best he could do to cope with the situation, to raise their daughter, with the poor hand of cards he'd been dealt.

He walked into the police station and told them he wanted make a complaint against her. They refused to take down the details and told him to go home; a poster as big as Walker sat proudly on the wall in the waiting room declaring, 'Domestic violence is a crime, don't accept it, report it'. The irony was not lost on him.

The shock of that day made Walker reassess his lifestyle. He attempted to knuckle down in the weeks and months that followed Victoria's disappearance. He cooked regular meals and the chip shop felt the financial pinch of their absence. The divorce was nearly through and he made an effort to be civil to Nat, and improve their relationship, the footings of a new life flowering before him. He realised that the past was behind him and Victoria was the most important person in all of this mess. The cease fire with Natalie was broken on regular occasions; the wound would never heal completely if he kept pulling the scab off. Walker knew the truth of the situation. He would have to do better for his daughters' sake.

CHAPTER 17.
CYCLES.

Walker felt lost, inert and was becoming bored with his new daily routine and life in general. Morning television was tedious with Richard and Judy sitting from up high on their pedestals preaching to the masses and they drove him mad with their empty mantras on how to live the good life. He was still only 31, he was young, he had to do something productive with his life. A single mother that lived nearby had been giving him the eye when he walked Victoria to school and had asked him out. She was attractive and sensible, able to make decent food so he decided to take her up on her offer and attempted to settle down.

Walker would take Victoria around to her home for a home cooked meal, whenever they were hungry, trying to prove to his daughter that he could lead a normal and domesticated existence. Walker could take or leave his new woman, there was no complexity in this scenario for him. He'd dated a couple of girls since Nat left and he ended up finishing the relationship with them all. They did not fix the hole in his soul; they made it worse and induced bouts of nostalgia for his lost life. When the firm dropped over to visit him, she would brew up and make sandwiches like a *'good girl'* and do what she was told. She was a carpet and subservient, but her main sin was simple: she was not Natalie.

Walker`s drinking remained problematic and caused moments that made her think he had issues that needed addressing. She explained his unpredictable behaviour to her concerned family and friends, explaining that, he had been through shit and was trying hard to come out the other end. When he turned over a charming side, when he was sober she told him she loved him. Good for you, he thought and ignored her. Events on the world stage improved and raised his mood. On the 1st May 1997 Mr. Blair was returned as Prime Minister after a landslide labour election victory. The hated Tory regime was finally at an end. The corruption and politics of subduing the poor was finally over.

Britain could enjoy the sun under Blair, as the grey skies and rain under John Major's conservatives were consigned to the history books. The level of his victory told a story about how the voters had turned against years of Tory misrule, against the regular recessions and the marginalisation of working class communities. The fat cats would finally have to pay their fee to be at the party, instead of always gaining entry for free. Their vote had collapsed; it was the conservative's worst result since 1832. The revolution was upon the country and surly, *'things would get better,'* as the labour election theme tune proclaimed.

Major had only 165 MP's left in parliament, the Labour majority sat at 179. Blair would be able to found a labour dynasty with that majority; it would take years for the Tories to reach parity. Walkers only regret was that Blair didn't get the opportunity to beat Thatcher in the election and nail down her coffin lid, instead of her minion politicians. He felt the result was a judgment and a reflection on her polices and political ideology.

 For Walker who loved his politics it was akin to Wolves winning the F.A Cup. Blair had been elected leader in 1994 after the tragic death of John Smith. Smith would have lead Labour to victory, but Blair was always Walkers first choice. He had charisma and a way of talking the made you believe in the sincerity of his political outlook. Perhaps his victory was a portent for Walker.

 He thought about college, and getting some formal qualifications. He thought himself intelligent so it was time to prove it, he made a decision and contacted Wulfrun College about courses and was accepted as a student. On his first day he arrived like a new school boy, smart and polished with a motivation and enthusiasm he hadn't felt in a long time. He'd chosen to take psychology and sociology in tandem, along with the core subject's of math's and English.

Walker took to the academic world as a duck to water. His essays were insightful and received excellent marks. Psychology was his natural subject. He would debate with the other students in the class and aid them in understanding Freud as opposed to Skinner. He would debate with knowledge about the competing methodologies employed and would argue the case for psycho-dynamics, taking umbrage with the behaviorists who thought you could achieve insight into the *'human condition'* with the use of replicated experiments and observation in laboratories. Humans didn't live in labs he would proclaim. They lived in the real world, and no matter what stimulus or variables you used, it was no substitute for individualism which kept us apart from the animals.

Sleep continued to be a problem, as he attempted to drop off he would think of ways to improve his essays and resulting critique. Flashes of inspiration would come and go. Walker ensured he always had a notebook and pen at the ready to capture them.

His parents were proud of him, Victoria was proud of him. His dad bought him a computer to aid his academic development; the last one he owned had been sold to pay his dealers off. Walker completed the course early, the credits required to pass safe in the bank, three months before required.

A graduation ball was arranged by the college with a local MP attending to issue out college certificates to the successful students. His mom and dad dressed up for the occasion, Victoria had her new dress on. Silks had donned his Hugo Boss suit, in order to celebrate the occasion. As Walkers name was called out and he walked to the stage, Silks was on his feet whistling and shouting 'go on Bruce!' His parents applauded and his dad videoed the occasion for posterity.

As he watched it back, a lump of emotion would rise in his throat when he saw Victoria jumping up and down cheering for her daddy, the camera rolling as he walked off the stage, pointing at her, banging his heart with his fist as he walked over and kissed her. It was all there on record no one could take it away from him. To celebrate Silks took him into town and treated him to champagne and clubbing with some pills thrown in on top. He had earned his night out Silks told him. He was fighting back and winning his battles. Walker knew it wasn't quite that simple and straightforward. His mind was still haunted. He had a long way to travel before he was cured of the problems that punctuated his thoughts.

Victoria was proud of him, he had not let her down, her daddy was clever and had proved it. He had 'A' levels now, four of them. He was ready for the step up to higher education. He was going to read psychology at Wolverhampton University

Walkers newly found confidence and positive outlook was not lost on Silks and his long time partner Julie. He was now a regular visitor at the, 'ranch' for meals. Julie had always liked Walker, but she'd told Silks he was 'unbalanced' at times. They became a tight unit, looking out for one another. Julie would offer Victoria a female outlet and played the maternal role that Nat couldn't fill at that moment. The other wives would teach her about makeup, clothes and female etiquette that Walker and Silks knew little about. Their knowledge was about football and beer, but it was equally important in her development and life education. Julie would pull a face when they would relate this fact and take Victoria away, calling them both a pair of idiots. Silks and Walker would laugh as they were at the bar; however they understood that she needed older female company to aid her development. Victoria was growing up and was no longer a child, their knowledge was limited and they could only take her so far with it.

They would spend their social time in The Coates a community pub to while away the hours. It was a family pub for Silks and Walker, a place to take the children and teach them the ways of the world. Victoria fitted in and would play games with the local children. Walker could keep her an eye on her and make sure she didn't go on another, *'mystery tour'*. This was a good socialisation period for Victoria; she met children from diverse backgrounds and cultures.

The Coates was a well known pub in the Wolverhampton area, it had a tarnished reputation with problems from the past that now rarely manifested . It was a community pub in the truest sense of the word. It was the focal point of the estate; it employed local girls, so it offered employment in the local community. The retired gentlemen would gather there to play dominos and cards, ensuring they had a social network. The youth would meet there and do whatever the youth did. The workers off the estate would meet in the bar and have a few pints in peace before they arrived home to their wives and children. Jobs in the construction industry were discussed so it was also an employment exchange. It offered Silks and Walker a home from home, a safe refuge away from the shit the outside world had in store for them. The bar needed a refurbishment plan but it did contain a decent pool table and dart board.

The lounge had separated alcoves, designated traps by the regulars. If you could secure trap one you were in pole position for the night ahead. It was: close to the toilets, (not far to do you drugs), It was closer to the bar (not far for the ladies to walk to fetch the beer) and it was close to the exit (clean set of heels if it came on top). The lads from the firm had started to use it before their Friday nights out in Wolverhampton clubbing. On a Saturday it was used as a venue for the children's disco night that was held in the lounge. Most members of the firm would gather there again for the family night out. It gave the kids and opportunity to dance to *'Saturday Night'* and enjoy their own party. The landlord would turn a blind eye when the parents would bring in pop for the children, happy to exploit the drinking habits of the adults.

If they were broke they could always organise a slate with the gaffer, or a slip a free drink from the bar staff. Silks was a respected face on the estate; Walker his side kick, they were well known and well thought of. The youth would come to Silks for advice on many subjects; he had a level head (mostly) and would impart good advice (legal) over a few beers. Victoria was experiencing the childhood Walker wished he'd lived. It offered him a support network and it offered him an opportunity to charm the local girls in his quest for new love. Walker had found a breeding ground for available woman; he would take full advantage of it.

CHAPTER 18
DUBLIN

Walker's primary thought and behavioural motive since his split and subsequent divorce from Natalie had been to find a replacement wife. He missed his wife and the bond that they had once shared, his mind airbrushing out the bad memories when he reminisced. Nostalgia never contained a nightmare.

He would look around the singles scene when he was out and about with Silks and realise that even though Natalie may have had her faults they were far outweighed by her pluses. It became an obsession for him to find the right woman to fill her shoes. Advertising would scream at him from every direction, from his television set in the evening and billboards on the side of the roads that having a partner and 2.4 children was normal and that he wasn't. It was not the first time in his life that he had felt on the outside of life, looking in upon the world feeling conspicuous with his own inadequacies.

When he did met a girl he would break off the relationship after two or four weeks, getting bored quickly when the excitement of *'first contact,'* had faded away with the realisation that this was not *'the one'* sunk in. He hadn't found a single girl that filled his personally exacting criteria and he would return back to square one in his private game, ever more frustrated that his search had again come up blank. Snakes and ladders played with real people and your own emotions was a difficult came to win, life simply had too many reptiles in the grass and not enough ladders.

Fiona Lee was an elegant black lady that drank in The Coates with her children and friends. First generation Jamaican. She had a degree in theology and was about to launch herself into a teaching career. Her clothes were expensive and stylish which helped her stand out from the crowd. The Coates was a boozer noted for its history, no its fashion sense: London, New York, Paris, Milan, Wolverhampton did not roll off the tongue. Walker knew she was interested in him, Silks had told him when he saw Walker eyeing her up once as she swayed catlike through the crowd to the bar, her presence was Eartha Kitt in her provocative prime, radiating sexuality. He looked over at her and weighed up his options.

Fiona had listened to Silks talk about his mate and his recent academic achievements and his strength at being a single dad, when they had enjoyed a lock in once upon a time. Silks liked to talk when he was on the Jack Daniels. He used the bar as his stage and people enjoyed his monologues. The ambient lightening and intimacy that The Coates offered after dark providing a fitting arena. She fitted the portrait painted with the stocky skin headed man that used the pub regularly and made the connection. She wasn't his *'usual type'*. Walker was partial to petite blonds that supported a bob styled haircut but she did tick most of his boxes.

 He contemplated the pros and cons for a moment. The bar was quite, a few couples were dotted around, three children were playing pool, arguing like sibling. They were dressed like most of the kids that used the pub as if they were little adults, name brands standing proudly on their caps and clothes. Silks and Julie were not in sight. Walker felt suddenly very conspicuous. He drank the rest of his pint, stood up and walked over to the bar for a refill.

"Give us a beer Neil, please mate." Walker was at her shoulder when he ordered his drink. Fiona heard him order his drink and felt his presence close behind her. Taking the opportunity to make his acquaintance, she turned around, looked him in the eye and broke the ice. "Hello mate, I'm Fiona, who are you then?" She held out her hand and Walker surprised by her London accent, paused before he kissed it and introduced himself. She started laughing, expecting a handshake off him. "You're a smooth one then!" He'd been taken aback by her forwardness and had been caught off guard, but Fiona thought him charming and cocky. He liked what she was wearing: tight black leather trousers, a black round necked t-shirt matched with a long black cardigan that went down to her knees with pointed black boots that gave her eye-to eye contact with Walker. It was a well-designed ensemble. Her close cropped Afro suited her perfectly oval face. She was not beautiful, but she was exotic. Fiona Lee looked sophisticated there was no doubt. Walker had found his next victim.

Fiona and Gary enjoyed instant rapport; she liked to talk about the academic world and showed interest in Walkers mind as a fellow intellect. Walker was happy to explore topical issues and enjoyed intelligent conversation. She was aggressive, in as much as she told him that she liked, and wanted him in a short space of time, just after they'd bought their third drink and perched themselves in trap three away from the crowd. That swift disclosure would normally have resulted in Walker taking advantage of her, thinking her weak and easy and discarding her quickly thereafter. It made things easier, he didn't have to play the charming game and go through the motions of laying the table and cleaning the silverware. He felt boredom might become an issue, but his mind was located firmly in the present and the future was still hazy. He had to admit though that she did have a certain charisma and earthy charm about her and this did interest him. He agreed to see her again, the drink making up his mind, chemical poly-filler. She nearly eat him standing by her front door after Walker had escorted her back home.

As he walked back to The Coates he mulled over their meeting and he had his doubts; she was far too eager and that was never a positive sign in his experience. He didn't feel that guttural pull, that kick in the stomach that signified that he was interested in a lady. Walker had to be made to work, he had to be challenged. He rationalised that the last time he listened to his *gut instinct* it had nearly cost him his mental health. After a couple of weeks of seeing him, Fiona fell head over heels for his wit and charm and told him she loved him.

She told him that she was an exponent of *'Wicca'* the religious cult of modern witchcraft and when Walker first walked into the pub, a voice in her head (her sprit guide apparently) informed her that he was the one. He put all this down to her first class degree in theology and the red wine, ignoring the alarm bells that started to ring in his head.

She was over eager and to quick to disclose information to him that he didn't need to know yet, her cards weren't close to her chest, rather they were six miles away. Walker required a girl that challenged him emotionally and made him feel that he was lucky and punching above his weight, he knew with Fiona that she was his, no matter what he did and that bored him, he felt no unsettling disturbing feeling if they had a drunken domestic. There was no barrier to stop his moods, he could wipe his dick on her face and feel nothing. On one Friday he and Silks had no money and landed in The Coates's in the search for free entertainment. Neil gave them a tab for ten pounds each, an opening stake to keep them in the game. Walker came up with a bright idea after he'd spent his and developed a fever for the flavour. Fiona was due to meet him in the bar at seven for their Friday night shindig. Walker convinced Neil that Fe would sort out the bill when she arrived to meet him. Six hours later she entered the pub looking like cat woman and asked for a glass of red. Neil charged her sixty pounds for the privilege and her eyebrows rose. "Fack me." She exclaimed. "It's only facking house red!" Her cockney twang apparent when she was angry. Neil informed her that. Mr. Walker and Mr. Coleman had been drinking steadily on her tab for a few hours, was she not aware of the arrangement?' She looked across at the pair of them, who'd wisely taken cover behind the pool table trying to avoiding her eye. She paid the bill and chased Walker around the bar and out onto car park much to the regular's amusement.

Fe could lose her temper with the best of them and when she was drunk she was a head case who could hold her own in a fight. She forgave him in less than ten minutes after he melted her heart with a lopsided smile and some more cheap lines before taking him to the cash point to give him a few pounds, so he could stand his round. Fe wasn't going to have her man begging for beer. Nat would have dumped him, never mind topping up his bank balance. She was his to be exploited.

Fiona Lee was a paradox, she was a career woman but accepted a subservient role in their relationship and this lost her respect with Walker. Woman who made the evening meal and accepted their traditional gender role were not his cup of tea. He liked women that were feisty and fiery. Fe's social philosophy made her very welcome in the firm. She would drink red wine like Ribena and would happily bomb speed and pop ecstasy all weekend, explaining that it enhanced her libido and made the physical experience *'god like'*. Behaviorally she was volatile, a product of the care system that failed to provide the support and safety network that children required to make them feel loved and included.

A feeling of hopelessness and an attempt to claw back control of her life had produced an attitude that stuck two fingers up at the establishment. She became embroiled in the gang culture that existed in south-east London, beating a rival gang member with an iron bar to gain *'respect'*. Her futile attempt to regain power and direction of her own life resulted in jail time at a young offender's institute. Here she had her epiphany, understanding the senselessness of fighting the system from the outside; she made a vow to change it from within.

Walker admired the way she'd changed her life around and wanted to help the kids that lived on the estates. She would give up her spare time to provide them with knowledge and an education that would help them stop getting into trouble with the police and helping them to navigate a road away from criminality. She offered them an alternative avenue, away from the gangs and showed the local youth that they could succeed legally. She wanted to break the cycle of social poverty. He found it hard to marry her intelligence and drive with the needy and clingy woman she became around him. Walker was often conflicted in those post Nat days.

Fe's main crime like many others that had gone before her, was that she simply wasn't Nat and he accepted that with resignation in his heart. They would sprawl around his flat and talk and discuss their future. When he was high on speed and grandiose he would agree with her and make plans about houses and marriage. Sometimes even believing his rhetoric. When she had left and peace descended, he doubted that they would live the dream, he knew he didn't love her it was that simple.

Silks son, James was a good footballer and played for the local youth club. As a hand across the water programme to promote unity between the two lands had been extended and an invite to play an Irish boys club over the Irish Sea in Dublin was forthcoming. Silks and Walker recognised an opportunity for the lads to have a long weekend away ,as well as a chance to support the local community. They could represent the estate and export their own values.

Silks, like Fiona liked to put something back into the community. The local youth were good kids who at times had been dealt a poor hand. Silks believed that given the right motivation they would not tread the same paths as he had. He was a good teacher, his time within the prison system giving him a valid platform to preach conversion. He wasn't born again, Silks realised that a life of crime was a waste of talent and would inevitably lead to a jail sentence or an early grave.

Walker's mom sorted out the booking details for them. The flights and hotels were all organised, they just had to turn up and behave themselves. The party was made up of four lads: Silks, Walker, Langley and Declan Flannigan, an Irish lad who moved to England when he was young and liked to visit the Emerald isle on a regular basis to keep in touch with his family. Walker knew he didn't hold down a 9-5 and was well thought off by both the Irish community and top football lads in Wolverhampton. He had a pretty sister who he warned potential suitors off, named Siobhan. She was petite and blond with an attitude and mouth making her the estates version of Kat Slater; she was certainly a good looking girl. Walker thought she was beautiful, but she didn't really know he existed. Lads that drank in the Coates where ten a penny and as Declan drank there she left them all well alone. Declan looked Irish, chalk white skin with close cropped hair that couldn't hide its ginger heritage.

Walker shouted. "Guinness and Irish stew all around please landlord," as they announced their arrival at the Irish bar in Wolverhampton town centre. The locals raised an eyebrow from the beer barrels that passed as tables, and raised a glass. This pub was not political, happy to welcome all with a good attitude who simply wanted the criac. The tickets were safely tucked away and their pockets were full of money. Everybody in the pub knew about their plans to storm Dublin and show the Irish how to party. Walker had managed to get hold of £800, Silks roughly the same to last them the weekend. After holding court and telling anyone that wanted to listen about their plans they finally managed to drag themselves away from the pub in high spirits.

The beers had flowed a little too freely and they nearly managed to miss the flight. A stampede of feet had greeted the cabin crew as they arrived at Birmingham airport, their faces full of smiles and excuses as they gratefully received their boarding passes. A pint in the departure lounge was downed in one before the scrum for places on the flight began. It was a cheap flight so seats were not allocated prior to boarding, it was first come first served. The lads managed to down three double vodkas on the flight over and toasted each other from their various seat on the planes, impervious to the anxious glances from other passengers, they didn't care, they were on holiday.

At Dublin airport while having another beer and waiting for the queue at the taxi rank to disappear, they bumped into 'Huggy Bear'. A.K.A, Antonio Fargas, an actor that played the part of the nightclub owning snitch from the hit seventies cop programme 'Starsky and Hutch'. Silks pulled Walker to one side to confirm that it was indeed the man in question.

Walker was a well known T.V addict and unbeatable at Trivial Pursuits. He glanced across and confirmed that it was indeed the man in question. They walked over and asked if they could have their pictures taken with him, passing over generous compliments to seal the deal. Antonio gave them tickets for the grand opening of a retro club that he was in town for and the reason for his visit to Ireland. Walker knew it was a portent for a good holiday; they had only been in Ireland for

thirty minutes and they had already had pictures taken with a
'Hollywood,' legend and had a free night out if they wanted it. They
made the journey into Dublin City Centre and booked into their Hotel.
Walker and Silks simply tossing their bags into the room before turning
round and heading back down to the bar to grab some food and take
in the local scenery. The rest of the evening was spent drinking and
showing some moves in the nightclub located downstairs.

Flan was pissed, more pissed that anyone had ever seen him; a few
bottles of fizz had been popped to cement the occasion of his return to
the homeland. Back at home he wasn't a big drinker, he would drop in
the Coates have a couple of pints before he went on his way to an
alternative shady location in the near vicinity. In Dublin he danced,
drank, laughed and had a riot of fun on that Friday night.

Breakfast was a damper affair, hangovers well in evidence on all their
faces as they sat round the table and leaned on the linen tablecloth.
The waitress raised an eyebrow when Langley asked for a full 'English'
informing him he could have certainly have a full 'Irish' if he wanted a
proper breakfast. He stumbled over his words before correcting
himself and apologised emit loud laughter from the table.

Silks asked the same waitress for poached eggs and the laughter went
up ten levels when a plate was placed in front of him with no toast on
it just lonely looking eggs, his face was a picture as she explained that
you had to order the toast separately as it didn't come as standard.
Walker and Langley nearly broke down as he was being pointed in the
right direction by the assertive Irish lady and he glared at them as they
hid their laughs under napkins, hands or anything else that was close
at hand to hide their mirth. His patience finally broke after another
comment from Langley and he chased them good naturedly around
the dining room, much to the staff's amusement.

The breakfast was good, the coffee was freshly ground not the freeze
roasted rubbish that was served to guests in cheap establishments.
They sat round the table making conversation, drinking a few gallons
of orange juice and hoping the aspirin they had taken would help the
thump in their heads. Finally they decided to motivate themselves and
headed off into the city centre to enjoy the delights of Temple Bar.
Temple Bar was a cattle market, full of loud northerners who were
queuing ten deep at the bar to order a beer and enjoy the local
culture. Tired of the tourist trap they headed off into Dublin centre to
find a proper pub with some proper people in it. Flan was suffering

badly from his Friday night exertions and headed off into the city centre to fulfill his family obligations.

Walker and Langley were also suffering badly from the night before and their enthusiasm for the day was starting to ebb. They suggested returning to the hotel, for a lie down to recharge the batteries ready for a big night out. Silks started to play his face, unimpressed with the proposed plan. "They were in Dublin." He told them. "They should be out and about, not sleeping in the room like a bunch of fucking old men!"

Immune to his motivational speech they found a taxi rank and asked the driver to take them to the Lower Rathmines Road. Walker relaxed in the cab, relieved to be out of the crowd. Langley held his head in hands and contemplated being sick. Silks wasn't finished with the day and after much vociferous coxing he convinced them to have a drink at a pub near to the hotel called *Roddy Boland's*. Walker ordered three pints and brought them over to the table which was in a prime position to watch the afternoon sports programme placing them down with a sigh. He was tired and fed up of Silks and his 'old woman jibes' and decided to have a word with his mate. "You're on top Silks, fuck me you're going overboard here." He had been on their case now for a full twenty minutes. "Wirr in the fucking pub ay we? Give it a fucking rest now man. You have got your own way".

Langley was silent, looking at his beer and gagging. The nausea at least adding some colour to his cheeks. "Fuck off Bruce you're a fucking lightweight, don't fucking start mate!" Silks eyes narrowed as he spat out the words.

"I'm saying what I'm saying. Fuck me mate, what you want everybody to toe the fucking line eh? It don't work like that. We get fucking hammered now, it kills the day." His eyes didn't move from Silks.

"The day will fucking last longer than you Bruce, fucking believe it. Yam a pussy mate." His finger was pointed at Walkers face.

"Fucking pussy! Yam having a laugh ay you?" Walker could feel his blood turn to acid. Tempers were rising. More words were exchanged between the two before Silks got up and left the table to have his tantrum alone nearby. His pint spilled onto the dark wood table and stained floor as he slammed it down.

Langley and Walker started laughing, surprised at his reaction and the fact he was sitting arms folded and was clearly sulking because he hadn't got his way. This did little to improve Silks mood, his face became darker and his stare fixed, aimed straight at Walker. They knew that an assault could be imminent. Silks was displaying all the signs that he was about to attack.

"Fuck it." Walker turned toward Langley. "If he wants a fight, I'm fucking up for it." They'd fought on many occasions previously. Silks had won them all until a bruising battle had taken place in a large pub that they sometimes visited. Walker had to be pulled off him, as Silks was dropped in the doorway that led outside. Their battle had raged from one side of the pub to the other and the locals picked their pints off the tables as the battle moved toward them. Accepting this new opportunity that had been presented to him Silks attacked Walker again as they were ushered outside and onto the street. They fought in the middle of the road and stopped traffic. Silks had his fingers pressed into Walkers eye socket right up to the knuckle, Walker rained punches onto his head, his eyes watering from the pain his mate was inflicting. Silks had some funny moves that he'd learned in prison and would win at all costs. Walker's mentality wasn't about winning it was about the taking part.

 Walker needed some Dutch courage and an anesthetic. "If he is going to start, I'm at least going to get pissed," he informed Langley as he headed off to the bar to refill their glasses . He bought three pints dropped one on Silks table and pulled face at Langley that started a fresh round of laughter. Walker sat down with his back to Silks.

 "What's he saying Daz?"

"He don't look happy Walks mate, you might be wearing your boxing gloves when we leave mate."

"Fuck him lets have another."

As they waited for Silks to attack they managed to drink their way through the hangover and started to enjoy the day. After a couple more pints Walker invited Silks to join him in 'a glass of the black stuff' and come and sit back down at the table. Silks agreed after Walker apologised for being *'rude'* to keep the peace, ensuring that war was averted.

They drank some more Guinness and raised their glasses to the locals and praised the Irish nation. Singing football songs to entertain the local lads, inviting them to have a beer and join in the fun. The Good Friday Peace talks were never required, the Irish and the English drank in peace on that Saturday. The locals wore Arsenal and Man Utd, replica shirts. After six pints of Guinness they were all Wolves fans.

As it got dark they bid farewell to their new friends and returned to the hotel to get changed, arm in arm, swaggering and singing to pedestrians. A Garda patrol care slowed down to observe them for a minute. They lowered their voices, smiled sheepishly and made the hotel without incident. Walker and Silks were back in the hotel bar almost immediately. Flan spotted them as he walked past reception and waited for the lift, he'd just arrived back to the hotel after visiting his Grandmothers. He declined a drink stating he felt terrible from last night's exertions.

"Champagne then?" Silks offered him a tall glass full of bubbles.

"Fuck, no man." He told Silks, looking suspiciously at the bottle. Silks had decided to show the locals what they were all about and asked for the wine list. He decided to order a decent Tattinger that was a mere £70 a bottle.

"A bottle of Tat with four glasses please." He ordered proudly and waited for the pretty bar maid with long black hair pulled back tightly into a bun, crisp white linen shirt, and an arse made for the black trousers she was wearing to return from the wine cellar. The few other patrons that were scattered around did notice, their eyes had been all over the room, now surreptitious glances were aimed in their direction as she placed the champagne in an ice bucket in front of them. "You'll need a sponsor form for all the walking yam going to do." Silks turned to the rest of the customers and raised his glass proclaiming. 'The boys are in town.' they were kings of all they surveyed.

After one bottle, ten minutes and thirty seconds later a fresh bright idea swayed into Walkers head. He waved over to the bar-maid a good-humored expression on his face."Could you send some hot milk up for the pussies in room 234 as well please." Walker asked. Tapping his nose with his forefinger in a conspiratorially gesture. Walker and Silks had started playing a few schoolboy pranks on the others to entertain themselves; one more wasn't going to hurt."It appears them having an early night!" Walker added for good measure.

Langley appeared five minutes later with his class of hot milk clasped firmly in his hand and a broad smile on his face."Pair of fucking jokers!" He turned to Maureen, (he was on first name terms apparently)."Can I have fresh glass please," nodding toward the bottle, succulent with melted ice making it appear even more refreshing. The cheaper the champagne the drier it is. This bottle was wet.

Walker and Silks looked at each other and made a mental note. There was mileage in this one they laughed as Langley left the bar to have a piss. They laughed even louder when Langley told them that Flan had accepted his and settled down to watch Noel`s house party in front of the telly. He glanced at the bottle and poured himself a drink. "What's the occasion with the champagne then? I thought we had done that mission last night."

"Wim on holiday ay we!" It was a simply answer. Silks didn't elaborate. Silks ordered more champagne and the barmaid got her promised exercise.

 A contractor that was stopping in the hotel, a lad from Huddersfield glad to hear English voices joined them at the bar. They exchanged some banter with him, swapping areas and tales about football. "What do you lot do for a living then?" he enquired

"About five to ten in the pen mate." Silks side-stepped the question and there was more laughter from the bar.

Walker pointed at Silks. "He likes to bite people's faces off mate." It was true, Silks did like to bite people.

Silks explained to the Huddersfield lad ."It's from my star sign mate. I'm a Leo, a fucking lion, King of the fucking jungle you understand me?"

"Yes mate," the lad nodded back nervously not sure of what to make of it all.

Walker turned to Langley. "What a load of bollocks the barmy bastard just needs an excuse to hurt people, when he hits them with a wrench does that make him a fucking plumber, fucking Leo the Lion-heart."

"Can I get you drink lads?" Enquired the lad from up north.

"Champagne please," they replied. They were not about to lower their standards to appease this joker.

"How much is that a bottle then?" He was trying to impress them as he opened his Velcro wallet and inspected the contents watchfully. Hoping his expression didn't give the game away.

 Walker watched with an amused grin on his face."Seventy punts a bottle mate." Walker said.

"I can't afford that" the meek reply was barely audible.

"We fucking can! " Walker stated as he opened his wallet and threw some notes on the counter, the others banged on the bar and laughed loudly."Get a glass, have a drink on us mate."

The night wore on and got better and better. Walker's and Silks behaviour became worse and worse. The bar was proving to be a popular venue with the revellers of Dublin. Soon the hum of conversation filled the room. The tables were full of glasses, the floor was filled with groups. A combination of smart chic, and elegant scruffiness.

The bouncers isolated them from the rest of the revellers as they chased each other round the bar, laughing like lunatics. One group that were standing in the corner started to make more noise than them. Silks went over to inspect them, he poked one tall lad in the back twice to gain his attention. The man thought ignoring Silks was the best tactic, maybe then he would melt into the woodwork. Silks pokes became harder, under the watchful eyes of three bouncers. Walker noticed that three more had appeared and were standing by the entrance.

He motioned to Langley who raised his eyebrows and hands in mock surrender. "What do you think you're playing at?" Silks asked the confused Irishman.

"Nothing." Mystified expression greeted him, from a roguish looking man with thick curls and eyebrows that needed attention."I don't know what you mean. His accent was broad, North Dublin and hard to understand.

" Do you understand me, senior, speaker da English."

Walker and Langley appeared at Silks side and managed to drag him away with smile and apologies. The bouncers looked on and made sure their presence was recognised in attempt to limit the potential for trouble.

Flan showed his face a few hours later and accepted the offer of a glass, stating he wanted a Buck's Fizz. It cost them another ten pounds for a jug of fresh orange juice but who gave a fuck they were on holiday. They drunk the hotel out of Tattinger after ten bottles, cementing themselves as the top bodies in the bar, they sang and asked people to join them in a toast as they downed another glass of champagne." God bless all who drink here," raising their glasses to toast their audience.

Flan bought another bottle before he headed back upstairs in an attempt to escape the mayhem.

The party continued in their rooms, as they left the bar at closing time. Silks dressed himself up in sheets and proclaimed himself to be *'Shaka*

Zulu' about to go to war with the white man. War was declared on Langley and Flans room. There had been pre-emptive strikes already, when Silks and Walker learned from reception by accident, (after they had lost the swipe cards for their room), that as they were lead names for both rooms so they could easily request a replacement swipe card. They saw an opportunity and requested a copy for Langley's room; they could now enter it at their own will. They hid their clothes and removed their bags and nearly had a heart attack when Langley said. "The hotel might be haunted." they laughed so much.

They would swipe open the door, run in and water bomb the *'enemy'* using condoms they'd brought with them from England, before making their escape choking with laughter in the corridors. Langley responded with a pizza attack that left the walls in their rooms scored with tomatoes and salami. Flan wanted an end to hostilities but the offer of a cease fire was refused and the battle raged on throughout the corridors. Walker called room service and ordered an early morning alarm call for half past four for room 234, with an added request for breakfast to be delivered to that room for five. Langley highly amused at being woken up for the second time told the waiter. "Could you make sure that this goes on to Mr. Coleman's bill please and give yourself a ten pound tip." he accepted the tray and sat down to enjoy his breakfast in bed. Ha ya bastards, he thought vengefully . Mopping up his eggs with freshly buttered toast and enjoying the free meal before he made his way to their room to wake them up. Walker opened the door to save Langley knocking it through. "What the fuck Daz?"

"Is that it now? All bollocks finished?" Langley asked. Taking a seat on the edge of Silks bed.

Silks had opened one eye to see what all the fuss was about. He was not impressed by his morning visitor so he flipped him off the bed and onto the floor. Langley landed on his neck with a grunt and decided to get out of harm's way and get back to the, *'safety'* of his own room, returning within the hour to complain about serious pains shooting through his neck. Langley was a soldier, not a man that would normally make a fuss. After another half an hour of loud groans and Langley telling them that he couldn't move his head, the thought emerged that he may have broken his neck started to register with them.

Walker dialled Emergency services who responded quickly to the situation. Within ten minutes the hovel that had become their room was full of police officers and members of the ambulance service. Walker glanced around the room, it was a fucking disgrace! The floor was littered with discarded glasses, empty bottles, pizza boxes, clothes, condoms and cigarette packets. The only space was on the bed. They hadn't realised that they had a kettle in their room until Langley told them it was, 'under all that shit,' pointing to a pile of discarded clothes on the dressing table.

The ambulance men unable to manoeuvre him out the room and down the stairs called the fire service to assist them, which they duly did to adding to the havoc in the room. As they pushed Langley out of the hotel on a gurney, his bare feet were sticking out from under a blanket. Walker in an attempt to protect his dignity placed a gaudy pair of socks upon them and Silks placed a cigarette into his mouth for pain relief. The hailed a taxi and followed the ambulance to hospital and presented at casualty. Langley was admitted for assessment.

They were ushered out the cubicle by nursing staff who told them 'they had work to do advising them to get a drink and come back in an hour. Langley looked worried, Walker and Silks felt the cold hand of dread touch their hearts.

"Fuck me Silks you better call his missus and tell her you broke Darren's neck."

"You call her Bruce please." The frowns on his brow were real. These were worrying times for the pair.

"You did it, you're the fucking brother-in-law, sort it out man." He wasn't comfortable in telling Sarah they'd just crippled the love of her life.

"She will take it better off you." Silks countered, desperately.

"Will she fuck, she'll get on a dam plane and we are both dead!" The debate raged on over coffees. They could procrastinate all they wanted. She had a right to know that Darren was not in great shape. Silks bit the bullet; he had done the fucking deed after all. He placed some coins in the call box, and dialled the number and tried to look positive.

"Hello Sarah, you alright are you?" She was not stupid. Sarah was very far from stupid, she knew that something had happened otherwise Silks would not be on the phone at eight in the morning. From the gist of the one way conversation and the deteriorating look on Silks face he knew that concerns were being raised back home.

"The hospital will sort him out, we'll call you when we know shit." He chucked the phone back into the receiver, as if it was too hot to hold."Fuck me, he'd better be alright Bruce, she will fucking kill us, I mean it mate she isn't happy!" Walker shrugged his shoulders, there was little else to do or say until they heard from the medical team. The nurse came into the canteen to find them and pulled them out of the hole they had dug for themselves. She told them that Darren had suffered a muscle tear, it would be painful for a week and he had to keep the neck brace on but there was no real damage. They nearly burst into tears as they thanked her for all her help. Walker thrust coins into Langley's hand as he was discharged and pleaded with him to put Sarah's mind at rest. Darren picked up the phone, checked the area code and dialled in his home number,

"I'm alright Sarah, I'm fine really.......calm down.....no you're right......no thanks to those pair of idiots. Yes I'll tell them. I Love you, see you tomorrow." He turned round to look at them having to rotate his whole body. It was a comical sight now he was safe.

 "Fuck me it's Frankenstein!" Silks laughed out loud clearly relieved the situation wasn't serious.

"Yeah you can take the piss now, wait until tomorrow." Langley pointed toward Silks. "Especially you mate!

"The rest of their day was spent watching the youth team play football, nearby to where skeleton of Croke Park was emerging over the rows of terraced houses. A national monument and the scene for the first 'Bloody Sunday.' When on November twenty first 1920, seven spectators were shot to death by way of reprisal for an earlier IRA outrage. When the taxi driver explained it, the lads listened and dropped their heads in reverence Their team managed to win the challenge match 1:0, with their goalkeeper playing a blinder. The Irish lads had superior technical ability; however for heart and passion they were nowhere near the lads from Wolverhampton. They were warned by the referee for their foul language and continued encroaching onto the pitch area totally immersed in the game. As the final whistle blew they celebrated with the players and danced a jig of joy in the centre circle. When they returned home to Wolverhampton and were walking through the train station Silks spotted the Langley family vehicle in the distance heading toward them and bolted quickly into a black cab to escape Sarah's wrath.

"Fucking pussy." Walker whispered as he received his lecture on good behaviour from her before he was dropped off back at home

BOOK THREE: MIND OVER MATTER
CHAPTER 19
MURDER

Walker's relationship with Fe deteriorated as he knew it would to, it was now based almost entirely on alcohol and drugs as they established a common ground. He had to be pissed to have sex with her and off his head to talk to her. She got on his nerves with her clingy and submissive behaviour. This caused them to fight occasionally, when Walker tired of her and became increasingly exasperated by her unwillingness to leave him the alone and afford him some peace. Her needed for both affirmation and validation at his hands was intensely sad, and in turn caused Walker to dominate her when he saw fit, or was bored and low. He knew it was wrong and manipulative, he knew they were stuck in a destructive cycle. He pictured them clinging onto driftwood like shipwrecked sailors .

Around Victoria they made sure they got their act together. Fe was good around children and Walker didn't understand the metamorphosis that took place within her when they were alone. As most couples they could hide the disjointed lines in their relationship and rationalise the drinking and drug taking by proclaiming to all who cared to listen that it was just a 'social activity when they were out together. They both chose to ignore the truth ; ignorance is bliss. When Victoria went over to visit Natalie,(which was every other weekend now), they would arrive home early on Saturday morning and continue to drink and take drugs throughout the rest of the weekend, safely ensconced in his flat. It didn't require a risk assessment to realise that alcohol might become a mitigating factor in the end of their tempestuous time together.

The children were on half term holiday, away from school and free of the shackles of convention. Victoria was playing with Silks' kids on the grass located outside The Coates, the boys kicking a ball, the girls sitting down and laughing. The usual faces were in the bar when Fe walked in with a big smile on her face. She tapped Walkers broad shoulder. "Hello you old baldy." She said with a grin, obviously happy to see him.

"Where's Vicky? She asked ."I've brought her a present." She reached into her bag and produced a watch. Walker thought it was a nice touch and a decent watch, which again cancelled out his misgivings about their future together

"Out and about." He pointed over to the grass outside the pub.

"Do you mind if in I give it her?" Fe asked.

"No, not at all, knock yourself out." He shrugged his shoulders at her. She went into her purse and past him a twenty pound note over. "Get me a bottle of red wine baby and whatever you and Silks want." They wanted a couple of beers with vodka chasers, they told the gaffer as they settled down for another free night on her.

The night turned into a party and the music played loud and long into the night. Fe was drinking her own weight in red wine and was becoming loud and obnoxious, getting on Walkers nerves with her, idiot like behaviour. It was getting late and Walker had drunk plenty, he wanted to go home, aware that Victoria was tired and yawning by his side, resting her head against his shoulder. He asked Silks to book him a cab, understanding that Silks was well known and a taxi would actually be ten minutes if he ordered it. Ten minutes later the taxi tooted its horn outside and Walker gathered Victoria up in his arms and nudged Fe to come along. Her speech was slurred as she said her goodbyes and kissed the cheeks of the girls left in the pub. On the way back to the flat she snapped at him a couple of times. Walker's lips became thin and his stare remained ahead as he managed to keep his temper in check. Victoria was sleeping and he didn't want a stand up row in public.

As they arrived back to the flat, he opened the taxi door and picked Victoria up to carry her to bed. Fe managed to get in another snide remark as he left her to pay the fare. Walker opened the door to the flat and took Victoria to her bedroom laying her down and pulling her quilt over her before he kissed her forehead and wished her 'the sweetest of dreams'.

Fe had poured herself another glass of wine and was sipping at it, sitting down in his chair looking out of the window as he returned back into the front room."You still drinking then?" Walker asked, his thirst had been quenched some time ago when she'd started to act like a dumb prick. Even the alcohol hadn't managed to air brush his mind through the evening.

"Yeah I am you wanker." The cockney accent in evidence, slurred but clear.

"What did you fucking say?" Walker didn't need a drunken domestic; he was tired and wanted to go to sleep.

"You heard me you wanker, you're both wankers you and your mate, Silks." Walker was confused. What the fuck was going on in her alcohol fuddled diseased mind? The last thing he wanted was Victoria to wake up and find her dad kicking fuck out the school teacher.

"Shut up keep you voice down, Shorts is asleep, leave it please." He attempted to placate her.

"Fucking wanker" She repeated the insult.

Walker was in not in the mood for her drunken, irrational behaviour, he was tired and drunk, his lethargy was rapidly metamorphosing into irritability. Walker stared back at her and pointed his finger at her head, his patience with her and their situation finally exhausted.

"You're a drunken fucking cunt, get the fuck out my yard. I don't want to see you anymore; I don't want to fucking hear from you again, do you understand what I'm saying to you?"

Fe rose from up from her chair and started walking toward him, she was staggering, the bottle of red wine in her hand. She reminded Walker of Dean Martin, without the humour. "Look at you, you fucking piss head," he taunted her. "Yam pissed and going to wake up single." He had the power in the relationship, she loved him and he could wipe his dick on her face whenever he wanted to and not give a fuck about it or her.

"At least I'm not a wanker!" She repeated the insult and poked him the chest, her voice getting louder. Walker was trying to think of a way out of this situation without the need for the flat to get turned over.

His thoughts about nullifying the situation brought a hesitancy to his actions. He brushed away her hand and considered his options.

Fe continued with her drunken tirade. "If I had a fucking knife I would fucking stab you." A brave claim Walker thought, he'd slashed up a couple of people. It wasn't as easy as it sounded.

"Would you?" He challenged her, looking straight into her eyes before going into the kitchen and picked up a scaling knife which was long, thin and evil looking. He thrust it in her hand as he met her in the entrance hall. Walker's thoughts was simple, call her bluff and fuck her off, she'd made a tit out of herself; the fucking dog. Arriving down uninvited and………………….

The wind left his body, it was strange experience, he didn't feel anything like pain. Walker just had trouble in breathing. It took a second before it registered with him, she'd stabbed him in the throat. Walker sank to his knees and collapsed onto the floor his shirt turning crimson with blood. He knew it wasn't an arterial wound, surprised at how calm he felt, he could see the ceiling and the blood was not splattering upon it. His hands were wet, sticky and covered with his own blood as he tried to stem the flow running freely from his throat, his mind losing focus again. He began to feel nauseous and weak, before slipping into unconsciousness.

 Fe brought him round slapping his face telling him to live. Shaking him and causing the blood to splatter over the walls. She'd opened the door to the flat and was banging on his neighbours doors. Begging the sleeping to wake, hysterically pleading with them to call an ambulance and the police. Why did she want the fucking police? He wasn't a narc, he still had a plan to get them out of this, even on his death bed Walker had a plan. He felt quite warm and comfortable as if he was floating on a gentle breeze.

Fe sat abreast of him again, her knees across his chest, crying and telling him to live.

"I fucking intend to!" He croaked, he couldn't speak or enunciate his words correctly and he wondered if she heard him? He could barely focus on shadowy images of people standing on the landing, he could just hear blurred conversation. Where they talking about him? Was he the one dying on the floor?

His fist connected with her chin, as the thought hit him; Fe had tried to kill him, while his daughter lay sleeping in another room. His instinct to fight flowed through his mind and weakening body. She'd stabbed him in the fucking neck. He punched her again. The force of his blows weak. He had no strength left in his body to hurt her. Fe continued to sit on his chest her hands around his neck attempting to stem the tidal flow of blood. Walker passed out again.

The paramedic brought him round in the ambulance, Walker saw a blue light with visions of men dressed in green overalls. He croaked out a question. "Am I going to live mate?"

Their reply was ambiguous. "Hold on mate, we're nearly at the hospital," a tear slid out his eye and crept onto to his cheek. His time had come; he would never see Victoria again.

His dad was at his bedside, when Walker awoke in the morning. His
throat was sore and he had trouble swallowing, the thought of last
night came sharply into focus. His hand went to the wound, feeling the
dressing. He looked up at his old man and wondered how the fuck he
had sunk this low? In the last few years he'd lost his wife to another
man, become a single father and got divorced. Lost and found Victoria,
coping with the fallout from all that in his mind and now his parents
had thought he'd found a half decent woman and she'd tried to kill
him! The hammer blows rained down on his head in quick succession.
In three years his life had sunk from near normality to a plot from a
soap opera.

"Where's Victoria?" He sounded like Marlon Brando from the
Godfather.

"She is at school Gary; she stayed with your mom last night. She hardly
knows anything, Just that you have had an accident and had to go into
hospital."

"Good, I don't want her to know anything, as long as she is fine?"

"How are you?"

"Don't know dad, I really don't know mate. It's all a nightmare."
Walker shook his head, the shock of nearly being a corpse lying on a
slab in the mortuary hadn't fully resonated with him yet.

"I've brought you in a change of clothes."

Walker realised that he was in a hospital gown and his arm was bruised
and hurt. He looked down at the plaster on it.

"What's that?" He asked.

"They had to give you some blood, it's OK".

"Blood?" The realisation of last night was still trying to break through
the invisible wall that protected the mind.

"Fiona is in custody, they want to charge her with attempted murder
and the police want to talk to you when you're up to it."

"That's great; does Silks know I'm here?"

"I don't know Gary; the nurses will tell you what you need to know. I
don't know that much to be honest, just that you needed some clothes
that's all. Look I'm going to leave you in peace, get things sorted son."
Walker looked terrible to his dad as he looked down upon his wounded
son .The massive weight loss in a short amount of time had made him
look ill. He knew he was drinking heavily to cope with life. Now he was
lying in a hospital bed with a dressing on his neck and throat to hide his

wounds, lucky to be alive. He passed him a bag containing, a t-shirt, jacket and jeans

"Thanks dad, I appreciate it." Walker tired to smile.

His dad got up and left, smiling sadly at him before he turned and walked slowly down the corridor. Walker was touched, that was the closest thing to a father and son moment they'd shared for a long time.

The nurse waited for his dad to leave and appeared at his bedside."Morning Mr. Walker, how are you this morning? You had quite a night by all accounts?"

"If the hangover is anything to go by." The flippancy masking his deeper, true feelings.

"Want a hot drink?" The nurse asked him. She looked kind, there was no judgment in her eyes. It was all in Walkers head.

"I could murder a cup of coffee." The ironic answer brought a smile to both their faces.

The doctor came to visit him shortly afterwards. He informed Walker that he was a lucky man to be alive. The knife had bent on the way in, missing the jugular artery on the one side and his main veins on the other. Millimeters had separated him from death. There was deep wounding to his throat, however they'd managed to stop the blood flow with internal stitching and he would make a rapid recovery. He had been given five sutures to close the wound from the outside and he had to be careful not to bang it. Did the doctor think he made habit of banging his fucking neck, he wondered?

"There is some internal damage and we don't want it to start bleeding again do we now?" Patronising advice from the doctor. Walker smiled and nodded back thinking, Of course not doctor, I'm a yob, doctor, a drunken anti-social thug doctor, three bags fucking full doctor! Walker continued to smile as he thanked him for his hard work. The nurses informed him, he would be kept in until the afternoon just to make sure that the bleeding was controlled. On discharge he would be given his prescription for painkillers and penicillin. The police wanted a word, was it alright to send them in?

"Yeah let's get it over with." Walker wanted to get these fuckers out the way quick sharp.

A burly man, with a shining head and an ill fitting brown suit smiled incongruously at Walker, as he stood next to his bedside. Standing next to him was a sour faced man with wispy blond hair. They didn't look like Crockett or Tubbs. The police wanted his version of last night's events.

Walker looked at them and narrowed his eyes, attempting to look confused. "What can I do for you lads?"

"We need a statement?" Shinning head asked.

"For an accident? Walker replied.

"Mr Walker, we have the assailant in custody, she has admitted stabbing you."

Walker held his tongue, the 'assailant' had a name and three children.

"She is mistaken, last night she was fucking hysterical, she was a tit head, pissed, off her trolley and obviously in shock. It didn't happen that way. I'll make a statement to that affect if you like?"

"Could you tell me how you managed to slip onto the point of a knife Mr Walker." Wispy hair joined in the debate.

"Because I'm a twat, now I'm tired and I don't want to answer any more questions, I'm presuming I'm not under caution. And as there are no other witnesses Its let her go time lads." Walker remembered when he' d tried to make a complaint against Nat. They hadn't wanted to know him then. They'd beaten him up in the past, spent time knocking on his door, which hadn't helped his relationship with Nat. Asking him stupid questions about crimes he knew nothing about. Now they wanted his help in putting Fe away! Probably, because she was black and he was a white man. He remembered the tales of Silks and the racial abuse he suffered at the hands of these fuckers who were meant to uphold the law. They excused themselves and left Walker alone with his thoughts, he didn't want to think, they were not contented images in his head.

Silks arrived at lunch time and looked at Walkers food and sniffed it dismissively and pulled a face. It must have been Friday, Walker thought, it was always fish and chips for lunch in hospitals on a Friday. The chips were dry and hard and in need of half a ton of tartar sauce to make them edible and hurt when he swallowed them.

"We can do better than that mate. I'll buy us some eats at The Gate. What the fuck did you do to her then?" Silks pointed at Walkers neck.

"Fuck all mate, she was off it. Simple as."

Silks searched under the bed and brought out a carrier bag, he looked inside at the contents. "Fuck me she meant it then?" The t-shirt and jacket were stiff with dried blood and nearly entirely red."You must have lost some claret man." Walker knew that Silks was trying to be flippant to cheer him up."We'll blow here and hit The Coates Bruce. A few people want to buy you a beer."

"I'm really not in the mood right now mate." Walker said as his stomach turned over.

"Show your face Brucie boy, show them you alive and show them you're strong. You can sleep tomorrow." Walker could see the sense in his words. They waited until his meds were ready for collection and left the ward. Silks flirting with nurses as he bid them goodbye. With a resigned smile Walker stepped back into the pantomime that was fast becoming his life.

When he walked in The Coates he received more than enough pats on the back. He had to warn them that if they hit him to hard they risked giving him internal bleeding and that didn't have a positive prognosis for his health. Walker felt flat; he had no emotion in either direction. It was a strange detached, mechanical feeling, he couldn't discover any enthusiasm for alcohol or the powder offered to him for free. He should be nearly murdered every fucking day if he got offered free Charles, he smiled to himself wryly. Silks nearly started a fight with some bloke from off the estate over money, an old beef, heads turned as their words got increasingly heated. Walker sighed and ambled over and Informed him that another blow to his neck and he could die, so could he leave out the violence for one day!' Silks saw the persuasive side of Walkers argument, relented and offered him a lift home. Walker wanted his daughter, he wanted Shorts. They made enquires and located her quickly, she was just down the road at his moms house.

Silks revved the car and they made the trip to pick her up arriving shortly after at his mother's house.

Walker knocked on the door, his mother opened it to him. Walker looked into her face and raised his hand. "Not now mom, please."

Walker shut the door to the flat behind him, happy to lock the outside world out. "Go and get washed before tea please Shorts . He stood in front of the wall and ushered her away from the 'crime scene'. He surveyed the flat grimly, the wine bottle was still lying discarded on the floor. He smiled sardonically and attempted to hide the blood stains on the wall from Victoria. He went to the kitchen, found a plastic bag and started to collect rubbish. He filled it with the debris from another glorious night out, hoping the activity would clear his mind of

the vision of the knife in her hand and the feeling of it in plunging into his throat. It was more vivid now than when it happened.
He turned and hugged Victoria. A small tear washed out his eye and ran down his cheek , just as it had in the ambulance. He would try to limit the drama for them, he had to for his own sanity.

CHAPTER 20
ABYSS

Days turned into weeks after the stabbing and Walkers mind attempted to come to terms with the latest sequence of events that had further derailed his attempt to integrate back into polite society. He became increasingly withdrawn after the attempt on his life. Making excuses not to go out when Silks called him, content to park himself in front of the television set with a can of cider and Sky Sports for company.

Victoria noticed a change in her dad; he appeared increasingly serious nowadays, his wit and humour were mechanical all previous spontaneity lost. When he did venture out, he would drink faster than ever and become overly aggressive with no valid rationale for his display of machismo. The sympathy he received was driving him insane. Did he have a sign over his head saying, *'loser'*? When he walked down the street did the general public push and nudge each other and point at him as he walked past, whispering about his private life, he felt transparent and vulnerable.

Walkers blooming academic career started to suffer, the few essays he'd submitted received excellent marks and his tutors reinforced previous opinions that he showed great potential in his studies. He didn't want to attend lectures anymore; they'd become hard work and a struggle for him provoking anxiety reactions. One morning he fought his doubts and the negative voices in his head and made the trip to university, walking around the campus attempting to find reserves of courage to attend a lecture.

His breathing quickened and his chest compressed, before he suffered a panic attack, outside the School of Social Studies. His t-shirt became stained with sweat, his brow glistened and exaggerated the cadaver like colour of his complexion. As he sat on a wall to control his breathing the shame poured out of him as his weakness was exposed to a public audience. When he arrived home and shut the door behind him he was relieved to be hidden from the outside world.

Walker pondered over what to do with his future in the long days and short nights mulling over ideas that may lead him to a better life. He remembered a conversation he'd with a tutor who was interested in him because of his passion for the subject and wanted to know what his motivation was to study Psychology. Walker told him that he wanted to help people discover the origins of their emotions and help them understand their thoughts and feeling. The tutor mentioned that Psychiatric Nursing was a good profession, maybe he should research it? Walker had never considered nursing as an option, he associated the profession with hospitals and illness, not troubled people and angst. Walker turned on his computer, logged onto the internet and typed in 'nursing'. There was a specific course for mental health and he had to apply to NMAS to have his application cleared. Walker understood the process because it worked that way to apply for a graduate course. Incoming mail detailed three universities he could choose from: Wolverhampton, Stafford and the University of Central England. He decided to list the U.C.E as his first choice. Birmingham was out of Wolverhampton, he was anonymous there and the change of scenery might focus his attention. When he was in Wolverhampton, the pubs were proving to much of a distraction for him and to get to the School of Nursing he had to pass at least six pubs he knew well and they would talk to him as he walked past. Stafford was carrot crunching country and travel was an issue. Birmingham and Solihull mental health trust was then the biggest in the country and big trusts equalled lots of jobs for when he qualified. Walker knew it wasn't too far away or too difficult to travel to and they had a diverse cultural and social mix that would provide him with a sound foundation for his professional practise. After an hour or two wrestling the decision over in his mind he made a decision, completed the paperwork and posted it off. He knew that a positive attitude would bring an uplift in his mood, he was on the path again and moving forward.

His fingers ripped the envelope open excitedly. It was marked from the University of Central England. Walker scanned the letter quickly and smiled and gave the air a little punch. They were pleased to invite him to attend an open day and meet with course tutors with a view to accepting his application. He got straight on the phone and told Silks, who was pleased that his mate had finally been given some good news for once.

The stabbing worried Silks, as his mate took another quick setback. He knew that Walker had suffered underneath all his displayed bravado and that didn't surprise him at all. Who wouldn't be a bit concerned that they'd just missed death at the hands of another? Especially your

girl and then only a short time after your wife had done one on you!
Bruce, you should leave women well alone, Silks told him over a half
one dark night. They were fucking about with his head, and he was
going through them at an alarming rate. They chatted about it some
more over a pint or two when Silks banned him from seeing any more
women off the estate.

One of his previous conquests, upset that he'd dumped her on
Thursday morning and he was with another girl in The Coates on
Friday evening had started trouble, threatening to shoot the girl he
was with. Silks knew her and knew that she had just come out of jail
and was capable of stupidity and calmed the situation down. He told
Walker he had to end this ruthless playing of the field, he had nearly
ended up dead once, maybe he wouldn't be so lucky next time. Walker
had to agree. His troubles were being exacerbated by the women in his
life, he knew he had to clear his head and focus on real life. Not some
dream that one day he might meet his fairy princess and they would
live happily ever after.

Walker was accepted by the University and they forwarded all the
necessary paperwork to him, detailing course structure, and
requesting his bank details so they could to pay him his bursary. He
neatly completed the enrolment forms and wrote the starting date on
the calendar that hung in the kitchen. He was now a student
Psychiatric Nurse, he had a title that didn't include the words: Mr.
Walker you have been charged with .....

His family were proud of him for showing ambition and starting out on
a good career path, his sister was a general nurse and it was a
respected profession. His parents understood that this was not a
grandiose fantasy as some of his other ideas appeared to be, this was
tangible and achievable. Perhaps their son had finally grown up and
had made the transition into adulthood.

The first three months of the course were academic in their nature and
a foundation into the principles and ethics of modern nursing. Walker
felt confident about the academic side, writing essays had never posed
a problem for him in the past. He was nervous about attending to
direct personal care whilst on a clinical placements and having to clean
up faeces, inject people and provide medical interventions. He crossed
he fingers and hoped he would cope with it all, not that full of
confidence.

When he sat down for lectures, he would sit by himself at the back of the theatre and when the lesson was concluded he would leave quickly without a word to other students, wanting to do his research alone. He didn't want to socialise with the student population he didn't want to answer awkward questions about himself or his past. Questions that would have to be answered if new relationships were to be formed. Walker would respond if he was approached, he would be polite, but that was as far as it would go with him. In between lectures other students would gather in the café to drink coffee and chat, he would watch them at a distance with his face set in stone hoping that his menacing facade would shout at people to leave him alone.

As his studies continued his social life slowly improved. When he was in the mood he could still fool people into believing he was coping with life and his sense of humour could paper over the cracks. Victoria now spent all her weekends with Natalie and in those moments Walker would feel isolated and drink for company, heading off to The Coates, when he'd drunk enough to feel like a man again.

 He was pleased that Natalie was making an effort to be a mother, pleased that Victoria had her mum back in her life, girls need their mother and Victoria needed to feel love off both her parents. Walker's biggest fear was that she would grow up to be like him, with his personality, character flaws and all his weaknesses' despite his efforts to the contrary.

 The fallout from the divorce had been placed behind him and his resentment emanating from Natalie's adultery had receded. Walker still felt the subtle wrench of regret when they met, as she came to collect Victoria or discussed her progress in school and in life.

Nat could not argue with his parenting skills. Walker had done his best, Victoria was well grounded, confident and a bright well mannered young lady. Nat couldn't disagree with the evidence that stood right in front of her and called her, 'mummy'. The only concerns she raised were about his lifestyle and the cleanliness of the flat and Walker couldn't disagree with her about his lifestyle, as the vultures of regret regarding certain incidents circled above him day and night.

It was a Friday evening, Walker was bored and the batteries on his remote control where about to expire as he randomly selected and discarded channels in quick succession. Victoria, bored with her dad's attempts to find a programme that grabbed his attention had taken herself off to her bedroom to read. As he was contemplating the night ahead the phone rang to end the debate. Silks was on the other end of the line demanding that his mate. 'Get his arse out the flat and come and have some fun. The local pub was a having a karaoke night and an eighties disco was thrown into the bargain and his presence was being requested. Walker weighed up his options, opened another can and decided that a night out couldn't do him any harm and shouted out to Victoria. "Come on Shorts we're going on our travels."

He started to run a bath for her and stuck in some bubbles for good measure, she popped her head around the bathroom door and asked. "Where we going Daddy?"

"To trip the light fantastic my daughter."

"Mommy's coming early tomorrow."

"And?"

Victoria looked at him with her hands on her hips giving him 'the look'. He started laughing, the resemblance between her and Natalie was uncanny at times. "Pack you weekend bag, we will have dinner in the pub then you can go to Nanas to sleep. I'll call your mum and arrange it." He picked up the phone and made the necessary arrangements.

Victoria and Walker arrived at The Coates and walked into the bar. Victoria spotted Silks and Auntie Julie sitting down laughing and ran over to them so say hello, accepting a bag of crisps before sitting down on the table with her mates and chatting excitedly. Walker got the round in and brought them over to the table on a tray and handed the drinks out, nodding to those he knew. Silks glanced across at his mate who was already supercharging his first pint, the alcohol relaxing him and lifting his spirits. His mood brightened even further when he saw Flan enter the bar. "You want a glass of hot milk as I'm getting them in mate?"

Flan gave him the finger and Silks laughed as he remembered the night out in Dublin and added little titbits to the story as Walker told their tale to the people who were gathered around. Walker noticed that Flan's sister Siobhan was sitting at one of the tables listening to the story. He was surprised ,as she was not a familiar face in the pub. She was laughing along with the rest and appeared to be enjoying his humour. The girl looked good, her clothes were stylish and a plan was already developing in his mind, further lifting his spirits. He offered the group another drink and looked at Siobhan. "Can I get you a drink?"

She looked back at him and smiled. "Yeah alright then." Walker breathed deeply and went to the bar, he was about to jump in again and spin the wheel of fortune.

They decided to head off to the karaoke night and Siobhan accepted an invite to join them, she sat next to Walker as they made the short trip to his mom's house to drop Victoria off. When they were alone she asked. "Where's Victoria's mom then?"

"With her husband I expect."

"Ok, Victoria lives with you then?"

"Yeah, she has done since her mom had an affair and fucked off."Siobhan looked surprised. "Most men wouldn't do that."

Walker smiled back at her. "I'm not most men."

Silks and Walker were on form for the rest of the night. Silks hugged the microphone and sang. Walker enjoyed a dance as the pub and the regulars shouted and clapped along, enjoying a good night out, amused by their antics of the pair.

Walker felt free and liberated for the first time in as long as he could remembered and wished you could bottle whatever it was and take it home confused as to why tonight he felt so good. Siobhan giggled as he told her stories of his and Silks past glories. Their money making schemes as he passed her over another vodka, whispering in her ear and flirting outrageously. She accepted the drinks and compliments with open hands and flirted right back. The landlord finally called time on the night and the pub slowly empted. As Walker finished his drink and got up ready to leave Siobhan grabbed his arm. "I know the gaffer, let's stay for another drink, he won't mind."

"Ok sounds good, I'm game" Walker didn't want the night to end.

Silks staggered over and put his arms round Walkers shoulders and kissed his mates cheek. "Great night Brucie Boy, fucking fantastic, back on level mate, you coming now, are you ready?"

"I'm hanging on here." Walker inclined his head toward Siobhan.

Silks patted his friend on the shoulder laughing. "Go on son, I'll cover you." He dragged Flan out of the pub with him, leaving them to enjoy the rest of the night without big brother watching them.

Siobhan was as attractive and she was feisty, she was confidant, street smart and Walker was impressed by her.

"Why does he call you Bruce? Your name`s Walker. I don't even know your fucking first name." She broke into howls of laughter at the thought.

"I'm Gary," he offered his hand, formally introducing himself and bowed.

"I'm Siobhan," she offered him her hand and he kissed it. The ladies did seem to love that romantic shit, Walker thought and added."I know who you are."

"You been stalking me then?" Another fit of giggles.

"Yep, and the fact I've just been away with your brother to Ireland."

"Oh God, yeah, that was you lot. You scared him to death." She laughed again.

"You want to come back to mine?" Walker put the offer on the table.

"Yeah, why not. No funny business though, I'm a good girl." Once again Siobhan laughed at her own wit. This amount of dizziness from a girl would normally have annoyed him, however Siobhan was somehow different. Walker was about to jump out of the plane without a parachute.

They spent the rest of the night around Walkers flat chatting and laughing at nothing in particular. They had chemistry and an instant connection, the conversation never becoming strained between them. She worked in the pub they'd just left, so no wonder she knew the gaffer. Walker poked his head and did a good impression Of Homer Simpson. "D'oh!"

"I wouldn't normally wouldn't touch a mate of my brothers , they're, all muscles with small brains, but, but you're different. You're funny and you make me laugh, you're not at all like I imagined you were going to be.

"So you didn't really know who I was then?" Walker faked anger.

"Yes, I know who you are. I've seen you about, you`re Silks best mate, Walker. I've heard the lads in the pub talk. They say you`re good lads who are best left alone. You, (she pointed at Walker and laughed) aren't quite right in the head." Walker smiled back and didn't confirm or deny it, he merely thought, wasn't that the fucking truth, the news gets around.

The sun came up and they both yawned, Siobhan held his hand and spoke gently. "I've got to get back home and get some sleep, I'm on shift at twelve."

"I'll come in the pub later and see you, if that's alright?" Walker's enquiry was polite.

"Yeah, I'd like that." She leaned across and pecked him on the cheek, a cheeky smile on her pretty face.

He arrived home after dropping her off, with that, *'guttural'* feeling in his stomach and a feeling, his search for a girl he liked may just have ended.

Walker opened one eye and stretched, yawning with a smile on his face. He'd slept well and felt refreshed for the first time in weeks. His watch told him it was one, it was time to get dressed and head off to meet Siobhan. He made his way into the kitchen to make a coffee, picking his mobile up on the way through. He had a missed call of Silks and voice mail. He listened to the brief message and returned his call and told him of the plan for the day.

He left the flat and pointed the car in the direction of the pub with Faithless pumping out from the stereo. *'I only smoke weed, when I need to, when I need to get some sleep...'*

Siobhan looked up as he entered the pub and smiled at him, a pint was waiting on the bar before he had reached the stool.

"You alright then?" Siobhan asked.

"Good, you?" Walker thought she looked great.

"Yeah, it's on the house," she said nodding at the pint. Refusing the offered five pound note, moving gracefully to serve another customer.

Walker approved of what he saw. Her hair was well styled in a bob, she was wearing a tailored shirt, with a pair of smart trousers. She had on a little too much make-up, but she had just spent a night on the tiles. She had a nice air about the way she talked with the punters. It was not a chore seeing her, it was a pleasure. She joined him back at the bar when she'd finished serving. "Where's your mate, thought you pair was joined at the hip?" the smile still played across her face.

"He's showing here soon enough, then you get double bubble, what time you finish?"

"Sixish, why what you got planned?" She winked at him and he laughed.

"Play it by ear and buy a cute bit of Irish totty a beer if she's up for it." Walker said.

"I'll phone my mom and see if she will look after Samantha for me." Siobhan replied.

"So I take it you think that you're the Irish girl in question then?"

"I've bought you a pint, now you have to get me one back and I don't drink at work."

"Check mate, you've have a date then Siobhan."
They willed away the next hour, before Silks made his usual grand entry with a broad smile and a hello to everybody in the pub. "Hello you two, good night was it then?" A lecherous smile and innuendo was written all over his face. They smiled back and ignored the implications of his question. Silks nodded to Walker and they made their way over to a table.
They sat with their heads together briefly discussing plans before Walker got up and made his way back to the bar. "Wim chipping now, I'll be back at six to pick you up." She smiled back at him as she was pouring a lager.
They drove round the estate and Silks made his moves placing a Henry in his top pocket. Silks pulled in at The Coates, eager for a toot and a tot. As they walked in Flan was already at the bar reading a paper and sipping at the last of his beer. Walker walked over to him and Silks went to the toilet.
 "Want another beer Flan?" Walker asked.
Flan looked up at him from the sports pages. "Don't hit her or fuck out on her, that's my little sister Walker alright mate? Don't make me look like a prick and don't make me look for you. Is that ok?"
Walker nodded back. "No problem." And ordered three pints.
Silks entered from the toilet, sniffing with a smirk on his face, eager to stir the pot. "Hello Flan, my man, have you met your brother in law then?" He was laughing as he pointing toward Walker.
Flan looked him up down. "Rather him than you, you fucking plastic Jamaican!"
 Silks laughed. "Exactly the racist bollocks I would expect from a plastic Paddy, all racist fucking cunts and Orangemen!"
Walker left them to it and sipped at his strongbow, relieved he had got the meeting over with before he was spotted out and about with Siobhan.
 Silks had found a wedding party for their evening entertainment that was taking place at a pub nearby. Walker picked Siobhan up and told her the plans and she nodded satisfied with the arrangements. There were a few lads off the estate dotted around the reception who looked surprised to see them out together. She stayed over at his flat for the second night in a row and received breakfast in bed for her troubles the next morning.

The next few weeks went like a dream for Walker, he liked Siobhan and the chemistry they shared was undeniable. Siobhan would tell him how weird it was that they had got on so well, so quickly. For a month they set sail on the sea of tranquility before they had their first domestic. It kicked off in The Coates', during an afterhours drink. She was pissed, feisty and didn't want to listen to what he was actually saying and wouldn't take a backward step. Walker was pissed and in the right and wouldn't let it go. She was never in danger of a physical assault, but the row escalated as they started to shout insults at each other. A bloke that tried to intervene nearly got swiped with a pool cue. Walker was bundled out of the back door to save the situation getting any worse.

Declan found out there had been trouble and like his sister didn't stop to listen to the facts and headed off to find Walker. Walker was more pissed off that he had split up with Siobhan than the fact the brother wanted to have a word with him. He got the phone call and agreed to meet Declan at a neutral venue to discuss the situation.

Flan told him that she was a '*head fuck,*' and he didn't like her himself half the time. She was a gobby cow, but she was his sister. If he, Walker wanted their friendship to continue he wouldn't see her again. The last thing Walker needed was a pissed off Paddy on his case and Siobhan was blanking him anyway, pissed off with his attitude and behaviour in the pub. She was adamant he was, a wanker and just like all the rest'. He nodded to Dec and said he could see the sense in what he said, they shook hands over a pint. Walker made some calls and hooked up with an old flame called Lyn, within a week of their break to get his mind off her.

Lyn had just finished attending to Walkers needs on a Sunday morning, when his land line rang, it was four a.m. Not used to early morning calls he made his way to the front room to answer it, worried that there may be a problem with Victoria or his mum. He picked up the receiver. "Yes" Walker was tense and it showed in his voice.

"Hello you Ok?"It was Siobhan, he was surprised, to hear her voice. "Hello you, to what do I owe the honour?" It had been two weeks since they had last spoken, and that was when she screamed at him to. 'fuck off!' Walkers heart started to pump pure adrenalin. Lyn shouted at him from the bedroom, he couldn't make out what she had said. He shouted back at her." Shut the fuck up will you, I'm on the phone here!"

"She is with you then?" Siobhan asked quietly.

"She?" He left the implication floating in the air

"You know who I'm on about, don't fuck me about." Siobhan explained that Declan had told her to forget Walker, that he'd moved on and found himself another 'squeeze'. They blamed each other for their spilt before the mood relaxed and they rode the waves of happy memories.

"Have you missed me Walker?" Walker knew the question was coming.

"You know I have Siobhan." He replied with feeling.

Lyn barged into the room breaking the moment, clearly irritated that Walker was still chatting on the phone. He motioned for her to leave with his hands. The look on his face leaving her in no doubt the bedroom was the safest place for her to be, if she wanted to make a scene.

"Tell your dog to stop barking or I will." Siobhan waded in.

"How's that going to help matters? Look I'll see you at yours later on, at five is that OK with you?"

"That's good, come round the back and get rid of her please."

"Yeah, yeah it's done." He walked into the bedroom and gave Lyn the phone and a fiver. "Call a taxi, I need some sleep." Lyn was gone.

They met at Siobhan's house and talked things through. Walker felt strange parking his car at the back of the house and walking in through the back garden. Siobhan told him they had to keep it quiet they were seeing each other again for a while, because her brother would be on the warpath as well as her mother.

"What the fuck have I done to your mother?" Walker looked blank as he raised his hands in confusion.

"I told her you was on drugs when we kicked off, and you use them all the time."

"What! Why the fuck would you say that for?" He couldn't believe it. Some women had big balls and even bigger mouths!

"You pissed me off Gary. I really liked you and I was hurt with what you said."

"Fuck me Siobhan, would you stab me dog as well as boil the fucking bunny? They both laughed at the image as the ice was broken, all warning signs and flashing red lights in his head ignored. They were in love with each other, it was as simple as that. Love would always find a way to make sense.

Three months passed by, the pressure on sneaking around behind
people's backs was starting to build and it was starting to show on
them both. Walker knew he was breaking a code of conduct and the
realisation that it would backfire on them kept him company at nights
as he grappled with his thoughts, his sleep patterns deteriorated even
further. When he had a pint in The Coates, he had to act like things
were normal, as the hole became blacker. His relationship with Silks
had become stressed. Silks didn't know why his mate was blanking
him, he hadn't told him about Siobhan and the weight of pressure
increased along with the guilt. It had become a strained atmosphere
when Walker entered the pub. Silks would nod at his mate and go
about his business, Walker would stand alone at the bar, his head
starting to melt under the heat. The only thing keeping the world
spinning for him were Victoria and Siobhan.
Siobhan was also starting to crack under the pressure, she'd been to
the doctors to pick up some pills to help her sleep. She told Walker to
be patient, that the dust hadn't settled yet in her mom's house. The
Irish were funny about family, but they would accept the situation in
time. Walker just wanted the situation over, they had been seeing
each other for four months now, managing to fit ten years of strain
into their relationship.
 Worse news followed. Silks now wanted his mate's blood. It had come
to his attention that Walker had tried to kiss Julie some time ago when
Walker was off his head on pills, bottles of vodka, and a few grams of
coke. Walkers world was collapsing around him again, too quickly for a
halt in the slide this time. Siobhan told him that Declan would like a
word with him to, one of the lads had spotted his car parked around
the back of her house during one of his overnight stays and had told
her brother they were back on. Declan had confronted her along with
her mother and now they knew it all. Walkers head was seriously in
turmoil, he knew he should have spoken to Declan about it, he had
wanted to and all the left over's were now being pushed on his plate to
finish.
 The thoughts in his head torpedoed his psyche and he started to drink
with more gusto than ever. The two main players on the estate were
after him, now he was a marked man. He watched them outside Silks
house jumping into their cars, when he was sitting in Siobhan's
bedroom and he knew that he was the topic of their conversation.
Siobhan had missed her period and asked him to come round, he had

missed a confrontation by a minute. She came into the room with the test in her hand and confirmed that it was positive. She was pregnant. They looked at each, sat down on the bed and hugged. There were tears in her eyes as she told him to keep the news quiet, that she didn't know what she wanted to do yet. Walker wanted the child, they should stand up and be counted, he wasn't sure of what they'd actually done wrong, he couldn't understand the situation. The perfect storm was upon them.

Saturday dawned, the nation was enjoying the European Championships and it was England versus Germany, they were playing the hated enemy. Walker sat and pondered his life with a can his hand, on his own in front of the telly. He had decisions to make; he had to sort out this fucking mess for his own head. He made his mind up, picked his keys up and left the flat.

Surprised looks greeted him when he walked into The Coates. Silks was at the fruit machine watching the spinning wheels, he looked up and glanced up at his long time mate as he made his way to the bar. Walker ordered a pint and stood next to him. "Where you watching the game?"

Silks shrugged. "Don't know yet" He'd made the move and broke cover. If he was to get a beating then it would be over and done with. The worry was worse than the bruises and breaks could ever be. They made strained conversation but the beating he expected was not administered, more lads walked in and nodded to him. Walker was not welcomed as before, but the reception was not as bad as he imagined. He thought he would be spat upon, like the pariah he had become in his own mind, the atmosphere gradually relaxed and they made plans for the day. The fight erupted on the car park, feet and fists were flung and insults traded. Silks and Walker had gone to a pub in a nearby area to watch the game and have a chat. Walker was so drunk he couldn't remember half of what he had said and his mate looked surprised when he broke the news that Shorts was going to have a brother.

The locals had taken offence at their loud behaviour and the argument spilled outside.

Walker left the scene more despondent than ever. Nothing had been resolved, the situation was considerably worse if anything. The doors in mind were slowly closing one by one. They last thing she had said to him was to keep his mouth shut and in less than twenty four hours it would be all over the jungle express. Walker knew it wasn't a good state of affairs and waited. The expected phone call didn't take long to materialise.

Siobhan phoned him two days later and shouted hysterically down the line. Declan had been round hers to read her riot act, and how the fuck did he know that she was pregnant?' She never wanted to see him again; she was going to get a termination and he could fuck off!

Walker's mind finally buckled under the weight and he retreated into his own head as he shut out the world. He'd lost all his mates. He had betrayed Silks, the man he loved, the man he called brother.

Siobhan hated him, and didn't want to speak to him. He'd finally managed after all those years of searching to find love again. Found the magic ingredient , despite the scars that Nat had inflicted on his soul and he'd managed to turn it into a living hell. She was going to terminate their child because of his erratic behaviour, his mistakes and poor judgment had just cost a life, his baby's life. What type of a dad was he anyway? He'd ruined Victoria's life with his drinking, drug taking and irresponsible behaviour.

Nat could offer her stability, when all he could offer her was more drama. He'd lost the lot once again and was truly on his own now. The past four years since the break-up had been a nightmare of stress and it was weighing too heavily on his head. He was beneath contempt and he knew the truth. He was a cunt, he was a drunk, he was a junkie, and he was a loser. His fingers were scaring the wall as he slid down the cliff face barely being able to hang on.

Life was painful, he came to his decision.

PART THREE: MIND OVER MATTER.
CHAPTER 21
MADNESS

Walker was aware of the change in his frame of mind. The burden of worry and anxiety that had squatted in his stomach for so long had lifted and a decision concerning his future was firmly established. For the first time in an age he was master of his own destiny. It had taken a few days to assess the situation and formulate a definitive course of action. He had to search his soul when considering his plan, listing all the pros and cons. These decisions were not easy; they had to be considered carefully. However as the fog lifted from his mind and he enjoyed a clarity of vision that had been absent from him for so long, he knew it must be the correct course of action. The plan was straightforward; it was genius in its simplicity. Walker always had a plan.

Morning broke, sun streamed in through the windows waking him, for once he'd slept well. He blinked and focused his mind, briefly trapped in the twilight zone between deep sleep and full consciousness. He rearranged the pillows and enjoyed the cool feel of his bedding. His bed really did feel comfortable today. He stretched and yawned, pondering the day ahead as he checked the clock on the bedside cabinet. It was time he woke up Victoria and attended to their daily routine.

Within minutes he'd made her breakfast and placed a cereal bowl filled with coca-pops on a tray, along with one piece of buttered toast. Shorts liked real butter, he filled a glass with orange juice and walked to her bedroom, breakfast in bed for the short-legered one. She deserved a treat. Since her mom had left her, her whole world had been fucking: *Alice in Wonderland.* He was more efficient than normal (whatever normal constituted) as he placed her freshly laundered clothes on the back of her chair, tutting gently as he switched her computer off. She'd been reviewing that new Encarta CD rom he had bought her. He brushed her hair away from her face as she slept. She looked so peaceful, she deserved some peace in her life as she gently stirred.

"Morning beautiful." Walker said.

"Morning Daddy."

"Your breakfast`s on the desk, your clothes are ready, your bags packed. It a done deal, all you have to do is get ready. D'you think you can manage that please." She nodded her head at him. "Okey Dokey, you have twenty five minutes, then I'm back with the bucket, we clear?" Walker smiled down at his daughter.

"Yes Daddy we're clear." Shorts smiled back up at him.

"Good."

He took Victoria to school and waved her goodbye, blowing her a kiss as she disappeared into the playground. He visited his dad and enquired whether she could stay over at his for the night. His dad asked why? Walker replied he had something on and winked, there was no need to elaborate on his plan. His dad sensed a difference in his son. Walker appeared very calm, not like Gary at all. Perhaps he'd taken control of his life and grown up, his dad didn't have the time to delve any deeper. There was gardening to be attended too.

Walker checked his jeans and felt the notes in his pockets, he had saved forty pounds to apply his plan; it was more than enough money for the job in hand. Baskerville was no longer with them, she'd died of cancer and he missed her as he walked to the shops to pick up his cigarettes. She had always been a good listener and he was aching to talk, to explain, to ventilate. He walked to the off sales and bought a case of cider, a bottle of Smirnoff, a bag of ice and a bottle of lemonade. He was having a party but he was the only guest invited. Walker visited both Lloyd's chemists in the immediate area and decided on extra strength painkillers, before he jumped in his car and paid a call to other chemists that were close by. The pieces of the jigsaw were all in place.

He collected Victoria from school as usual and walked her hand in hand back home to the flat, already a little drunk. He wanted them to spend a couple of minutes alone so he could tell her that he loved her, to let her now he always had and he always would do. She thought it strange; he was not like Daddy, he hadn't been himself since the stabbing. Today he was different and she couldn't put her finger on it and it nagged at her as they jumped in the car to go to his dads. Walker made sure that she had everything she needed for her slumber party.

After he'd dropped her off, he steered the car toward his mum's house and turned up there to tell her the same thing. His family was getting used to his weird and eccentric behaviour, his ambivalent moods and though they thought it strange, it was nothing to worry about. His mum simply wondered, if he'd been drinking again? As she closed the door she took a moment to reflect, before she sat down with her cup of tea, troubled but not knowing exactly why.

Walker was in total control of his thoughts and actions, he was enjoying the power and assertiveness it afforded him. He arrived home, sat down on the sofa, pressed the button on the remote control and Gary Numan appeared on the screen. Walker had decided to watch Numan live at Wembley, a concert he'd scheduled to say farewell to his follower's way back in 1981. It had been a magical occasion for his the legion of fans.

Numan was a compelling presence on stage. The music and the power of his words, in addition to the backdrop of a gigantic rig made it the definitive moment in his career. It was Gary's finest hour. This brought a smile to Walkers face. They were both Gary's; it was both their finest hours and both their farewell concerts ensuring perfect symmetry. Sitting back and relaxing with the music, he drank the last of the cider, lit up a cigarette and opened the vodka and listened to Numan pronounce: *"Tell me of your pain, love it, love it. Show me the new way, love it, love it, it's so unusual. But all I find is a reason to die, a reason to die."*

Walker nodded his head in agreement. The visions about his life added to the nostalgia filling the room. He looked at the wall, there were many pictures of Victoria, a pictorial record of her life. He'd taken down all the pictures of Nat long ago, but the flat still reeked of her presence. There was a picture of him, Silks and Langley sitting at the bar in Dublin, arms around each other, their faces full of smiles. He thought about Nat, about Fe, Siobhan, Silks, the lads and finally Victoria the love of his life. He'd experienced good times; he had lived through bad times, and no one lived for ever.

Walker safely negotiated the child cap on the first bottle and swallowed the first pill, taking a swig of vodka to help him swallow. The peace and tranquility slowly ebbed into his mind, silent tears rolling down his face. They were not tears of regret, they were tears of relief, etched with a tinge of sadness that his life hadn't worked out and his plan had failed. He swallowed the momentary guilt that he was leaving Victoria and rationalised: he was doing her a favour by fading away. He was the black sheep of the family, the one everybody pointed to at family occasions, the old drunk in the corner that told everyone. 'He could have been a contender.' He despised himself for his weakness, his use of drugs and his reliance on alcohol. Once he had been a solid lad, he wasn't anymore. He'd lost his personal war and he deserved to die for his mistakes. He was the jury, he was the judge, he was the executioner. The thoughts flashed through his head in quick succession.

Walker sat back, trying to relax and regain momentum. His heart pumped blood and poisons, the adrenalin flowed around his body, he closed his eyes and tried to stop the pounding that was ricocheting in his heart and his ears. This is why he chose this course of action, to rid himself of the constant torment and pain that life offered him. He lay back on the sofa. It really was very comfortable relaxing his mind, blocking out visions of life, he concentrated on the blackness of space. He opened another bottle carefully placing the pills in his mouth and imbibed more vodka. He got up from the sofa as the video finished, his head felt light and his mouth had a strange coppery taste. For a moment he looked at the blank screen of the telly and a stranger looked back. He needed company for his encore.

Walker remembered that Siobhan had bought him a U2 compilation. That was perfect he thought and laughed ironically at the joke; Irish and from her, the killer of his child. The curtain would go down with Irish music in his ears.

He hit the volume button and pushed away sad memories from his mind. Wiping away the tears before he picked up a pen and started to write, taking more pills and vodka. In the background Bono sang. 'In the name of love:*"Free at last, they asked for your life, they could not take your pride."*

He felt his heart rate slow, the beat was no longer a thud, it was a flutter, the thunder in his ears had stopped, his eyes were growing heavy and a beautiful mist entered his dreams. He closed his eyes and waited, soon he slipped into unconsciousness. It was all over.

Walkers eyes were hazy, his vision blurred. Some cunt was slapping him round the face and telling him to move. Who the fuck was that? Was this heaven? It was not peaceful, there weren't any angels playing harps and sitting on white fluffy clouds. Where was the peace and quiet? Perhaps he was in hell? Could well be, he had done some bad shit in his life. Why the fuck was he on the floor? Who were these fucking people?

"What you taken mate?"

Who was this man? "What?" ....Confused
"What have you taken mate?" The stranger asked again.
"Who the fuck are you?"….. ....Disorientated.
"Tell us what you have taken?" He was aware of more people in the
room, his t-shirt was off and he was bare chested . There was a room
full of people and the electronic buzz of gadgetry.
"Who the fuck are you ordering around? You fucking prick!"…………
Angry.
This was not how the plan was supposed to end up. This was not
heaven; he was not resting in peace. He had a room full of people in
his flat, uninvited gatecrashers that were trespassing. Walker didn't
want to be back in the land of the living and struck out at the
paramedics that were trying to save his life. They struggled with him
briefly, as the reality of the situation hit home in his head. Unable to
control his behaviour they called the police, who were waiting like
Pavlov's Dogs outside, primed and ready in anticipation of some sport.
 Walker couldn't think, his head was lost, on another planet, in an
alternative reality. His memory was stuck like a scratched CD; it would
play a line and then stick again. He slowly tried to unravel the tune in
his head and finally asked. "Who the fuck called you lot?"
The police with the help of the ambulance service managed to remove
him from the flat. It wasn't the first time he had an audience as he was
taken out of his home by the emergency services, he was becoming
better viewing than Eastenders. Walker spat at the men holding his
arms, attempting to fight back and resist. The police advised him to
'calm down,' they didn't want to hurt him, panting as they dragged
him outside to the waiting blue lights. The ambulance drivers were the
target for his anger, it was their fault he was alive. His arms were
hurting and he wanted some peace, he turned to the police officer and
promised to behave himself, the police let him sit on the back of the
ambulance and stood in front of him as a human screen, they were
dressed like extras from the movie 'Robocop'.
They got to close and Walker shouted irritably back at them. "Don't
fucking touch me please, I'm alright!"
Two officers stepped back to give him some space, judging he was
obviously psychotic and that mental illness was a virus they could both
catch. Walker took his opportunity and attacked one of the
paramedics, hitting him his face, he staggered and went down on one
knee. Walker attacked him again, he turned and ran down the street

with Walker in pursuit, followed by the police. It must have looked comical to the viewing public; it was a scene straight out of 'The Keystone Cops'. Walker would have enjoyed the show himself if he wasn't the main actor staring in the production. At the bottom of the road he rugby tackled the paramedic, wrestling him to the ground and getting in a couple of quick punches before the police dived on him and hauled him off.

Walker wasn't going quietly. He continued to fight and the police had to call for further back up to bring the situation under control.

Finally they managed to haul him back to the ambulance ready for his trip to Bedlam. He fought on, spewing out venomous insults, unable to move as they held his arms to his sides in a vice like grip.

Victoria turned the corner into their street. She'd heard the sirens and watched the police cars turning into the street she called home. She had sensed something was wrong with her dad when she was at her granddads and decided to go back at the flat to make sure he was OK. As she heard the distant sirens she intuitively knew they were coming for her dad. Victoria blinked at the sight that greeted her; she saw her dad raving and fighting in the street with an army of uniformed man and ran toward them. "Leave my Daddy alone!" She demanded.

The police stopped, Walker stopped, the sight of a twelve year old girl crying in the street stopping them all in their tracks. Walker's personal battle wasn't completed; he took the opportunity to get in another punch in a futile attempt to escape the ambulance.

 "Daddy stop it!" Victoria held her arms straight down by her side, her hands balled in a fist. He stopped dead and sat down on the back of the ambulance, breathing heavily, taking a moment to look at his daughter as he begged God for forgiveness. This was not meant to be happening, what had gone wrong? He'd arranged for a friend who lived down the road to visit him and pick up some stolen goods, he was meant to find the body. Victoria would be spared all this drama and taken to her mother's to start a fresh life in a better, *family environment,'* to live in a house that didn't experience his endless tragedy. He must have arrived earlier than anticipated and saved Walkers life, Walker didn't thank him his timely intervention.

Armed with renewed vigour he started abusing the emergency services once more and Victoria hit him, the slap echoing around the streets. His anger evaporated as he looked at Victoria's tears with his hands raised in surrender. Walker sat down on the tailboard of the

ambulance and mouthed. "I'm so sorry," he stared sadly into his
daughter's eyes as they shut the doors to the back of the ambulance.
He didn't know what else to say to her.
Four police cars followed the ambulance into Accident and Emergency,
as they admitted him onto the ward.
Walker's behaviour deteriorated again as he tried to go on a second
rampage around the hospital. The police waited with the nursing staff
for an hour until he calmed down, his adrenalin and anger now shot.
They gave him a black (charcoal) substance to drink, which made him
throw up and he kept vomiting long into the night. The retches were
deeper than any feeling he'd ever experienced before. He didn't know
if the tears running down his face were as a result of sadness or the
pressure of the convulsions as his body tried to rid itself of all the
toxins. He finally slipped into a troubled sleep.
 Walker didn't know how long he had been out when he was woken by
a pretty blonde haired lady with a notepad and pen in her hands. In
hospital days and night were one. His brain broke the news: he was
now in the hands of Wolverhampton Psychiatric services.
 Natasha introduced herself to Walker as he lay in a foetal position
under a NHS blanket on a hospital gurney, hypnotised by the lights
above his head. She was a CPN from the Psychiatric Liaison Team who
were based at New Cross Hospital.
Walker stared back up at her unsure of what to say. She was wearing
the uniform of the Psychiatric Nurse, black trousers and a tailed shirt.
He knew he was about to be sectioned under the Mental Health Act,
aware of the process even if he was a first year student nurse only a
few months into his course. Walker wasn't meant to be here today;
maybe fate, destiny or whoever else ran the universe had another plan
in store for him. The anger of being cheated yesterday had vanished,
his suicide attempt had failed and the feeling that he had the power
and control over his life again had evaporated. He was empty and left
with the thought that he couldn't even end his own life properly.
Walker felt naked and vulnerable, finally there wasn't a place left for
him to hide.
Natasha attempted to create small talk with him, he knew she was
endeavouring to generate a dialogue before she explained the way the
service operated and moved on to the text book questions he knew
would follow.

"What had happened that had made him decide to commit suicide?" She discussed his past and what he thought the future held for him. He told her about his history, the feeling of inadequacy that had prompted him to start searching for a way to feel involved and stop the constant fear. He told her about the present and the awful mess he'd created in his life, a mess that had turned his life into a docu-drama without a resolution. Walker found it strangely cathartic to discuss his use of alcohol and drugs with a neutral face, understanding that maybe he needed an outlet to explain his mistakes. An avenue for him to explain the problems he'd created with Nat, Siobhan and Victoria. He wanted an answer for the rationale behind the violence and mood swings that had caused him so much anguish in his life. He wanted redemption and somebody to give him a reason to fight back. What he couldn't speak about was about the future and what direction his life would take, he was alone in a black tunnel with no light in the distance to guide him on his journey.

Natasha continued with her assessment, she paused and asked him. "If he had any intention of hurting himself or anybody else?"

Walker answered honestly. "I don't know, I'm not going to hurt anybody else that's for sure. I don't know what the fuck I'm going to do, it's all such as fucking mess." She pulled the curtains back around him to afford him some privacy and left with a promise that she would return soon. The nurses brought him a hot drink and he sipped at it gratefully. Last night's events and the abuse he'd thrown at them forgotten. The ward sister had told him he was disgrace as he abused anybody in earshot ejecting a torrent of hatred from his mouth. He remembered telling her, to fuck off and did she want some too? He couldn't contain the vomit as another wave of nausea hit him. He buried his head in a receptacle that some kind sole had left for him.

Natasha arrived back and asked him how he felt about spending some time in hospital.

"The nut house?" Walker had finally arrived in, *One Flew Over the Cuckoo's Nest.*

"No," she replied. "A specialist unit that addresses the need for people who are in crisis."

Blah, blah, Walker thought. Spin it how you want. He was about to be admitted onto a psychiatric unit. "What other option do I have? Can I refuse to be admitted?"

"I would advise you to accept the admission. Gary, you have obviously experienced a tough time recently, it couldn't hurt you to have some time out and receive support. You have told me that you might try to harm yourself again. You could be admitted informally, or I could call a doctor and they could admit you under a section of the Mental Health Act."

"If I leave now?"

"You might be arrested over last night's events, or we could detain you under a section two, a twenty eight day period of assessment. If you come in informally you might be out in a day, a week dependant on assessment. Its open ended depending on how you respond to treatment. If you are sectioned it is twenty eight days, no less, before the powers that be decide if you are well enough to return home or consider you require further treatment. You are not psychotic and you have insight, you appear to be very low in mood, probably suffering from clinical depression, accept the help Gary." She looked him in the eyes.

"Admit me then." He knew when he was beaten and resigned himself to his fate.

Walker was transferred from Accident and Emergency to Wrekin House the psychiatric unit located on the main hospital campus, he was able to walk into captivity. The door to the ward shut behind him and clicked, locking him away from the outside world, all he fucking needed now was a straight jacket, he told the humourless nurse as she lead him to his room.

Walker spent most of his time in hospital alone in his room. It had en-suite facilities and a bed but it closely resembled a prison cell, except the door was unlocked, allowing access to the other screaming case studies on the unit. The food they served looked inedible and didn't motivate him to eat, even if he could raise an appetite. The environment was harsh, unwelcoming and didn't encourage him to leave the safety of his new sanctuary.

A place the staff tagged a day room, was populated by people rocking back and forth, talking to themselves and laughing out loud for no apparent reason. The nurses where stern and stood with their backs to the white painted sterile walls, their feet firmly planted on the white linoleum floors. They were not full of smiles as were the nurses that were portrayed on NHS recruitment posters. They walked around the ward in pairs, with panic alarms in full view and keys hanging down from their belts. This was a jail, a lock up for mad people to live in.

On regular occasions an alarm would sound and Walker would listen to the shouts that echoed in the corridors with the sound of running feet. The nurses would tell the patients to move away, go to their rooms and stay there until they were given the all clear. Walker could see the door to the clinic from his bed area, he watched it being opened out of normal medicating hours. Two nurses would leave with a kidney dish covered with a towel or paper, signifying that some poor soul was about to get the *'liquid cosh'*: an intra muscular injection of Acuphase straight into their gluteus maximus. The documentation would reflect that the patient was being *'aggressive'* and *'not responding to approved de-escalation techniques'* so they required *'sedation'*.

On his brief trips out of his room to discover his new environment he would notice some patients staring into space like zombies. They looked drugged up to the eyeballs, they had to be to look like that, Walker thought. Surely these people were overly medicated, how could you assess a patient if he was out of it from the amount of drugs that were prescribed? His questions fell on deaf ears and the nurses told him, it was none of his concern. It reminded him of when he was off his head on heroin.

Walker remembered when he and Bamford were on the back end of another mission and needed a *'pharmaceutical intervention'*. They had called a man that was in the know to sort them out some cocaine. He had landed at the local pub and informed them he had no Charles but he had some brown instead. They could pay half price for the gram and sample it. They stumped up the money and cut it into lines snorting it deeply into their nostrils.

About thirty minutes later both of them felt like shit. The bar stools were glued to their arses and they were afraid to move, both badly needing to go home and lye down. As they made their way unsteadily to Bamfords house, projectile vomit kept them company on the walk. Bamford could hit a lamp post from fully ten feet away. Walker just wanted to lie down on the sofa and sleep. The feeling he was experiencing resembled the come down off a million pills. That was how these people looked, drugged up out their minds; they looked like he had felt on that night, *'fucking overly medicated'*: the drugs turning their minds into mush.

Scheduled key sessions to talk and explore your problems were in short supply on the unit, the nursing teams appeared too busy to have an opportunity to spend one to one time with the patients on the ward, the people the system was supposed to support and care for. Their main concern when they talked to you was, were you taking your medication?

Walker was informed by a severe looking lady brandishing a clip board that they would sit down in the next day or two with each other to go through his care plan. None of the qualified staff made any real attempt to get to know him, to ask how he was and how he felt. The only real contact he experienced was with the ubiquitous nursing assistants. They would make an effort when they spoke to him asking him, how he was, how he was settling in? Was he hungry? Did he want a drink, with a smile on their faces. The nurses were crammed like sardines into the office or patrolling the corridors. While in the office they would write furiously into brown sleeved case files, or look seriously at each other as they talked into the phone. He made a promise to himself that if he did ever qualify he would not be a seat and office jockey. Mental health was about the clients you served, engaging with people and showing an interest in that person.

He'd spent half an hour in three days with his named nurse and he still wasn't sure of her Christian name. The care philosophy was spurious, as the unit didn't provide care; it was a dispensary for psychotropic medication. After five days he was called to a ward round to sit in front of the consultant psychiatrist; the head of the team. The nurses, handed over their progress reports pertaining to his time on the unit. They talked about him and then invited him into the room to listen to their professional evaluation of his presentation and assess his recovery. Fucking psycho-babble and euphemisms constructed by bureaucrats as a language that would confuse clients and demonstrate the lines of demarcation. He was in the system, but his voice appeared lost. They had never once asked him about his feeling and how he felt and now he was supposed to disclose it all again in front of an audience of people he'd never met.

"Do you think you will hurt yourself again?" The psychiatrist looked up over his pad at Walker and finally acknowledged his presence in the room.

"No." lied Walker. "I have had my moment, I want to move on, stop the drugs and carry on with my nursing studies."

The psychiatrist nodded, seemly placated before informing Walker that he had exhibited no signs of a psychotic splinter from reality, he had insight into his illness and it was obvious that he was looking toward the future. They asked him to leave the room again, avidly whispering to each other, before inviting him back into the room to sit in on a meeting that decided his future. The psychiatrist informed him he was being discharged into the community, on the proviso that he had to visit his doctors to schedule follow up care with the local community mental health team. He would personally make the referral. They would take his case and provide ongoing support. Walker was given a letter and told to hand in to his doctor when he presented for his appointment and informed that because he was low in mood he would be given his script weekly to reduce the risk of him overdosing again. Bit of bollocks that, thought Walker. I can walk into the supermarket, a chemist, even the fucking garage and get more than enough shit to end my life, and you're going to give me drugs that could fucking kill me anyway. He would have laughed it was that ridiculous, but perhaps they might have thought he was experiencing, *a psychotic splinter!* With the clothes he was wearing when he was admitted into hospital he walked onto the car park, looked at the skies and headed back home.

"Hello mum you OK?" Walker picked up the phone and called his mom as soon as he arrived back at the flat. He'd felt self conscious about walking back onto the estate and he made the trip with his head down and his eyes locked on the pavement. His heart pounded as the gap to his front door closed. He'd nearly made it, the sweat pouring down his back. He was sure that everybody would be twitching their nets and talking about him, pointing and laughing that the nut job is back in town. Kids would point at him and yell, It's the mad man from down the road. When the door to flat closed behind Walker, he felt the relief wash over him. He blew out and tried to breathe deeply, to regain his composure. He was safe. His flat would provide refuge from the outside world. He needed a safe haven to keep him away from life and the harsh exams that society scheduled. Exams that he had decided to sit and sadly failed. If he didn't engage with the outside world he could not get hurt again, it was simple logic in his mind. The flat looked much as he remembered as he glanced around. He remembered being dragged out of it screaming and ranting. The sweat beaded up on his brow and he felt sick.

Bottles and cans littered the floor discarded and alone. His note, his last will and testament stood on the table untouched and unread. The pill bottles were discarded nearby. His life or death, the effort of thirty four years was encompassed into the radius of a few feet. "Hello Gary, how are you?" His mom answered her phone and broke the sad memory.

"They just let me go; can I stop at yours for a few days please?" The thought of having to deal with everyday tasks was above him. He didn't want to walk to the doctors and then to the pharmacy every week. Through the crowds that knew he was mad, people who would stop and stare and move their children out of his way as he walked past. In case they caught the disease he had.

"Of course you can, I'll pick you up now."

"Can you come when it's dark please?" The streets were quiet and lonely when it was dark, he could escape unnoticed.

He sat down with his mom and explained the situation as best he could. How could you explain to people that you'd wanted to die? You were too scared to go to the shop and wanted to avoid any situation that could cause you to take another overdose because you couldn't cope with it. How could you explain that you're self esteem and confidence were so low you wanted to end your life, unable to deal with the constant rejection and attacks that his mind had received over the last four years. How could you explain that leaving your house and going outside was a terrifying experience? That he felt scared and exposed. That he felt guilty and ashamed at the
trouble he'd created.

His mom informed him that, Victoria had gone to Shrewsbury to live with her mom. The vision brought another round of thoughts that he couldn't cope with. The struggle to bring her up correctly was over and he'd failed at his most important job. She would hate him along with the rest of the world now. He'd failed at that, he'd failed at everything. "How is Shorts?" He had to ask the question. Not really wanting the answer."

Upset and worried Gary, you scared everybody that night, even Nat was worried when she came to pick Victoria up."

He didn't need to hear that, the guilt rushed over him and broke in a tidal wave of sweat and nausea.

"I called her." His mom emphasised the word her. "And told her what she had done to you"

"Who? Siobhan?" Walker didn't need her to say the name; he knew who she was on about. She was simply the last straw the broke the camel's back. He told his mother about the medication and how he didn't want to pick it up. She took the script off him and jumped into her car heading off to the chemists to get it filled. They had prescribed him and anti-depressant for his mood; a hypnotic to help him sleep and a benzodiazepine for his anxiety. He sat alone on the sofa and appraised the wreckage of his life. Where the fuck was he going to go from here?

Walker spent another week at his moms, he didn't want to see his dad, he couldn't look him in the eyes. He picked the phone up on numerous occasions to call Victoria. It always ended up in an aborted call. He couldn't explain what had happened; he couldn't explain that it had seemed like a good idea at the time. He was left with the shame and stigma that was attached to his actions.

The nights were terrible; he would avoid the blackness of sleep and the nightmares he would suffer. At dawn when he was exhausted Walker would finally turn to his medication and take a Zopiclone hoping it would kill his dreams. After talking to his mom they decided that he needed to go home. He had to start to face up to life and fight back. Walker wasn't sure if he was ready for the fight back just yet, but he didn't want the continued looks off his mom and the continued autopsy surrounding his mental health. There was a doctor's appointment coming up, then a consultation with the community team. He had to make a step on the path.

Treading water was not going to help him.

CHAPTER 21
DARKNESS

Walker was nervous when he arrived at the surgery and he was thankful that he didn't have to wait long for his name to be called. He glanced around the large waiting room and found a place on the long built in imitation leather sofa that afforded a semblance of privacy. No one seemed to know him, his pulse rate returned to a 110.

The waiting room was filled with old people and young mothers, their children playing with the few toys that had been donated by generous benefactors. He'd arranged the appointment for eleven, so the morning school rush would be over and the net curtain brigade would be safely inside watching *Trisha* 'with their cups of tea safely in hand. He picked up a magazine and held it as a shield, hoping that prying eyes didn't notice the gleam of sweat that was escaping onto his brow. His thoughts were broken by the receptionist.

"Gary Walker, room two please." Walker stood up and nodded, raised his hands and opened the door to his future.

The doctor looked up as he entered and smiled. "Please take a seat Mr. Walker, what can I do for you this morning?"

Walker handed him the letter, the doctor opened read it, read it again, placed it on his desk and looked at Walker. "You've had a tough time, depression, drug abuse, alcoholism, how do you feel?

Walker sighed did he really have to do this all over again? "Not that great Doctor, but not suicidal anymore." What more could he say?" It had taken all the motivation he could muster to make it this far: his sleep was poor, his mood low, his appetite nonexistent He couldn't concentrate, and he was tearful and experiencing intrusive thoughts.

"Not going to hurt yourself?

"No." The doctor scribbled into his notes.

"Good, I will give you a repeat prescription that you can only fill on a weekly basis for obvious reasons, is that clear?" Walker nodded. He was ill not fucking stupid. "I will make an appointment for you to meet with a CPN: a Community Psychiatric Nurse. Do you understand?" Walker understood that if this man kept fucking patronising him he might well walk out the fucking office. The doctor requested that he make a further appointment for next week so that he could meet with his community nurse for an initial consultation. Walker confirmed that he would prefer that the meeting was held at the surgery. No way were they coming through his door to intrude into his world! That would mean having to tidy up and clean the flat, fuck that, he thought. It was an effort for Walker to move off the sofa let alone start acting like Mr. Sheen around the place.

 The week passed by in a slow journey up a mountain with no summit and he presented for his next scheduled appointment. They had warned him that time and resources were precious and if he didn't turn up they might come to his flat and complete another mental health assessment. Another assessment! How many did they feel he fucking needed? Walker kept his thoughts to himself he didn't want another evaluation into the state of his mental health and he didn't want another spell in hospital.

Walkers flat and existence became a self imposed prison as he retreated further from contact , he didn't go out, he avoided phone calls and knocks at the door. He attended his meeting and answered the same questions over and over again. His answers were now verbatim. His CPN explained he would refer him to alternative services for a further detailed evaluation. This would take a few weeks, maybe a month with the waiting lists the way they were.

Walker's days were taken up with thinking about the past and a constant diet of television and videos to distract him from the present. When it was time to go to the doctors and hand in his repeat prescription he would wash and attend to his hygiene, he didn't see the point at any other time, it wasn't as though Walker had or wanted a busy social agenda. The thought of leaving the flat was painful. He didn't want crowds, they induced panic.

People going about their lives and daily chores; laughing and coping made him feel even more inadequate. Perhaps a beer would give him the courage he needed to cope? Alcohol had always worked for him in the past, he knew he was lying to himself, but the boredom of his existence needed alleviating. Night fell and Walker left the house and jumped in his car to find an off sales where no one knew him; anonymity was a cloak that would protect him from prying eyes that would certainly see deep into his soul and notice that he was psychotic and an alcoholic. Walker completed his mission to the shops and succeeded in finding his goal.

To fetch his beer he had shaved his beard and head and put on some clean clothes, the smell of the others made him retch. The motivation had left him tired, but the craving overcame his exhaustion. It had been a long time since he'd smelt fresh air and he eyed the street suspiciously from his window, standing to one side as not to be seen. Reviewing his appearance into the mirror he decided he looked 'normal' but once again he didn't recognise the stranger standing there looking back at him. He listened at the front door for a moment, there was no sound from outside, the landing was quiet. Panting, he slammed the door behind him, ran down the stairs and made it to his car. The street was still quiet. He could make out a man in the distance walking toward him. With shaking hands he opened the lock, fired the engine and gunned it, unaware he was talking to himself. Half an hour later he, was back at his flat, safe with his goods. He shut the door behind him and locked it. Afraid that it might open and he would be caught guilty in the act of drinking, compromising all the care and efforts he'd been making.

Walker was talking quietly to himself and offering reassurance, hoping to calm himself down. He was home, he was safe and crowds had not chased him with torches and pitchforks. In fact the shop assistant didn't even seem to notice that he was mad. How could she possibly miss it, he queried? As he sat down in his chair, not on the sofa, a semblance of esteem rose In hls throat as the thought that he could survive illuminated his thoughts, people didn't appear to notice how disturbed he really felt.

Walker hypothesised into the future as he opened a can and drank alcohol for the first time in weeks, feeling the familiar confidence rush through his system as he felt 'normal' for the first time in a long time. Walker considered the word, normal. What was a normal person? He should stop using it to describe his appearance and feelings, one persons normality was another's abnormal. He was an individual. Perhaps he should find an alternative adjective to describe himself, one that didn't have a negative undertone.

 The feelings of confidence and optimism didn't last long, after a few cans, the murky thoughts would return and he would make a visit back to the shadow lands. After a few more cans, night would fall in upon his head and he would think over his failures and look inside himself once more. He knew he had to make a plan and make painful decisions to move his life forward. Lying on his sofa all day was not working. Walker picked up a pen and started to construct his own care plan. Firstly he would write to Victoria and explain what had happened; his first step to beat the illness was to get back the thing he missed most. His letters tried to cover up the depth of his pain. He would sit and think before he put pen to paper. Walker would take hours writing them and felt relieved that he could still accomplish small tasks, contented that his words offered him respite for the daily torture of introspective analysis.

 Three weeks went by, three weeks without drugs or alcohol and he managed to pick up the phone and dial the number to Natalie's. Nat answered and put Victoria on the line. He was expecting a confrontation with her and he didn't want to have to cope with that. Harsh words may have broken through his first line of defence and the walls he was carefully constructing. She merely called their daughter and soon he heard her voice on the end of the line. Memories flooded back, he had to breathe and compose himself to get his words out. He told her he loved her, having to cut the call short, when his voice started to break with emotion.

 Walker wrote to Siobhan and Silks to explain what had gone on, he couldn't handle talking to them in person, sure that the conversation would not go well. Siobhan wrote back to him.

It wasn't the kindest letter he 'd ever received and highlighted and exposed his own feeling of self -distain. Walkers fragile recovery compromised, he took more pills and alcohol. This time there would be nobody to find him. Walker woke up two days later, with a memory of broken dreams, covered in vomit. He looked in the mirror and asked aloud. "Was this it?" If he was going to die, pills were obviously not the way. He tried to hang himself but the beams weren't strong enough to take his weight. Pondering about the best way to kill himself made him laugh as he declared to his walls."Fuck this bollocks, if I showed this much effort in living as I am trying to die perhaps I will fucking make it." To die is easy, to live is hard. The fight back for Walker had started. Walker had avoided opening his post. It would only bring further anxiety and another circle of doubt in his mind. He bit the bullet and opened a letter marked U.C.E. The university wanted clarification as to his status after he had missed a complete module. He turned on his computer and wrote them an e-mail detailing the fact that he had experienced, 'personal problems' and could he make an appointment to see someone to discuss his options. Further appointments had now come through the post scheduling a visit to the Addiction Psychiatrist that would help fill his schedule. Walker picked up a pen and noted it on the calendar, hanging above his desk. It wouldn't do to miss and appointment because of a memory lapse.

Filled with determination Walker put on his coat and went out into the daylight. It was the first time he had seen the outside world for two months, he breathed in the fresh air and looked up at the sky, blinking softly and trying to squash his anxiety. Walker lived on take away food delivered to his door since his discharge, the cash he needed was supplied from nocturnal visits to the cash point, cash points you needed a car to get to. His mom would pop round with chips and supplies on a weekly basis and receive an up to date handover into his health, she would stay an hour. Check his cupboards, fuss and tut. Paradoxically it helped him, providing a focal point for his week: a target. The motivation driving him to at least clean the floors, wipe the surfaces and polish on weekly basis. It added to his routine and provided structure. It had been nine weeks since he had been released from hospital and four weeks since his last failed attempt at suicide. It was time to face the outside world.

The expedition to the shop was completed with minimum fuss. He purchased stamps and posted his letter to Victoria. Familiar faces glanced at him as he walked, he nodded, and they nodded back. It wasn't as bad as he imagined it would be. Perhaps that was the answer to his problems, stop imagining how bad it was going to be and actually go out and experience life again. He had always experienced troubled thoughts and feeling but he'd always managed to cope with them.

He picked up the phone and dialled Shrewsbury, calming his shaking hand he talked to Natalie and arranged to see Victoria. He made plans to take her out for lunch and work on their relationship from there. He sat on the sofa after the phone call, drained. Easy tasks were so hard, but they were getting easier.

The anticipation for the day ahead woke him early; he had been dozing on and off all night on the sofa, trying to get a good night's sleep, listening to the news, imaging a halcyon future, all efforts failing. Walker still found it hard to go to bed. The silence brought unwanted images into his minds-eye. It had been years now since he had fluffed up the pillows and felt like he was relaxing in the clouds.

Today was different; today he had something to look forward to. He glanced at his watch, it was half five. It was time to sort out himself out and run a bath and get his clothes ready.

Walker was nervous, this would be the first time he had seen his daughter since the ambulance doors had shut on him and ended that chapter of his life. That's how he would view it; just another chapter in his life. He took his medication as prescribed. The zop's and benzo's had been stopped. They were short term medication and a short term remedy. It was never a good plan to give a substance abuser a dependant forming medication. The diazepam didn't work for Walker as well as beer at curing anxiety anyway. Alcohol still took the nerves away for a few hours. At times he would feel straight headed, however the cider did open up the door to a memory chamber he didn't want to access and he would watch his life unfold like a tragic film before him. Films had happy endings; he crossed his fingers and prayed his life would.

He had stopped listening to Numan; the words were too real for him. He listened to the radio as he made the journey over to Shrewsbury, to Nat's new house. The stack of CD's on the passenger seat were avoided. Any song that bought back a painful memory was hurriedly turned off in an attempt to keep his mood on a level. Songs triggered memories, memories emotions and Walker was still in his infancy regarding this stage in his recovery.

He had stumbled and fell more times than he wanted to remember. Natalie had given him directions to her new house, realising that he was no longer a danger to her or her partner. That spark was extinguished. What was the point he asked himself?

Had violence and being a, 'geezer' ever impressed Nat? An emphatic no was the answer.

That lifestyle had brought about his downfall. The drugs and the violence had provided him with a high at the time but they had left gaping holes in his soul that he had to fill now. He had used them to hide his own insecurities, now he had to stand up a view the planet and the real world without a distorted perception on life.

One step at a time, one day at a time was his mantra Walker had to be realistic, there would be days when he wanted to cry, there would be days when he would feel normal. The balance would return over time. Walker located Natalie's home without a problem. It was a modern semi-detached house on a new estate. He nodded his head in approval; she had done well for herself. Breathing deeply Walker summoned up his scant reserves courage and walked down the path, knocked on the door and hopped from foot to foot while he waited for the door to open. His ex-wife opened the door; she looked older and more serious than he remembered.

"Hello Nat," he tried to sound casual.

"Gary, how are you?" She nodded at her ex-husband. There was no warmth in the question. Fucking mad and beaten he wanted to reply. You started the process four years ago; you put the knife in first. He managed to keep his thoughts to himself and managed a smile that didn't rise to his eyes. "Fine Nat, you?" She nodded her head and turned away.

"Victoria you're dads here."

He heard footsteps and he saw her emerge down the staircase. Walker smiled and looked at his daughter. "Hello Shorty, how the hell are you?"

She smiled back at him "Hello daddy." the ice was broken. Walker turned to Natalie.

"I'm going to take her shopping and buy her some clothes, is that alright?"

"Of course Gary, she is your daughter too." He pushed emerging memories aside when he looked at her. That was bollocks, he told himself. He knew the thoughts emerged from a safe memory, a place where he had been and a time when he felt settled. He wasn't in love with her anymore. He was in love with a memory of a previous life. "Come on then Shorty let's make a move." He didn't want to be in Nat's company anymore.

They made small talk on their drive into Shrewsbury town centre. It was relaxed and the words were not forced. Victoria didn't ask him what had happened on that night. Perhaps she didn't want to be reminded of it. Walker knew those events had to be resolved when it was fresh in both their memories. He broached the subject gently and told her that Daddy was ill, but he was getting better and he would make a full recovery. It would just take time.

It was no different from him having a physical problem, when you required an operation to cure it. Daddy's illness was just in his head, lots of people experienced this particular illness and he would beat it."
She listened to him and took on board what he said before she replied. "Ok then, now can we have burger at McDonalds." She had accepted his reason and they returned seamlessly to a previous level.
He didn't know anybody in Shrewsbury so the paranoia that Wolverhampton induced was reduced and he felt a sense of comfort

as he walked through the intimate streets of the medieval town and the small shopping centre. Anxiety levels came and went but the power of rationalisation helped him in overcoming their symptoms. Walker bought her some new clothes. Victoria wanted the latest in teenage fashions.

 Walker remembered she had just turned thirteen. He had been unconscious at the time, or hoping to swing on a beam. He smiled and ignored the voices in his head. The past was the past. They walked and talked some more, enjoying the winter sunshine.

   They stopped at an old book shop that pricked his interest, a book sat in the window. A novel by Alexandre Dumas: *The Man in The Iron Mask.* He thought momentarily and gestured Shorts to follow him inside. The book was an adventure about a man who had to overcome many hurdles to reach his goal, a man who had suffered a terrible hardship to get where he belonged. An iron mask covering to his face, hiding his real identity from the outside world. Walker bought the book, and he threw in some other books for good measure as she wondered around and took her time in choosing some appropriate material. She still had a veracious appetite for reading.

Over a drink in a small café, Victoria informed him she was making friends at her new school and was still doing well with her studies. His daughter was exhibiting all the fortitude he had been unable to in his childhood. Her strength of character was undeniable.

Maybe his job hadn't been wasted, maybe the lessons he had taught her had not been wasted and this was the end product. He watched as she confidently asked questions of the shop assistants and swallowed tears of pride. She refused his hand as they walked back to the car.

"I'm not a little girl anymore Daddy."

Walker smiled sadly, wasn't that just the truth.

The day was therapeutic for Walker, he felt like he had recaptured a moment in time. However the emptiness closed in on him as he drove home. He missed Victoria terribly and decided to get a beer to fill the void. "Only a couple though," he reassured himself. Just enough to help him sleep to take the edge off his feeling. He continued to whisper quietly to the fictional audience, attempting to reinforce the situation and take the positives out of the day. He had taken a big step and he was on the pathway moving forward.

The beers brought fresh tears, he knew they would. They were tears for the desert of his past, not for the vision of his future. Walker could now discern the difference. The light at the end of the tunnel was minute, but a crack had appeared in the darkness.

Walker scheduled appointments were appearing over the horizon thick and fast providing a focus for his attention. He was expected in Cannock to see his addictions psychiatrist and he had to meet with a counselor from the U.C.E the following week. Psychology had been in touch. informing him that they had received his referral and an appointment would be forwarded to him shortly.

Walker drove into Cannock and found the hospital quickly. He looked at the signs and was directed down linoleum corridors to a depressing waiting room. Finding a seat he viewed the other people sitting around, they looked tired and disinterested. They were addicts, drunks, shoplifters and thieves. All in the same position as him.

He was no different and no better than they; this was what he had become. His name was announced and he stood up and made his way into another consulting room.

A middle aged, well dressed lady looked at him over her glasses. Her hair was tied back in a bun and she invited him to sit down. Briefly she looked into a folder. It was probably his life story, but why ask him, when she had words to read? Her eyes looked up and she started asking him the same questions he'd already answered on myriad occasions. Questions about his past, when had he started taking substances? What he had been on? What was he on now? How long had he been clean? Was he suffering from withdrawal? Was he experiencing perceptual crisis? Perceptual crisis? What the hell was that he asked her!

Walker informed her." No I didn't see pink elephants." He wasn't rattling and he had been clean for about two months. He still drank and that was probably his primary problem. She didn't delve into the reasons that explained how he started using drugs initially. That wasn't her job, and her role was to stop him using drugs inappropriately. She explained. " His alcohol intake was a separate issue from his drugs and that problem would be subsequently addressed by a separate team." She promised to send an urgent referral through to alcohol services.

After making a few more notes, she declared. "Because you are clean and not experiencing physical side effects associated with substance withdrawal she really couldn't offer him a service. It appeared he was making an effort to address his own problems."

Walker frowned when he asked how long would it take for his referral to alcohol services to come through?

She didn't know, it was dependant on the severity of the problem and their case load.

"That doesn't fucking help me, I'm pissed off with telling my story to a host of people sitting around their desks and no fucker wants to help me yet. I've been taking my medication and It's had been a few months since they let me out of the bin and discharged me from hospital and nobody seems bothered. I tried to kill myself for fucks sake! Would it help if I went to the pub, got pissed and glassed some cunt and then took an overdose? Would I get help then?" Walker spoke with a passion he hadn't felt in quite some time.

"That sort of talk and language is frankly counterproductive, do you intend on acting on these thoughts?" She replied coldly.

"So if I glass some twat, that's a risk and you have to address it? But if I tell you I drink and take drugs because of some problems I had in the past, that's a problem that psychology has to deal with? "Walker said.

"In a nutshell yes. I can handover the urgency of the situation, but I can't act outside my professional competency. Unfortunately that's the system." She raised her hands in acquiescence of his frustration.

"What a load of bollocks," he told her with hard eyes and thin lips. "By the time I'm sorted, I would have cured myself." Walker, stood, shook his head and slammed the door on his way out.

On the drive home he realised that he had taken another step forward, the spark of anger had shown passion, an indication that he wanted to get better and he had been assertive in the process. Small steps, one day at a time he told himself.

Walker was getting tired of telling his story to people that made a pretence of listening but then never seemed to want to follow it up, or would pass the responsibility onward. He had to visit Birmingham and meet with the universities counselor and explain his, 'personal problems' to another audience. His appointment with psychology was a month away and he didn't have to meet with his CPN for another two weeks. By then he and nature would have gone a long way to sorting his own head out.

Boredom was becoming a problem as he continued to improve. Walker knew from past experience that he had to find an outlet to fill his day, his past clearly teaching him that when he was bored he would find some way to fuck his life up. He didn't want to drink on a regular basis anymore, aware that it had caused him problems and opened up internal conflicts and depressed him. Alcohol had always been a precursor to his difficulties. The root cause lay in his warped and paranoid thoughts but alcohol was the catalyst that lured him over to the dark side. It would open up a world of paranoia and insecurity to him. He walked into his bedroom and eyed his weights and bench. Perhaps he should get fit he asked himself? Research suggested that if you exercised, it released chemicals into your brain that helped when you were battling depression. Small steps again he told himself. The journey was not about the end, it was about the steps on the pathway to recovery. Walker picked up a dumbbell and started to curl.

His relationship with Victoria had virtually been repaired. He had visited her on a couple of occasions since his first visit over to Shrewsbury to see her. Walker could cope with life around Victoria and his mum, other social situations caused difficulties. His mum wanted to go to the pub and eat lunch occasionally, she thought that it might assist him being out and about. He held his head in his hands and thought of a way he could explain to his mother that he was battling alcohol and drugs and the pub signified all these to him?

When he was sober he felt naked stripped of his armour, vulnerable and scared like the boy that had once been the target of the bullies. The pub was not what he needed at the moment, he had to reintegrate in some other way and though he still did use alcohol to cope with stress occasionally, his reliance on it was being gradually broken.

When the feeling of inadequacy charged through his defence mechanisms he didn't run straight to the bottle anymore. He wrestled with the feeling for as long as possible before he turned to alcohol. Tears would well up as he walked to the shops to buy cider, his brain taunting him and telling him he was a, 'weakling. 'His strides on the way home longer and quicker than they were on the way to the shop, at times he would nearly break into a trot.

He was sure that people would know he was using and that they could see the transparency of his weakness. Walker would drink the first can in record time and the alcohol would slip seamlessly into his system without a ripple to take control.

The weakling that was Gary, the man that was scared to live life would slip away and the real man Walker would take control of the wheel while the bender lasted. He made a pact with himself that he would not drink in the week. He would limit his alcohol use to Saturday nights, that would be his, 'treat' day and then only if he adhered to his own care and exercise regime. The journey back to good health was slow, sometimes it was trench warfare, but he would conquer his demons, fight his battles and win the war.

Today it was the U.C.E's turn to hear his story. These people had to know what had happened, this was work and this was his future. He wasn't sure how deep to go, how much of his story to unveil. If they deemed he was, 'damaged goods,' would they remove him completely from the course instead of simply deferring him? The trip to Birmingham was safely negotiated and Walker used the time to go over the scenario in his head. He parked the car at Occupational Health walked to the imposing Victorian building and pushed a button to announce his arrival.

"Hello can I help you?"

I fucking hope so thought Walker. "Gary Walker, I have an appointment with Ann Morris for eleven."

"Come on up, it's the second floor."

The door clicked and Walker entered. He located reception and booked in, picked up a magazine flicked through the pages without interest and waited. "Gary?" Walker looked up. A woman with a friendly face looked back at him. She was small, neat and smiled at him. In this game he was used to androgynous behaviour. The smile eased his angst and he smiled back at her and answered. "Yes that's me."

"Would you like a drink?"

"Yes please, coffee."

"Sugar?"

"Two thank you"

Ann Morris in her opening gambit had done more for him than Wolverhampton Psychiatric Services and Cannock Addiction Services. Walker didn't relate to his CPN. How could he talk about his weakness to another man when he was a man himself? Silk`s footsteps had left their mark in his mind. The CPN hadn't constructed a rapport. He was overly clinical and aloof. Ann Morris appeared that she was concerned, that she valued his opinion. It was a strange phenomenon that humans form an opinion of a person after an initial seven second contact period. Some people can grow on you, but in a majority of cases if they don't like you at first, they never will. You never get a second chance to make a first impression was a true statement. Walker liked Ann Morris's approach; a smile was always a good way to start a conversation.

She returned quickly with two steaming cups of coffee and handed one to Walker, he tasted it and was pleasantly surprised. With a warm welcome and decent drink he was ready to tell her his story. She beckoned him to follow her as she led them to a comfortable room with two chairs and a single table with various magazines looking up at him. She offered him a seat and Walker sat down facing her.

"Morning, I'm Ann Morris, a psychiatrist working for Birmingham and Solihull Mental Health Trust. I've read your letter Gary, would you like to tell me in your own time what's been going on" In my own time he thought, it could be a long day he hoped she had cleared her diary.

"Where to start," he paused, looked at her and started at the beginning. Ann listened and asked if she could make notes and waited until Walker had given his permission before she continued. Walker didn't elaborate on his childhood relating, 'he had a few problems at school that started him on the road to drugs'.

However he had primarily been a recreational drug user and drinker until times of heavy stress. He explained the problems he had encountered with Nat, Victoria, single parenthood, Fe, Siobhan, the termination, Silks the list went on and he felt responsible for them all. She looked up at him from her notes.

"That's a heavy burden to carry around with you, Gary."

"A man has to accept responsibility for his actions Ann. It's what being a man is all about."

Walker knew the truth, he also knew that hiding under a tidal wave of alcohol and a pile of powder wasn't exactly, *'accepting responsibility'*. He moved on to tell her how he had felt he had betrayed Silks his best friend. The situation with Declan and becoming a hunted animal, the guilt and shame he felt until he finally decided on a way to end the pain. She listened without interruption, allowing him to ventilate with no spurious interruptions enquiring about, *'perceptual crisis'*! She allowed him to exorcise his soul and confront his personal demons. When he had finished and sat back in his chair, she looked at him.

"Quite a life you have had Gary. What do you want from life now?"

"I feel I'm getting better, time away from everything has helped me reflect. Sure I miss my mates and portions of my previous life. I would be lying to you if I said I didn't. Victoria and me are getting on better than I expected, after what I did to her. I have a good relationship with her and she comes down now every week to see me. I want to be a nurse and make her proud of me. Make everybody proud of me for a change. I want it for myself to, as proof that I can come through this and emerge on the other side. I want to finish my course; I can use my experiences to help others." "You don't think the stress of the job and other peoples stories will open up painful memories for you?"

"No, not really. I can step back and remain objective in that sense. Life experiences help the process of empathy and that's what being a nurse all is about. I want to help people, it's that simple. I had a bad time, but I came through it. I know people can recover, that must help when you're talking to a client, being able to understand?"

They passed the ball around for a while until Ann informed him that their time was up.

"I will write to the course director and submit my report detailing some recommendations."

"What recommendations?"

"Simple ones, it's up to the director and the Dean to make a decision based on the evidence.

You have had problems and addressed stress reactions and situations inappropriately."

Walker could feel a sinking sensation. "However I believe that you should be allowed to continue your studies Gary. You have been honest in addressing your issues. You have engaged with mental health and addiction services. You are going to seek help regarding your issues with alcohol. I'm glad you are going to psychology to help you with your thought processes. I will recommend that you have to come here every three months so I can continue to evaluate your appropriateness for the course. If you don't attend, I will pull you off it with no questions is that clear?" Walker nodded and Ann continued. "I want permission to contact other professionals involved in your case for their feedback. You are going to be working with complex clients and I'm sure you want to be a positive influence around them. It will also give you an opportunity to talk to me about the course and how it's progressing and how you are dealing with stressful and complex situations." Ann finished and looked at Walker.

"Thank you. It's a deal." Walker knew it had to be.

"I will ask that you be placed in the September intake, that's six months away. Do you feel that's appropriate?"

"Yes, it gives me a target to work toward."

"Good, we will confirm it by post Gary. I will give you your next appointment now. It will be before you start of the programme, to make sure everything is progressing well. Are you happy with that?"

"Very, thank you."

"You're welcome. But Gary as I can recommend you continue on the course I can recommend that you can be removed. So it's hard work do you understand that?"

"Yes I do." He appreciated her honesty. He knew where he stood, she would help him. If he continued to act like an idiot he was out. Walker needed direction. Ann Morris had provided him with parameters, he could work within them.

Walker's appointment with psychology arrived and he hypothesised regarding the approach they could use with him. He was interested from both perspectives both as a student and a patient. He hoped he could be assertive and debate with the psychologist about the methodology they would employ. He had an idea what would work and what wouldn't; more than that he just hoped they could find a reason for his behaviour and mind set. If they could provide him with answers then he could build from there. All patients needed to know what was wrong with them, in order that a cure and peace of mind could be found.

Walker was no different. He knew that he had suffered a serious depressive episode that much was evident. However he had underlying problems that had plagued his thoughts for years and these thoughts were not just the result of substance abuse or symptoms of depression.

These thoughts had provoked his actions since he was child, he knew that the bullies were a mitigating factor, however he wanted validation to prove that he wasn't mad and his issues were real and not imagined. He told his story again and waited for the light to shine down upon him.

Walker sole form of social interaction, his only outlet was his mother and Victoria, his entire social structure was now based around them. He knew he had to spread his wings in order to flourish and continue with his forward momentum. He discovered an outlet via the internet, when he was surfing online one day and he discovered chat rooms. The world of cyber space appealed to him. You could be anonymous on a computer, the screen protecting your identity and masking your weakness. The web page informed him that he required a screen name; he paused and thought before typing in, *'Jo the Waiter'*. That was the song that was playing on New Year's Eve when he and Nat had decided to conceive Victoria.

The words in the song were a stark reminder of his life. They sang about confused roles and identity, loneliness, drug abuse and mental illness the name seemed apt for him. As he logged on and explored further, he discovered the sad flotsam and jetsam of society. People who were sadder and lonelier than he. He would log on and answer stupid questions like.

"Hello Jo, are you a waiter then?" He would explain that it was just a song and they would either get it or they wouldn't. It was better than some of the idiot names that were used such as: *'Big Boy', 'Gangster man' or 'sexy girl'*. He found some people online that seemed to understand what he said and where he was coming from. They would type back sensible comments and he realised that not all the people that used this medium were weird or eccentric. He started to look forward to their e-mails and online conversations.

Walker started to feel increasingly confident about going out into Wolverhampton, but he still made sure that he had his eyes on. He didn't want to bump into people he had known previously, awkward questions might be asked and he wasn't ready to give answers yet. Small steps one day at a time he repeated to himself. Walkers exercise regime continued to progress, he would spend three hours a day training: one hour on the walking machine, one hour doing free weights and an hour finishing off with press ups and sit ups. It didn't matter how many sit ups he did, he never achieved his dream of a six pack. His shoulders and chest that were already large became defined, his arms showed the results of his efforts. When he finished his work out he would look in the mirror and he had started to like the reflection in the mirror.

Walker was content to attend his psychology and assertion classes they were aiding him to addressing his problems and he could feel the progress that was being made. He had jettisoned anger counselling after two sessions. He was aware about counting to ten and not putting yourself in a situation where you could lose your temper. It didn't help you once you had lost the plot and you were in full battle cry. It was obvious to him that your decision making skills were debilitated and subjective when the red mist descended in front of your eyes. It was not an epiphany to understand that you knew what got on your nerves, so you should distance yourself from stress inducing events. The bloke that took the class was a prick in Walkers opinion. He would never put himself in a situation beyond his control because he advocated avoidance. Walker wanted skills that helped him address life not avoid it. This bloke wanted people to run away. Can you image he thought? All the work to build your self esteem and then you run at the first sign of danger! That would beat at his head quicker than any hammer.

Perhaps he was getting the message wrong but he didn't respond positively to the group and offered his opinion to his psychologist. The assertiveness and anxiety classes helped him; they offered knowledge that was tangible and pertinent. Knowledge that he could explore it further. It was common sense not some theory an idiot relayed verbatim via a text book.

Walker enjoyed his sessions with the psychologist who had advised him to research childhood links into drug related behaviour and return with his own view, review his symptoms and see what he thought. Walker had been too long in the world of, *'paralysis by analysis'* to think this was a viable alternative. He had discussed with the psychologist how he had thought a label for his , *'condition'* would help him explain his behaviour and help him understand his problems, The psychologist explained he already understood enough about his own condition.

 Walker had created his own alter ego. Finding a way to survive in the harsh environments of life, he had generated tools to cope. Unfortunately all the ways he had identified were considered maladaptive. His bullying and need for subsequent acceptance were a defining point in his life. He needed to find another avenue to seek acceptance. His academic success had brought about a natural rise in his confidence and self esteem resulting in an increase in his ability to exert himself and be assertive, join the dots Walker was advised. The violent acts at football and the drug seeking behaviour were ways to submerge his fear of ever being vulnerable again. He had a misconception and this was as a result of an inappropriate adolescent socialisation period. The psychologist could give him alternative mechanisms that might negate his thoughts that caused his destructive behaviour but he needed a voyage of self discovery to find his own personal answers. There was a high possibility that he suffered with a personality disorder, which affected his thoughts, control and impulse processes. This was exacerbated by drinks and drugs which had affected his ability to make rational decisions. He had made progress and had come to terms with his problems and was taking steps to address them.

Walker furnished with his new found knowledge arrived at occupational health for his pre-course evaluation with Ann. She smiled and asked. "How are things going?"

"Very well," he replied. He was engaging with psychology, assertiveness and anti-anxiety classes. His referral from alcohol services had come through and he was looking forward to attending that appointment. He had been clean for months and was feeling positive for the future. He still had bad days, his sleep was poor, but that had been the case for many years now since the breakdown of his marriage.

Walker continued and asked, if she understood the term: *'personality disorder'*. Ann nodded her head she did, but she didn't like labels adding: "Personality disorders couldn't be treated by pharmaceutical intervention and were just the submitted hypothesis of the individual professional, however with all his paranoia, drug abuse, alcohol abuse, forensic difficulties and problems with relationships there had to be something that defined his problem." The rhetoric was the same as used in psychology. Walker explained he required an understanding of his life.

Ann explained, that a label could be counter-productive however it was crucial for him personally to come to terms with his past, she continued. "With your socialisation, drug seeking and forensic behaviour there is a possibility that you do suffer with a personality disorder. Again if I had to make a classification I would say you fitted the profile of borderline with anti-social traits. Borderline can replicate depressive behaviour.

However your breakdown was a direct result of deterioration in your
mental health that can be attributed to external stress factors.
Your alcohol and drug abuse obviously made the situation worse, if
you can control that aspect of your presentation then you should be
able to control your behaviour."
"So I'm not mad then?"
"If you mean psychotic, then no. You have insight and understanding.
You are intelligent Gary, you require focus. I believe that nursing may
well provide you with that focus. You have fulfilled the criteria I was
looking for. You are making an effort to address your needs. You are
clean and your no longer drink to self medicate. I would like you to
totally abstain. But you know the signature that starts you on the road
to problem drinking."
Walker nodded, he understood, he knew when he was on the beer it
was because he was unhappy and wanted to block things out. His
relief was audible in the room. He got up from his chair and ignored his
instinct ho hug Ann, instead he smiled polity and offered his hand as a
gesture of thanks. "Thank you Ann I appreciate your candour."
 She looked up smiled and accepted it, nodding back at him.
 Walker had found an answer, for years he had been questioning his
mental health. He had been worried that he had a serious mental
illness that could see him locked away in an asylum for years.
Electrodes glued on to his temples, strapped to bed, barking like a
rabid dog. Yes he had serious issues, but they were not unique, others
suffered with the same diagnosis as him and managed to live fulfilling
lives. As he aimed toward Wolverhampton he felt like a door in his
mind had been closed. The long hours lying awake only the dreadful
ring of his inner monologue for company. The awful feeling of
inadequacy when he skulked to the shop to buy beer, his own voice his
biggest detractor.
Only Walker really knew the depths of his sorrow. He was the only
man that understood the schism that his soul had suffered. He had
always had his own finger on the red button marked, 'self-destruct,
god knows he had pushed in enough times. He had been happier to
sink into oblivion than to take responsibility.
That was the easy way out. Blame was a game, not reality. You could
always point the finger and accuse life and circumstances of affecting
your destiny, your future. The sweat stains on his sofa were clear
testimony to his reality, the scars on his arm a topography to his

determination to abstain from life. His rehabilitation was nearly completed. He was very close to stepping out in company again. His exile was coming to an end.

CHAPTER 21
RECOVERY

Walker laughed sarcastically to himself as he thought, if he had been sponsored for all the visits he had made to competing professionals over the last few months for his ongoing therapy he would surely have saved the rainforests by now! He was preparing for the last dissection into his past with a trip to the Staffordshire Alcohol Advisory Service. "Only one more to go," he told the mirror his tone alive with relief. In the long months since his breakdown, he had managed to control if not beat his lust for alcohol.

He no longer ran straight for the bottle if a stressful situation arose, he would make an effort to sit down and try to work through the problem with a level head and not through the haze of alcohol. He had taken onboard what people had advised him, to put structure in his day and made a plan, using his time constructively. Trying to find other ways to entertain himself other than getting of his tits.

Each day he would write down his schedule and tick off his chores one by one as he completed them, the highlight being when he spoke to Victoria every night, over the phone and asked her about her day at school. Nat could teach her many things but her academic future was still his responsibility. Walker knew he had travelled a long distance in the intervening nine months since his self imposed banishment and discharge from hospital.

Nine months of exile, it wasn't a long time in the bigger scheme of things. He looked fit and healthy, the dark eyes were gone and the blue eyes that looked back at him where his and no longer that of a stranger. Stafford was the last port of call for him, maybe the last piece in his personal jigsaw, he certainly hoped so aware that his recovery had to take years and not months. It had to last him the rest of his life for it to work. He had to introduce control, when he was out of his depth he drowned, the math wasn't hard.

Walker wasn't sure what service they could offer him, a lot had passed through his mind since his suicide attempt and he had developed a toughness and pragmatic attitude that he thought was previously beyond him. His thoughts were mainly his now. He was trying to leave his insecurities outside his front door along with his trainers. His thoughts weren't clouded by a daily assault of chemicals. The blur they created lifted the haze and fog of war that his mind had created disappearing. As he left the house he hoped they had the key to finally lock Pandora's Box.

Walker drove into Stafford, parked and located the building after asking a lady who was out doing her shopping. He didn't feel weak and transparent any longer, his walk was that of a man, not a robot. The alcohol services was located in a grubby building in-between a flower shop and a butchers. You could get your girl some meat and some flowers by way of apology when you had fucked up on the drink. He shook his head this was no time to introduce negative thoughts.

The butcher had some good deals; perhaps a thick sirloin would be a nice way to end the day.

The service was located in a ramshackle part of the town centre, hidden away down a side street, obviously they had to be careful with their budget he thought as he entered and introduced himself to the receptionist and was subsequently offered a seat in reception. He looked around the room, stained walls with the mandatory posters pinned up in abundance informing people of the perils of alcohol abuse or covering the neglect of the building.

Papering over cracks, was that a euphemism? Walker waited patiently before being called and shown to a room with two sofas, a dirty carpet and awful green floral wallpaper. "Fuck me sack the decorators," Walker said under his breath. He viewed the counsellor who obviously shopped at, 'stereotypes are us' and dressed accordingly. He was re-splendid in a ridiculous green jumper with blend ed into the wall paper, only his tweed elbow patches made him stand out. He had chosen to match his bright ensemble with brown cords and suede hush puppies.

Give him a chance, he may dress like a cunt but perhaps he talked sense. Walker crossed his fingers and hoped for the best.

There were two of them sitting down facing him, pens and pads at the ready earnest looks upon their faces. His assistant was dressed entirely in black with a face full of piercing, and she forced a smile as he introduced himself. Fuck me" he thought I'm in a room with, 'Marcy the mortician' and 'Tim nice but dim' but at least my sense of humour is returning. Walker fought the feeling that this was a waste of his fucking time.

During his endless rounds of meeting and appointments with a plethora of health professionals, who had advocated this method, that

intervention and the other strategy, only two had really impressed
him, their words having a resonance: Ann Morris and his psychologist.
They had shown interest, knowledge and compassion in the story that
he had to tell. They had taken time to listen to him, before they started
imparting advice and offering guidance on how to start growing as a
person. It appeared they realised he was an adult and had lived, so
they didn't treat him as a child and make him feel patronised. Walker
lamented that the many people he had seen, appeared more
interested in their professional persona than in actually helping him.
They seemed to be more concerned in their professional status and
appearance, than the value of the advice they professed would help.
Unfortunately in his opinion, they were not there for the benefit of the
clients who turned up with reserves of courage to relate accounts of
abuse and reasons for their emotional distress.
They used their position as a social platform, a vehicle to impress there
liberal friends, boasting freely about. "How they helped the poor and
marginalised classes and made a difference in society. "Their hypocrisy
and genre was easy to spot as they sat and drank designer coffee from
Starbucks and read the Guardian with a furrowed brow concerned
about climate change and the demise of the indigenous tribes that
lived In the Amazon Basln.
When they arrived home they would drink a nice Sancerre and dine on
chicken in a white wine sauce, before adjourning to the living room to
further discuss world events and the rain forest.
Walker was aware of the negative processes involved in typing and
labeling, but his experience at the hands of psychiatric services had not
been a positive one and he was talking from personal experience as a
man that had been to numerous services and had been batted back
and forth like a tennis ball. They wanted kudos for doing a job that was
a calling, not a career move and that shouldn't include demeaning the
clients that they engaged with.
He would rather use a service that employed people who had life
experience rather than careerists who had gained an 'A' in their
written examinations.
Laurence finally introduced himself and Emily, who sat with a fixed
smile on her face.
Walker was tempted to ask her. "What the fucking joke was?"
Laurence looked insincere as he asked the requisite questions: past
and present alcohol usage, stress triggers, with no enthusiasm or

warmth. It was standard material, they were reading the blueprints from the manual. With their script completed they sat and congratulated one another on yet another stellar performance. Walker was finding the same line of questioning invasive and at times offensive. He had told his story a few times to a few people over the last year.

Where were Laurence and Emily when he sat sobbing on the sofa and wrote his suicide note? Where were they when he lost everything? Not fucking there that was for sure.

Walker asked them. "What should I do when the craving hits me and I wipe away the tears as I walk to the shop to buy the magic liquid that erases my painful memories, and I experience all kinds of unhappy felling? Purchasing shopping I don't need to do, so the lady on the till wouldn't think I'm a degenerate drunk, trying hard to cover my addiction like behaviour; the feeling of worthlessness that wells up when I take my first drink."

Could they explain that to him?" He continued his verbal assault. "What did they think about the premise that, he didn't drink for fun but because he needed alcohol to repair the damage that life had caused his fragile psyche."

Could they, please explain to him, the feeling of power, alcohol gave him as his personality changed, before he crashed down on the rocks below him and wanted to die? Could they put it into fucking context for him why he had been so weak? Why had he been chosen to suffer? Knowing that he was taking a step backwoods but unable to stop the thought and need processes that made him drink." Walker sat back, fully aware that these questions could not be answered but happy he had got it all off his chest.

Laurence pondered over the questions that had dropped onto his lap, he leaned forward and spoke with a voice that exhibited little confidence. "That's a personal choice, but that you have to fall back at times to recover."

Walker interrupted him. "fallback? Wasn't that regressive? Didn't that signify a step backwards? Wasn't that negative?" He knew he was being difficult but he was enjoying flexing his own muscles.

Laurence continued to stumble over his words a little. "He meant that appropriate coping mechanisms should be utilised."

"If they don't work?" Walker enquired.

"Explore alternative avenues, "Laurence imparted some more ground breaking advice.

Walker could have punched him right on the nose and watched the blood spurt up the walls. Fucking prick, he had no understanding, he just quoted the manual. Yes he was making the right sounds but show some fucking empathy for the bloke sitting in front of you. Listen and try to understand before you quote the addiction and social model. Walker's internal monologue was drowning out the insipid claptrap that was intended for his ears. Walker informed them that, 'he had formulated his own care plan.

He exercised to release natural endorphins to improve his mental health and self esteem and to add an alternative 'coping strategy' to his growing portfolio of them. His drinking was down to one day per week. He didn't self medicate with alcohol when stressed anymore. He knew the dangers both to his mental health and physical health; he knew the effect that alcohol had on the central nervous system and the physical damage it caused. He was aware because he had damaged his liver and kidneys with his alcoholic behaviour and suicide attempts. What service could they offer him? His drinking was still a problem he used alcohol as a motivational tool, for fucks sake, he told them. What could they do for him when the craving started?'

"Have you considered AA?" Laurence countered.

"Fuck that twelve steps bollocks and higher power bullshit." Walker snapped back.

"The idea of a sponsor might help you though, as a support network. However you had to be in the service to be allocated one unfortunately. Your drinking appears under control so you don't qualify for detox and rehabilitation."

"I don't want or fucking need that anyway. More time on an acute unit and then into the country for six months before you dump me back kicking and screaming into society?"

Walker wanted someone that would stop him drinking when he was hurt and fucked up in the head. Walker knew that person had to be him. He had to be his own sponsor and his own counsellor. Laurence continued. "You're doing well; I'm not sure what more we can do for you, you appear savvy and on top of the problem. If you want another appointment you can book at reception."

Walker thanked him for all his, *'help'* and left. His anger and frustration and his own failure had found a target. His time in therapy was over. It was time to step back into the sunlight.

Walker packed his bag with all the trapping of university life, leaving nothing to chance: A4 pads, rulers, ring folders, plastic pockets, black and red pens where checked off as he placed them carefully in his new bag purchased specifically for his trip through university. This was his future and he was ready to meet the challenge. The last year had taught him discipline and he would use the experience to flourish at, *'school'*. He turned on the radio and listened to the irreverent chat on the morning breakfast show, enjoying the banter that distracted him from nervous thoughts. He checked the rear view mirror as he pulled out and left for *'work'*.

The drive over to Birmingham was uneventful and Walker arrived early for university, he quickly located a free parking place, locked his doors, hitched his bag round his shoulder and made his way to the School Of Nursing. As he arrived in the lobby he looked around remembering it from before and closed his eyes and breathed. He pushed open a door and found his group`s notice board and weekly timetable. His fingers danced over it before he found the location of his first lecture.

Walker did some reconnaissance around the building to get his bearing and found the room. He knew that if you were prepared it reduced anxiety. With time to kill he made his way to the canteen and viewed the options on the board before he decided to try a cappuccino, that made the boast it was, *'freshly brewed'*. He tasted it and paid, thanking the lady at the till. He stopped and looked around the room, even though it was still early there were students sitting and chatting in little cliques.

He could tell the new intake from the third years. It was simple: the way they moved, the way they sat, it was all about confidence in his eyes. Time moved on transparently and Walker would let it carry him past the finishing line. He walked outside and lit a cigarette and drank the rest off his coffee before he headed off to start his future in room 101.

Room 101 was a traditional lecture theatre. The seats were banked steeply and were arranged in an ark formation. Walker was reminded of terraced ends that were situated behind the goals at many football grounds up and down the country.

Ends that he had once stood on with confidence and for a brief moment he was transported back in time.

There was one other student in the room, who was sitting alone and arranging folders and pens into position and then starting the process all over again, a sure sign of nervous tension,

Walker knew the signs.

He walked up the steps and sat in front of the lad turning to offer his hand. "Morning, I'm Walker, your first day then?

"Morning." The man with the glasses and neatly cut hair smiled back." I'm Rich, pleased to meet you. Can you tell it's my first day then? Fuck me I'm shitting bricks."

Rich shook the offered hand, Walker could feel the sweat on his palm. "Nice to meet you Rich. It's not rocket science you know. It's your first day mate. Unless I'm in the wrong room and the numbers on that door are a foot high." Walker nodded toward the Exit.

Rich looked to where Walker was indicating and laughed. "Yeah it's too hard to miss!"

"You mental health Rich?"

"No, I'm doing adult."

"Fucking adult, all that shit and bollocks with ill people in hospital?"

"That's right yeah." Richard laughed again. "I am going to be a nurse that's the territory."

"Rather you than me mate, sort out the mind and the body will follow, without shitting and bleeding all over you." Walker noticed he didn't have a local accent. "You're not local then?"

"No I just moved down from Leicester with my girlfriend, she is from Sandwell"

"You like football?" Walker was about to go on about a past life and his love of a Saturday afternoon.

"Yeah but I prefer rugby, the tigers, union."

"I watch the five nations, it's good that." Football could wait for another day.

Walker had wanted to fit in this time and not sit at the back on his own and play Hannibal Lector. He was pleased that he started University life again and the last year was behind him. Within an hour he had found a study partner, as well as an adult to talk to, away from the computer screen. It was amazing what you achieve with a positive attitude His recovery was nearly complete.

As the course programme continued, Walker and Rich added three others to their small study firm. A lad from Birmingham called Colin who was boring and organised and two girls; Rachel a pretty redhead from Redditch and Annette a plump former hairdresser from Wolverhampton.

One day the pair of them had been sitting behind Walker in a riveting lecture about personal development when he felt and a hand on his shoulder and looked around. A girl smiled at him and asked if he was from Wolves because of his distinctive accent, they got chatting and Walker found out she lived on the same estate as Silks, but didn't drink in *'The Coats'* because of its, *'colourful reputation'*. Walker liked Rich and the girls and felt comfortable in their presence, he suffered Colin. Colin and Annette took their studying very seriously and spent long periods in the library doing research for essays that weren't that taxing. This was foundation, he would tell them and they weren't even in branch specific yet, a bemused look on his face. Annette had informed the rest that if he had drunk in, *'the Coates'* he was rough because that place was full of criminal types. Walker would laugh and tell her he didn't frequent, *'dens of inequity'* anymore. With his looks and language you didn't have to be Sherlock to come to the conclusion he had a past.

They arranged a night out starting in the student union and them moving onto Broad Street to take in a couple of clubs and invited Walker to join them. He politely refused, using Victoria as the rationale behind his decision making. These were nice people, they were civilians not the type he would chose to drink with normally. If he got the fever for the flavour what the fuck would they think of him? He had started with a clean slate it was best to leave it that way, he concluded.

Walker started to pick Annette up in the morning to give her a lift into university. Walker enjoyed her company and they would talk on the way in. Walker did disclose some snippets from his past. He did drink and had done drugs but he didn't reveal the extent of his problem to her. She was off the estate and knew some of the people he mentioned in passing, he liked the fact that she was grounded and understood what he was talking about and the intricacies of life living where she did. He laughed when she told him that Siobhan had used to pick on her when they were on the bus going to school.

Walker turned down the stereo and reassured her. "She is short sighted, so no worries Net, you're studying to be a nurse, she will amount to fuck all, believe me."

Walker enjoyed academic life and completing his essays, deriving pleasure when he would read the finished article before he submitted them. The first module was coming to an end and the first round on exams and assignments were due. Walker was relaxed and confidant and did very little preparation for any subject. Annette worked like a beaver and would study for hours. She didn't have Walkers natural flair, but her work ethic was second to none.

When the results were posted and released, throngs of anxious students would congregate and push each other to view their results. Walker wasn't arsed, he would sit down smoke a cigarette, wait for the herd to dispense before finding out what mark he had been awarded. He passed them all with no drama. He hugged Annette when he saw her brandishing her results and skipping up and down on the steps outside the faculty office.

She deserved everything she got with her hard work and dedication, she beat him in two out of six subjects they had sat together. Not bad for a girl who communicated the fact she was, 'thick'. She was only a small percentile away from his marks in Psychology and Sociology which surprised him. "Fair play Netty," he told her with a smile and without being arrogant,

He was happy that all her sweat and tears had paid off. They decided to celebrate in the union. Walker again excused himself. He was enjoying the course and wanted to avoid any complications. His first placement was just around the corner they were finally going to let him loose on patients.

His personal time remained quiet. His trips to University had cured his boredom and provided him with adult company and a social outlet if he chose to use it. His home life had become a mill pond. Victoria visited every weekend and they would relax on the sofa watch films, discuss her studies and eat pizza. He would show her his essays and ask for her feedback. He handed a piece over that detailed the: 'Transposal of Psychology onto Modern Nursing Practise'. She looked at it and tutted, got up shook her hair which was now a mane rather than the neat bob she used to support. She walked over to the desk that had managed to survive every incident that had occurred in his front room. Rummaged round in a drawer and held up a red pen triumphantly. Victoria had a grasp for English language and would punctuate his work for him and tut at obvious grammatical errors. "You're their and there's wrong. There is a difference between to and too. Why is there a comma there? It should be a full stop." She looked across at Walker who puffed out his cheeks.

"Change it then." He looked across at her. "What, you want a medal?"

"No, you to learn."

"Learn!" Walker laughed. "I've got an A level in bloody English!"

"The examiners must have been having a day off."

"It was continual assessment actually, good work over a long period." Victoria pulled a disbelieving face. "Where you drunk at the time or where they?" Walker laughed. "Don't get lippy girl." He pointed his finger at her and laughed again. "Go on I dare you, I double dare you." He pulled out a pizza menu. "Do something useful; read this and order food I'm hungry."

Walker couldn't argue with that logic. Her grades at school remained excellent, despite the distractions that teenage years offered girls, such as mates, makeup, boys and rubbish music that that they had to play at 100 decibels. She listened to Eminem and told Walker. What a great song writer he was. He shouted at her to, turn it down. Today's music was rubbish pre-processed and packaged. It wasn't a patch on the artists that performed in his day. Walker had finally turned into his dad.

Walker still chatted to people on the Internet and in particular one girl called Monica. They had become friends during a chat line debate on psychology and he was impressed with her intelligence and fluidity of thought and had started to e-mail her. She owned her own business, providing a secure and nurturing environment for pets when their owners were away on holiday and additionally providing security for their properties and ensuring peace of mind.

This line of business left her house bound for days at a time. The contract (she had written) stipulated that the sitters' that worked for her had to be in the property for a minimum of twenty hours a day. So she had to get her social fix via the net too. She had little spare time, as she was just starting out in the business world and was driven to succeed. Walker learned that she had achieved a first class degree in psychology from Wolverhampton University and this added to his curiosity and interest in her.

One day when they were talking on line and he had asked her if he could call her? So they could communicate as, 'normal' people do. Walker tutted there was that word normal again. After a modicum of persuasion she had agreed and they had been talking on the phone as friends ever since. He weighed up the options and debated whether he should meet her or not. He had talked to her about his thoughts and his life and didn't feel reticent about disclosing his vulnerability to her. Perhaps it was the anonymity that helped him talk frankly about his past. It was a cathartic exchange for both of them. He had found a psychologist, and she had found a nurse.

Monica had issues she needed to discuss. She wanted to disclose them to him. Slowly her confidence and trust in him increased .Walker would listen without judgment and pass over snippets of advice. Walker found her: intelligent, sharp and witty. Walker asked her to describe herself and she had told him that she had plenty of male attention in the past but was no longer interested in the cattle market of the dating scene. Smart girl, decent personality face like a battered cod was probably closer to the truth he thought. They had been talking for some months now and he decided that he wanted to meet her in person so he broached the subject and she agreed straight away.

 "Yes the time was right, she was in Wolverhampton on business on Friday, was he free in the morning?"

 Walker checked his schedule, he had a diary now and he chuckled as he reflected that not so long ago he would chat with a call centre operative to break the monotony of his life.

"Fridays good," Walker said and crossed out his lecture concerning tissue viability. She would land at his at ten. "I'll look forward to it," Walker said.

Walker was up early on Friday morning. He went round the flat sniffing to detect any stale ordure's and wasn't impressed with the smell. He searched in the kitchen and found some air fresheners in the cupboard that boasted it could turn any room into a country meadow.

Go on then give it a try. He emptied the canister into the air and sniffed again, deciding he couldn't discern any wild roses but it did smell better than before and headed off into the bedroom to get changed. Before she arrived he inspected the flat one more time and nodded his head satisfied. He opened the fridge and inspected the contents. The milk was still in date and fresh, he had juice and other refreshments.

Bored, he sat down switched on his desk top and checked his e-mail to see if the world loved him this morning. His box was full of spam. Some company was asking him if he wanted to improve his sexual performance. Walker felt the summer meadows could do that for him well enough as he sniffed the air again and thought that he didn't require a penis developer and switched off his computer.

The door knocked at a couple of minutes before ten. A gentle tap, not the thud like some folks used.

They sounded like coppers, the heavy handed idiots. All noise and bloody drama just to get some attention. Monica was on time; he turned off the T.V and made his way to the door making out her silhouette through the glass. She didn't appear to have humps and two heads. He opened the door and smiled.

Monica was small with blonde hair cut in a fashionable bob, she was attractive and pear shaped. She did have a big arse and chunky legs, but her face was easy on the eye.

Smiling he formally introduced himself. "Morning, how's you? I've left my axe in the torture chamber, you do hear some weird shit about people you meet over the net."

She smiled back. "You got a big chopper then?" Walker went red, her eyes never wavered, full of confidence. "You going to invite me then? It's taken four months to get me here and now you're going to leave me outside."

Walker stepped back with a smile, he was amused. "Sorry."

"I should bloody think so to." Monica Gillard entered with a flourish.

The next hour went as their phone calls had and Walker sat on his chair relieved with the way things were progressing. She laughed when he cracked a one liner, and listened when he spoke. She liked his coffee and even mentioned that the stains on the cup added body and flavour. Walker got the joke and invited her back for dinner. She agreed without pause.

They arranged a date for five days time. Before she left he insisted that she inspected the kitchen to prove he did wash up. Walker had cleaned the kitchen and was proud of his efforts, as he leaned on the kitchen surface Monica inspected more cups.

Most of the girls, that come back don't care about the state of the cups, I don't offer them a coffee, you see I have had worse pigs than you here." Walker said. He didn't mean it like it sounded and immediately realised his error and stuttered. "I mean…. his face turning red."

"That………"

Monica took pity and decided to give him a hand out of the hole he was quickly digging for himself. "That the other girls were pigs and didn't appreciate the surrounding or your smooth talk and chat up lines. Don't worry, I've dated men that were more Neanderthal looking than you! "She stood with her hands on hips and smiled back at him. Walker was impressed with her lines and laughed. "Yeah ok point taken. You remember 'Pinky and Perky' the puppet pigs that were on telly a while ago?"

Where was he going with this pig thing? She thought I know I'm not a size zero! Monica managed to hide any misgiving behind a hazy smile and answered. "Vaguely." Beginning to look confused by his train of thought.

"We have nicknames now, you can be Pinky, and I'll be Perky. Sorted?" She continued to smile and nodded at him. "If you like that sort of thing, you've had bloody worse pigs than me here indeed!"

Monica had to leave to visit with a potential client. Walker sat down and reflected on their meeting. He was interested in her. She had made a good impression and he was looking forward to cooking her dinner. Walker decided to go to his mums on the afternoon. She had cable installed and he wanted to relax and watch a film. As he was now experiencing life again he didn't relish spending all his time in the flat on his own. In the dark days of his depression the flat had provided sanctuary, but it also had become a prison and an isolation cell for him. It was full of memories some good, some not so good. He had spent fourteen years there, if the walls could speak they would have some stories to tell.

On the drive to his mums he had to pass nearby to where Silks lived. He had pondered whether to call him or not, a few times over the last few weeks as he continued to feel his confidence grow. He missed his mate and the bond they had once shared. He was humming to a song on the radio when he spotted a familiar car in the distance, as it got closer he saw a familiar face sitting behind the wheel. They looked at each other as their cars passed. When he arrived at his mums he paced around the living room for twenty

minutes, trying to form the words of what he would say in his mind. He wanted Silks to absolve him. That was the final piece of his puzzle.
 He found Silk`s number in his mobile and hoped that it hadn't changed over the last year.
The phone rang twice, and then Walker heard a familiar voice answer."Hello."
"Hello Silks, how are you mate?"
"Bruce?" Walker could hear the question in his voice.
"Yes mate it's me."
"Fuck me you`re still alive then?"
"Yes, I'm still here, still about," Walker was tense. He didn't know what reaction his call would have on Silks.
"Ok then." Walker read between the lines and translated his answer as. 'What you want me to do? Fucking applaud you!'
"What you up to?" Walker asked.
"Fuck all, having some food round Jules."
"Fancy a pint?" Walker asked.
"When?" Walker remembered when he had first met Silks and how hard it had been to get him to bloody talk. He hadn't changed. "Meet me in the gate in ten?"
"I'll be there."
Walker was nearly back where he belonged.

CHAPTER 24
RETURN.

Walker placed himself at the bar and ordered a cider. He vaguely recognised the barman who looked at him twice, recognition shining in his eyes. He appreciated the taste, aware that there was no need to 'get *the fever for the flavour'*. His drinking was under control, but there was no need to push his luck.

Alcohol became a problem when he was unhappy, in a bad place in his life. He wasn't exactly tripping the light fantastic. It had been a year of battles and he wasn't in Berlin just yet. The pub was empty. The only sound was the electronic music coming from the gambler in the corner.

Walker was nervous. He felt around his collar and decided to unbutton his polo t-shirt. Today was about comfort, not fashion. He could feel the slight trickle of sweat running down his back, he breathed in deeply and slowly, he knew the drill. Slow the heart rate, send out a message out, and relax, no panic. It felt like a job interview waiting for a man who had been his closest friend, his brother. He wanted absolution, he needed this.

Silks was late as usual, he worked on his own time scale, Jamaican time. Walker had been in the pub for half an hour and had sipped two pints before Silks made his entrance. He felt a presence on his shoulder, turning round to investigate he saw a familiar face looking at him.

"Hello Silks how's you mate?"

"I'm good Bruce. I'm always good, you going to buy me a beer then?" Walker gestured to the bar maid and ordered two pints.

"Still power drinking then are you?" Silks nodded to the empty glasses she took away.

"Not like I used to mate, lots changed since then." Silks nodded at that. If his mate hadn't sorted his head out it would be a short conversation.

"It had to Bruce, didn't it really mate. It was all fucked up man? You lost the plot eh?"

"I've been some places mate, but I'm back now, not as before, but do you want me to go and fucking bore you about psychiatry and all that jazz?"

"No time for it, Psychotherapist, break it down Bruce, psycho the rapist mate. They tried to get in my head. I fucked them off, I didn't like it."
Walker nodded. He knew Silks wouldn't want a detailed explanation of his time in darkness.
"What you doing now, you sorted your shit out?"
"Back at Uni, still going for the nursing mate. It's what I want. It's what I want to do." Walker reinforced the point.
Silks nodded. "Safe, a man's got to do what he has to do to make a living."
They made small talk for a while. It was strange talking to Silks again after a year, after all that had passed since their last pint together. The conversation was polite nothing more and they fished around without catching anything. Silks looked at the time and told Walker that he had to be elsewhere, he looked at Walker as he stood up to leave.
"Good to see you out again Bruce, don't be a stranger."
"No mate. I won't."
Walker made the short journey home with a lighter heart, he felt more than satisfied with the day's events. When he was unwell he had made plans and created a timetable. First and foremost it was to get his head sorted out. He had to reboot and rebuild his mind and thought processes. If that didn't work out for him the rest of his plan was doomed to failure.
The second stage; was to return to university, fit in with the student population and build a career for himself. He had started down that road and he was succeeding. Finally it had been to resume his friendship with Silks, he had made contact and had broken the ice: small steps, one day at a time.
The events that had caused the breakdown of his mental health and the dark days of solitude as he recovered were becoming distant memories. Time does not stand still. Time was about exporting history into the present and remembering the journey.
Saturday arrived and so did Victoria. He was excited about meeting Monica and Silks in one day and spoke to her about it. Victoria told him. "I'm not concerned with your love life. I had enough of that when I lived with you." She did smile when she heard that he had been out for a drink with Silks even though her face clouded briefly when she asked many he had drunk.
Walker smiled and raised his hand signifying four. She nodded and looked again to make sure he was telling the truth. Victoria knew her

dad missed his best mate and she also knew he had to find his mate again to make a full recovery.

They decided to go and visit his mom for a change of scenery and jumped in the car. Victoria taking out her dads cd and putting in one in of her own. He scowled but didn't argue, it wasn't worth the effort as he listened to her latest taste in music and thought what a load of rubbish.

He pulled on to his mothers drive and she opened the door to greet them, hugging Victoria who pulled away and shouted. "Nana, I'm not a baby! Daddy tell her!"

She's not a baby mom," he turned and looked at Victoria. "Happy?"

After Walker spent an afternoon moaning at Wolves latest defeat and performance, his mom asked them if they wanted to go out for a curry, he looked at Victoria and she nodded.

"Yeah go on then." Walker felt the need for a Vindaloo.

An hour later they were sitting around the table in the intimate Indian restaurant, an establishment they had frequented for years, for as long as he could remember anyway.

Walker had enjoyed his first curry there without his parents, when he was eighteen and the pubs had kicked him and a mate out for the night.

It was early evening and only a few couples were dotted around. They were polite enough to keep the conversation low. Walker never understood why people had to shout to get attention. The waiters serviced the tables efficiently with genuine smiles and traditional Indian dress. Walker felt relaxed as he picked at his popadoms, dipping them in raita and chili pickle. He looked down at his class of coke, full of ice and lemon and smiled,' a bloody coke' he thought.

His mom and Victoria where about to start another war about fashion and modern teenage angst. Walker sighed and interrupted them." I'm on placement soon, they're sending me out on the wards. Walker blew air out of his mouth. " I'm a tad nervous to be fair. It's easy at Uni., sit behind a desk, write an essay or two. These are real people, I might go on bloody holiday to get over the trauma."

Walker was joking but his mom picked up the point " Shall we go away for Christmas?"

"Yes Nana." Shorts interjected, always happy to go on a trip to the beach, her memory of their previous disagreement consigned to the selective memory compartment that all teenagers posses.

Walker nodded. " Why not, I've got some time off after I finish my placement, stay in England for Christmas day and then go for New years."

The plan was tossed about as they finished their dinner. When Walker and Victoria returned home back to the flat they logged on to the net and searched for holidays. Now that it had been discussed Walker realised how much he needed to getaway and think about fuck all for a change.

They found a bargain and Walker phoned Nat to check dates and got the go-ahead. They would fly out on Boxing Day. His mom couldn't go for the full two weeks but would travel for the first. Walker was happy with that arrangement. Victoria was flexing her adolescent muscles more and more, taking offence when his mum treated her like a child and he had to act as a referee one more than one occasion, it was mentally draining.

Walker could see Victoria's point but he stepped in when she got to vociferous with a firm. "Victoria shut up, that's your Nan you're talking to, show some damn respect!" He would point his finger at her and she would sulk quietly for ten minutes head down in the corner. Silent rage emanating in waves.

Walker knew that his mum needed to come to terms with the fact that Victoria was nearly fifteen and no longer a baby. Walker's mum had never got to grips that Victoria had been raised on a different stage to him. Victoria's life had been tough and my little pony had not been her best friend when she was child. She had been raised by Walker in an environment that was alien to his mother and the cotton ball world she lived in.

As he drove Victoria back to Shrewsbury on Sunday evening, she asked him if he didn't mind her staying in Shrewsbury next weekend. "I want to go s out with my mates." She said. "No problem Shorty, got a boyfriend I need to know about then."Walker looked askance. "No!" her eyes narrowed as she looked across at him. "Ok, ok, give me my head back,"

Walker knew this time would come. The time when she wanted to spend time with her mates instead of her middle aged dad. He also knew that she had waited until he had regained his health before she dropped this on him and he would always be thankful to her for that. He turned to her. "Shorts you got that Eniemen cd handy?" she nodded back." Stick it in then, let's see what Marshall Mathers the third had got to say for himself then."

Wednesday dawned and his dinner date with Monica was planned for the evening. They had enjoyed a pleasant conversation on the phone after their first meeting and she had pulled his leg about his chat up lines and calling her, 'a pig', Walker laughed and waved the white flag. He told her about having a pint with Silks. Monica listened without interrupting, he had spoke about his friend at length to her, previously, and she knew that Walker needed closure.

"I'm looking forward to cooking dinner." Walker said. "What's on the menu then Mr. Chief, what surprises have you got in store for me?" Walker was elusive. "It's a surprise," was all he would say, adding. "You can be sure I'll wash the dishes and make sure that the flat complies with food hygiene standards."

"Thank you for your diligence, I appreciate the effort you're going too." The ironic slant of her voice brought a smile to his face.

He finished shaving his head and washed the shaving foam out of his ears before checking his appearance in the mirror, smiling and nodding at his reflection. Searching through his wardrobe he had laid out a dark blue Armani shirt and some beige casual shorts with flip flops as footwear. The look was aimed at smart casual and confidant.

Walker glanced out of the window it was a beautiful late summer evening and the sun was starting to set and he looked at his watch. It was time to stick on a tune, pop a bottle and do his stuff in the kitchen. Numan was keeping him company from the CD player as he started his prep work and even though he loved the music it still could transport him to a darker place and time. Numan was a regressive step tonight. Add that with beer and bad memories and the night could become bleak for his guest.

He clicked open the cd and placed in a Massive Attack album and smiled and sang along with the music. Walker had selected a tried and true menu that had worked well for him in the past when he had entertained: Smoked salmon on fresh rocket with balsamic roasted vine tomatoes, to start. Followed by, beef stroganov with wild mushrooms, dwarf beans, baby sweet corn and asparagus. His tip was to use French instead of Dijon mustard in the cream sauce, it made it richer and subtler. Vichy carrots added a different and contrasting sweetness, with a bed of saffron rice for texture.

The desert was always champagne and strawberries. This combination had never let him down and the ladies loved the extra effort and attention to detail that Champagne seemed to offer.

Walker concentrated hard on the task in hand, rolling up the salmon without it tearing it and placing it strategically over the rocket. He was deciding on whether to add a creamed horseradish sauce when the buzzer rang. Walker checked his watch it was nearly eight and she was on time, leaving the kitchen he pressed a button to let her in, waiting at the top of the stairs with an open door and a smile on his face. Monica smiled back.

She looked nice, she had applied a touch of makeup, styled her hair and changed into a lady rather that a pet sitter.

"How are you Pinky?" He laughed and hoped she got the joke.

"Fine, I suppose you have laid out the sty so I can eat at the trough then?" She smiled, easy with the banter and obviously relaxed.

"Yeah it's all set, complete with dirty cups, come in." Walker invited her through into the front room and she looked around. The table was set with a linen cloth, silver cutlery, and crystal glasses with a floral centre piece. (All borrowed from his mothers).

"Very impressive, though I have the distinct feeling that you have had a few dress rehearsals before me."

"Shakespeare wrote a draft before he released Romeo and Juliet you know Pinky," Walker countered seamlessly.

"Romeo and Juliet eh, you expecting romance?"

"I'm expecting a good night with a beautiful lady, some witty and intelligent conversation washed down with some nice wine." He hoped she wasn't knowledgably with Shakespeare as that play didn't have a happy end.

"I'm driving I can't drink, and do those lines work with 'the other pigs'?" She had moved her Knight and was threatening his queen.

"You are over twenty one and I do have a spare room if you want to sleep here. I'm easy with that. Do what you do Pinks, as long as you eat the food, I'm not fussed." 'Got you', he thought as he took her Knight and moved his Rook in for the kill.

"Very smooth, you got a plaster for all those sores?"

"I'm a nurse aren't I?" Nearly check mate.

"So you say." She moved her knight for the last time.

"Let me get you a class of wine, it's a sauterne. I remember you said you liked a sweet white."

She looked at him as he poured her a drink in a sparkling glass that had come pre-cleaned by his mom and accepted the drink. Walker held her eyes in his and thought, check mate.

Monica enjoyed her dinner; apparently she wasn't usually into posh food and thanked the chef as she cleaned her plate and asked if there was any 'seconds'. Walker smiled and thanked her for the compliment as he cleaned the table and suggested they had dessert on the sofa. They had drunk a few glasses of wine by now and she started to laugh when he made the suggestion.

"Does this approach work then?" Monica asked.

"What approach would that be?" Walker answered.

"This set piece seduction technique from the novel of corny one liners?"

"Actually it does my dear, and as you're half pissed and sitting next to me. I would suggest that it's working well tonight."

"I suppose you have got Champagne and strawberries for pudding?"

"Why?" He looked innocent. His school boy impression was ignored.

"Because if you're going to do it properly you have to take me into the bedroom with Champagne and feed me Strawberries, that's the way the plan is meant to work isn't it?"

Bloody hell she was good he thought." Well not quite, we're meant to watch a Gary Numan video first and explore my mind, you find out I'm a complex but decent man blah, blah and want to get to know me. The real me and what makes me tick." They both giggled on the sofa.

"Well get the bottle and lets go to bed, forget the strawberries I'm not really that keen on fruit.

 By the time he returned with the chilled bottle the front room was vacant and Monica had adjourned into his bedroom. He would have fun with this one he thought. He could see it on the cards. He sighed and with a smile made his way through to the bedroom.

Monica had to be up early for work, and Walker groaned as the alarm on her mobile went off. They hadn't had sex because he didn't go, 'dressed for dinner' and had no condoms.

Walker told her he didn't use them, they ruined the moment. Monica had done a dissertation: It had been about AIDS of all things and told him. "If he wanted her, he would either wear a condom or get a test."

He had laughed at that one. 'Fucking get an AIDS test!" Was she on crack? He was clean.'

She did plant a seed in his mind as he thought. 'You have been with a few girls now mate, some with worse morals than you mucka. That's all need, to get back into the swing of things and find out I'm fucking dying of AIDS. But if she wants to give me blow jobs all night I ain't the type of bloke to say no.'

Walker knew she would break before he did, all girls did. They would always use the condom bit as an opening gambit to show they were responsible. It soon became a bore for them, when they needed a fix, or felt that they were missing out on the pleasure. He felt good regarding the situation, he felt positive about Monica.

She was independent and assertive, she was intelligent but didn't use it as a platform to preach and promote her own mind. He found she was one of the few people that would happily listen to others ramble on, rather than to try control a conversation, comfortable with her own intellect rather than having to sing it out from the rooftops. As she had a first in psychology, Walker tried to debate with her, she would giggle and dismiss him by saying she couldn't remember half of it but he could read her essays if he was that interested. They established early parameters and were both were in agreement as to the shape of their relationship.

There was little ambiguity and lots of honest talk. He relaxed in front of the telly after she left and smiled, they had arranged a date for Sunday lunch and he was looking forward seeing her.

Silks was on his mind. It had been nearly a week since they had met for a beer and he wanted to see him again. Friday night was around the corner and Walker fancied a beer. He didn't know if he was up to being in one place with all the lads, Walker still experienced feeling of guilt about his actions and was embarrassed about his breakdown.

He picked up the phone and made the call.

"Bruce?" Silks answered

"Yes Silks how's you mate?"

"Good, good and busy what can I do for you mate?"

"What you up to tomorrow?"

"Bit of shit in the morning, around and about in the afternoon, the usual," as always the man provided a wealth of information.

"You want to hook up and grab a beer and some lunch?" Walker knew you could always entice the man with the offer of free food."

"Yeah could do, sure why not. Meet me in town at one." He gave
Walker the name of a pub they had used in the past that served a good
cheeseburger and hung up.
Walker was in town at one and Silks was already in the pub standing at
the bar reading his paper with a pint in his hand.
"Alright mate?"Walker joined him at the bar.
"Safe Bruce, get the beer in then." Silks swallowed the dregs and
waited for his refill. "Let's sit down and take the weight off," Walker
suggested. He wanted some privacy, conscious that he still wasn't the
finished article in this, the harshest of environments.
They parked themselves by the window and watched the world go by.
Silks knew people that walked past the window and acknowledged
them with a nod. After a few more beers and a couple of large
cheeseburgers, they started to relax and joke with each other. Enjoying
the greasy meatiness of the meal. They wiped their hands on napkins
threw them on the plate and drank their beers, sitting in silence for a
moment. Rituals had to be followed. Walker threw Silks a fag over and
offered him a light. Old days were being recaptured.
 The mention of Walkers past year was touched on briefly. Silks probed
for a short time, still unsure what had happened to his mate over the
last months, or how far down the well had he fallen. Silks was
Interested to hear what had happened, he wanted to test the water
for traces of madness. Evaluate how far his mate had come.
 "It's old ground, it's been harvested. There's no real need to go over it
again, what's the point? Done and dusted," Walker said.
Silks nodded and raised his hands in agreement, there was no need to
harp on. Walker had grown a backbone, and realised now that you
don't necessarily need to talk to be heard.
 As the alcohol took effect Walker agreed to the Friday night hedonistic
tour of Wolverhampton and realised that nothing had really changed
in the last year. It was the same old faces and the same old pubs. He
had moved forward, the rest had, but at the same time stayed still. He
felt differently when the lads welcomed him back. He didn't feel he
needed to belong, he felt that he did.
He had an inner strength that wasn't present previously. He had been
down, to a place where not many return from. People might ask you
to describe the torture of mental illness. It's impossible to do so when
well. Moods and feeling change like the wind. To describe a living hell,
where do you start? It would cheapen the whole experience in attempt

too. Walker knew he had beaten that episode. His wounds had been exposed, and stitched. While the others laughed and joked, he smiled, a reserved smile of inner wisdom. Silks understood. He had been to dark places as well. They stood silently together and watched the merriment around them.

 "Come a long way mate."

Silks nodded back at him. "Good to have you back Bruce. "Walker had returned. There was one more week left to go before he had to start his placement. Next Monday he was due to start work on an elderly adult psychiatric unit in Birmingham, his day of the text book was over, it was time to start nursing properly.

CHAPTER 22
STUDENT

The film wasn't grabbing Walkers attention, his mind kept slipping away to Monday and his first placement. Walker knew this day would dawn and his restlessness was matched only by his nerves. One thing he had learned from painful experience was that dwelling on the problem would not improve the situation. He decided to jump in his car and meet the challenge head on. Walker recognised the importance of being proactive in the process and making a good impression was paramount in his list of priorities.

His only previous knowledge of a psychiatric ward was from behind the subjective standpoint of his own experience, he wanted a fresh perspective to clear any bias from his mind. He needed to reinforce the difference in his own mind that he was no longer the patient.

The hospital loomed into view. It wasn't what Walker had expected, he had imagined a foreboding sinister building, hidden away in dark ominous grounds. A reclusive setting concealed from the prying eyes of the British public. Walker thought back to the misconceptions printed in the press vis-à-vis football hooliganism and reflected that middle England was still prone to accept the intolerant views of the right wing press. Blinkered individuals would read about a, 'madman' who had been discharged from services by a, 'do good' doctor and was free to rampage across society. Less than 1% of all violent crime could be attributed to clients that had used services. Go to prison and you served a fixed tariff, go down the mental health system and you could be in hospital for life for the same crime.

Maximum security hospitals were no holiday camp. Walker understood that diving into dark water was scary, but it was the job of the press to provide balanced coverage and reduce the stigma attached to mental illness, not prey on the fallibility of the uneducated and persecute those that they simply didn't understand. Mental illness was not catching. It was not a viral infection and it was not consigned to a specific socio-economic group: that was a simple fact of life.

The building was modern, bright and located away from the main hospital campus with a slip road siphoning off visitors to the unit. It resembled a comfort inn rather than a hospital, red brick and well maintained. Walker nodded his approval, as he noticed the difference in atmosphere from when he had spent his time in hospital. There was no oppressive atmosphere hanging like a chain around both the nurses and patients necks. Automatic doors welcomed visitors into a main atrium that boasted a coffee shop and restaurant.

There was a small shop that sold papers, snack foods and toiletries. It reminded Walker of better days, when he was checking out duty free shops in the departure lounge of an airport. There were clients sitting in wheelchairs talking to with staff, who were recognisable by their displayed name tags that stated their designation. He could not hear any screams or cries, the noises of the night that had kept him awake when he had been admitted to his own personal hell.

He found a sign that pointed toward Amber Ward and wandered toward it. Amber ward was located two floors down in the bowels of the building. Away from the main entrance, the building started to resemble a hospital the further down he walked. The smell of disinfectant, the linoleum floors and the locked doors. On his way down he noticed a room marked *'treatment suite'*. Walker was drawn back into the specter of the asylum and frontal lobe lobotomies.

On his chauffeured tour of the hospital, he asked the guide, 'what's the treatment suite'? He replied.' It's where they perform ECT. Electro convulsive therapy, or as the public know it. Electro Shock Therapy. ECT was a last resort for patients who were not responding to traditional methods and anti-depressant medication. They were plugged into the national grid and had their minds, *'rebooted'*. It was a disturbing sight for Walker as old people where laid down on a gurney and had electrodes placed upon their head and had currents conducted into their brain. When he witnessed it had it left a bitter taste in his mouth. More than one professional told him ,it worked better than drugs for kick starting a recovery, Walker was not sure that was the way forward in modern mental health and naively thought that talking and showing compassion might have a positive effect on the patient.

Three floors down, he found the entrance to Amber Ward. Tried the door and found it locked. Pressing a button to signal a visitor had arrived. A professional looking lady, who appeared to be in her early forties walked down a long entrance and opened the door with a click. She was wearing a panic alarm which was attached to her belt, he heard the keys jangling as he walked and he looked back into his past.

"Hello there, can I help you?" She had a gentle Irish accent and greeted him with a smile and warm eyes. Her name tag identified her as Bridget: staff nurse, Amber Ward. Walker introduced himself. "Hello I'm Gary Walker. A student nurse, due to start a placement here on Monday. I just wondered if I could have a look round and meet my mentor if he is on shift? I did phone to tell you I was coming."

"Hello Gary how are you?" she offered him a well manicured hand and he shook it smiling back at her. "Come on. Martin isn't on duty today, but I will be happy to show you round and give you the guided tour. I'm Bridget Callaghan; it's very nice to meet you." She appeared friendly and there was an amiable ambiance on the ward. He felt a sense of relief that maybe his role here would not be that of an oppressor.

Walker had completed his research and was aware that elder adult was far removed from acute psychiatry but a smile and warm welcome would always get you further that a scowl and tepid outlook in his experience. As he followed Bridget onto the ward he took the opportunity to soak up his surroundings.

The nurse's office reminded him of the bridge on the star ship enterprise. He was greeted with: banks of computers, fax machines, copier's, phones and filing cabinets placed strategically on top of a single long curved desk. The office was large and airy with a glass paneled frontage that allowed staff a 270 degree vision of the dayroom,; a small seated area with tables and corridors which accessed the exit to the ward and bed areas.

 Bridget told him that Amber was a mixed sex ward with 21 clients, a majority of whom had their own room. All rooms had private toilet facilities but most didn't have shower facilities as some clients were forgetful and prone to flood the ward.

The ward contained three large communal bathrooms where clients could attend to their personal needs with assistance from staff. The ward was spacious and light and didn't have the claustrophobic feel to it that he had encountered on his previous trips into hospital.

The day room had numerous armchairs, a warm pink carpet; floral sofas' and wide open French doors which lead out to a sizeable garden containing two patio sets. This surprised Walker as they were three floors down. Bridget told him there had been extensive excavations at the back of the building when the hospital was first built. The gardens were enclosed by seven foot high wood paneled fences and he could hear but not see voices behind them.

The patient's rooms were small and allocated on individual requirements. One large dormitory had three beds in it; these were for high needs clients that required regular observations. They had to be placed in one location to ease the pressure on staff. The ward had its own kitchen where you could prepare basic food and drinks. Nursing assistants where in abundance, sitting with the clients and making small talk. Other patients were reading the daily newspapers or watching the television. Nurses were looking through files in the office and answered incoming phone calls. Walker was aware that the qualified staff still acted as administrators, while the assistants attended to basic nursing provision. Bridget informed him of the daily routine and smiled when she learned it was his first time on a ward.

"You'll soon be in the swing of things Gary." She found his name on the off duty Rota and wrote down his shifts for the next two weeks before she handed them to him.

Bridget was a good advertisement for the ward, he liked her easy going manner and when she was showing him around Amber it was evident that she had a rapport with the clients. She knew all their Christian names and when she greeted them they would respond to her with a smile and a gentle comment about the weather and what was for lunch.

He walked back to his car with lighter footsteps. On the way back into Wolverhampton, Walker phoned Victoria and arranged to pick her up from the train station. As she sat in the car on the drive home, Walker described the ward to her, she smiled back at him and went through the motions of listening and feigning attention before she worked out her strategy.

"Do you get paid any more money for working on a ward then dad?"

"Why" Walker waited and wondered 'how much?'

"I could to with some new cd's and a trainers"

" Fine, leave it with me, I thought you were looking scruffy anyway Shorty my girl." Life was easy for teenagers. The parents worked and their children sponged off them. Walker smiled and listened to the car radio, he was happy to be *'normal'*.

Walker's first shift on Amber Ward was an early. He had to be on the ward for 7:30. On Sunday night he had gone to bed and tried to go to sleep in the quiet of his bedroom. After an hour of tossing and turning he grabbed his quilt and made his way back to the sofa to turn on BBC news twenty four and let his mind focus on the news. At least his grasp of current affairs had improved considerably since his break-up with Natalie, he thought as he closed his eyes.

When he woke in the morning he double checked that his bag was packed for the day ahead. Satisfied, he pulled his new shirt off the coat hanger and buttoned it before stepping into a pair of pressed black trousers. On his way out of the front door he paused and checked his reflection in the hall mirror and said a little prayer before he headed off to ease the suffering of the mentally ill of Birmingham.

Walker arrived at the door to the ward half an hour early and pressed the buzzer to alert staff of his arrival. A large black lady that looked tired and overworked shuffled down to the entrance and didn't look overwhelmed when he introduced himself to her. She nodded at him and introduced herself as." Ella the night nurse." He followed her into the office and ignored the yawns from four others who were sipping on hot drinks and nodded back at him as he introduced himself.

"Show…." Ella looked puzzled and rolled her hands.

Walker stepped into help her "Gary."

"Gary." She repeated his name. "Show Gary the kitchen and how to brew up, it's your first day on the unit mate, learn how to make a drink it's the student way."

Walker followed an unenthusiastic lady into the kitchen and she pointed out where he could find: tea, coffee, cups and pots." Better do trays love, the others will be on shift soon."

Walker nodded and attended to his first task on the ward as the tea boy and thought it's all downhill from here. He loaded the tray was with cups, a pot of tea and coffee and milk and noticed other people arriving onto the ward. He adding more cups to the tray and made it safely back to the office without a spill.

Walker introduced himself to the room again and was welcomed with more blank expressions. A staff nurse checked the communications book and finally acknowledged him with a smile. "Ah we have two from the U.C.E , welcome and hello." Walker smiled and the rest of the team thanked him for their hot drinks, before they found a vacant seat and sat down.

Walker looked around and identified three women who were staff nurses and five others who were pinning nursing assistant's badges onto their shirts. They laughed as they spoke about their weekend and

Walker realised that he was the only man in the room and smiled occasionally, briefly trying to translate the female language into English before he gave up and daydreamed, hypnotised by the clock on the wall. Ella came back into the office and the hum of conversation trailed off and silence finally settled. She picked up a hard backed A4 pad and offered it to a colleague and started handover.

Walker learned this was the time when the nurse coming off shift, would discuss the patients with staff starting their shift and talk through the care they had received and their recent behaviour. Ella discussed all twenty one patents without a break or without referring to notes and all of the team listened intently. Walker tried to keep up with her and act like he knew what she was talking about. Some of the terms were lost on him. He worked out for himself that. "Jack opening his bowels." meant that he had been to the toilet for a number two. He blew out his cheeks and made a note to learn this new language as soon as possible.

His mind became alert when Ella used the term. 'Overly Medicated'. He understood that phrase. Ella pointed that there was a case conference scheduled for ten, as several nurses had raised concerns over a patients (Elizabeth) medication. She appeared tired and lethargic and this might be as result of the sedating effect of her prescribed medication. Walker realised that maybe the power on the ward lay with the nursing staff after all.

Ella continued about ECG's and CAT scans and unpronounceable medications as his thoughts drifted away again. He was returned back to the land of the living when a stressed looking girl panting heavily, knocked on the office door and entered with a flourish introducing herself as Leanne the student. She was wearing a self conscious smile. Walker recognised her from lectures but had never spoken to her. She sat at the front and insisted on asking questions at the end of lectures when it was time to leave and beat the traffic home. The nurse in charge informed her that she should be on time in future and left it at that. Walker poured a cup of tea and smiled at her and she accepted the cup gratefully. Students of the world had to stick together and watch each other's backs.

A nurse who had her head buried in the office diary, noticed their presence and looked up at them before she waved over toward a middle aged woman who waved back and came into the office. "Can you take our students into the kitchen and show them the ropes for breakfast please Maria."

They stood to attention as they were given a ten minute briefing on the rudiments of making tea. Walker was allocated toast duty and tutted at, when he started the task without putting on an apron and warned with a wag of the finger not to leave the toaster unattended. Leanne was asked to inform the patients that breakfast was served ushering them into the dining room and checking what they wanted to eat.

Walker was feeling confident and tried to boil the kettle at the same time as buttering the toast and forgot about one load of bread that was starting to caramelise nicely. The alarms sounded as the smoke curled its way up to the detectors and his face turned as red as the fire engines that were now speeding toward the hospital. Staff rushed around the ward to locate the fire point and then reassured patients they didn't need to evacuate the building, pointing toward the kitchen and saying. "It was the bloody student! He had burned the toast and there was no need to worry."

One kind face smiled at him after the panic subsided and told him. "It cost a fortune for the fire service to respond but not to worry as he wasn't the first person to do it and it happened all the time."

Leanne smiled at him, Walker thought. That was one all, in fuck ups and it wasn't yet ten in the morning.'

As the shift neared its conclusion Walker breathed with a greater degree of freedom. He had made it through his first day. He had been shown how to make a bed with nursing corners and shown where to deposit the dirty laundry after he had stripped down the beds.

He had done a better job at serving lunch and had started to smile at the patients as they enjoyed their meals. He even learned where the sluice room was for cleaning bed pans and getting rid of urine in receptacles, breathing a sigh of relief that he had not encountered any faeces or other body fluids yet.

The NIC called them into the office and asked them how their first day had gone, amused at the relief on the faces when they replied. "Happy they had survived it." She smiled at them and thanked them for their hard work and added. "Make sure that they knew what shift they were on tomorrow (looking at Leanne) and to familiarise themselves properly with the morning procedure (looking at Walker).

As they both left the ward, they leaned on the wall outside and exhaled loudly. "I'm glad that's over!" The relief was easy to hear in Walkers voice. "So am I, I was shitting bricks before today and then I was late like a twat."

Walker laughed. Leanne appeared down to earth and appeared normal, (anyone that used foul language appeared 'normal' to Walker).

"Look on the bright side Lea, that's our first day of proper nursing over and done with. It should get easier from here on in. You'll look back on this day when you're qualified and laugh when you see a first year student hiding in the office."

Yeah you're right, I'm just glad it's over." They turned and left the building, feeling ten foot tall.

CHAPTER 26
POISE

During the course of the next few weeks Walker got to grips with the fundamentals of the ward. The basic provision for him was to provide care and make the patients days go as well as possible with a smile and a laugh. He would offer people an ear, listen and be attentive. Show interest in what was said to him. He gagged when he had to clean soiled sheets but hadn't yet been faced with a dirty bum to clean. With the help of Leanne.

Walker had started to do patients rounds. Documenting physical observations and recording them in their notes. Walker had learned to take blood pressures manually (after twenty minutes practicing on the nursing staff) and take a pulse. After reading the, *Marston clinical guide* he had started to understood what the readings indicated and correlated them with the patient's physical health.

He learned their names and learned about their lives before reading their case history. If a client told him they didn't feel well or they didn't appear there, *'normal self'*. He would check their notes for the past few days, check their medication and take baseline reports and document the facts, after seeking advice from the NIC. His mentor was impressed with his progress.

Walker enjoyed talking to the clients. They all had a story to tell. As his confidence increased he would make a circle out the chairs and encourage as many people as possible to join in activities and play games.

He remembered when he used to collect Nat from the care home she worked at, it was an awful and depressing sight; old people sitting around and waiting to die whilst defecating in their underwear. He saw one old man who was so weak that a care assistant had to hold his cigarette for him as he smoked.

Natalie was constantly ill because of the infections passed on and he didn't want that environment where he was working. Life wasn't just about existing it was about living.

During one afternoon Walker decided to make them all rich and organised a game of, *'Who wants to be a millionaire'*. He went round the ward and raised quite a crowd, after a few attempts they finally reached the million pound question and were all about to retire on the proceeds to Benidorm. The audience waited with baited breath as he drew the card and looked at the question and asked. "What is Donald Duck's middle name?" What type of question was that? Walker thought. He didn't even know that Mr. Duck had a bloody middle name let alone what the hell it was. He could see by the sea of blank expressions on the faces around him that maybe they felt the same. He looked at the answer and announced with a laugh that. "Its Fauntleroy after Little Lord Fauntleroy." Walker's laughter proved infectious and soon the whole circle was laughing. The nurses even left the vacuum of the office to investigate the melee. When they learned what is was all about they had to smile and started to laugh. Walker had been accepted.

The nurse's confidence in him and his ability improved and he was delegated increasingly complex tasks. He was asked to, go and fetch prescriptions, support nursing assistants on patient's escorts to other hospitals and go to medical records. The NIC would allocate him one to one clinical interactions and ask him to lead handovers. He was being trusted and he thrived on the responsibility. His ability to document clearly and with detail was noticed and the staff nurses hardly read his entries after a while, before they counter signed them.

Walker had managed to avoid cleaning dirty bottoms, until one day when the task was inescapable. Mary was a lady who had the look of death about her. She cried a lot and was demanding at times. They would leave her to sit in the chair and watch her weep quietly to herself. This made Walker feel uncomfortable and he would talk to her and receive no reply through the tears. He came to comprehend the tears were evident, because she needed the toilet and didn't want to soil herself. Who the fuck could blame her?

Walker thought. If I needed a shit and couldn't find a toilet and had to go in my pants in public, I might well have a tear or two in my eyes. Walker knew that it breached her dignity and it was poor practise to leave her. The nurses were always too busy to help, writing reams of notes making sure they adhered to endless edicts issued by faceless bureaucrats.

Walker had learned not to blame the staff nurses anymore for the long periods they spent in the office, he had learned how time consuming their paperwork was. It could take over an hour a day to write up a few lines in each patient notes. Added to the rest of the paper work they were expected to finish before the end of the shift they had little

option than to spent 90% of their working days writing. When Mary
started to cry Walker knew she wanted the toilet. He would grab Lea
and another female student nurse and they would help her to the
toilet while Walker would wait outside. The girls could clean dirty
bottoms all day without a problem. They would wipe it from end to
end without a blink. Walker bowed his head in respect, he only had to
discern a pungent odour and his gagging reflex went into overtime.
Mary managed to catch Walkers eye as he was chatting to Bill; a
veteran of Normandy who now lived alone. Twelve story's up and
whose only view was of past glories. Mary's finger curled as she
beckoned to him to come over. He looked around the room there was
no other member of staff for Walker to delegate to. Oh shit, he
thought and the literal meaning was not lost on him as he got up and
searched the ward and found everybody was busy. Leanne was in the
bathroom already cleaning up a patient, the qualified staff were busy
in the office and all other nursing assistants were busy attending to
other tasks. He walked slowly back into the day room and Mary again
gestured for him to come over to her. She could stand and move small
distances unaided so he hoped that she could maybe make the short
trip alone if he could get her close. Walker assisted her to sit on the
wheel chair and
wheeled her over to the toilet.
"Ok Mary I'm going to take you to the toilet, don't worry we will make
it." Walker spoke to her gently. "I just want use you use your arms to
stand up and get yourself onto the toilet is that ok?"
Mary nodded back to him that it was." Mary, you don't mind me
helping you because I'm a man? Would you prefer to wait for a female
member of staff to help you?" Walker played the get out of jail free
card and Mary indicated that she was fine with him helping her.
Walker managed to help her on to the toilet and as she sat down he
noticed she was wearing an adult nappy and a *'strong'* smell had
started to flood the room. Walker remembered the film. *'The Silence of
the Lambs,'* particularly the scene in which Jodie Foster had pushed
some vapour rub up her nose to lessen the smell of a dead body during
an autopsy.
 He looked around the toilet and his eyes fell on the liquid soap
dispenser. He pressed it and placed the soap up his nostrils and
resisted the urge to sneeze." Ok Mary I'm just going to take down your
pants, there is no need to worry." As he tugged at the pad the contents

spilled out over the floor. It was sludge, it was thick and it was all over the place.

 Walker lost his breakfast in the sink and subsequently slipped in the sea of shit and hit the ground covering himself. He apologised to Mary before he threw up again. He heard a knock on the door and Leanne announced her arrival. "Gary, you ok in there mate?" She knew Mary was about to burst, Walker had informed her with panic in his eyes. "Not really Lea I could do with a hand for a minute if that's ok?" Walker felt sorry for Mary, how must this look to her? She was on the toilet with her pants down around her ankles and he was having a swim in her waste and throwing up into the sink.

"Open the door then you plonker," Lea had a laugh in her voice. Understanding that he wasn't in control of the situation. He opened the door and she looked at him, on his knees and covered in shit. "Bloody hell Gaz, you alright down there, you look and smell and great mate. Take me to the pub on Friday night or leave me forever!" Now is not the time for joviality Lea," Walker gave her the look as he inclined his head toward her. Lea looked back at him and waved her hands, a small smile on her face. "Get out the way and... and.... go and have a wash or something."

A staff nurse who was leaving the ward investigated the situation. She looked into the toilet and put her hand over her mouth to stifle a smile.

"Bloody hell Gary, what have you done? Are you Ok Mary?" Mary nodded. "I fell over Sue. "Walker volunteered the information, surprised he wasn't receiving the sympathy he deserved.

" Are you ok to deal with this Leanne? I'll get you some help to move Mary."

 She turned back to Walker and again tried to stifle a smile. "Gary it's only a couple of hours before your shift ends mate, I suggest you go home and have a shower and get out those clothes. You don't smell very nice."

With a red face and the smell of shit following him round the hospital Walker left and tried to avoid the raised nostrils of people he passed on the stairs.

The remainder of his placement was a good experience after the trauma of that day. His mentor had commended him on trying to protect Mary's dignity, pausing before he informed him. "That in future always wait until you had appropriate help to complete any and all tasks."

Leanne had christened him the, *'muck spreader'* and his kudos increased as the staff were aware that he would literally get, *'stuck in'* to help. He formed a pact with Lea. He would deal with the aggressive patients and she could deal with shit. Lea wasn't as confidant when it came to diffusing potentially volatile situations.

During their time on the ward, two ladies had been admitted who did present with behavioural problems. One lady came from Wales. She had moved to the West Midlands years ago and had managed to avoid the Brummie lilt in her voice. She suffered from Alzheimer's and now required assistance in most areas of her life. Her name was Alice and she was a big physically powerful lady, who would shout loudly at staff in a strong welsh accent. Walker told Lea.

"It's like having a bollocking off Dylan Thomas, don't worry about it." as Lea backed off from her again. Alice was a former school teacher and the students under her tutelage must have been well behaved as she was the brawniest lady he had ever met. All Alice wanted to do was go home and she would constantly attempt to leave the ward despite being informed this would not happen. Sentries had to be placed at the top of the corridor to stop her efforts at leaving.

One day she had screamed and banged at the door and it shuddered under her onslaught. It was a distressing sight and upset the patients. Some would leave the dayroom and go to their rooms clearly disturbed by the scene. Alice would scream at the top of lungs. "I WANT TO GO HOME!" Pushing out violently at staff; who were attempting to calm her, without violent intentions. She managed to push one nursing assistant to the ground. Walker watched as three more pounced on her and escorted her to her room. He was shocked that it had taken so many of them to achieve their aim and one member of staff had actually appeared to derive pleasure from the altercation.

Walker didn't understand why they needed such a, *'heavy handed'* response. There had been no malice in her actions and the need for three staff to march her to her room had send out a message to rest of the patients, who was in charge on the ward. Their actions simply made her scream louder and fight back harder. She was obviously scared and didn't understand that she couldn't go home. Her husband was no longer able to cope with her at their house and a home in the community was being sought, which would be able to provide a specialist service for her.

When staff, *'tackled her'* she would become increasing upset and this would make her struggle with increased vigour. The fear fuelling her strength. Her frustration would boil over and she would chant over and over again that she wanted to go home. Sometimes the chants would become shrieks and this made uncomfortable viewing. When she aimed toward Walker, when he was on *'sentry duty'*, he would merely look her in the eyes, fold his arms in front of his chest and speak assertively. "Alice you don't want to do this, let's go back and have a cup of tea. Your husband will visit you soon, but at the moment you live here and it's against the law to let you off the ward because you might get hurt." He could see the flicker of understanding in her eyes as she looked into his. Gently he would take her arm and lead her back into the day room and get her a hot drink making sure that she couldn't launch it over anybody else. Sometimes she would try to push past him and he would place his arms behind his back and block her. She was strong, but after negotiating with her quietly she would make her way back into the day room, understanding it was futile to attempt to get past the immovable object. Walker could understand that members of staff could be intimidated by her but in his mind, she was an old lady and having three people jump on her was a tactic that made him uneasy. He pointed this out to his mentor who nodded and explained that with the risk aspect and the effect her behaviour had on the other residents it was a valid intervention. It was a persuasive argument and he could see the point made. However he didn't totally concur with this assessment.

Perhaps he was being too soft on her but he thought that it was a bullying manoeuvre and some staff were dishing out pay back for the push. There were times when he heard the nursing assistants and some qualified staff talking to the patients like they were children and treating them as such.

There were people who had mental health problems, who could live independently and with support from the community teams could stay out of psychiatric units.

It seemed a paradox to Walker that the local council who were responsible for housing them, deemed it appropriate to place them in high rise flats on the top floor. It was the Tories who had started this process with their, *'care in the community'* policy. In Walkers opinion it was a way simply to reduce the cost of the health service and place the poor with mental health problem in poor housing. The rich could provide for private health care and were not at the mercy of local services. What was the point of placing an old person on the twelfth floor of a tower block, surrounded by residents who had their own problems? What was the point in housing them on estates that were plagued by the gangs and other anti-social elements? How were they meant to go to the shop and then get their groceries up twelve flights of stairs? It was a hard enough task when the lifts worked, let alone if they were out or order. Young people intimated older folk even if their motives were honourable.

Statistically if you were a young male you had a higher chance of being mugged than any other demographic. The Middle English press would go into overdrive when a pensioner got mugged and plant their picture all over the news and profess that Britain was lawless under the new Labour government. It was party political posturing aimed at votes rather than exposing the cruelty inherent in society.

Walker understood that these individuals should be targeted and punished to the full extent of the law. In Walkers and Silks circles, these people would have been singled out and punished so badly you wouldn't have needed the legal system. All this achieved was to increase worry and isolate whole communities of old people who were now too scared to leave their houses. You scare them and then place and them in poor accommodation in high crime areas. It wasn't hard to make the connection between social isolation and an onset of a depression disorder.

What a way for a country to treat the generation that had won the first and second world wars. These people were ill not stupid and didn't need to be patronised in Walkers opinion.

One client who had been admitted was simply violent and her actions were behavioural. She had attacked numerous staff on her many visits to hospital, ripped pictures off walls, to aid her to assault people. Stockpiled ammunition to use as missiles and flooded her room to cause maximum disruption. She had become a famous name in mental health. She was admitted on the last week of Walkers placement and he was interested to see just how unpleasant she really was. The admission had been planned for a week and the handovers were detailed, to inform staff of policies and procedures pertaining to her admission.

Risk assessments were in place and the ward battened down the hatches and waited for the storm to break. When she finally arrived, you could tell from her demeanour that she could represent a problem. When Walker asked her how she was, she spat in his direction. It was evident that she viewed the nurses as the enemy and vice versa.

This must had been a result of all the previous battles that had raged when she had been an in-patient. Walker broached this point with his mentor at his final assessment. He nodded and told Walker that he understood the point that he was making. "However it was simple, they could not be held accountable for previous behavioural dynamics, she had a catalogue of assaults against staff and it was their responsibility as a team to make sure that all those who lived and worked on Amber Ward could expect to come and go without being the target for assault."

Walker checked her case history. Her behaviour was poor when she was well and living in the community. She had a long list of arrests for assault and drunken conduct. Walker could see the logic in the recommendations, but he also knew that she was in hospital for a reason and they had to try and help her. She was different from Alice, he tried to talk to her and she would tell him to. "Fuck Off."He found it amusing and would ask her to call him Gary not 'Mr. Off.' Her negative association must had stemmed from past experiences and the cycle had to be broken.

All his efforts were in vain and despite his kindness she continued her abuse. Whilst doing his rounds Walker noticed water running out from under her door. She was obviously flooding her room to cause the staff more problems. He knocked and entered. She was waiting for him and popped a greenie straight between his eyes. He wiped the sputum from his face, avoided the fist that was aimed at his head and backed away slowly, his eyes never leaving hers as he shut the door behind him and informed the NIC. He watched as two nurses drew up an injection know as a 10:2 (haloperidol and lorazepam) and place it in a kidney dish and cover it with green paper towels. Three qualified staff entered her room with two assistants in tow and held her down on the bed, removing her undergarments to allow access to her bottom before they plunged the needle in.

Walker didn't hold grudges and this seemed excessive. He struggled with the scenario on his drive home and concluded, there was no way

that it could have been avoided. They had attempted to limit the extent of her poor behaviour. The nurses de-briefed him and told him it wasn't nice but in extreme circumstances it had to be used.
It was hard the first time; it had been hard for all of them. His placement came to an end and he felt sad as he left the ward on his final day. He had enjoyed the real world of mental health nursing; it was so much more than the text book world of university.
Walker and Victoria had enjoyed a quiet Christmas as they were leaving for the Canary Islands on Boxing Day from Manchester airport. He had enjoyed a quite period after his placement, enjoying two days with Monica and a raucous night out with Silks. Monica wanted to meet Victoria. Walker was reticent, he didn't want to introduce her to another woman while the specter of: Nat, Fe, and Siobhan still hung in the air like the ghosts of Christmas past. He explained it to Monica and she understood his reasons. He wasn't sure where they were heading. He liked her, but the settled feeling wasn't satisfying his needs. Walker knew he liked Monica, he also knew he didn't love her.
Boxing day dawned and Walker was up bright and early with his cases packed. He woke Victoria up and dragged her out of bed encountering her normal resistance to the start of the day. He had picked her up from Nat's Christmas afternoon and they had spent the rest of the day checking their packing, tickets and passports before they headed off to his mums to spend the night there. His mum was excited to see them as he parked his car on the drive and kissed Victoria making her usual fuss. Victoria looked on definitely and explained. "Nana I'm not a child," for the hundredth time. Walker let them get on with it and went to make a drink. The running battle continued in the lounge for a few more moments before he intervened.
"Mother, stop treating her like a child and you might get somewhere. If she is giving you some cheek slap her, don't bloody negotiate with her. You are the adult Ok?" He looked at them both and they nodded their understanding of the situation.
When they arrived in the Canary Islands, Walker thought it surreal as he walked down the steps of the aircraft. He had woken to fog, ice and breath bellowing out his mouth as he de-iced the car. Now it was seventy degrees and sunny. Walker had to check that it was still Boxing Day as he unpacked his suitcase and viewed the pool from his hotel window.

He was happy to see that they had a poolside bar and quickly dressed in his shorts and trainers to enjoy the start of the holiday. "Mom, Shorts I'm going for a pint and a swim." Walker announced as he headed off excitedly down the steps and off to the pool.

"Ok don't get drunk though, remember we're going out for dinner soon." He had already left the room .

The bar had cider on draft and it was well stocked, with an attractive lady called Sonia who worked behind it. The accents round the bar were southern in their origin, bordering on London. One excessively large lad spotted his tattoo and enquired curiously. "You Wolves then mate?"

Walker looked down at his arm. "No I'm Albion kid, I just thought I'd have a Bulldog tattooed on my arm in a wolves strip to impress the lads," Walker said it with a smile and a joke in his voice. The bloke got the joke and laughed.

"Point taken"

"Who do you follow then mate?" Walker asked as he took a gentle sip of ice-cold cider, it tasted delicious.

"I`m Tottenham geezer." All chirpy cockney spar
row."Fuck me, yam a yiddo, I suppose I better getter the beer in then." Walker nodded toward the pumps. "You want a beer?"

"Go on then I'll have a lager, who you out here with?"

"Me Ma and baby, they'll be down soon moaning because I'm at the bar, who you with?"

Walker laughed and joked. "I'm meant to be on the wagon."

The big Londoner pointed over to a few ladies and a couple of gents were sat, burnt and under a sun umbrella , grateful for the shade it provided . "Them lot: the wife, her brother and his wife, and his mate and his knock off"

"Knock off?" Walker inquired

"Yeah, his wife`s a cunt, so fuck it, let him play away."

Walker laughed out loud and wiped his mouth as beer spilled out. He liked the bloke's honesty and stuck out his hand. "I'm Walker pleased to meet you."

About 18 months ago he was vomiting up painkillers, his head in a black hood waiting for execution. Now he was round a bar, in the sun, making hay with strangers. Confident and alive.

"Keith, geezer." He shook Walkers hand. "I'd better fuck off, the wife
is eyeballing me and about to bend my head that I've had a few beers.
I'm always round and about come and have a beer when you spot me."
"Ok Keith I will do, avoid the rolling pin mate."
"I'm a past master at ducking Walker believe me geezer. "
Victoria and his mum arrived twenty minutes later, both dressed for
walking down the town not standing at the bar having a beer. They
took a seat under an umbrella and soaked up the ambience as Walker
brought them over drink. It looked a nice place to spend two lazy
weeks. They sipped their drinks before making and exit and heading off
into town to explore their surroundings.
Walker enjoyed the feel of the sun on his face as he dozed by the pool
and thought about how quickly life changed. One moment you're a
nutter, the next your about to have a cocktail and chat up the barmaid.
The bar by the pool was the heartbeat of the complex and there were
little cliques all over the place.
Walker had started talking to a Dutch holidaymaker called Vernon and
a rapport between them had grown as they sipped their drinks,
watched the sun go down and waited for their respective companions
to dress ready for dinner.
Vernon was an easy going chap. Six foot two, blue eyed with short
blond hair. He laughed when Walker called him German. Vernon
informed his English friend that if the English hated the Germans the
Dutch hated them twice as much. They found a common enemy and
would laugh as they told anti-German stories.
 Vernon's wife was a new age type who would arrive at the bar with a :
swish, long hair, sandals and flowing dresses and talk about crystals
and candles before she took their two sons on a journey of spiritual
enlightenment.
 Walker and Sonia had started to talk while he sat at the bar. She
laughed as his jokes and gave him a couple of free drinks. He nodded
his thanks and looked her in the eye, she smiled and looked straight
back. An older Dutch man was always seated at the bar. He would play
chess against himself and Walker would watch with Victoria while
waiting for his mum to come for a pre -dinner drink before they would
head off into town in search of a nice restaurant.
 Vernon translated for them and the Old Dutch man taught Victoria
how to play chess. It was relaxed atmosphere and Walker enjoyed the
break.

After they had eaten and looked around the shops at night. Victoria and his mum would have one drink besides the pool with Keith and the gang before adjourning to bed. Walker would stay an extra hour. Careful not to get drunk, he didn't want the anxiety that could be a result of an extended stay at the bar. He liked to chew the fat with the London lads and their wives and talk football.

During one mission he and Keith had stayed late up until the bar was due to close. Walker had lapsed for the night. They were both drunk having been on Tequila slammers for the last hour. Walker invited Sonia to join them in a drink; she politely refused and said. "I'm not allowed to drink at work."

"Are you allowed to drink when you're not at work," Walker asked. Sonia nodded back at him.

Her eyes looked shyly toward the floor. Walker knew she had played this game before. Still it wasn't a bad time to play. The stars flickered in the sky. The small lights dotted around the garden made for a romantic ambience, highlighting the small cactus plants. The sound of crickets, and the beautiful turquoise sheen of the pool added to the atmosphere. Walker smiled and licked the salt off his knuckle, swallowed down the sprit and sucked on a lemon.

His eyes watered. "This is good Keith. I ay really done slammers before. It's a rush man."

He smiled again at Sonia as he caught her looking at him out the corner of eye. She was wearing a tight white vest that showed off a good figure, her cutoffs displayed well toned muscled and tanned legs. He liked her smile, it suggested mischief. After six slammers he would have liked her if she was a pig. He thought of Monica back home and shook his head.

He wanted fun, not an operation. Anxiety could wait until morning. They arranged a trip into town, after the pool bar closed, Sonia told him. "She would show him the sites."

Keith laughed. "You pulled boy."

Walker didn't see it like that but laughed along as well.

"Wolverhampton charm me old cockney sparrow".

Sonia showed him to a bar which was owned by a couple of middle aged gents she knew, who dressed up like pantomime dames to entertain the holiday makers. As the night drew to a close Sonia invited him back to her apartment,. Walker had never been unfaithful before and his thoughts briefly focused again on Monica as he agreed. He

crawled in at seven just as his mom was opening an eye to the
sunshine. "You just getting in Gary?"
"Yes Ma, had a few with Keith and them then we went onto a club.
"She looked at him "Ok then," evaluating his mood. Everyone did when
he had a night out now. He was no longer a piss head. He drank
socially now. He didn't stay in and load up on cans and rock in his seat
and look for ways to die.
"You fancy a breakfast" Walker didn't want an inquiry as he felt guilty
about his actions. As he walked around the supermarket and his eyes
opened at the prices of English bacon and sausage he again felt the
pangs of guilt in his stomach. His life had changed when he had been
the victim of an affair and even though he and Monica where not
married they were a couple. He wondered if the last years had taught
him anything. He was about to step on the feeling of another human
merely so he could have his fun. He decided that he would have to be
frank with Monica when he returned home and discuss how he felt
and not abuse her feeling toward him. Being mentally well, did not give
him the right to return to previous mistakes of his past and ignite his
insecurities over again. He finished his shopping and paid the bill.
Over the rest of the holiday he and Victoria spent their time relaxing
and enjoying the company of Vernon. Sonia knew he had a daughter,
and, as his mum had returned home, understood he couldn't join her
out on the town. She accepted it and laughed with them at the bar and
gave Victoria free pizzas and drinks and spent her days off with them.
Walker got a guide, she got a lunch and free drinks. It was a suitable
arraignment.
 On their penultimate day there she treated them to a trip to a seafood
restaurant that was perched on a cliff overlooking the Atlantic. It was
off the tourist track and frequented only by local connoisseurs. Walker
looked at the waves crashing into the rocks below and contemplated
the fragility of human existence before he slept with Sonia one more
time.
He had come through the tunnel it was time to enjoy the light. In two
days he would be back in the real world and the holiday would seem as
a dream. This time next week he would be back in a lecture theatre
starting year two of his studies and Victoria would be back in
Shrewsbury.

He would have a word with Monica to cleanse his conscience. All good things come to an end.

PART FOUR: PROFESSIONAL STANDARDS
CHAPTER 27
PSYCHIATRY

Year two was focused on acute psychology, the cutting edge in mental health and Walker felt ambivalence toward it. This was the field he wanted to specialise in; this was the area where his worst nightmares had taken place. He remembered the alarms going off, the sound of angry voices and running feet. The aloof attitude of the nurses, it was a pressured environment with an undercurrent of them and us and a daily ritual of, *'who controls the corridors.* To Walker the philosophy was simple. The lunatics have not taken over the asylum. I'm here to help. I will be straight with you. I will be honest. I'm here to support you, not constrict you. I'm not a jailer. I am a nurse.

Lectures were aimed toward teaching students about psychosis and the relative symptoms associated with: schizophrenia, bi-polar disorder, psychotic depression and personality disorders. Lectures were becoming tedious for Walker. They were uninspiring and unimaginative and didn't compare to the actual experience of delivering good health care or watching as a client responded to you. Seeing an improvement in their mental health until finally all the pain and suffering had been eased and a discharge was around the corner. As a student: you walked in, sat down and were given a hand out that detailed the entire contents of that lecture. Mapping out the next two hours with answers to the questions posed printed in black and white on page 12. The theme was not about constructing an argument and debating the methodology, it was about raising your hand if you didn't understand and being taught parrot fashion. At the start of the module you were given the assessment criteria with a list of points you needed to include in your essay to achieve to pass mark of 40%. The premise of independent research was lost on the course director. He had listened to his mentors whilst on placement and they were critical of the course structure; thinking that it over focused on the academic side to the detraction of clinical skills and experience.

Students had to pass six clinical placements, a final professional placement of sixteen weeks before they were awarded their PIN number and let loose on real people. The mentors thought that it frightened away potentially good candidates, because they didn't feel that they could cope with the rigors associated with the academic side. Walker did see the argument for and against.

However, the university could not be accused of over complicating the educational format; students were offered and received enough support academically. Walker speculated that they should sit down together and search for a resolution. He personally thought that the placement option was the best policy. That is where you learned your craft: on the shop floor, that was where the art of mental health nursing was illuminated to the student.

It took time, effort and money to attend lectures and the course work was not tasking. Walker decided to start selecting which lectures to attend and which he could afford to miss. With his assignment criteria safely tucked away in a file next to his P.C, he wrote his essays without too much head scratching. Added or deleting information as he saw appropriate and waited for the submission date. On his brief trips in to university, he would listen to the rambling of the students becoming bored with the same monologue exuding from the mouths of overanxious nobodies. He understood about journeys in life, and felt the exaggerated stress they displayed where a puerile attempt to promote their own thoughts and find a niche in the crowd.

Placement allocation was a day that Walker looked forward to. He would eagerly view the next stepping stone on his path toward the Holy Grail, and plot the course of his studies.

Today as he approached the office, his stride did not have the same length to it, he hesitated before opening the envelope to reveal the name and address of ward he was scheduled to start work on. Shaking the cobwebs of anxiety ay, he read what was on the paper and blew out his cheeks. As he walked to the café for a coffee he spotted Annette and Rich sitting at a table surrounded with files and text books and joined them Rich waved at him and he walked over to the table with a smile. He missed them, now they were on a branch specific to them and their paths only crossed on brief occasions.

Where they sending you the Gaz?" Allocation day was the same for mental health as well as adult nurses. "Ward one, Pearl, male acute, Nightingale House."

At that moment a seconded student, who was walking past their table overheard the conversation and patted Walker on the back. "That's a war zone mate, good luck and enjoy it." Walker didn't want him to elaborate, his stomach started to churn.

The unit was situated in an inner city area of Birmingham, where there were daily reports of shooting and gang related problems. Walker correlated that the demographics on the ward would reflect that and he would be in the minority. He researched the unit and spent a few hours on the internet researching psychosis and conducive clinical environments; thinking hard, with his pen stuck in mouth scratching his head as he constructed a study plan to show his mentor that he meant business, when he sat down for his initial interview.

Walker was ready for his biggest test, back on an acute ward as a staff member, not a patient. The unit like many others in modern mental health had a generic feel to it. The new designs were aimed at eliminating the system of its asylum and institutional tag, inherited from the big hospitals left over from the fifties. Institutions such as Highcroft and St. Mathews.

The mini-hospital contained three wards: male, female and ICU (Intensive care units). Walker didn't want to work on an ICU with its daily rounds of restraints and liquid sedations to control patients as the nurses patrolled the corridors in pairs. When he arrived in Birmingham for his first day, adrenalin rushed through his system as he approached his destination. He quickly found a parking space, opened the door to his car and vomited bile onto the ground. Hoping the cameras hadn't caught him on tape. He had noticed the CCTV towers they added to the prison feel. Walker pulled himself together, thought of Victoria and used her as a motivational tool and strode to the front of the building. After inspecting a panel in the morning gloom, he pushed a button on the intercom and introduced himself to the voice that replied. The door clicked and Walker felt like Alice in wonderland stepping through the looking glass.

This building did have the feel of a hospital to it. There were no sliding doors that welcomed you, no coffee shops and happy visitors milling in the lobby. The floors did not have carpet. It was clinical and it was naked. Signs pointed the way to prayer rooms and psychology interview suites.

All the doors away from the main atrium were locked and he felt the intense atmosphere that hung like mist in the corridors. His ward was located on the second floor and with leaden legs he made his way up the stairs. He found Pearl unit and buzzed to gain attention. The doors had glass panels and he could see straight through to the unit. All he could make out was a long corridor with an occasional closed door.

A large man, black as Silks made his way to the door, inserted a key into the lock and the door clicked open. Walker tried to enter the man didn't move. "Can I help you?" He stared straight at Walker. "Yes I'm a student nurse here for placement" The gentleman looked him up and down, there no welcoming smile yet. He paused for a second and invited Walker through the entrance to his past. He was ushered into to an office that was five steps to the unit located opposite the *'dayroom'*. The dayroom was an unwelcoming sight with seats placed against the wall, as you would arrange them out for a game of musical chairs. There was a magnolia lino floor with a TV and video on a shelf on the wall, locked behind a glass cabinet.

It was early, just before seven am and there were four lads already sitting down smoking. Three were black lads in tracksuits, caps and trainers, the uniform of *'the ends*. They reminded him of the youth he knew that hung round, *The Coates*. One white older man with long hair was sweeping up frantically.

"In here mate." The *'bouncer'* invited Walker to step into a small office that doubled as a staff room. A woman looked up from her notes that she was busily writing and did manage a small smile which didn't look completely sincere. Her name was Jackie and she had dreadlocks. A hard face with large brown eyes. Her cardigan was rumpled and she looked like she would fight a dog for a bone."Fresh meat on the ward from the university, welcome to Pearl."

Walker smiled back and offered his hand."Hello my name`s Gary," she accepted it. He was surprised by how strong her hands were. "Well you look the part Gary; you should fit in well round here." He had wondered how a shaven headed man with an England tattoo would fit in around an area full of Jamaican lads. He rubbed his head and said. "I'm bald, it's not a fashion statement," he tried to lift the mood. "Good job. Round here mate they love skinheads. Pour yourself a brew and sit down. You look scared to death."

Walker was a bit on edge and had hoped he had covered any overt signs of nerves with his stone faced approach. He didn't know who worried him the most, the rugby player marking the door, the Rasta in the office or the gang members in the day room! These were not the same type of people that had greeted him on elder adult.

A middle aged lady bustled in to the room with fresh energy and full of vigour. She was wearing a green jacket that did nothing for her, and smelt of cigarettes. She hung her coat up hurriedly and Walker was reminded of a mouse with the way she snatched at her movements. "You made a fresh brew Jack or have I got to do it?" "Make a fresh one Dot, take him with you, (she pointed at Walker), and show him the kitchen. He is a student so he must know how to make a cuppa, am I right err?" Jackie paused and waved her hands at him.

"Gary" he provided the answer for her,

"Gary..........I'm no good with names.......sorry." The apology was insincere.

Walker followed Dot off the ward and into a nearby kitchen, her keys jangling as she walked. She explained to him as she washed out teapots that they didn't have their own kitchen on the unit adding with a agitated smile. "This lot would have a field day with boiling water and an entire canteen of unsupervised cutlery."

He helped her make the tea and coffee and he pushed the trolley back onto the ward and into the dayroom, Dot popped her head round the corner and cheerfully said morning to the lads sitting around. "Hello Dot," they answered back, except one lad who was looking at the floor with his head in his hands.

"What's up with you then? Had a bad night have you Luke?" Luke looked up at her and pointed to his head. "Alright love, I'll make us a cuppa later and we can have a chat".

Walker immediately liked her, she was happy and bright and the lads in the room were automatic in acknowledging her with no apparent resentment or hostility. When they sat back down in the office, Dot explained to Walker that when Luke was pointing to his head, the voices were disturbing him and he wasn't happy. She passed on this information to Jackie who made a note of it.

She tasted the tea that Walker poured into a cup and handed to her. "Let's hope your tea improves in the next nine weeks you're with us student! Oh and you're lucky enough to have me as your mentor!

How's that to start your day then?" Walker raised a thumb and smiled back at her.

Jackie was a veteran of Birmingham Mental Health and charge nurse on the unit. She had learned her trade in the big old hospitals and had plenty of experience in, 'challenging environments'. She waited for the room to clear and asked to see his portfolio from University. She quickly flicked through it before she focused on his study plan. "Very good .

Gary, but I'll be honest with you, all that is bollocks. You can write about it, but can you do it? It will take a week for you to find your feet here. All I want from you in that first week is to get to know the patients, the staff and how the ward runs without me babysitting you. I will show you round and all that but I want to see you in this environment and how you cope with it. I can teach you how to give an injection, give out medication etc but to feel comfortable and be a natural communicator, that I can't do." Walker agreed with her. That was his thinking and personal philosophy. He kept his mouth shut because he didn't want to come over like a student swat. He was happy that she was a straight talker and came to the point, he could work with that.

After his initial assessment he walked around the ward to get his bearings and view his new surroundings. The ward had a bar football table with very little else to stimulate its sixteen guests. That was their world until the psychiatrist decided that they were well enough for a return to their lives on the outside. A day room, a dining room and chill out room. Sixteen bedroom doors, each one with different story behind it.

Walker introduced himself to the qualified staff, there were three of them. The ward manager popped her head around the dayroom door to welcome him. Her name was Elaine and she hoped he enjoyed his stay with them. The patients all welcomed her, before she had an opportunity to say hello to them. Walker enjoyed the moment, it showed certain camaraderie between staff and clients and despite the initial feel of the ward it did appear that the lads had a good rapport with the staff.

Walker started to thaw and introduced himself to the lads sitting and staring vacantly at the television set. A couple of moody black lads asked him if he was NF and he laughed and told them he was bald and not a skinhead and if he had hair it would be longer. They nodded back at him and accepted what he had said. One complemented him on his shirt (Lacoste), "nice threads man."

"Cheers mate, it was a present, I ay got many good shirts so I thought I would stick on me best clobber to make an impression."

"Safe, my names Granty." Walker had been accepted.

Walker got on well with the older man who had been sweeping the floors since the break of dawn. He was quick with the one liner and had lots of banter with the other lads on the ward which raised the mood and kept them all amused. One Asian lad bounced on the ward at lunch time saying "Safe, safe, safe" to any one who would listen to him and started chucking cigarettes around. One hit Walker on the chest and he thought it rude to refuse so he accepted it and lit it. Jackie's head appeared round the entrance and she nodded toward him, Walker gave his cigarette to a man sitting next to him, who thanked him and took a deep pull.

"Well, what you think then student fresh meat?"

"I'm glad the first day is done and dusted, I was shitting myself this morning."

She laughed at his honesty, "Yeah it was showing a bit but you did Ok, you went in the day room and didn't hide in the office like some students do and read the notes. So take a bow you did alright. You got your shifts for the week?"

"Yeah, yeah"

"I've put you on with me for three days a week, the other two you find your feet and show initiative, is that fair enough?"

"Yeah that's fair"

" Don't worry Walker I've looked in the diary we have another five students starting next week you will be an old hand by then, it will be your turn to rip the piss . Get your coat and have twenty minutes on me. I've cleared it with the gaffer."

"Thank you," Walker said.

"Don't thank me mate, you have a long way to go yet and I've failed more than one student.

I expect you here twenty minutes before shift tomorrow morning. I'll do your schedule and what I expect of you and you can dump yours." Jackie smiled at him. "Welcome to acute mental health and Pearl".

Week one on acute progressed as well as he could have expected. He had moments when his arse flapped. One lad, a Rasta man had taken a dislike to him and when Walker went into the day room to either wish everyone a good morning or good afternoon he would scowl at him and ask. " Why you look upon me so?" Walker told him no offence and would leave softly and go into the office for handover. The routine on the unit was relaxed: receive handover, check all the rooms make sure you had a full complement of patients. It wasn't good if you lost one during the night (Jackie told him). Check the board to see who your client was for the day, (the nurse in charge allocated this duty and you were expected to attempt to have a one to one with that client).

 Most nurses didn't because they had better things to do, most nursing assistants did because that what was they were paid for. Walker appreciated the logic behind this. It meant that all staff got to meet all clients and rotate their knowledge. He did point out a problem to Jackie that maybe some of the lads might get pissed off with different faces asking them the same questions (he had when he was on the other side of the fence). She said that this was factored in when allocation was made. One member of staff would make toast and tend to the tea trolley for breakfast, a trolley would then be delivered onto the ward and they would go and knock on doors to make sure everybody was aware that breakfast was being served.

The food was good and plentiful, Walker had to admit. He never felt like eating when he was unwell; the food offered, didn't motivate you to eat. On Pearl you had a cooked breakfast: with scrambled eggs, sausages (bacon twice a week) either beans or tomatoes' and as much toast as you could humanly eat. Fresh fruit juice was also on tap with a selection of cereals.

It was also nice to see that the staff ate with the clients and they mingled with each other without a second thought. Lunch came three hours later and was a waste because most went of it went into the bin. Most people were too full from breakfast. The lunches again, provided good meals and specialist diets were catered for; with West Indian meals such as curried goat and salt fish. Walker tasted them, they weren't as good as Silk's mums, but they were still very tasty and better than he could manage.

The first time Walker saw problems on the unit was when two lads wanted the same meal, staff were on hand quickly and the problem didn't escalate. The evening meal came three hours after that and again was hot and plentiful. Complements had to be paid; they eat better than most people did on the outside. Walker's confidence increased and he became part of the team and enjoyed the thrust and energy needed to survive on an acute unit.

He understood that he had a long way to go and many greater challenges lay in front of him. He would enjoy his beer on the weekend, he felt like he deserved a few with Silks and the boys.

He woke early on Monday morning. For once there was a feeling of anticipation not trepidation in his stomach, as he shaved his head and got dressed in his shirt and trousers. He could get into work early via the motorway network and he left the flat with a spring in his step. Walker was also aware that they had new students starting today and already he felt like an old hand on the unit. He was the first member of staff to arrive for the morning shift and had made an early tea trolley up for the lads and the staff. He took the NIC (Nurse in Charge) a cup of tea into the nursing station. She was manning the phones and struggling to find staff`s cover, when he glanced at the allocations board he noticed a new name written on the staff board, a charge nurse named Maggie was on duty; they should have named her Ratchet.

CHAPTER 24
ETHICS

Walker detected a subtle change of mood when Maggie Patel stepped onto the ward, the needle of the barometer gently moved to low pressure. The banter in the day room reduced a notch and the horseplay in the staff room became non-existent. Maggie Patel was in her mid thirties, good looking and not a traditional Indian lady. She wore smart designer clothes, sported a salon cut hair style and if you checked her in the pub you would look twice and offer her a bed for the night, it would be rude not to. She had been born in Yorkshire, and despite her salon look she kept the harsh lilt of her accent. The way she enunciated her words added to their severe message she carried. Walker later learned she hailed from Rotherham. He had visited the town during his time following Wolves and hadn't been overly impressed by the welcome he received there.

Maggie Patel was loud. She laughed at her own jokes and amplified arrogance. As she walked into the office, she viewed the new faces and joked about students to the regular staff. She tutted and moaned about university allocations, while the nervous students smiled anxiously and waited. Her insensitive attitude started to boil at Walkers brain, even though he had to admit, you did have to sell tickets to get a seat in the handover room. Still she didn't have to make them feel any more self conscious than they did already, it bad enough that they had found Bedlam and he was run by nurse Racthed.

The goal in mental health was to move away from the vision of *One Flew Over the Cuckoo's nest* model of care.

Her thoughts on producing a contemporary and holistic environment would indeed have been interesting. She was a bully and she stank of her own self-importance.

She interrupted the handover while the other staff nurse was in mid flow, explaining she had been away on leave for two weeks and could she be more specific in her dialogue. Walker knew it was lever and meant to resonate with the students with a, *'look at me I'm in charge* metaphor behind it. The Asian lad who had met Walker, by throwing the cigarettes around the day room on his first day, entered the room ten minutes later. Maggie thanked him (sarcastically) for being prompt.

His eyes met Walkers and vice versa and they looked quizzically across the room at each other. Walker had thought he was an in-patient, he had thought Walker was on day release and also a client. He introduced himself as Foz. Walker immediately liked Foz. He was a decent man that had served time in jail and exuded patience with the patients on the ward.

He would bounce around the corridors with a bright and sunny persona and always offered assistance with any job that had been delegated. If it did kick off, he would be the first to respond, and always ensured that it didn't escalate to an inappropriate level. Foz had life experience, having spent some time in young offenders institute and walked with real people when he was off duty.

This always gave a man (or woman) an extra dimension in Walker opinion. You didn't need to have served prison time or been in front of a magistrate to fulfill this criterion; however it did appear to add an extra degree of empathy to your practise if your personal experiences assisted you in relating to the clients. Some *'career nurses'* chose this profession as a means to accept the kudos that came with the title: R.M.N. There weren't many of their kind and they appeared in mental health more so than general nursing.

They were intelligent and adept at the scholastic aspect involved in the occupation, able to work their way through the plethora of complex documents that punctuated nursing. They were able to relate to the psychiatrists that met with their patients for twenty minutes a week, after they had completed eighteen holes on the golf course and charged a ridiculous amount for consultations in the private sector. Walker didn't begrudge them a piece of the pie, hard work, drive and ambition deserved reward otherwise life would become a stagnant pond.

The paradox for him was the insincerity that was evident in the office when discussing patients, their illness and social circumstances. Some comments showed a distinct lack of understanding into an individual's situation and they would flow gently into the river of care without a ripple on the surface. Walker found this a disingenuous stance and remembered the originator and tempered his attitude accordingly. Nursing was a caring profession; in the public's eye they were considered, *'angels'*.

In later life, Walker would start his personalised training courses with the question: Should nurses be able to relate to the clients they cared for? A balance had to be achieved, and some did attempt the concept of empathy. On his career path Walker was unfortunate to meet some that did not, appearing more concerned at reaching the top of their profession at the expense of care delivery and their ability to communicate with and learn from their patients.

Handover completed, Maggie made her way into the office to check the diary and communication book, two other staff nurses opened up the clinic and started the preparation for dispensing morning meds. Walker asked Foz if he needed a lift and they struck up a rapport from that moment onward. The new students unsure of the routine hung around like sheep and a few NA's felt sympathy and pointed them in the direction of the housekeeping cupboard. Walker did the rounds with Foz to check that all who were there were well and left the ward to attend to breakfast.

When breakfast was completed, Walker invited the other students to help him tidy up the canteen, as they cleaned the room he introduced himself and explained the morning routine. The dayroom had started to fill up with clients and the buzz of conversation took precedence over the clinking of dishes. The dayroom was the only room on the unit that allowed smoking and as such filled up quickly and became the heart beat of the ward. Foz was already there handing out cigarettes and enjoying his banter with the lads. He was quick witted and capable on the repartee front. Foz was able to generate laughter.

Walker listened and applauded, he understood that if people are laughing, then they weren't crying and focusing on the negatives. The atmosphere helped the nervous students integrate and broke the ice effortlessly. Maggie's head appeared at the door to investigate what was going on, she paused for a moment with her hands on her hips and then pointed at three students including Walker, her fingers like the barrel of a revolver, the students her prey. "Come with me if you don't have anything to do. I'll find you some work." They looked at each other and followed in her wake. "Who's done a depot before?" Walker raised his hand, feeling like he was back in class. He was confident of sticking someone with a needle.

He had been allocated depot clinic whilst on community placement and had injected hundreds of patients in a week to become proficient in the skill. She nodded her head at him and ordered the other two to find out the procedure for admitting clients onto an acute unit. The sections and protocols involved and to write it down and bring it to her before shift closer. She opened the door to the clinic and looked at Walker. "You done many depots then?"

"I did the depot clinic when I was on PCL (Primary Care Liaison) for a month, so I've done a few."

"So you're an expert then?" The tone not lost on Walker, he breathed and didn't rise to the bait. "I wouldn't go that far." Walker smiled, attempting to add some humour as she was starting to make him feel nervous.

"Draw up some Depixol for me, the dosage is in his notes," Maggie did not return Walkers smile." Then you can inject him and I will observe to make sure that you are Z tracking correctly.

"Ok."Walker replied.

The drug was hard to draw up as it was diffused in vegetable oil which made it thick, inhibiting its passage into the syringe. Walker knew that you had to agitate it, but it could be difficult at times. He managed to draw it up correctly, changed needles and left the ampoules on the side for verification that the dose was correct, covered it and awaited feedback.

"Are you going to inject him here, or in his room?"

I was going to ask him?"

"Why?"

"Choice and options and all that. " Walker had worked hard to build a rapport, this women was us-and-them, all over the fucking place.

"It is better practise to perform the procedure in the clinic. It's a sanitised environment and you know if the client has a weapon."

Fuck me, Walker thought a weapon? What was she on? Did she think he was off the boat and just starting? He knew she was making a point at how tough and dangerous the job could be and she was queen of the fucking place, but stroll on she was making a bad job difficult here.

"I'll go and ask him then." Walker left the clinic and knocked on Dwain's door, he was up and about, tending to his personal stereo.

"Morning Dwain you Ok mate? It's time for your depot, can you come to the clinic please. "Maggie on then?" He looked at Walker with resignation.

"She is Nurse In Charge, yes." Walker answered.

"Thought so, you giving it me?"

"I'm easy like a Sunday morning mate. If you want me to I'll do it."
Walker opened his arms.

"It's your choice me old China."

"Yeah man, I don't mind if you do it."

Walker winked at him. "Cheers mate. I've done shit loads, no need to worry."

Dwain followed Walker back to the clinic and Maggie wished him a good morning with no warmth, she was as sterile as the clinic itself.

"This student is going to do your injection Dwain. " Walker thought, I have a fucking name, or did you just want to pull rank?

Dwain nodded and shrugged his shoulders at her. "Cool, no problem."
Walker sorted his head out and breathed, she was making him uneasy. He concentrated and pulled the skin back, inserted the needle quickly and counted to ten as he released the meds into Dwain's upper right quadrant of his glutinous maximus. When he withdrew the needle he applied a plaster as a spot of blood that had just started to leak out from the small needle prick.

Walker thanked the heavens that Dwain wasn't a *bleeder*. He placed the used syringe in the yellow sharps container, thanked Dwain for his co-operation and waited for applause and congratulations. She nodded and left the clinic without a word. He locked up the clinic, and dropped the keys and medication folder to Maggie off to her in the office. "Will you sign my clinical competency sheet please?"

"I'm not your mentor, so I can't. I will hand over how you did, who is your mentor?" "Jackie." A flicker lit up in Maggie's eyes. Perhaps she wasn't as proficient at intimidating his gaffer.

"I'll have a word with her." The phone rang and Maggie was off to fry bigger fish. Walker was wary of her and relieved that her attention was off him. He wasn't sure he would impersonate her interpersonal style any time soon. Maggie lay off him off for the next two days, her persona casting a shadow over the entire ward. It appeared that she didn't understand the therapeutic premise of happiness and deemed laughter and banter as skiving and not getting the job done. Walker didn't understand her stance. His second week was completed successfully and he didn't broach the subject with Jackie; when she asked him how he was doing, Walker replied. "Fine."

Monica had a week off work and she was squatting at Walkers. He was at work, completing his shift patterns and working on his placement portfolio, so it was no strain on his brain that she had tried to add a 'female' touch to his home. Walker enjoyed the thought of intelligent conversation when he arrived home and a person to share his day with. They had been seeing each other for nine months now and unlike his other relationships this one was steady with no real dramas. He had resolved the guilt he had felt about his short fling on holiday. He had confessed, been admonished and walked out the other side. He didn't enhance her reputation with him.

He hadn't really have to beg, Monica had forgiven him in under a day. Once she had caught him the girl's toilets of the Fitre doing a line or two with Silks and hadn't passed a comment, again the term carpet could be associated and this was causing some conflict within him. As with Fe it appeared that university graduates became subservient when in a relationship. He wasn't sure that this was a valid study, but in his experience this was certainly the case. He knew he wasn't that irresistible to women. He could not understand why the ones with a first class degree would pass over his obvious shortcoming and lose all rhyme and reason when dealing with him. Was it Text book dating? Walker knew that wasn't the way to go.

Use your gut instinct, remember evolution. Walker had never been a social anthropologist but the origin of the species had defiantly been a work that defined nature. Presented a case for eugenics and had spurred on many to find an answer to weak chromosomes. The population was ageing. Some lessons of the past were being learned.

The Fitre had been christened by the locals that lived around his Tudor visage. It was a quaint looking pub, all wattle and daub and located next to a large green that became a hub for families and lads in the summer time. It was a new venue that the lads used regularly and had been renamed from the sign on the board outside due the fights that could erupt there on a Friday, Saturday and Sunday. This was when the firm was in full attendance, their numbers now swelled by a new alliance with a Sunday league football team which Langley had started playing for.

When Walker was in the pub, Monica watched him quench his thirst with gusto on her trips out with him and the lads on a Friday. Despite his past indiscretions with alcohol she was easy on his ear, with no judgment call on his social habits.

Monica was aware of his triggers and antecedents, so perhaps she was doing a study on him? Again the dichotomy of feeling began to sow the seeds of doubt into his mind. She didn't push him and provoke him, there was no rollercoaster ride for his mind to endure. On the other hand it also made Walker uneasy, was he settling for her? She did evoke some passion within him? As Nat and Siobhan had punched him (metaphorically) to the ground and caused his emotions to burn, Monica did not. He had the feeling he could take her or leave her at any time. There was no angst involved in the relationship. He pondered on the question; did he love her? He was nearly 36 perhaps it was time to settle down? Walker also knew if you had to ask the question. Unfortunately you already knew the answer.

For years Walker and Silks had been attending Sunday league football matches staged on parks in and around Wolverhampton. Langley was a sought after player, tenacious in the tackle, and hardworking. He was the epitome of a Jack Russell terrier on a football pitch. They had always followed the teams he played for, excited by the prospect of a Sunday with all the trimmings.

Walker would turn up with a bag of beer containing Strongbow and Carling and hand them out. Silks would run the line, the flag firmly in his hand, his mouth running with him up and down the pitch, spitting insults at the opposition players and supporters. A few lads would show to support their mates and they could muster a good twenty soldiers on the sideline for a match.

Their behaviour was already causing the local FA concern. Players would suffer intimidation from the likely looking lads on the sidelines and there were regular pitch invasions and the fines started to mount up. They considered it banter. The rest of the world called it Hooligan behaviour. Walker could never seem to rid himself of the adrenalin that was associated with football. It didn't matter how many sessions he had attended, how many books he read, some traits were in the blood and even Darwin couldn't explain them. Human nature was Human nature. The mind like water had a way to find its level.

The club was owned by a local entrepreneur who had made it on the back of the rave scene via club promotion and finally diversifying into different avenues, all mainly legal. He was a sharp financial player and an astute business man, now a millionaire, but he had never forgotten his roots as he boarded planes that conveyed him to glamorous locations around the world. He mixed with animal charm with the lads that supported his club, enjoying the rowdy banter and making sure those that needed a drink had one. He ran his business with his two brothers, who possessed the good manners and bright smiles that kept them above the rest. They were a top firm in the criminal food chain which marked Wolverhampton out for the rest of the country. When Walker mentioned Wolves, when he was on one of his jollies around the Med, lads would always nod their head in reverence and respect. Sunday football became a social occasion, the wives and children would turn out. It became the best day of the week. The kids would bring a packed lunch. Walker subsequently added pop and fruit juice to his shopping list. Silks managed to find a couple of air horns to add to the atmosphere. They would all join in the chants from the side lines .Silks and Walker devised their own anthem and the kids would sing it as the parents looked on with smiles, backing them with air horns. It was like the, *Nou Camp* on match day. After the game had finished they would all adjourn to the *'Fitre'*. Drink laugh and eat, a family day in paradise.

Silks would pick Walker up at nine and they would start the day from there. "You carrying mate?" Silks looked across at Walker."I had a good night, spent all my dollars on a Henry and few lap dancers." Walker smiled and shook his head. The bloke never appeared to suffer from hangovers or a come down off the party gear. If he laid his head down at four after a bender, he would have five hours sleep and be up the next morning hopping about like a spring chicken. Walker rarely did a two day bounce now.

His body was packing up with all the abuse it had suffered. He experienced severe gout attacks and ached to an extent were he couldn't walk at times. Toxins could not be processed with the same speed, his kidneys and liver had suffered damage from all his previous excesses. The poisons in his body now had a physical edge. Walker would grimace and the pain would stop him from repeating the abuses of the past. Even if his mind still had some way to go. The darkness of his past had been replaced with new vigour and a new anger to expel demons as they nested, there would be no mistake about internalisation, Walker had opened new doors, but new rooms offered a different set of conundrums on how they needed decorating.

Silks and Walker had a system that was set in stone. If one of them had money, the other had money they would split the bill or run up each other's slate. Walker had showed at the pub to pay off his debt and his eyes widened when Disco (the gaffer) told him it was into three figures.

Walker had been expecting to hand over a score. Silks had entertained a young lady and was short of the folding stuff and had used Walkers tab to cover their date. Walker had done the same in the past to Silks, it was tit for tat and became a badge of honour until Disco had stamped it out, unless he had prior instructions from both parties that they had authorised the expense. Walker paid his bar bill with a frown, ordered a cider and double and asked

Disco to stick it onto Silks tab. They always paid within the month and on the whole would not take liberties.

Silks had ten pounds in his pocket, Walker had a purple. Thirty was enough for a starter and get them in the pub. They could speculate from there. Silks indicated and maneuvered the car over to the curb. A sign in the window of a small corner shop suggested they had bargain inside. In five minutes they had 24 cans, twenty Bensons and enough left over for an hour in *The Fitre*.

 Walker got on the phone and invited Monica; she would be good for a round or two. He got his mum to drop Victoria off. He could hear her moaning in the background. She didn't do football now, she was all girlie girl, her tom boy nature had never really had a foothold in her mental make-up. Walker listened for a moment and shook his head. "Mum just brings her, no debate, not arguments. You`re the adult. She comes now!"

The beers and abuse flowed on a sunny morning that was crisp and fresh. The laughter reached new levels as the cleverest put downs showered over the opposition. Their boys did the job and had turned over their opponents with ease. Walker had been told by Langley to get off the pitch at least ten times, a new record even for him. Victoria remained in Langley's MPV, playing with his children with the heaters on obviously not enjoying the fresh morning air. Her face set in a frown and her shoulders hunched, the look of rebellion easy to see. Walker opened the door and tossed in a shopping back full of: fruit , crisps and pop. Maybe that would raise a smile or two. Short`s eyes softened as she started to thaw .Just like her fucking mother, he laughed as she accepted the bribe.

The Fitre was empty. They had made it in first and were already merry. "Give us three lagers, a Hand-glider, two cokes and a blackcurrant cordial please Disco." Silks leaned on the bar.

"One round each today," said the big man with the messy blond hair, and a face like a sailor. His complexion was rugged ,as if he spend too

much time outdoors exposed to the elements. He pointed at the pair.
"You nearly up to your limit."
Silks smiled back. "Cool Disco, sort you out next week mate, its pay day
mate." He rubbed his hands signifying he had done well.
 Walker and Silks were satisfied with the arrangement; they knew that
something would turn up. Disco was fair and the best Gaffer of any
pub they had known and they had drunk in many. Within an hour they
had busted their credit and abused the kindness of a few more lads.
After a brief confab they decided to head off down to, 'The Coates' and
try to blag a beer down there. Silks had smiled when the pair sat back,
finished off his parcel.
"New gaffer down The Coates Bruce, let's see what's he about eh?"
"New blood eh? Always welcome round there." The sarcasm was
unmistakable in his tone."
"Let's hope he has sense of humour." Walker added with a grin.
"He knows me, met him before." Silks smiled at a distant memory.
 Silks went back indoors and shouted at the tribe to get their gear
together. In a bundle of bags and banter they managed to leave The
Fitre in one piece. The rest of the drinkers didn't want to spend what
was rest of their Sunday on The Chatsworth estate.
 They piled into the cars and headed off the short distance to The
Coates. A short distance by car, a lifetime of social economics. Walker
called Monica and informed of their new destination, she was waiting
on the car park when the convey pulled in. The bar had the same faces
in the same chairs as they entered with bluster and noise.
The new gaffer knew that Walker and Silks were good punters and
liked in the area, he had done his homework, after a brief negotiation
he agreed to sell them some bottles on credit, at cost and throw in the
occasional round for the ladies. Walker and Silks played pool all
afternoon with a top lad called Cordial, a large mixed race man with a
penchant for pool. He played money games against the Indians, men
that drank in the small drinking clubs that were dotted around Wolves
and belied the wealth of those who socialised inside. He was a
respected face on the estate, who didn't push his position onto others.
He didn't need to.
They had two bottles of Smirnoff and a bottle of JD on the table to sip
on as they liked. Victoria, Monica and the rest of the ladies and
children had gone round to the lounge to play bingo and have a girlie

chat and discuss the irrelevant topics that women can talk about for hours without getting bored.

Monica would pop her head round the bar room door every now and then to ask what time they were leaving Walker would tell her, 'soon' and go back to playing pool with the lads. The bottles were empty and the three amigos were very drunk and increasingly loud.

Silks had lost a week's money on pool. His devilish scheme to get Cordial pissed was backfiring as he was drinking more sprits than anyone else. He checked the bottles for dregs and lurched over to the bar and ordered three more bottles. The new gaffer shook his head. "The bar bills over a hundred for the afternoon."

"That's fuck all mate, give us some beers now and we will settle up on Tuesday." Silks was expecting a result on Tuesday and in all fairness always sorted his bills.

"No lads you have had enough now."He placed both hands on the bar as a gesture of assertiveness. Walker's eyes widened with amusement and a hint of surprise. Was he making a stand?

"You what mate?" Silks shook his head, needed a translator he didn't understand the word , no. Walker recognised the subtle change in tone in his mate's voice and knew that there was a problem and walked over to the bar."What's occurring Silks?"

"How long we drunk in here Bruce?"

Walker rubbed his nose and looked at the man, who was now looking increasingly out of his depth. "Fuck me, years mate, why?"

"Have we always paid our bills." Walker eyed the gaffer, his eyes narrowing.

"Fucking right, we always do, why?"

"This joker says we can't have anymore." Silks pointed at the man's chest with a violent stabbing motion. "Fuck him let's get a carry out and trap them." Walker was easy, he knew Silks was pissed up and looking for a row."No. I want a drink here before I go, give us some beer gaffer." Silks spat out the word, *'gaffer'* his tone heavy with derision. Walker looked at the bloke. "Just another round three pints then we are gone OK?" Three pints was fuck all after the ocean of beers he had just given them on tick. It was a reasonable solution to the problem. Silks would be happy with one more before he passed out. Cordial was on a freebie anyway, so he didn't give a fuck. It was only another fiver and honour would remain intact for all parties.

The few customers in the bar had gone quietly away they knew that trouble was in the air and probably on the way.

"No lads sorry, you have had enough." This was not the time to make a point. They were drunk, perhaps he should have considered his options three hours ago when they started on their binge.

The glass smashed into the mirror that was just behind the bar sprinkling shards of glass onto the now nervous publican. He looked around quickly, his eyes were white and indicated his weakness.

"Stop it now or I will call the police, I mean it." Shit thought Walker. Don't threaten Silks with the Old Bill. It was bad enough that you had refused to serve him in his own backyard, but you didn't understand the 'out', with the offer for one round to pacify the geezer. Now you want to call the police on a man who had done years in prison? What a fucking cunt, Walker thought.

The second glass was launched and took a few bottles down. "Fuck it mate, give him a beer now and it's done and dust kidder." Walker tried one last attempt at peace negotiations.

"You're both barred." Walker had done fuck all but try to preserve the peace and now the twat was barring him!

"Fuck you!" The table went over: bottles, glasses and ashtrays hit the floor with a loud crash.

Silks laughed ,as he looked around at the noise."Go on Bruce fuck him up." Silks aimed another glass at the bloke and took out some more glassware. Walker turned over some more tables.

The bar was now empty, all the punters safely out the way. The gaffer was hiding under the bar. Victoria placed her head round the door to see what the fuss was about and saw her dad and uncle turning the furniture into fire wood and shouted at them to stop. Walker turned and saw her and Monica, both wide eyed staring at him. They smashed up the last table and walked around to the lounge as if nothing had happened.

Walker pointed at Victoria."Get your stuff ready Shorty please, we're leaving . He looked across at Monica who was still pale and mouthing words with no sound." Start the car now let's go home." Walker knew they had outstayed their welcome. Silks beckoned to his lot to move out in regulation formation, they laughed as they exited 'The Coates'. It was the end of a fantastic Sunday and it cost them fuck all.

Monica wasn't used to that behaviour, she tried to reason with him and explain that's not what was expected on a Sunday trip to the pub. Victoria knew her dad and Uncle Silks all too well and even though disappointed with his behaviour, she understood this was not the right time to confront him with logic. This was nothing to what she had witnessed in her short life. Her dad had been well behaved and on an even keel for years now. She knew that this wasn't a symptom of any mental illness, this was just him and Silks playing up .People had different value systems. It didn't mean they were mad. She understood the difference, she knew her dad. If you left him alone for half an hour he would calm down, sleep and be straight headed by the morning. Monica pushed the situation to its limits and Walker unimpressed by her persistence looked at her with bored resignation, her time had come."

Shut the fuck up or fuck the hell off, you're a fat cunt anyway and past your sell by date. "He folded his arms, looked out of the window, anger flowing off him in waves. She dropped them off at the flat, apologised to Victoria, ignored Walker and drove off into the sunset.

Walker wasn't bothered, he tried to rationalise his behaviour to Victoria he wanted to explain what had happened. She listened briefly, told him he was a dickhead and went to bed. He laughed and went to sleep in front of the TV, the Discussion was concluded.

When Walker woke the next day, he was greeted with the familiar pangs of guilt and anxiety. These moments lived long in his memory, as his drunken stupidity became clear in his mind and disapproving thoughts would provoke a rush of guilt in his stomach. Walker was trying to come to terms that he was two different people: two competing personalities, personalities that lived poles apart from each other.

Drunken Walker could be a violent, cruel, cold bastard of a man. Sober Gary was kind sensitive and reasonable with a good sense of humour. He understood the premise concerning the adoption of his alter ego. It didn't help him resolve his eternal conflict; that both his personalities didn't like one another.

This was the foundation and the basis of his concerns. Walker wished he could find a middle ground for them to meet and exchange a point of interest. Unfortunately Walker liked drunken Gary. The man could look after himself and cope with the rigors of modern life. Most people liked the sober version of Walker, who was intelligent and listened before making a rash decision, thus adding to the dichotomy of feeling cloaking Walker. The general consensus of opinion with his friends was he was a paradigm. There were occasions when Walker got drunk and didn't make the transition into Mr. Hyde and remained *'sober 'Gary'* those that were out in his company enjoyed a better night of revelry. Walker had existed for years as a dog chasing his own tail round in circles to find a solution to his complex behaviour.

His year in therapy had resolved many issues harboured deep in his unconsciousness, but a cure for his perceived weakness hadn't yet been discovered, his internal battles would simmer on until they boiled over.

Walker continued to impress on his acute placement. Walker and Jackie formed a good working relationship, each trusting the other in a short space of time. Jackie trusted him to do the medication rounds with only minimal supervision, after two weeks of faultless performances. Walker completed two weeks of nights shifts and completed all the tasks, the nurse in charge was accountable for without drama: the night register, notes and handovers. Jackie observed him and nodded her head in approval. She had a calm, firm and assertive ambience that surrounded her as she walked down the corridors of Mental Health.

Unlike her peer, Miss Maggie Patel, she still managed to have a laugh with all the staff and clients without detracting from her supervisory status. Jackie would motivate Walker and as he grew in confidence, he would want to accept increased responsibility and take on increasingly complex tasks.

Walker came to the attention of the ward manager, who asked him what he was planning to do post qualification. Walker paused for a moment and answered her. "Acute nursing, to work on the ward, to help those that need it. I want to serve my apprenticeship.

Being a student teaches you how to be a nurse. When you qualify you have to learn how to become a nurse."

She smiled at him. "Exactly," obviously impressed with his answer. "There are always jobs on Pearl ward. When one comes up, I would suggest that you apply." Walker was aware that at the end of your three years study, you had a sixteen week professional placement; the transition from student nurse to qualified staff. He had already chosen where he wanted to spend his time.

He told this Elaine over a coffee and an informal chat and she replied that she would be happy to have him back on her ward.

He owed his rapid progress to Jackie. Walker need strength around him, he needed a good example to follow. She was respected where Maggie was feared. Walker knew which he preferred to be.

His patience finally snapped with Maggie on a Sunday afternoon when he was nearing the end to his time on Pearl Ward. Sundays were quiet days on Pearl, if the weather was sunny the staff would organise a bar-b –que for Sunday lunch. Elaine was always generous with the ward`s petty cash and would go the extra mile to make sure that the lads on the unit were looked after.

Maggie didn't look happy when Walker arrived for his afternoon shift. She moaned about staff and lack of responsibility to the few that were seated in the office awaiting handover.

Staff levels were relaxed on the weekend, and her co-nurse had phoned in sick making her the only qualified staff on the unit. Walker was super numerate and didn't count as an official number and two NA's had also phoned in sick. She had called the bank to advise them they were short staffed, and was having no luck in finding cover. After handover she motioned to Walker to help her dispense medication in the clinic. For the first time since he had known her, she addressed him politely, which worried Walker." There are a few lads bubbling up, we haven't got the staff numbers to cope with them, if they kick off. So start putting some 5: 1 (Sedation),into tots and we can dish them out PRN(meds when required)."

"Who's bubbling up?" Walker was interested; the ward had been settled for days. "Some will, when they realise that we're down to a skeleton staff level. This way we can cope without trouble."

"You want me to 5:1 the lads before they have kicked off?" Walker wasn't sure what she wanted, but he didn't feel comfortable with her request.

"Yes, they are written up for it."

"But only if they need it though. The ward seems Ok; they all appear chilled out at the moment Maggie."

"So you know do you? You're a second year student, I'm nurse in charge, can you do it please." Her tone changed from polite to bully, as she realised her charm offensive had not turned Walker into a co-conspirator.

"No I can't. I'm not sure as to the protocol involved and would prefer it if you didn't ask me. As you're aware, as a student I'm not meant to complete any task I don't feel competent and comfortable to do. That's underpinned by the NMC and university rules. So I'm sorry I'm not prepared to do that."

"Fine then, I'll talk to Elaine in the morning and tell her you refused to follow my instruction."

Walker knew that she was trying her bullying ploy but he was unmoved. He wasn't about to sedate the entire ward so she could have a quiet shift.

If they needed to pull the panic alarms they had two other wards full of nurses that could help out. She wanted to knock them out so she could sit in the office and do fuck all, all day, not on his watch.

"Talk to Elaine, I'll talk to her too, as well as the University and Jackie too clarify procedure here. I do not feel comfortable with what you are asking me to do and I don't feel comfortable with you giving out a knock out drop to lads that aren't presenting with behavioural problems. I'll discuss it with Jackie tomorrow."

Walker turned and left the clinic. He knew that Maggie was a veteran and Jackie though not completely happy with her attitude, accepted that she knew the job and got it done. Walker felt confident in his stance and was not about to medicate the entire ward. How could he look the lads in the faces when he was knocking them out for fuck all? He wasn't a grass; he didn't like bubbling anybody but this wasn't right. He would go to Jackie and ask her advice in the morning.

Walker approached Jackie about the incident the following day and even though she tried to remain passive, he understood that she was not happy with the events that had taken place.

"Leave it with me Gary I'll have a word mate, trust me. You did the right thing in telling me. You don't take it any further though, it will be like committing professional suicide. Maggie has worked the trust for years and has friends. Let me handle it, I promise I will."

Walker was disappointed, and asked himself the question, so this was the way of nursing then? He had found some aspects in his two years he had been a student, hard to digest. The sitting in the office, the way some staff spoke to the clients. They way some male staff liked to get involved in a restraint when the panic alarm sounded. But to deliberately overly medicate the clients so you could have a quiet shift, that was bollocks and he had told her so.

She looked him in the eyes and fixed his stare and repeated herself. "Trust me Gary, ok?"

Walker sensed the steel in her tone and did. He later learned that Maggie returned to her home up north, after requesting sick leave soon after this incident. She should have been struck off in Walkers opinion, he knew that Jackie had watched his back and sorted out the problem politically, to limit the potential for bad press. He was barely satisfied with the way the situation was resolved and it did leave a caustic aftertaste in his mouth. Nurses that entered the profession had an obligation to provide a standard of care that was exemplary, to work to the best of their ability, to improve standards with the framework. It was an uncomplicated premise in Walkers mind.

They were supposed to rise above personal dynamics that affected the rest of society. They were angels in the public eye. Walker understood that was a utopian vision that was probably unachievable back down on Planet Earth. People were human, with the inherent frailties that came with the territory. The burn out rate was high for nurses that worked acute psychiatry, five years was the sell by date. The absence rate, for those that made it past six years, was higher than the national average. It was a stressful environment; it was abusive and it was violent at times. However you were masters of your own surroundings and if you attempted to change it, to diffuse the *'us and them' mentality'* that could permeate the clinical setting it would go a long way to resolving the stresses that affected nursing staff.

The government had spent many millions of pounds on changing the mental health system: there was a new (1983) mental health act that had started to address the problems in the system and reducing the attached social stigma. Ridding the public of the perception of asylums and *'mad'* people, being chained and shackled in overcrowded wards. There were inquires into staff attitudes after a black male was killed while being restrained by staff in a predominantly white area. Studies were done as to the disproportionate percentage of black males in the system. Did mental health have the same problems as the police force had encountered, Walker queried? Cultural differences had to be taken into account when assessing a patient from initial contact at PCL level to Home Treatment involvement.

Walker didn't know how you initiated a recruitment campaign to encourage more members from the afro-Caribbean community to enter psychiatry but he did understand what was required for an equitable system.

He did know that many ingredients made a good meal and that what was needed, a good meal for the British public to digest instead of the diet of fast American bollocks that the authorities seemed content at feeding the masses. The change had to come at grass roots level ,from the universities, the students and the mentors. All the white papers in existence could not alter institutional attitudes and prejudice.

Nurses like Maggie were a cancer that had to be cut out, a tumour that affected all around her.

She affected the staff, students saw her in a position of power and in some misplaced attempt to claim success and be accepted by their peers, imitated her. She bullied the clients, the very people they were there to help, that was unforgivable and in Walkers eyes made her the lowest of the low. He would stick her on a section forty three with the sex offenders. She would rather sedate patients than interact with them. The girl should have made a career in the police force instead of nursing.

Walker rationalised that was probably unfair to decent officers who had their hard work ruined by the actions of a few fuckwit bullies that wore the uniform. She had been moved to a different ward but was still in a position of power and her bitterness would probably extend to the poor souls that worked with her and the problem would continue. Nursing was politics and Walker reflected he must have been naïve if he had ever thought differently.

He wanted to be a carer not a politician and while he was on the ward or in the community he would try his best to put patient care above his own interests. It was a halcyon view and he didn't know if it was inexperience talking. He didn't know if he would feel the same after years of being in the system? It had opened his eyes but he would not let the situation poison him and his feelings toward the profession. He would challenge bad practise it would be as simple as that.

Walker passed the rest of the second year, his essays still receiving high marks and his placement portfolios were of a standard that was rewarding his hard work. His personal tutor was concerned about his attendance at lectures but was pacified when Walker explained the financial limitations, travel problems and the fact he was a single parent. His tutor safely manipulated and in his pocket, Walker started his third year in good spirits this time next year he would have his PIN number and would be ready to save the world.

CHAPTER 29
PROFESSIONAL

The third year of Walkers training passed by without drama or further conflict in his personal life. It was a strangely tranquil time and he wondered when he flicked on the television at night did he actually enjoy peace and quiet? Was serenity all that it was cracked up to be? Even in times of peace, Walker could conjure up some kind of personal conflict to pass the time. His efforts were now being channeled into his studies, the realisation that in less than twelve months he would be accountable for his own practice excited him.

The last three years had blown by like a stiff wind. He was surprised how easy the third year was becoming, all that changed was the essays got longer and the placements easier. When he presented to a new team, either in the community or on the ward he was expected to tenuously understand the nursing processes and be able to polish up on the gaps in this knowledge and refine his practise accordingly.

His mentors enjoyed his enthusiasm, and drive. When they arrived on shift they would find him with his nose buried in the notes, annoying their colleagues for answers to questions such as: What you would do in that situation, what was the protocol on that scenario, what would be the consequences of that decision be or simply sitting in the day room enjoying a laugh with the patients, practicing his stand up routine.

Walker enjoyed one on one interactions and was slowly building a good interview technique, which was based on warmth and not clinical guidelines. He didn't study the patients with an over worried frown and complex questions about mood, his legs crossed with a notebook and pen at the ready and his hand supporting his chin. Walker would relax with his clients and enjoy the time he spent with them. Their dialogue they introduced was what he needed to listen to, in order for him to learn. The art for Walker, was to get a person talking freely without feeling they were being analysied. It wasn't rocket science in his mind.

Walker would laugh and tell his mentors, he elicited his information in a' *social context'*, when they looked in through the window occasionally and witnessed the laughter, the game of cards, or some other shenanigans that Walker was using at the time. They would shake their heads with a smile and a look of interest on their faces as they dissected his notes for salient points . Walker knew that the nursing professed to utilise the *'Holistic'* approach. To him this meant more than simply asking the question: where the voices bothering you? You had to understand the client as a person not just as a set of symptoms. Not all agreed with his methods, some hardened practitioners would tell him he was *'fading out'* the lines and *'not establishing boundaries or exercising parameters'*.

Walker would listen and ensure that he laid his cards out on the table and explained his motives and drives for entering his chosen profession when he met a client. For him there was no us and them, there were no clear lines of demarcation when he came to healthcare. He was not on any side. He knew you could be assertive and retain your sense of humour and individualism.

His next placement was an unrewarding experience based on an elder adult's ward. The ward enjoyed a poor reputation within the trust after a series of internal investigations after two separate scandals. The team walked around the corridors and dayrooms as if they had already been beaten into submission and were resigned to their fate. His mentor's morale was so low and his practice so inhibited with fear that Walker filled in most of his own paperwork to avoid the man bursting into tears, he was so stressed with the extra pressure of looking after student and all it entailed. It was a sad and de-motivating sight.

The charge nurse had no respect for him and had again been molded in the image of nurse Ratchet or Patel. She was in love with her voice and thought that patients were conscripts, and that discipline equated to good practise. During their initial interview as Walker asked questions regarding the philosophy of the ward and the model of nursing practice they used. The stressed man who professed a love of Cliff Richards and comfortable jumpers pleaded with Walker not to ask him any questions in front of her.

He explained there were negative dynamics on the ward, covert war had been declared due to the cloud hanging over them and she would be condescending over the purported gaps in his clinical knowledge. He was on a level 3 observation when a client fell and broke her hip. Her family had complained and another investigation was formally initiated. Rather than supporting their colleague, they pointed fingers and compounded the problem.

That attitude did little to improve his decaying confidence and marginalised some elements in the team, unfortunately it was wolves versus sheep. Walker's eyes opened with surprise when his mentor spilled his guts over coffee in the first six hours of his placement. What was he going to learn here? He didn't understand the attitude. If he wasn't confidant with his practice, what was he doing on a ward?
 His opinion of the team wasn't further enhanced when during a handover his mentor was conducting, when the charge nurse`s patronising tone was unmistakable. She interrupted constantly and his face turned redder and his stammer more pronounce with every new slight . At one point she even spoke over him to discuss fashion accessories with her female clique. Such was the schism within the team. The man was one step away from extended sick leave.
Walker`s smile was not once of amusement, it was rather one of despondency, that this was the state of health care provision on this particular ward. He brushed off his discontent and did the job as best as he could and delivered the same humorous health care that he was making his trade mark. He assisted the first year students who wondered around like lost sheep and supported his mentor who he found to be a caring if unassertive nurse. The ward was Walt Disney without the flowers, the flying bluebirds and little Bo Peep. Walker kept his head down for the most part and did his job. But the unit was an advert for burned out practitioners and institutionalised care provision.
The other nurses looked on with hand and their hips and startled expressions as he organised dance and quiz afternoons, motivating the other students to assist him in the activity. The students laughed along with him and their practise didn't feel the oppressive weight of asylum nursing.
Walker built up a good relationship with an old Irish fellow named John. John O'Brien was a feisty Dubliner who had moved to England in the fifties to find wealth and fortune on the plethora of building sites that helped to shape modern Birmingham and rebuild the economy after the second world war. John had just stared the slide into dementia, but for most of the time he was lucid and enjoyed a bit of banter with Walker. His loss of memory and the frustration he would feel caused him annoyance. He used to be a builder, and enjoy a trip down the pub for a pint of the black stuff with his mates. Now he sat in

a dayroom, on a chair surrounded by old women knitting and was spoon fed a diet of pills and daytime television.

 It was no massive leap of faith to understand why he could be troublesome at times. He would shout and play up if he didn't get the attention he demanded and some nurses slid away from him, worried about the sharpness of his tongue. He was high spirited, he was angry and more to the point he was aware that soon his faculties would desert him, his mind would leave his body and he would simply be the shell of the man he once was. However the weight of his illness hadn't crushed his sprit yet and he fought on, hoping his feisty character would thwart the dying brain cells.

 John didn't like being in hospital and he wanted to go home to his neat little semi in Bordesley Green that he had bought with his hard earned wages. He didn't want to spend his final days in hospital or a nursing home. Unfortunately he tended to wander off after a trip to the pub, or to the shops and the police would find him shouting, swearing and distressed as he struggled to come to terms that he was lost and he couldn't remember where he lived. Walker hoped that death would take him before he fell afoul of Alzheimer's.

 If you lent John an ear and treated him like a man, he would tell you what the problem was, relax and laugh. Talk down to him and be a patronising shithead and he would let you know what he thought about you. Walker felt this was a fair and equitable arrangement. If you came to work on a psychiatric unit it was your duty to listen, help, support and improve the quality of the patient's lives.

Walker spent two days away from the ward relaxing on his sofa and ruminating over how he should approach his debrief with his clinical assessor. His misgiving over the poor health provision on the ward was starting to cause him a conflict that he needed to address to shut up the constant debate rampaging through his mind, as he waited to fill in his portfolio. Several times he picked up his pen and then doubted his words. He didn't want to be totally negative about the ward and his mentor, he had enjoyed parts of the placement. He wanted to be objective and wanted to be positive about his mentor, the man wasn't a bad nurse, he was in a bad environment. He chewed over the problem with his pen in his mouth and went to bed to try and sleep on the matter.

Walker bounced back onto the ward two days later, relaxed as he had determined his course of action. Whistling loudly he made a drink and pushed the trolley into the day room, laden with tea and coffee made with hot milk. He added some biscuits he surprisingly found in the kitchen cupboard.

"Morning every one; did you all sleep well and enjoy your breakfast?" Walker looked around at the sea of souls who were in the departure lounge for the one way trip to God. It broke his heart that this was all some older people had to look forward to in the lives.

"You have the full English Joan? I heard they got a new cook and he can fry up some white pudding eh Jonny boy?"

Joan looked up from her knitting. "Morning Gary, full English. I haven't seen a sausage since I was a young girl. It was bloody porridge again. I told them I don't like it." She looked melancholy, perhaps the daughters she loved to eluogise over, would pay her a visit today?

"The British empire was built on porridge oats my dear." He turned to John who had his cap lodged at a jaunty angle on his balding head. "What you got to say eh Johnny boy?" Walker looked at his Irish side kick, who held his side and didn't answer him.

"Not to worry Joanie, I'll see if I can rustle up a hobnob or two, they have had a biscuit delivery today." Walker pointed at the plates filled with custard crèmes and chocolate bourbons, and added." I'll put in a request for some extra toast with strawberry jam.
Is that Ok with you?

"Thank you Gary." She smiled back at him, before she went back to her knitting. "You're welcome as always beautiful."Joan laughed and brushed her hair. Walker was relieved that she remembered to let go of her knitting needles and laughed along with her.

Walker looked over at John; it was unusual for him not to take the offered bait and have the criac. He walked over and bent down in front of him. Walker noticed that John was pale and sweating. He appeared to be in pain and rasped when he breathed out, as if he was a twenty a day Capston full strength smoker.

"You alright there John?" Walker asked.

John shook his head and moaned.

"Give me a minute kid, I'll find out what's going on." Walker went to the main office and handed over his concerns to the charge nurse. She explained that he had fallen two days ago and had been checked out appropriately by the Nurse In Charge. Walker unsatisfied with her reply continued to raise a concern. She huffed and puffed and told Walker to take him to x-ray if he was that worried, too busy with her own reflection to be fully aware of the situation.

Walker arranged transport and he presented with John at the radiology dept. He was seen quickly and without fuss. Walker waited for the results and handed them over to the qualified staff on his return to the unit. John had suffered a pneumothorax (punctured lung) as a result of his fall, the nurses had failed to spot he had a broken rib and had left him in a chair and associated his complaints with his usual demonstrative behaviour.

Walker informed the NIC that John had been admitted to a general ward as an emergency admission. The *qualified staff* looked at each other and passed the buck around, as if it was a game of pass the parcel. The present being a wrapped bomb that was about to explode, covering their already tarnished reputation with more shit.

Walker had suffered three broken ribs when he and Silks had met their match in Wolverhampton City Centre when they had been on a night out. Silks had (under the influence of twelve pints and a bottle of vodka), gone toe to toe with a heavyweight boxer of all people and got knocked out. Walker trying to defend his mate had got battered, his boxing ability not as smart as his mouth. They had ended up in custody, then casualty.

To recover from his bruises Silks took the opportunity to go to Jamaica to visit his family.

Walker suffered on the sofa back at home in the cold. It took him half-an- hour to initially move his broken body up off the sofa ,one step at a time, wincing with every movement. He took him half-an-hour to complete a journey that would normally have taken him ten minutes. It was a crippling pain, it hurt to move and it hurt to breathe. God knows how John coped with the pain when he was hauled up by the staff.

The charge nurse looked surprised at the news, said. "Oh," and left the office. Another trip to the toilet to check her makeup Walker speculated.

Walker handed it over to the ward manager and completed a report at his incident. The whole ward was going to be taken down, it was time to cover one`s back. The whole place was under threat of closure because of the catalogue of mistakes and the bad practise that afflicted it. It was a bit late-in-the day for transparency but the manager had been appointed to sort the mess out and calm down the media scrum that was about to explode over their health care provision. Paperwork had to completed, it didn't make a difference if it was by a staff or student nurse ;transparency was transparency. Walkers report would merely be another piece of evidence to nail the coffin lid firmly shut.

His final placement was with the Home Treatment Team; the elite of mental health nurses.

They were the key to the door that allowed clients either off or onto the ward. They did the assessments that governed the care pathways and were all experienced RMNs. Walker was impressed with the way they went about their work. They made him feel like a student on the start of his path, with gaps in his knowledge that had to be filled and he appreciated the feeling that he was being trained again. They taught him a lot and he learned as much as his limited time with them would allow.

They were a good team, there was no doubt about it and Walker left them with sadness. His (last) professional placement took him on a return journey to Pearl and Jackie welcomed him back with a smile and trip to Handsworth on a Friday night.

Walker was dressed like a prison warden, armed with a list as long a week's shopping to collect some Caribbean food. He was sure she had laughed herself to sleep when she thought of this task, as a way of welcoming the return of the prodigal son. Well, he thought, if she needed a certificate of his commitment, this trip to the twilight zone was defiantly proof enough.

He got some strange looks from the queuing customers. Handsworth wasn't used to a big skinhead dressed like an off duty screw with keys jangling in their pockets. He ignored the stares and brought back the food: curried goat, mutton, snapper and rice and peas with a smile on his face and a heart that was thumping against his chest. Her mouth full of mutton, Jackie smiled as she informed him he was still her student, so he should be prepared to walk on glass for her. Now was his time, he had to step up to the plate.

In three short months he would be accountable for his practise. There were to be no easy rides for him she would make sure of that.

Elaine was still the ward manager and she continued to respect the manner with which Walker interacted with the clients. Over a coffee in her office, she informed him with a smile that there were posts available in the near future and he should apply for a job with them and become a real part of the team. She passed him an application with a smile and Jackie helped him to fill in the form when they had a break during a quiet night shift. Walker's eloquence was lost on the pragmatic charge nurse and she tutted at him as she questioned the wording of his personal statement. Two weeks later he received an interview date. He was to be interviewed on the ward, it was a home tie. Walker knew a job was just around the corner. He could hardly believe it, he was going to be an RMN on one of the most respected units in the city. Unfortunately a week later, Birmingham and Solihull mental health trust decided to employ overseas nurses to fill vacancies and not wait until the nearly qualified students received their PIN numbers. His dream job had been snatched away because of a hole in the budget which limited the new posts that were available.

Jobs had been cut as the system was being *'restructured'*. This caused Walker a bad week and a lot of beers. His thoughts turned back to his previous experiences as he sat on the sofa and stared out of the window, the dregs of a can of cider running down the stubble of his chin and dripping onto a dirty t-shirt. He had to be more resilient than this. One setback didn't make a depressive episode, his anger moved him forward there was no need to dwell. He dragged himself forward by his bootlaces.

Walker wasn't going back to the path of self destruction again. Armed with his new strategy and self belief he hit web sites and was afforded another interview based at a forensic unit in Birmingham, a unit he knew off. On the morning of the interview he retrieved his suit form the dry cleaners, carefully rehearsing his answers as he filled his car up with petrol. Ignoring the looks of other motorists as he became aware he was talking to himself.

He arrived ten minutes early, and smiled nervously at the receptionist as she showed him to a seat in a bright and well aired room. He looked around, picked up some NHS leaflets on the patients liaison service and tried to relax. He stood slowly and breathed heavily as a large women with a chest the size of an oil rig invited him to follow her. After ten minutes in the room, he calmed down and remembered why he was here. His answers became as crisp as his shirt as he smiled through the nerves and gave text book answers to questions that were not taxing when you thought about them. Three hours later his mobile rang and his face flushed with happiness as he was offered the position. He calmed down his breathing as he accepted; nodding into the phone as they told him HR would be in touch.

He was a staff nurse for the NHS. His time had finally arrived. He phoned his mum, called Shorts and drowned out their congratulations with his own excitement. With no one left to call and tired after a hard day he sat down and flicked through brochures for cars. Walker was satisfied with his lot as he looked at new model Mercs, beamers and Jags. After a brief period of imagining himself behind the wheel of his status wheel he closed his eyes and ruminated on his path to qualification. Life was short and whatever shit it chucked at you, with a good attitude and perseverance you could pull through the bad times.

He received a letter from the trust two days before Christmas Day, informing him that they had withdrawn the job offer due to poor references. When he challenged their decision they told him it was a reflection on his poor attendance at University and the reference reflected this; after due consideration the Human Resources department had decided to go with a candidate that had achieved a 100% attendance record instead. The ward manager apologised and explained they were inert in the recruitment processes. Big brother was alive and well and living in an office in Birmingham.

Walker fought the decision and wrote to the university, the trust, to anybody that would listen to his story about justice, all the time cursing himself for his laziness in not catching the train, or spending his bursary on the 'high-life'. He explained about his post-placement interviews, he explained that he had advised his tutor of his situation. The university was aware of the problems he had encountered attending lectures. It fell on deaf ears. His personal tutor spent five minutes with Walker before he waved his hands in the air, with a gesture of hopelessness. He gazed with a hint of guilt into Walkers eyes.

Walker felt like knocking him out, the train ride home was a glum affair. Motivated by the injustice and his anger burning brightly Walker made a further appointment to see the dean, the head of the school. His word was law. It would take him ten minutes to open up the world for Walker. His Parker ink pen could write him a personal reference. His efforts fell on a hard rock of policies and procedures and an inability to set a 'precedent' .The university regretfully informed him they could not traverse the rules for an individual case.

Walker sighed, looked at God and made a vow to take the latest
setback in his stride. He buried his pride and signed on for
unemployment benefit. He failed to wallow and blame life, the bad
days came and went and he remained strong, optimistic and confident
in his ability to fulfill his role and persevered. Walker scanned the job
pages eagerly and spotted a vacancy working for a mental health
charity in the West Midlands. He applied and received an interview
with their homeless services based in Wolverhampton, who engaged
with complex and challenging clients. Clients who's behaviour brought
them into conflict with the law. They had no fixed abode and used
alcohol and drugs to get them through the day.
He understood that pathway and he spoke with eloquence in the
interview. Walker was offered the post and accepted the job with a
jump and a punch in the air, to the people that didn't believe he would
achieve his ambition. He was now a case officer with his own clients.
He would work in a hostel network and sort out the lads heads.
They gave him a diary and a competitive salary. He would pay his bills
and be a productive member of society. The dream for as long as he
could remember achieved, his targets met. Walker had arrived.
 After a month and a smile Walker received his first pay slip and
decided to go to the bank to arrange a current account. He wanted to
pay his bills via direct debit, that's what the advertisers proclaimed was
the 'British way'. Walker was now a member of society and he was
eager to prove that he could move flawlessly into polite company. He
wasn't sure that his past financial blemishes would allow him a chance
to gain another step on the ladder, that lead up toward his goal of
'normalised behaviour'.
 He eyes widened with shock as the advisor at his branch smiled and
told him his credit history was clear and yes he could have a loan, a
platinum account and a credit card if he wanted. He walked out of the
bank with three thousand pounds on a personal loan, a credit card
with a thousand pound limit and a five hundred pound overdraft.
Nearly five grand for half an hour's work. He smiled sadly and thought
maybe he should have tried the legal avenue earlier, it paid better.
With a tank full of petrol and a wallet full of cash he aimed toward
Shrewsbury and fetched Victoria from Natalie's.
She had passed her all her exams and was officially intelligent in the
government's eyes. He parked at a travel agent and blew a fat chunk
on two week holiday in Cyprus, scheduled for later that summer. In

three months they would be by the pool. Sipping on a cold cocktail, eating at fine restaurants, the past a blur, the future idyllic. One more stop off on his pathway to glory was to collect probably the most expensive pizza in history.

Victoria had done well and she deserved a reward, her victory was as sweet as his. She had passed her exams despite the setbacks of divorce, watching her dad nearly killed by his girlfriend and witnessing the specter of mental illness that had risen when the ambulance and police had taken him away on that evening. Walker cried with pride when she told him of her exam results. Next on the agenda was sky television a mobile phone on a contract and then he would see about that new car. He was a kid in the sweet shop of life and he was about to get fat.

Walker and Monica got back together, split up and reunited. She loved him despite his obvious issues. He drank excessively and his moods could turn black when he was drunk, insecure or simply bored and looking for stimulus.

Walker had always exhibited a cruel streak. If he was in pain then so was everybody around him. He now used his talent at reading people, to open up their internal scars for his personal pleasure. His training had simply given him another weapon when he was called upon to protect himself. He wasn't proud of the fact, he knew it was inappropriate. He wasn't sure if the frustration and focal point of his anger was indeed Monica. But she did present a target with her nagging and the fact that was now indelibly etched in his thoughts, that he was settling for her, his shame was directed at both of them. The tinge of regret that another relationship had failed was eased by the plaintive hope that these episodes took place when he was pissed, even though now he was well aware of the premise of denial.

He asked questions. Maybe HE didn't need to be in *out of control love* to forge a relationship, when he was acutely aware that HE did. Perhaps these constraints were the last remnants of his previous alcohol reliant lifestyle. If you reduce all the questions then you should be left with one answer.

Walker attempted to totally give up alcohol on several occasions; once he went five weeks without a beer. Monica knew about his past and his diagnosis of personality disorder and wanted him sober and clean. She told him that his heath was fragile and he was prone to extreme mood swings when melancholy and drinking heavily. Walker knew that compared to his past he was now remarkably sober and clean. He slurred at her for the umpteenth time. 'Shut the fuck up or ship the fuck out,' bored with her and her endless attempts to perform a detailed analysis his behaviour. She was not Anne Morris.

He was the professional. She should learn that once and for all. After delving into her psyche she decided to stick with the trip, being with Walker was an emotional roller coaster and tiring for her. Monica crossed her fingers and hoped that the man she loved would finally banish the ghosts of his past and accept his life with her.

She would wrestle with the complexity of what should be an easy situation and pondered on the fact he didn't love her and deep down she knew it. When another night turned into an autopsy, she looked back sadly and walked away, sold her business and decided to fulfill her ambition of travelling the world to escape from the mental prison that she had sentenced herself to.

She booked up to travel for a year, starting her trip in South East Asia before visiting Australia, New Zealand, the South Seas and America. They kept in touch via e-mail while she was away. Walker missed her at times, she had become a good friend but that was all she was to him: a friend. She wanted more than that, more than Walker could offer her.

Their relationship went into terminal decline and he finally jettisoned all contact with her.

CHAPTER 26
KATHY.

Walker continued to exude calmness in the work environment, a calmness that had remained alien to him throughout in his personal live. His thoughts and actions belied the gaping chasm that had once existed in his mind-set. He enjoyed the challenge of promoting his own practise and devising work-shops that would benefit the lads he worked with. He fitted in with the staff, they enjoyed his blend of humour and the honesty in the way he worked.

Walker could be frank in the way he spoke, but his agenda was never political. Within a matter of months he had built a good rapport with the clients, for many of them the term *'staff'* was not synonymous with Walker. He would spend his days in the day room chatting about their lives in a language they could easily understand, he would laugh at their jokes and talk common sense without the help of a textbook. When they had a problem he would wait until they were alone, nod his head and they would go into the office to see if they could find a solution together. The lads that lived the *'social dream'* didn't see him as staff, they saw him as a man that wanted to help them. For many it was easy to see that he had lived a real life, his words didn't spring from clichés, they didn't walk off the type-face of a page buried deep in a lifeless book, they came from the heart with a semblance of good honest common sense thrown in.

Walker was confident in the environment and worked diligently to prove his obvious worth to his employers. Not long ago he had been set in that life, using drinks and drugs as a coping mechanism, facing up to regular court appearances and dealing with the rubbish that life hurled at him far too often. Despite the many problems he encountered Walker understood that he had been lucky.

His mother had provided him with a solid support. His friends though squashed in the distance had only been a phone call away if he really needed them. Without the support of his mum through those dark days he could easily have ended up homeless and right up to his neck in social quick sand, and sinking fast.

Walker knew that if he had become a government statistic he would have ended his misery with a bottle of cheap vodka and a tonne of pills, relieved to slip into the abyss, asleep with a note placed on his chest, a note that nobody would read, or attempt to understand.

Walker realised that now he had come through his own personal darkness, if he were having a bad day, somebody, somewhere was having it worse than you and taking it right up the arse. Stop feeling sorry for yourselves he would think, hiding his irritation. Self-pity was a depressing magazine that more people than needed to had a subscription for. He was paid to listen, most people didn't give a flying fuck about the problems of others.

Every morning as he was brushing his teeth, shaving, or attending to some other chore that was beyond him five short years ago, he would quote his mantra for the day."There by the grace of god go I."

Walker had never been a religious man. He didn't consider God as a way out, as a confidant, but at times of trouble he did pray. Didn't everybody? He did wonder what the big man upstairs had install for him.

Life were going as well for him as he could remember, at least since the days when he had first met Nat all those years ago. A lot of water had past under the bridge since that hot August day when they had first seen each other; in the days when Walker was waging war on his mind, his body and Leeds fans. He didn't feel any older than he had then, he was due to turn forty soon, the big four o. He still felt young, but his thought processes had altered.

Deep down he knew he still *'wasn't right'.* He could still enjoy a tear up with Silks, he still used a substance every now and then, had violent thoughts.

But the nagging feeling that maybe these traits were not so unusual now kept him company at night. Once his thoughts spoke of isolation and exclusion, now they were about integration, acceptance and inclusion. Perhaps he had found his niche in life, he prayed again to a faith he never possessed

Walker was happy with his current life. The sun was out, the sky was blue, the grass was green and the birds were singing in the trees. Walker was about to do what he did best. Meet a girl he knew was trouble and jump out of the plane without the requisite parachute. Enter a blonde Irish beauty with a history that was more colourful than his.

Enter Kathy O'Fallon.

Walker had first met Kathy years ago in a pub located in Wolverhampton city centre. A small pub with a smoky interior that was used by most of the towns criminal fraternity. She and Silks had history. They had been mates for years and would act like giddy teenagers when they were around each other. She would breeze into the pub, armed with a fresh faced grin and an arm full of shopping bags. With an angelic smile she would settle herself next to them at the bar order a large Bacardi, lit up a Sliver Cut cigarette and ask for the local gossip.

Kathy would rag Silks like no one else Walker had ever met. She was a confident lady with a quick mouth. Walker could see that Silks respected her. Her dizzy blonde act was a mask that covered, a rapier mind, predator like cunning and a brain that could work out a situation in a micro-second.

Kathy O'Fallon was a one woman risk assessment and a force of Nature. She would talk quickly about crime and what was going down on the street, unaware she sounded like a Martina Cole novel, unaware she lived the life that others read about in Cole's crime novels. Kathy's appearance was all social worker, her thoughts all criminal. She was as hard as they come.

Over the years she would show up like a will-of -the wisp in the pub, her happiness at being out-and-about in Wolverhampton; with people that she grown up with, guaranteeing a good day and a vivid assault on the senses. She would hand Walker numerous twenties from her well stocked purse and smile sweetly at him as she asked him to fetch the beer from the bar while she and Silks nattered about the old days, their heads huddled together as if they were in a rugby scrum.

Kathy liked dangerous men. Dangerous black men and had one at home, the term psycho was specifically developed for him. She had four children off him and one more off some other dimwit who got her pregnant when she was sixteen and decided that at that tender age she was old enough to be beaten, fucked and impregnated. When her mother found out she was having a black baby, she was shown the door and had stood on her own two feet ever since.

When the father of her first child broke her nose after a bout of paranoia, she showed him the door. It was not the last time that some idiot would think that being with her was a tag of ownership. Some men were stupid cunts, there was no doubt in Walkers mind.

When she came into the pub, a breath of fresh air would sweep through it. She would sit down on high-backed bar stools and regale them of her adventures around the country. Giggling as she passed them over wraps of MDMA powder. Ecstasy in its purest form.

You could love an Albion fan on that shit, with no problems at all! They were all mates and when she had real problems and was looking at a long sentence, Silks jumped in and tried to offer assistance. He offered to pay bail, his offer was refused by the wise men that sat in judgment.

Walker as a nurse provided her with a character reference, it was read out aloud in court. The judge didn't give a fuck about her past, he didn't care about poor environments, social deprivation, domestic violence, or the fact she had raised her kids alone. He didn't take into account the long years of abuse she suffered. Without a ray of emotion he sent her down for four years.

Kathy earned her money from nefarious activities and she earned well. Society had not given her the option of earning legally, so she took her piece of the pie the only way she knew how, through illegal activities. She had kids to feed, a man at home that was fucking useless unless you wanted your head kicking in or a tip what horse would most likely lose the 3:50 at Kempton park.

Kathy wanted a slice of the good life, a nice little house, a garden and a mortgage. Her last gamble was to move pills around the country and she was busted down south with a few thousand in her possession. Silks was not happy with the result, his face told the story.

His paranoia burst open like a dam as he thought she had been bubbled by her London contacts and he went looking for revenge. Kathy calmed him, gently holding his hands with a resigned smile on her innocent face and a tender kiss to his cheek.

She understood that prison was an occupational hazard accepted her bird and sent them both VO's. They would spend an occasional Saturday going around the country to visit her in whatever jail she found herself to be in at the time. Walker didn't enjoy the visits, neither did Silks. It was akin to watching a bird in a cage with its wings clipped.

Silks would always give the screws a hard time when they landed at the various prisons Kathy was locked up in. It was his MO, he had memories that time wouldn't heal.

Kathy liked Walker, she liked him because compared to the lads she knew, he was a soft white lad that didn't know about the deeper darker side of life. His naivety about real crime was refreshing to her. Walker was a petty criminal, he was married and loved his wife and child. She looked confused when he told her he was a single dad. He was not a man on her usual radar.

As she got older, she got bored with getting beaten up by her partner and made a stand and ended the relationship, ignoring the tears of her tormentor as he begged for another chance. Kathy was a strong lady and had balls that most men would be proud of.

She was Irish, mad, and as pretty as could be. Katy O'Fallon was the sharpest lady Walker had ever met: she was a force of nature, of that there was no doubt.

As Walker's life started to pass without drama, Silks became the bearer of bad news. He'd been arrested for yet another driving offence that looked like he was going for yet another lie down at: Her Majesties Pleasure. His last few convictions were all for driving whilst disqualified and driving whilst drunk. The judges were fed up with his constant disregard for the law and kept sending him to jail for his offences.

Silks and Walker didn't see driving as breaking the law. Robbing a bank, selling drugs, beating up a granny were all offences that required a custodial sentence. Driving a car without insurance or a license and sometimes under the influence wasn't criminal, it was *'high sprits'*. Silks had just laid his head down for a month before he was arrested again for drink driving whilst banned, racing his three litre Vauxhall Omega through the streets of Pendeford as if The Ryefield was Monaco.

Walker was sure that he was going away for a year this time or maybe longer. He let Kathy know when he was drunk and emotional, she calmed him down laughing down the phone telling him. 'It was only a fucking driving offence, Silks hadn't shot anybody.' She would always find time to attend court to see her Silks. Somewhere down the line she had exchanged numbers with Walker. Silks could see them getting closer when they were out and about. He called her and asked her to leave his mate alone, he could see an accident waiting to happen.

Silks went to court sure he was going away for at least three months. They booked in at the court with the usher and decided to have a quick tot at the Irish pup nearby. They walked with slow steps through the town centre. This may be the last time they would get to have a drink with each other for a long time. Walker ordered two large Brandies RSVOP, lifted the glasses to the sky and wished his mate a safe journey.

 In court the judge took half an hour to make his mind up. Silks looked at Walker, Walker looked at Silks. His defence reinforced the point that Silks was a business man, that he employed three people. If he received a custodial sentence they wouldn't be just be sending Silks down; they would be sentencing the families of the three men he employed as well. It was a pervasive argument and it nearly worked. The judge gave him six months and Walker watched with emotional and angry eyes as his mate was led down to the cells below.

It was not a good experience for Walker to watch his mate taken down. Walker loved the bloke, loved him like a big brother and to watch him hand-cuffed caused a response in his head.

 For the rest of the day he called people and arranged times to meet them in all the pubs they used regularly, a pint in his hand and vodka on the bar. A glazed look in his eyes and his temper on overdrive, how he didn't end up in a cell himself was pure luck. Maybe he had a fight, abused some people, Walker lost a few hours and woke up on his sofa with a kebab clasped to his face like an alien and a guilty feeling in the pit of his stomach.

He had been so drunk he couldn't remember what had happened the night before. People filled in the blanks for him from time to time with amused looks on their faces and Walker would laugh and shake his head.

Walker always got emotional when Silks got into trouble; he thought he would be immune to it by now because Silks got lifted on regular occasions. He was like a fucking magnet for coppers. Jules always fretted and moaned when he got locked up and would call Walker. Walker would arrive at the station armed with as many broadsheets as he could carry and a change of clothes. Silks did not like to look like a bag of rubbish when he was in the dock, even though his fashion sense had never really improved. Days in the cells were boring and Silks liked something to read while he was locked up and had ample time to complete 'The Times crossword.'

When he went to see him in jail it would cost Walker money, more money than when he was on the street. Money for petrol, time off work, but he never missed a visit.

Silks would scowl at the screws, sit down wink at Walker and put in his orders for newspapers. Lots of newspapers to keep him amused. Walker would leave the jail and track down a local newsagents that delivered to the prison. He ordered Silks papers, armed with his cheque book to pay for them, for the time he was serving.

He didn't mind so much, but if the delivery went wrong Silks would give his mate a hard time when he was next visiting the jail, as if he were the fucking paper boy. Walker would take it on the chin and buy more coffees and Kit Kats with a forced smile on his face, a nod and a mental message to breathe deeply.

Kathy had been unable to attend court, she wasn't going to give up here business elsewhere in England to for a driving offence. Armed with her number and a hangover, Walker called Kathy to inform her that Silks had been send away again, she didn't have time to talk. Walker knew she must be up to no good. After a brief conversation she suggested they meet in Wolves for a beer, she was back there soon. She picked the time and Walker the place, the date was quickly arranged. Walker was looking forward to seeing her. It was always a party, she always had a tale to tell and he could talk about Silks honestly.

Jules would go into overdrive about his irresponsible attitude and what a cunt he could be. Walker wanted a friendly face, he was already missing his mate. Thursday came around quickly. Walker packed up from work early, changed in the shower room. Ignored the lads who were laughing outside with a shake of the head and a don't ask wag of his finger.

The pub was busy when he walked in. It was a large boozer, sold cheap beer and tasty food. There was the normal crowd of old folks drinking mild and couples eating lunch. He waved a twenty at a white shirted barman and ordered a pint. Before he had time to look around, he felt a presence close by. He turned around and Kathy was at his shoulder with a smile that would have resurrected Jesus if his dad hadn't already been God. "Fancy a drink Kathy?" He was pleased to see her. "Get in a couple of vodkas and tonic Walker, Christina's here." She nodded over to a small kiosk where her cousin was sitting down examining her fingernails with avid concentration.

Christina was a lovely girl from the East Midlands whom he had met several times before. Walker raised his hands and waved. Christina looked up and Walker got a smile and a wave back in return.

"Two large vodkas please mate, one bottle of tonic, enough ice to chill it and not kill it." He turned to Kathy. "Go and sit down I'll bring them over.

He watched her walk back to the table, her hips swinging, the jeans she was wearing tailor made for her arse. She turned around and caught him staring and smiled, a mischievous smile that was both saint and sinner at the same time. He bought the drinks over and sat down beside them.

"You put a bit a weight on eh Gaz, good living mate or what?" Christina smiled at him and added. "Ta for the drink," as she measured out tonic as if it was a chemistry experiment.

"Yam welcome, its muscle Chrissie though not fat. "Walker laughed. Kathy leaned over and felt his bicep."You're tonk now init Walker. I like my men that way. She squeezed his arm and thigh seductively.

Walker gulped down his beer, blushed and ordered a large vodka. Was she making a move or having a rise with him?

They went to a pub with music and the beers flowed and the flirting continued unabated. Walker finally asked them if they wanted to go over to his side of town and have a few there, then go back to his for vodka and some '*extras*.' Christina wasn't sure if she wanted to head out of town. Kathy nearly jumped into Walkers lap and exclaimed. "She was up for it."

They landed in a few more pubs and more alcohol flowed, further loosening the mood. Kathy had some base, which they dropped and got high.

Walker and Kathy got to know each other and enjoyed a memorable night. He woke up in the morning with a dull ache and a happy stomach. As he turned over in bed, she was lying next to him a peaceful expression on her face. God she looked like an angel, pale and serene. Her mouth gently moved as she spoke a silent word and for a moment he considered phoning in work as not to wake her. He dismissed the idea as he walked on tip toes into the kitchen, to make a coffee. He had to go to work and support a client in a ward review, it was duty over desire.

He made his way back to the bedroom and gently woke her with a cup of tea and a smile. She accepted with a throaty. "Ta very much," and look of slight confusion.

On the way back to hers, he told her she was beautiful, and they should do it again. Kathy blushed and looked down at the floor and then out of the window. Had he hit a nerve? She mumbled that yeah they should, as she shut the door to the car and struggled with her front door key.

Walker never expected the phone call to come. He knew Kathy and he knew that she was a free sprit on the lookout for laughs, not love. His phone beeped three hours later. It was a message from her. She wanted him to meet her at Wolverhampton train station. He quickly pressed the keys on his mobile, pressed send and waited. His phone beeped three minutes later and the date was arranged.

Twenty minutes later Walker met her in the station foyer with a smile. "Hello Kathy I'm safe. How are you?"

"I'm fine. I sort of missed you."

"Really?" Walker raised his eyebrows and tried to hide his surprise."It's only been a few hours."

"Yes I know I ain't thick, blonde but not stupid." Her smile lit up her face.

"What you up to then?"

"I'm off to salsa, you want to come with me?" she asked, shyness written all over her face. Walker laughed. "Fucking Salsa? Yam having a bubble ay ya?" When I went raving I was off my tits before I had the bottle to boogie and you want me to go to a dance class and wear spandex?"

She looked disappointed as he escorted her to the station cafe and bought her a coffee while they waited for her train to Birmingham. When it was time to leave she gave him a peck on the cheek and disappeared into the throng.

Walker reflected that she was different and a bit shy when she was out of the pub and he liked that about her. He received a phone call four hours later telling him she was back in Wolves what was he up to? Any other girl and he would have blanked the call it was late, just after nine, but then she was different gravy. He dragged himself off the sofa and picked her up from the station.

She had a ten pound draw and she asked timidly. "Did you want a smoke?" Walker nodded at her. "Let's go back to mine then." Walker was as game as a football match between Wolves and Albion. They arrived at his flat and she laughed dizzily when she learned that he couldn't skin up and built them one apiece. They smoked cannabis, laughed and talked before they slept in each other's arms. Walker and Kathy O'Fallon were a couple. Who the fuck would have believed it?

CHAPTER 31.
PROSPERITY

The door to the office knocked a light tap that was repeated in quick succession. The sound reminded Walker of a cuckoo. He looked up from the flat screen and sighed, he had been hoping for some peace and quiet to get his paperwork completed. It was taking him longer than expected to complete this support plan and risk assessment for a new client who had the worry of the world upon his shoulders and needed a hand to unburden the weight he was feeling.

A tall man with a heavyish looking beard was stooping to look through the square glass window that was built into the heavy wooden door. It had to be heavy in case the lunatics tried to take over the asylum. You could always tell if Trevor was in trouble by the length of his whiskers. Today must be bad because he looked like Moses.

Walker clicked the minimise icon on the screen, thought for a moment and then pressed save. The door knocked again, Walker motioned with his hand that he was coming and checked the screen. His Wolves screensaver appeared, confidentiality had been preserved.

Walker hitched the catch and opened the door with a smile. "Mr. Bishop what the hell can I do for you at this time of the night?"

It was just after eleven, the sleep in support worker had gone up stairs for the night. Walker was lone working and there were still eight lads in the lounge and conservatory watching telly and DVD's that Walker had donated. He generally set curfew for twelve, tonight the lads had requested an extension so they could watch one of the many films he had lugged in from home. He was arranging a succession of film nights followed by group sessions, enabling people to express themselves via the medium of the plot.

Hopefully providing insight and highlighting the problems associated with their own and other people life styles. Walker had selected *Train spotting* for the heroin addicts, *Nil by mouth* and *Once were Warriors* for the drinkers and exponents of drunken violence. *Midnight Express* for those lads who wanted to deal in drugs.

Walker wanted films that didn't glamorise the life, he wanted films the provoked a thought rather than a laugh and a semblance of understanding. He had designed the posters on the office computer, he was never going to make it in the high-tech world of IT. Computers simply spoke a different language and it wasn't English.

His attention focused on the man at the door. "Mr. Bishop how are you?"

" Not good Gaz?" Trevor said with a mournful look on his face. Walker stepped aside and invited him into the office, pulled back a seat and indicated with a nod of his head that he should sit down.

"What you mean Trev? What-a-go-on." Walker liked to mimic Silks when he was trying to get the clients relaxed.

"She has been on to me again." Walker smelt alcohol on his breath, his eyes were glazed, his cheeks flushed.

"What did you say you were going to do Trev eh? Go on sit down buddy, you want a coffee? "Bishop nodded and wiped his eyes. Walker boiled the kettle and spooned Nescafe into two mugs. "You eaten today?" Bishop shook his head. Walker pursed hips lip and blew out a silent stream of air as he handed over the mug to Bishop, hiding his frustration. "What did we agree on eh kidder? Oh Trev, this only works when you do as you say you are going to do mate." Walkers tone was soft the message was unmistakable.

He walked over to the American fridge freezer that was in the corner of the office and rummaged briefly around inside. He produced some fruit, cheese and bread."Make yourself a buttie when we done here OK? And eat the bloody fruit."

Walker received a nod by way of reply."Come on then what she said to you that's brought about this reaction? "Walker asked.

She was Trevor Bishop's wife. She had burnt him badly, took his money and fucked his friends. Kicked him out his own house and basically fucked his head up. He had been in the hostel for nearly five months now. Walker admitted him after the CAT team had placed a call. Bishop had been sleeping rough for two months. His heavy social drinking had flipped over an acute use of alcohol as a way of escaping his thoughts and minds-eyes visions of what she used to do with his mates while he was out at work.

Bishop was a sparkie by trade and had used to command a decent wage, live in a house and watch sky sports on his new flat-screen telly. Now he lived in the clothes he was wearing, bunked down in a twelve by eight room, with a single bed and an old wooden wardrobe to keep him company on the long lonely nights. Compared to a bus shelter, shop doorway or a field it was luxury. On one occasion he had gone to sleep on a small field located in a rougher part of Wolves.

The local youth, bored and looking for entertainment had used him as a football as they played, *kick the tramp*. Walker assessed him in hospital, threw away the rules and admitted him. He would have been dead in a month otherwise. His mood was heading south. He was a mess, both physically and mentally.

Walker had picked him up and tried to re-build his wall of self esteem. His drinking bouts were becoming farther apart. His mood was holding even if he did have to have a row with Bishops GP. The doctor had prescribed him, Dothiepin. An old anti-depressant that contra-indicated with alcohol and was toxic and lethal in an overdose. It was just the right drug to prescribe to a depressed alcoholic, with suicidal tendencies, Walker thought with a scowl and an agitated shrug of his shoulders. After a *'full and frank'*, the doctor changed his script to Cipramil, a newer drug with improved beneficial therapeutic effects.

Bishop showed Walker his phone. He looked at the small screen and wiped his mouth. "What did you expect Trev? You know she can be cruel mate. You have to let go of this women." Walker said.

I can't Gaz, I love her." Bishops shoulders stared to shake as the tears flooded his face.

"Trevor calm down mate. You're pissed and tired son. We have talked about alcohol and what it does to your noggin. It ain't rocket science mate. I ay saying its easy kidder but you have to look after number one here son. You have kids mate. Think about them. "Bishop looked up, his eyes were red. "I'm sorry Gaz." He said sniffing and wiping away the tears.

"Don't fucking apologise to me Trev, you ay done nothing to me mate. " Walker smiled. "Stop apologising full stop mate. We come a long way in the last five months. When was the last time you was on a mission?" Bishop stroked his beard and looked up. "Two weeks."

"Really, that's more than four days growth on your face Trev. I've been off for a week now and you was alright when I went on leave."

"Two weeks Gaz, I promise you. You went on leave and then I called her. She was nice and then...............and then.............she let me down again."

"Can you see a pattern forming here Trev?" Forming, it had formed like the Himalayas.

Bishop nodded. Walker stood up and went to a small filing cabinet. Ran his fingers over a selection of ring binders, chose one with a whistle, picked it up and sat down next to Bishop. He looked at the index, flicked through the sections, found what he was looking for and placed a wedge of paper onto the desk. "Here's your diary Trev, have a look and see how much more positive your are when you haven't had a drink inside you." Bishop picked it up and read through it.
"Shall we do it again now? No time like the present."
Bishop nodded. He spend the next twenty minutes recalling good times with his wife, crying and apologising. Walker put his feet up on the table, sipped his coffee, listened and swallowed his frustration, taking the occasional note to jog his memory. He would re-write what Bishop said twice. Once as a key session and then when he documented their interaction in his daily record.
 Bishops was going round in circles. This was the same ground they had been walking over for weeks now. His wife had manipulated him again and crashed his mood. He let him get it out of his system, before he raised a hand as Bishop started to wallow in self-pity about his lost life. If he continued to suffer verbal abuse he would never find a new life.
" Stop right there please Trev, we're getting nowhere mate. You have to break the cycle. Only you can do it, talk to me before you talk to her again. Talk to me if you feel like you need a swig mate. Talk to me if you want to discuss how fucking awful Wolves are playing.
"You understand me?"Bishop nodded.
" Here is a pen a paper. I want you to write down how you feel, bring it down to me in the morning, yes? " Bishop nodded again.
Walker smiled. "It will get better Trev, yam along way down the road now mate. Things are never going to be perfect but now you ain't drinking all day, every day and getting the shit kicked out of you. Think about how well you doing mate. Focus on the positives. Now go and eat. Oh and Trev, have a shave and a wash mate. The grunge look don't become you son."
 Walker shook his hand Trevor he left the office. A disturbance over a remote control broke his concentration. He walked out of the office, and jumped down the step into the large lounge area. Two lads in tracksuits were having a row over what channel to watch. "Yam meant to be watching a bloody film not having a hissy over the bloody telly." Walker pointed his finger and looked sternly at two lads who now were looking sheepish.

" Behave yourselves or it goes off at twelve you understand what I'm saying Rich?" Rich nodded.

"John?" John nodded.

Walker muttered to himself as he let himself back into the office with his key." They like bloody children………….. He opened the file on the PC and started to type, rubbing his eyes and yawing.

Another day in paradise…………….

Professionally it continued to progress smoothly for Walker. His talent for working with complex cases was without doubt. The lads who lived within the hostel network and on the street respected and liked him, enjoying his banter and obvious understanding of their plight. He would always hand over a pound if they were hungry and give up personal time if they required additional support. He was their advocate in meeting and he didn't subscribe to the systemic approach and play the game. He would pursue fellow professionals to ensure they did what they said they were doing.

He would pursue Wolverhampton homes to locate stock so his lads could be re-housed. Walker was serious when it came to his clients and their well being.

He spend time listening during key sessions and all his paperwork was completed daily though not to the detriment of the time spend mingling with his clients and getting to know them all. Walker would arrive early and finish late. If there was a problem in the hostel they would come to him to sort it out. He had snouts on the shop floor and he knew who was doing what to whom, who was back on the gear and who was getting fucked up.

Politically, he wasn't the greatest. Walker was outspoken, he would fight his clients' corner, negotiating veraciously when it was appropriate. His reputation preceded him, and career professionals from other agencies treated him wearingly. Those who put client care first liked him and admired his passion and motivation to the cause.

He recognised the premise of objectivity and establishing parameters but he also knew when he was right. Those around him knew he was newly qualified and had talent, hoping he would calm down in time and play the game accordingly.

They viewed his success in creating a network with the local drugs and alcohol team and his political short falls and militant steak were overlooked.

The hostels catered for all sorts of people, mostly ex-offenders and drink and drug addicts. If you had a simple diagnosis of mental illness and didn't have a related condition this was not the place to live; because you would soon develop one. It was a very different environment from an acute unit. These lads lived in the real world, on the street and were not observed twenty four sanitised hours a day to make sure they were out of harm's way.

These lads would come home with all the marks that were a result of living life on the street. They would come home with black eyes, bruised knuckles, arrest sheets, court dates and a story to tell. They would OD on the sofa as they got high on heroin after rattling in jail for six months. Walker would sigh, place them in recovery, hit 999 clear the room and wait for the paramedics. It was tougher than an acute unit it was that simple.

The hostel was located in a tough area of Wolverhampton and the local youth knew who lived within those walls. If they were bored they would target the residents and blame them for the woes that would befall the local area, ventilating their own frustration of the social depravation they experienced on the very people that should have been their peers. All crime in the area was attached to the large terraced house with the white painted exterior and the large bay windows.

 It wasn't like the locals lived in a demi- paradise and didn't have the daily struggle with the police and were discriminated against for the way they dressed and acted. The pack always hunted the vulnerable and the weak and Walker knew that the local youth were responsible for far more crime in the area than the residents. On some days running battles could ensue on the streets as the more assertive of the residents took umbrage at the abuse that could pass their way. All age groups lived in the Hostel and a bond had started to exist between the residents as the workers tried to instill a sense of community and cooperation.

Once upon a time the drinkers would look down on the smack heads and vice- versa. After time both groups sensed the futility of waging war with each other and helped Walker start a five-aside team. They started to realise that there might be a future for them after all. Walker was proud of the lads as they accepted responsibility and represented their home in the wider community, and he was proud of all their hard work. They had developed a bond and a sense of inclusion. For all the work, they did. Walker would reciprocate it. These lads understood the difference between actions and words. They could sense a fraud from a mile away.

After a tip-off Walker began to provide escort to one resident, a man that was younger than Walker but looked twenty years older. He was physically and mentally wrecked by his childhood and the alcohol he imbibed on a daily basis. It was hard to understand what he said, he had developed his own unique language. He didn't understand the rhetoric of the nurses and the support workers. No amount of cognitive therapy, no ABC (Antecedent, Behaviour or Consequence) diaries would work with him. He simply wanted to get drunk and his ability to process information was severely compromised.

He needed input from the learning disability nurses and their team; they prevaricated after Walker referred him. He provided a risk, he didn't respond, all the excuses *'professionals'* would give, when they simply couldn't be arsed or the case was to complex. Walker tried but failed to hide his displeasure. He didn't play politics and was warned about his tone, even if his manager accepted the rationale behind his frustration.

The man didn't want a lot out of life, a few beers and warm bed. He wanted to be dry in the wet and fed when he was hungry He need his giro, he had bills to pay, beers to buy. The local youth had mugged him and ran away laughing with their booty. He kept to his routine, unable to understand Walkers advice as the muggings continued. He refused to change his routine, the post office he used or accept support in opening a post office account. Residents advised Walker of the situation and he would go with him to cash his cheque, even if it was his day off.

It only took ten minutes and because the man wanted an early start on the special brew, and as Walker still didn't sleep like a baby, it wasn't a problem for him to drop in at work, have a coffee with the lads and a walk over the park.

Walker deliberately walked; he could have driven but he wanted the youth to see the big bald bloke and fuck off to pick the meat off the bones of other carrion, the fucking jackals. A few years later Walker was reading the local paper, his eyes settled on an article and he found out with sadness that this man been murdered in the small town centre just ten minutes walk from the hostel. He had been beaten to death by two local youth, who thought it was tough to beat up on vulnerable people.

 Walker wished them well in their life sentence in tough jails, and crossed his fingers and hoped that they bumped into a *'decent honest criminal'* such as Silks.

Walker enjoyed spending time with the staff. They were good honest people, without conceit and without arrogance. They were dedicated and they lived the job. Walker added another chapter to his practise. He had little experience with drugs and alcohol and listened with interest to the veterans of the hostel network who had studied on the shop floor and given University a miss. He learned about emetic drugs for alcoholism. He learned about subutex and methadone for heroin withdrawal.

 He listened to the lads who explained what *'rattling'* was all about. He became knowledgeable about the criminal justice system and DTO'S. He had spent enough time in the dock but now he got to meet with probation as a professional and silently laugh at the thought that he used to sit on the other side of the desk not so long ago.

In return Walker taught them about traditional methods associated in mental health, about hearing voices, olfactory hallucinations. Cyclic episodes associated with Bi-polar disorder and together they built a solid foundation and prospered as a cohesive unit. Together they made a good team.

They were separate from Wolverhampton NHS (and its condescending attitude to all things not operated by central government) and as a charity they worked as tightly together with a siege *'us and them'* mentality which helped in getting the job done. Their manager was a Rottweiler called Rachel.

A focused forty something lady with steaks in her hair and a jowls that wobbled when she talked. Walker would find himself becoming hypnotised as he focused on her flesh as she went into a diatribe about the failing of society. She had a penchant for off the peg black suits, high heeled black shoes and bags that were that large it appeared the kitchen sink came to work with her. She was passionate and committed,

Walker never felt more at home than when she took off her ubiquitous black jacket rolled up her sleeves and got stuck in. Her talent had been recognised and she was about to accept a promotion and make the move up into senior management. The team was unhappy that she was leaving. Walker had only been on staff briefly but knew good team spirit when he saw it.

They just hoped that the new gaffer had her philosophy of: get it done, do it once, and do it properly, then have a laugh. The residents came first, they came second, and they came third.

She would work more hours than any of them and also do sleep in shifts. There was no job in the hostel that she didn't do. She was off the production line marked 'old school' and Walker liked her, more than that he respected her. Walker had to respect someone in order listen, if you were stupid or arrogant then Walker became deaf. Rachel had offered him the job and after a short induction period, she knew she had made the right decision.

His handovers and case notes were top drawer and he had a knack of motivating the lads. He spoke their language. What she didn't understand, what she didn't know, was that it was because he had lived their fucking life and then some more on top. She even smoothed over HR when they called him in to head office to discuss his CRB and past indiscretions. He was a good worker, the past was the past. Walker was a team player.

The team consisted of: resettlement officers, domestics and support workers. Walker was the only nurse on staff as they needed clinical governance when addressing the needs of the clients who experienced mental health problems.

The NHS handled the community side, Walker handled the everyday nuts and bolts and the fundamental care component that the more complex clients required. He received little support from the community teams who thought that a monthly meeting expedited their duties with due diligence. The CPNS's and Social workers were meant to fight there wider cause in the community, as there service offered an internal support network and a safe environment, not direct intervention. They sat and listened when Walker attended community reviews and said very little; nodding intelligently, with their diaries clasped proudly in their hands.

The kudos of the service improved when you had an RMN going to community reviews. Walker could talk the language of psycho-babble. He had formal training and he knew the score. He had a card off the NMC and a title.

The support staff came off the street with no formal training and received it on the job. There were gaps in their education but that was more than met by their willingness to go the extra mile for the cause. The resettlement officers were bright and had some formal qualifications. One had a degree in philosophy and Walker enjoyed their intellectual exchanges. He cared deeply about his job and found an ally in Walker when they went to meeting to complain about the service they were not being offered by Wolverhampton Homes.

 The charity provided a good training programme for all their employees and Walker put his name down to go on various programmes. The training was diverse and in his opinion you started to learn when you qualified. It was a road that you had to keep walking down. If you saw the finishing line it was time to retire. What Walker did know was they all knew their job and they all did it well.

There were no Maggie's on staff and that made him happy. A new manager was appointed and all that changed for the worse .Walker`s personal life continued to exhibit serenity. His salary paid his rent, all the bills and left him enough over to buy nice clothes and go out on the piss when he wanted. He could make trips to ASDA and not be bothered about looking at the prices.

He could give Shorts the things she wanted. He recognised that material things do not make a family but it was nice to take her shopping and be secure that when the door knocked it wasn't the bailiffs or the law. They had a holiday to look forward to and it was a good time in his life. His one concern was Kathy, she was a variable that that he didn't have a contingency plan for.

They got on. They got on very well and spent all their time with each other. When Walker wasn't at work he was with her. With Silks locked up in jail and most of the firm settled down in their world of domestic bliss, his absence wasn't noticed. He knew he was smitten by the girl, he knew he was into her big time and she told him the same thing when in a moment of weakness he let his feeling slip. She smiled with a glint in her eyes and held his hand, and for a moment, he knew what it must be like to look into the eyes of a cobra.

She was cool and demure and used to have men eating out of her hand. Walker doubted that her feeling rivaled his. He kept up the pretence of aloof charm and undetached love, underneath his skin the river ran strongly.

They would go out and have great times; they would stay in and have great times. It was the perfect summer for Walker as he danced on cloud nine. Walker introduced her to Victoria when they came home, loud and merry with the look of teenagers about them. She rolled her eyes twice, smiled sickly as she was dragged to the pub for an evening of merriment and a buy one get one free dinner.

Her eyes opened at the demure looking blonde who eat her meals like Audrey Hepburn and spoke with builder's language and laughed like a hyena. Her presence was infectious and Victoria laughed along at her course humour and down to earth intelligence.

When Walker was away at the bar getting drinks, Kathy would impart words of wisdom that reinforced her sharpness and attitude. She would laugh and kill Walker with one liners when he tried to be too clever. Shorts liked her immediately. Kathy was savvy and quick witted and Victoria understood her.

She didn't bow down to her dad, she challenged him and this interested her. Kathy was no carpet, she was strong and assertive. If Walker was being loud and obnoxious, she would stand up to him, talk sense and in ten minutes the storm would have blown over and a happy house would be left in her wake. Walker appeared to be settling down with a woman he loved, his contentment shone through

His eyes sparkled for the first time in years. What she didn't know was that Kathy had lived a different life and had no brakes, nor had Walker. When you have a car with no method of stopping it is inevitable that one day there would be an accident. Walker didn't focus on that, why should he? His life had been a dark cloud, they were happy, why rain on the parade? At the back of his mind, tendrils of doubt curled around his thoughts, he knew she was complex and it could all end in a heartbeat.

It was time to pick Silks up from Manchester; his jail sentence had come to end. Walker packed an anxious Jules into the car. She looked at her watch constantly as they drove up the M6 to Manchester. Walker wanted quiet on the drive up and smiled and nodded as she went through her personal anxiety reaction. Walker was deep in his own thoughts. Silks did present a problem.

Kathy and him had a *'relationship'* that went way back. They both knew that they had to break the news to him eventually that they were seeing each other. It was anybodies idea how he would react. He had been against them seeing each other and hadn't been shy in telling Kathy. Walker felt they had timed it badly, waiting for him to get banged up and then jumping into bed. Silks had no ties on her. She had never been his women. But the feeling that somehow they had betrayed his trust hung in the air when they spoke about him.

They would discuss it when they were in bed and would debate it in the pub, finally coming to a rushed decision that if he wasn't happy with them going out together that they would call it a day. Walker thought about it for about ten seconds, then slapped himself. If they were serious about being a couple they would find a way. Silks would be happy for them.

Walker would wait for him to come out of jail and break the news then. Today was the day. Walker sent a text out, when his mobile beeped with a delivery report, it would mean that Silks was back on the street. They arrived in Manchester early, Jules was still talking two to the dozen. Walkers ears were becoming numb. He spotted a McDonalds restaurant and decided that maybe a cup of tea and a meal might shut her up for ten minutes. He ordered two big breakfast meals, an orange juice for himself and a cup of coffee for Julie. As they sat down his phone beeped. Silks had turned his phone on, he was a free man.

 Walker shook his head as the panic flooded off Julie. "Calm down Jules, he is safe, we will be there soon enough. Take your breakfast with you, eat it in the car and bring your coffee."

Walker had looked inside the box and raised an eyebrow. Big breakfast? He thought there may be a case to answer if he took his case to trade descriptions. Silks would enjoy the meal after spending the last four months eating prison food. With a sigh he followed Jules out to the car.

Silks was on the car park when they arrived in a storm of dust and a screech of wheels. Walker slid down his window and shouted over to his mate."Oi, time to leave mate, come on. You just spent six months in that shit hole. Come the fuck on you tit. "Silks looked confused for a second. "Bruce, new wheels mate. Very nice. You brought a beer and a bag?"

"Of course mate, in the back. You like the ride then mate?" Walker had invested in an Alpha. Leather seats and sleek Italian design .He nodded his head, and then frowned. "Tarts car mate."

"Yeah, yeah. It's better than that heap of shit you drive round in, come the fuck on. We got the pub to go to and we arranged a party for you. Big turnout kidder."

Silks nodded. "Where's this bag then Bruce?"

"Beers in the cooler, here's your pressie." He passed him over a white parcel. "Columbia's finest." Walker hit the accelerator. They were back in Wolves in less than two hours.

It was time for Walker to fess up.

CHAPTER 32
SCHISM.

Walker parked his slate grey Alpha outside a large Victorian pub that was located in a suburb full of social deprivation, a mile outside Wolverhampton City centre. The pub was hidden away in rows of terraced housing; the occasional tower-block clouded the horizon. The pub was a contradiction. It hadn't tried to be fashionable, yet more customers who shopped in the designer outlets in the city centre gathered there, preferring its ambience to the hip-bars that Walker hated.

The pub had moved away from the generic feel of the trendy gastro-bar that were now spotted around Wolverhampton. Bars with brushed concrete floors, and shelves that sat behind the bar with stylish bottles that were illuminated by soft lighting.

Optics apparently had gone out of fashion. They had menus chalked on bistro blackboards, dishes with a French slant that proudly proclaimed that their food was: *a diffusion of this, and a sprinkle of that*. Meals were served on a bed of...... not a plate. All vegetables were seasonal, organic and fresh. Fresh, did most pubs serve vegetables that were off then?

The Manager had returned to polished wooden floors and a traditional feel. A large black container sat proudly next to the bar, containing two gallons of stew and the offer of crusty bread to lap up the gravy. The menu was not cheap and offered traditional fayre, the food was home cooked and didn't arrive in vacuum sealed bags ready to be micro-waved or flash fried.

 The local youth who had a fondness for baggy jeans and firearms had been priced out of the market, allowing the *'beautiful'* people to while away their Saturdays nights and eat their Sunday lunches over a pint of real ale.

The beer garden had been completely revamped and if it became too busy, bar staff would take orders and bring the drinks over to the punters. It was simple, it provided good customer service and it worked. The football team had started to use it, now it was a venue that fitted in nicely when they were on a decent pub crawl

Silks was already a little drunk and high when they arrived. He had managed to get through four pint bottles of Bud and half- a –gram of cocaine in the hundred minutes the trip home had taken.

The few customers that were in the bar on a Wednesday lunch time looked up from their papers as they landed in the pub. Walker ordered two lagers and a Strongbow from a pretty girl who had hair which was impossible to describe and a bored smile on her face.

Jules placed her-self at a long wooden table that was situated underneath a large window. Her face was a picture of concentration as she moved sauce bottles to accommodate her handbag. "Check mate Jules," Walker said as he arrived with the beers.

He placed them carefully onto the table and pushed one toward her. Ta Walker," she said as she took the head off her pint with relish. She was relieved that Silks was bubbling along happily, dropping out one-liners to anyone that wanted to listen; his relief at being back in his home environment evident.

Walker had joined in the banter. It was clear that having his key-spar back on the street had brought a smile to his face. However, he had to clear his mind. It didn't matter how long or loud he laughed, he had business to take care of.

He waited patiently for Silks bladder to fill, or his nose to empty. He didn't want any gear yet. He needed to approach this with a head that was clear of Charlie. After an hour and three pints Silks decided now was the time to pay a visit to the gents. Walker stood up to follow him and Jules cackled gleefully. "You pair of girls, you even go to the toilet together."

Silks looked across at Walker and raised his eyebrow. "People will talk."

"Fucking let them." He looked across at Julies and smiled. "Man time Jules, get the beer in then," he passed her a twenty over. That should buy her silence for a while.

"You want some of this?" Silks held out the wrap.

"No mate, not yet."

"You're turning down gear Bruce, what-a-go-on?"

Walker looked over at Silks. "I've got something to tell you mate."

"What's that then Brucie Boy?"

"Somebody I've been seeing," Walker said .With more confidence than he felt. Perhaps he should have dropped a line after all. However, he knew Silks would respect him more if he did it straight headed. The words were still the same, but they resonated effectively if the speaker had the balls to speak without a pharmaceutical intervention.

"You been seeing Kathy mate, I know."

"How?"

"Fucking obvious Bruce, you got a new squeeze and when wim sitting across the table in the visitors room you're more concerned with my diet and fetching the fucking kit-Kats and coffees than you are at talking about your new tart.

Why didn't you want to talk about her? I normally can't shut you up when I'm banged up. You evaded the questions and changed the subject. That ain't you mate. Never has been. Yam the first to squeal when you got some fresh pussy on the go. I went back to my cell, lay down on my bunk and thought it through. You have time to think when your locked up."

"So?"

"So what?"

"What you think?"

"Fuck all mate. Me and her are mates Bruce, we go back. But listen mate, she a great girl. But she's nuts." Silks jabbed his finger against his temple." She is not settling down material."

Silks looked at Walker and held his eye." Don't lose your head over her." Walker let out a sigh of relief. Silks continued." What, you thought I was going to kick off over a bird?

"Walker nodded his head forward with a serious expression written all over his face and replied. "I won't lose my head mate, now pass me the parcel then."

Silks laughed. "You and Kathy eh, fuck me you're a strange couple. Is she showing later?"

Walker keyed some powder and inhaled deeply, holding the bridge of his nose. "Yep. I'll call her now."

"What, she waiting at home to see how the land is lying?" Silks said with a hint of sarcasm in his tone.

"Sort of."

"You pair of cunts. Come on then, let's have a beer and a game of pool. I haven't had a beer with me old mucka for time. I'm not going to waste me afternoon on this.

He left the toilet. Walker followed him. That had gone better than expected.

Walkers' new manager was everything he despised; a careerist that sat on his arse and didn't spend any times working with the people he purported to support. When he arrived at work he would swing round on his chair and make sarcastic comments about the clients, before he left to head off to the company HQ in Wolverhampton to brown nose senior management and eat subsidised breakfasts.
His working day ended at two when he would pack his bag and head off home.
The project was ran by the other staff and morale lowered both in the office and with the clients on the coal face. The teams got their heads together and passed on their reservations to the operations director and were shot down in flames. Those that put their head above the trenches got it shot off.
Walker started to resent the hypocrisy of the company and the double standards of his boss. He was never going to be a diplomat and his feelings were well known to the manger.
Good team members were moved around the system as he brought in his own people and Walker found himself in front of a disciplinary panel on various spurious charges. The team split into factions and Walker never worked harder to prove his worth. He worked 80 hour weeks and came up with clubs and developmental activities for the lads; they were never supported by the management. Walker used his connections to finance them.
Others concerned at the managers appalling practice, looked into his past, his qualifications were poor and there was a cloud hanging over him from his time in the East Midlands.
The original team thought he must have something on the group director and battled on against the tide. The last straw came when Walker arrived on shift to cover a night shift. The manager's chosen few, who now were allowed to perform initial evaluations and risk assessments on potential clients without formal training, had admitted one lad straight out of jail.
Walker had eyed him up when he first presented at the hostel and had waited around for an hour, looking on in the background as he attended to some left over paperwork.
He was cocky and dropping out names that well were known on the street, major players in Wolves. But then anyone that wanted to be a gangster in Wolverhampton would profess that they knew Tom Dick and Harry, thinking the mention of their names would be kudos for

them. Name droppers were fucking despised in the criminal community. Stand on your own two feet and who gave a fuck about who you knew.

Walker asked him if he heard of 'Gary Walker'. He thought for a moment. "Is he from Wednesfield?"

"No you tit it's me?" It got a laugh but Walker could see the blag. The two other support workers that in the room were too busy making him coffee and asking him questions about drug use, when the emphasis' should have focused on his forensic history. Walker frowned, he had an attitude. Not an old lags attitude, but the prison mentality of the youth, the king of the yard mindset that resonated with violence. He passed a note over which read: 'Watch him'. The sun was just going down, the streets were nearly deserted with only the occasional couple standing at the bus stop or walking the dog. Walker parked his car or rather his wagon on the street next to the hostel.

He had invested in a SUV. He flicked the fob and the lights flashed and the alarm gave out an electronic bleep, he loved the sound. He would aim the fob at the car and shoot it as if he was a gunfighter from the Wild West.

Walker paused for a moment, he thought he heard a noise from the squat next door; he cocked an ear and heard silence. He would have a word with the lads after handover. If they were using it to get pissed and jack up, he would shut it down with a smile and a shake of the head, saying. "It's a bit close to home isn't it eh lads.

As he entered the building the new arrival pushed past him with a pedal bike in his hands. Walker looked around as he slammed the door behind him. "Easy fellow, calm down my son." He got no response in return. Was that blood on his knuckles?

Mary the support worker was still on shift, she had done a twelve hour stint and looked tired and harassed. She had performed this morning assessments and her expression exuded worry.

Walker lifted his head. "What up? Did he have blood on him?" Walker jerked his thumb at the door." What the fucks happened?"

Mary shook her head. "I'm not sure Gary. We think he has beaten up Mark next door."

"Have you called plod?" Walker said with a sense of innate calmness. He s surprised how in control of his emotions he actually was

Mary nodded her head.

"What they saying?"

"They will get here when they can." Mary replied.

" Pricks!" Walker exclaimed. The Old Bill were like buses. If he was committing a crime there were half-a-fucking- dozen of them zooming around. When you needed one, the streets were empty.

"Where's this happened, here?" Walker required clarity.

"No next door." Mary replied.

Walker opened the front door and stepped outside, it was now dark. The street lights glowed ominously.

"Gary ,you know protocol, we can't act if it hasn't happened on site. It's against the rules."

Mary loved to quote policies and procedures. She wasn't a bad girl. She just spent all her time reading the rule book. It circumvented her common sense at times.

"Fuck the rule book." Walker said as he broke into a trot.

Walker arrived next door, pushing through a tired old gate he viewed the scene. Mark`s body lay in a pool of blood, surrounded by empty bottles, cans and newspapers. There was an old lime green sofa sitting alone in the centre of the room and the whole place smelt of damp and desolate decay. Mark was breathing but his respirations were shallow.

Walker shouted. "Hang on Mark, helps coming and ran back to the hostel and hit the 9's.

"Emergency which service please." A crisp, fresh sounding voice greeted him.

"Ambulance and police PLEASE, we have a man that has been beaten, he is in a bad way."

Walker handed over basic details and put the phone down, valuable minutes were being wasted. He called the number that Mary had used to notify the police. He got through to a pedantic sounding officer who said tiredly. "We will respond when we have officers available."

"Make them fucking available, there is a man dying next door!" Walker shouted, trying to reinforce the seriousness of the situation.

Mary and her co-worker kept the lads inside the building, safe in the lounge, with hot cups of tea and food as the drama unfolded.

Walker's co-worker Anthony arrived and assisted in trying to achieve some sort of order from the chaotic events that were unfolding.

Anthony was a pragmatic, Jamaican lad, who followed orders and did what he was asked. Walker both trusted and liked him.

The night was punctuated by blue flashes and anxious faces. An hour later a serious looking inspector arrived in the office and informed Walker with a grave face. "We have launched a murder enquiry."

The police wrapped tape around trees and lampposts and sealed off the side street. Walker asked permission to move his car. A somber looking copper nodded his head. Walker breathed in and looked at the stars and shook his head. "There by the grace of god, go I," and said a prayer for the dead man.

Mary and Annette stayed over until 11 to write up their reports, they were in shock it was obvious and written all over their faces. The best thing they could do was go home, drop a sleeping tablet and hope for six hours blessed oblivion. They had done their background checks, they had contacted probation. Nobody could have foreseen the extent of the violence that had taken place next door and heralded a new face into the hostel.

The manager had the final say, he had given the go-ahead, they needed a full home to make the senior bosses happy. He had buckled under financial pressure.

Walker sent them both home, he hugged them as they left. "Don't fucking cry girls, save the tears for when you get home, show no emotional, you will start them all up". Walker thought they were on the verge of breaking-down. He had enough to contend with and the lads were starting to roam the building with bad intentions in mind. He called his manager. Protocol dictated the procedure. Walker explained the situation.

He was met by the manager's terse voice. "Is he dead"?

"Yes." Walker replied simply, the emotion draining away his energy.

"I'm on leave now. Call the senior management team and they will handle it." The manger replied.

"You're not coming in then?"Walkers blood was turning into pure acid.

"Nothing I can do is there?"The same smug, supercilious voice.

Walker slammed the phone down. "Fucking cunt." Walker said with venomous intent. He looked across at the squat black man that was sitting on the desk shaking his head, as if he was in a daze. "Do me a favour T?" Walker needed his troops, give this man something to concentrate on and he would snap out of it.

"Safe Gaz, what man?"

"Get the lads together; tell them I'm going to talk to them please."

He nodded and left the office. Walker thought he was a gem. He was calm, didn't panic and did what he was told, without the need for a fucking conversation.

The mood was sullen after Walker broke the news, the lads sat around and excepted the gallons of tea and coffee that Walker provided.

He gave one lad a tenner. "Get some snap, you got ten minutes OK?" The lad nodded back at him. Walker kept them occupied for another hour before he started to usher them to bed as the murder squad arrived on site and started to take a statements.

At five in the morning the birds started to sing and the tentative strands of sunlight started to part the clouds.

Walker resisted the urge to cry, he was filled with a sense of sadness, anger and frustration. He was disgusted with the attitude of his manager. He'd picked up the phone and called the Senior Management Team to tell them he was in control, he'd completed incident reports and passed the press over to them. They thanked him candidly. At seven the next morning he started calling staff that were due on shift in an hour to lessen the impact of the tragic news when they arrived. They needed to hit the ground running, the whole place was starting to stink like a mortuary.

At eight o'clock Walker was called by the CEO and given two days paid leave as a reward for his performance and informed that they would deal with formal investigation. Walker communicated his misgiving about the managers lack of support and was brusquely informed his manager wasn't duty bound to come in as he was officially now on leave."

Walker left work with his morale as low as ever.

To cheer up the place and improve the mood Walker formed a cooking club. The lads could have a themed night once weekly when they would all put together and work as a group. He approached the manager and was promised five pounds a week. Five pounds! It was an insult. The money was in petty cash and earmarked to be spent on improving the feel of the service. Fuck the cunt, Walker thought and paid for the ingredients himself.

 It became a day that the whole place would look forward to. Lads would shop with the money they had raised and bring Walker receipts; the shop lifters would add their bit and Walker would turn a blind eye.

The staff would get involved and the manager would sulk and leave even earlier. Shortly after Walker came into contact again, with HR over some nonsense that didn't need their involvement. He ignored the satisfied smirk of the man that called himself a leader. Walker had to hand it to him. He played the political game like a pro.

After a chat with Kathy he decided to jump before he was pushed. His time as a CPN was nearly over. He reviewed the job pages and applied for a job as a ward manger at a new private hospital that was opening nearby

The relationship with Kathy exploded along. It was a ride that was for sure. When they argued it was hostile when they didn't it was loving. At his flat she was a different lady, in company she was hard. Walker told her he needed to meet her kids. It was the proper thing to do if he was serious about the mother. She hadn't previously introduced men to her *'boys'* in the past. They could be difficult to any potential suitor. She agreed, she knew that it was the, *stand up thing to do*. If they were sneaking round it equated to they must have something to hide.

 After an evening in the pub, Walker landed with half a dozen chicken baltis and a crate of beer to break the ice. Her lads were big, mixed race and made their money without the need for a national insurance number. That was fair enough for Walker to accept, he and Silks had walked on that ground. He had made his money that way but these lads made a career out of it and were on a different level. They liked Walker, he knew the score and had been honest about the way he had felt about their *'Ma'*. They wanted her to have a respectable boyfriend with a good job and not some old ponce off the streets. Her eldest was in prison and he was a serious player.

Walker was happy that he could break bread with the rest before the leader of the pack came into view and 11 months into their relationship Kathy asked him to move in with her, they sat down and drunkenly planned to get married.

They were serious about their motives, they professed their love for each other. Walker doubted that their plans for domestic bliss would ever come to fruition.

 For Walker it was a good and stable period for his head. His job was going well, he had found a woman he loved and now he was going to live under the same roof. Her house, though small was located in a nice area of Wolverhampton. He reviewed his options and said yes. Silks shook His head and warned him not to. That was her yard not his, her house was her house , she will use it when you have a row, why upset the dynamics in the relationship? He reinforced the point that she was nuts. Walker didn't listen and blanked out the common sense argument. He knew his Kathy and she had changed, she was no longer the women from the past that Silks knew. Silks helped him move with a sad smile and a shake of the head.

Their relationship deteriorated steadily. Walker booked a trip to Cyprus so they could spend some time alone with each other, some time alone without the constant oppressive feel and pressure of her family. At times they still connected and would laugh like lovesick teenagers.

These were the faint points, like starts in the night sky. You looked up and knew they were there, even if the reality of seeing one was a dream. Walker became ever more frustrated with her change in attitude though; she no longer treated him as her true love and he came second every time to her boys. Walker accepted that the bond between mother and sons was a special and sacred connection. But now he felt more and more like Cinderella.

The day of the holiday dawned and Walker woke with a happy step and a smile on his face. Two weeks away from Wolverhampton, two weeks alone, two weeks to recapture those untroubled and rapturous days when they first went out together. On their first night there they had a stand up row in a restaurant.

The restaurant had been specially selected by Walker, a restaurant that overlooked the sea, with the moon glancing off the ocean. Kathy forgot she was Audrey Hepburn and turned into Janine Butcher and stormed off into the distance.

 Walker sat and looked at the other diners, couples with children who were laughing and enjoying their holiday in paradise. He felt vulnerable and alone. All the feeling he had submerged for years started to flood over the dam he had created in his mind.

Walkers temper simmered as he got a taxi back to the apartment and waited in the room, his face sat in stone, his mind locked on course. He sat on the balcony sipping vodka and viewed the surroundings, his anger growing, as the feeling he was trapped and his paranoia as to her real motives rose.

 All the days in therapy were temporarily forgotten. When she arrived back to their four star apartment with no word of apology he made sure that she knew he was unhappy. He terrorised her for an hour before she escaped by jumping over the first floor balcony onto the grass below and ran to a security guard and hid behind him for safety. Walker looked on, his eyes set in stone. He turned around, shut the door and turned out the light. He didn't need to beat her.

Walker was good with his mind and he used it expertly. She had been beaten by harder men than him and was desensitised to that approach. From that moment on she was wary of him, she thought he was mad. The holiday was punctuated by Walkers bad behaviour. He fought lads from London because she liked cockneys. She never looked at him the same again.

At home the pressure was telling, Walker working longer and longer hours. He was dedicated and loved his job and when he arrived home there was always a house full of people, lounging around, smoking weed, talking bollocks. He hardly got to spend quality time alone with her. He wasn't used to crowds and big families. Walker was used to his own space. On his days off he would take Kathy into Wolverhampton and they would spend hours in the pub. Walker just wanted to escape from her home. The bills were piling up. Kathy was on the dole and her boys didn't contribute, Walker paid more than his fair share.

She was trying to find work; he couldn't fault her on that. She had taken some voluntary shifts for a local charity that worked with abused woman and was doing well. However it didn't provide an income. Employers would not give her a chance because of her criminal record. Most companies wanted a CRB now which detailed your criminal record. Walker knew all too well about that. His was long and he had had to explain it to university and HR when it landed on the respective desks. He smiled and hoped that someone would give this lady a chance, he wouldn't walk away.

One day they had another domestic over nothing. Walker tried to make the peace, she was having none of it and told him to leave. He went to the pub to dress his wounds angry and hurt. He called Silks and had a beer or two.

Silks wasn't interested with providing relationship counselling. He had warned his mate not to move, he had explained that she was mad and not settling down material. If he hadn't listened to him then, what was the point of going through it again? Move out of her house and move on, Silks told him the answer and he wasn't going to spend the whole afternoon repeating himself.

Walkers' mood darkened when he received a text telling him his stuff would be in black bags on the lawn ready for him to pick up. He was now fucking homeless! His temper was about to blow, he snorted some more cocaine and left the pub in the suburbs, heading toward the city centre in his new 4x4.

He wanted blood, he wanted her blood. He checked all the Irish pubs and she was not about. His frustration at not finding his target boiled over and he headed back to his end to find Silks.

Walker was driving too fast and he didn't give a fuck, deliberately going through a couple of red lights, other car horns blazing at him, tears of anger on his cheeks. As he neared his destination one car decided to try and beat him to the punch. He rammed it deliberately, the crash and impact bringing him round from the red world he had lived in for ten minutes.

There were looks of shock on pedestrian's faces as they ran to help the occupants of the other car he had hit, which was a terrible mess. Walker drove off and escaped, returning a few minutes later to watch the scene from a nearby pub car park as the emergency services with blues and twos blaring arrived, like the cavalry.

Silks looked across at him. "Did you fucking do that?" As he pointed at the wreck of the car. "So fucking what!" Walker had lost the plot and Silks knew it. He gestured to a girl that Walker was tight with and had been for years. They had met eight years ago when she had moaned to him about her life and he failed to take advantage of an obvious offer when she told him she loved her husband. Walker dropped her off at home and told her to talk to him, maybe they had a chance.

"Take him to yours and keep him there," Silks ordered. She drove him home and built a strong cannabis joint to calm him down and knock him out. Mandy had been friends with Walker for a long time and knew what to do to calm him. She had seen him lose the plot on several occasions. She knew his moods were introverted and she was never in physical danger when he came to see her with his red face. Walker had never been a bully. If he was angry he would more than likely pick on the wrong man and end up with a black eye, sore lip and a tale to tell in the morning. Walker still had the ability to self- harm, he just got others to do for him now.

Walker sobered up and went home, back to Kathy's. His bags were not packed, but his time at hers was over for him. Silks had bought a house and was renovating it. It had a bed and that was all. For all intents and purposes it was a building site. Silks told him he was welcome to stay there and pay him a bit of rent, life was not free. Walker looked at his surrounding and pondered how he had managed to go from the best area in Wolverhampton to living in one room without a carpet in a building site in a drug ridden area of Wolverhampton where gang warfare was strife; shouldn't the steps be in the other direction? Walkers phone rang and Kathy's name was on caller id. They had not spoken since the day of the crash and had made tentative steps at reconciliation, but the magic had never really returned to their relationship and they were both aware of the fact. She told him that Old Bill had landed on her doorstep and were looking for him in connection with his recent accident. Flushed with anxiety Walker gave Silks a ring and told him about the new development. Silks advised him to give himself up and get it over with. Walker knew it was the right thing to do but it didn't set well in his head to voluntarily go into custody. Walker wrestled with the quandary and the date with which he was going to attend the police station was constantly delayed. He was busy at work and when a window arose he would make the short trip into the cells. Walker had always been a past master of procrastination.

A letter dropped through the door two days later requesting that he attend an interview for the position of ward manager. The excitement of moving on and upwards pushing the thoughts of any pending conviction into the distant horizon. The premise of failing his upcoming interview never entering his head; on the day it was due, his suit was as clean as his mind as he headed off to sell himself, revising his answers on the way. Walker had prepared and was confident that he would succeed. He answered the questions that were posed and left with good feeling in his stomach, intuitively knowing he had *'nailed'* it. His opinion was confirmed as he was offered the post.

He and Silks toasted: Gary Walker Ward Manger. He had managed to pull it off. Walker liked the sound of his new title, it satisfied his ego. He had made a promise to himself when he qualified that he would buy a Jag and live in a purpose built apartment in a red brick development with the rest of the beautiful people and live this normal life that he had craved for so long. Perhaps his recent trials and tribulations was fate`s way of deciding if he was prepared to move up to the plate and accept the responsibility that leadership entailed. Walker and Kathy recaptured their lost youth for a brief moment and giggled like teenagers as they misbehaved round town, it was a weekend from the old days and Walker felt the nostalgia.

 Monday dawned and his hangover and memory receded as the old bill landed at his new address, three cars strong and looking like they expected resistance. Fuck me, Walker thought. Am I a terrorist? It was an RTA that was all. Talk about a worthless show of force from the boys in blue. Walker stepped into custody, confirmed he was the driver, received his court date and was bailed to appear before Wolverhampton magistrates. It had been a long time since he stood in front of the beaks and it pissed him off.

He deserved the arrest and didn't moan out loud. With his head bowed he received 100 hours community service and a heavy fine. Walker knew he deserved a lot more. Sometimes he would wake up when he felt the impact of the crash. He knew at that moment he didn't care if the occupants of that car died; the thought that he could kill somebody haunted his thoughts for a long time afterward. Luckily the occupants of the car survived serious injury and for that Walker lit a candle and thanked God.

What he didn't know was because he had been convicted of an offence where a person had been injured the courts had notified the NMC and the fitness to practise panel would investigate. Oblivious to the thunder clouds forming, he bought himself some nice new clothes that cemented him in his new role and pushed away thoughts that he should notify his new employers about his recent brush with the law.

CHAPTER 28
REMOVED

Walker enjoyed the title ,Ward Manager and he attacked his new role with gusto. The home manager had promised him near autonomy to train his team. He was now in charge of six support workers and it was his job to identify areas of potential growth. Three years ago he had been about to qualify now he was captain of the ship. Silks sang the Funboy Three song: *'The lunatics have Taken Over the Asylum'* ,as they celebrated his promotion through the ranks in the many pubs that seen their custom over the years. In a quieter moment Walker reflected that he would use his experiences to make sure the clients under his care were afforded respect and treated like humans.

His allegiance and empathy would always be with them. If he caught any member of his staff with Maggie's' philosophy, then they would have to reconsider their career options, because a place in Walkers new order of mental health would simply be untenable.

As his work environment improved, his relationship with Silks as his landlord deteriorated. Walker was searching for an escape route from inner city gangland Wolverhampton and even though his salary was good, it didn't provide him with vast resources to move to the leafy suburbs just yet. His time with Kathy had left him with a few bills, his financial prudence not tempered by her ability to help him spend his money. "He was a big man," she would tell him. "If he wanted to blow his wages that was up to him she wasn't about to tell him what to do." Walker loved the trapping of his success: new clothes and nice cars, mobile phones and plasma televisions.

 Spending money had never been a problem to him. As their friendship continued to sink behind a cloudy horizon, Walker and Silks got into another squabble. Kathy angry with Silks attitude told Walker to pack up his things and move back in with her. He took five minutes to make a decision and jumped back into the frying pan, his love for her again blinding him.

They decided to find a house that was a neutral venue. Walker didn't understand that where Kathy went, her boys would surely follow. They searched for a house and Kathy came back with a three bed roomed terraced that was bigger on the inside than it looked on the outside and fitted their needs perfectly. Kathy liked the new house, the area was less than salubrious, but when you shut the door from the world it was safely locked outside.

All thoughts of austerity in the budget were lost as Walker went on another spending rampage to furnish the new house: new bedroom suites, a new cooker, an American fridge freezer, a smart patio set, carpets, wood floors and a new flat screen television and sky in every room pressed his already struggling bank balance to the limit. The centre piece was a dining room that was fit for the meals that's Walker provided.

An eight seated glass table with high backed champagne leather chairs took centre stage. Walker would open the door and gaze upon the home he had provided with pride. He wasn't overwhelmed when her boys, all of them, decided to move with them. They were her children, they were adults. This home was a stepping stone to their lives.

He was becoming a positive role model, with a resigned smile he stepped over the sleeping bodies as he made his way to the kitchen for his morning coffee as prepared for another long shift at work. Kathy never understood that at their age maybe they should be doing things for themselves, as his generation had been taught to do and stand on your two feet.

At a younger age he had moved out from under his parent's wings, married Nat when she had become pregnant, worked and paid the bills. He smiled sadly and felt old, as if he was from a different generation, and a different world. He had turned full circle from the boy who had become a man.

The time allotted for serving his community sentence was getting in the way of his work and paying the bills and his social life. Kathy liked a weed and Walker found a drug that served a purpose of calming down his volatile mood and perpetual anxiety state. As alcohol served as a catalyst to his mixed emotions and escalated minor inconveniences into tidal waves of problems; problems that blended with his inherent paranoia and insecurities to form a volatile concoction. Marijuana would slow him down, giving his brain time to adjust and reflect on the problem.

Kathy loved him when he was stoned and hated him when he was drunk. She knew he was Dr. Jekyll and Mr. Hyde and accepted her fate. When the bad thoughts strolled casually into his mind he would use his experiences and training and control them. Walker would push them aside and wait for the drift off to blessed oblivion. His sleep patterns had never returned, he always felt tired and blamed Natalie for the legacy she had left him.

He hankered after the sleep that smoking drugs bought him, and accepted the night's rest with a happy and relieved smile. Perhaps Walker in his wisdom should have realised that drugs, ALL drugs provided the snakes, the opposing force to life's ladders, in his perpetual search to reach his grail.

His years of using alcohol as medication to cure his resident anxiety had left an deep-rooted mark.

The courts had been in contact, he had breached his court order and a warrant for his arrest had been issued. Walker dismissed it and continued to work and smoke, the weed providing a camouflage to his responsibilities. His new role was stressful and time consuming, Walker averaged 60 hour working weeks at work, such was his determination and motivation to succeed at his job.

On his days off he was too tired to spend his time dredging canals and painting toilets. He just wanted to relax and have a beer with Silks or a smoke with Kathy.

He never realised that breaching a court order was an offence that judges would take seriously as he was not a career criminal. He breeched again and was warned of his behaviour, he managed to knuckle down and reduce the hours to ten, working on all his days off. The relief that he only had one Sunday to go was a like a balloon sailing away into deep blue skies. Saturday night came around and Walker decided to have a couple with Silks before heading home to Kathy.

A couple became a few, a few became many and many meant that he was too drunk to drive home. Silks put him in a cab and waved at his mate who was slumped against the window, refusing the urge throw up and his head span. When he woke up he felt like rubbish, his head felt as if somebody had plugged in an adapter and inflated it to its limit and it was about to go POP. His mouth felt like nails had been hammered into it and he had been French kissing a moose. His tongue was furry and he didn't have much motivation to move. His car was five miles away and he was four miles away from probation.

He rolled over and decided to spend a day in bed with Kathy and decided to roast a joint and smoke one too. It was a far better idea than circumnavigating Wolverhampton in the rain. Walker would sent in a letter explaining his absence for community work, the process of prevarication alive and well and working in his hung-over mind. He blew away the anxiety and made a coffee.

Kathy was sleeping, he would spend a day cooking and smoking, he had Monday off, he deserved a couple of days rest. He had been working non-stop for the last fortnight. He left the letter to the last minute and relied upon the vagrancies of the Royal Mail to deliver it. Unfortunately probation received it one day late. The wheels of justice were already turning in motion, aiming straight at him. Warrant offices descended on their house and Kathy covered for him when he was on a twelve hour shift.

He accepted her phone call in his office . Shook his head and dismissed his problems as a minor distraction from the job in hand. He quickly weighed up the pros and cons and again dithered about handing himself in.

Professionally he was accelerating like a Ferrari; personally he was strictly a Skoda.

Walker was arrested while putting out the morning rubbish. The two large men wearing stab proof vests stood on his doorstep and he knew his time was up. He considered running or simply denying he was Gary Walker, that idea evaporated when the taller one of the pair smiled at him.

"Morning Gary, aren't you fed up with this lark?" He had nicked him at Silks the last time he had failed to appear. Walker shook his head. "It appears not lads can I get dressed and tell the missus please?"

They nodded and followed him inside. The smell of stale cannabis was evident and hung in the air. Walker was relieved that there was not the perennial body stretched out on the soft leather sofas he had nearly paid for or wedged up against the door.

They waited downstairs, looking uncomfortably at BBC breakfast news as he walked up the steep stairs with heavy footsteps. He gently nudged Kathy, who opened one deep blue eye and looked confused. "What you want, what time is it?"

"Warrant officers are downstairs I'm being lifted for breach. I'll be back soon.

She yawned and turned over in the large leather bed, that he hadn't quite paid for and pulled a pillow over her pretty head.

Kathy wasn't fazed that he was on his way into custody. Men in her life had a habit of receiving early morning visits from the authorities. Walker felt initial relief that it was over.

The thought that he was 'wanted' and the axe could drop at any time was a stress he didn't really need. He only had ten hours community service to complete, he would stand in the dock and inform the judge that he would book annual leave and sort the remaining hours out next week and the problem would be duly solved. He was a professional and productive member of society, what was the worst thing that could happen?

" Mr Walker, those ten hours will be the most expensive ten hours of your life, you will go to prison for ten days."

 Walker thought he had misheard and shook his head. He was perplexed as he was taken down back to the cells. He turned and asked the screw if he had heard correctly.

"Has he just sent me to jail mate?"

The guard nodded and smiled sadly back. "Yes mate, bad luck."

"Did I get ten days?" The guard nodded again.

"Fucking cunt," Walker said, he still couldn't believe it.

The lads in the holding cells eyes opened with surprise as he was deposited back in with them. Walker sat down on the wooden bench still slightly shocked his brain trying to formulate an escape route.

The three men who remained in the cell, looked at each other slightly mystified by the sentence. "He gave you ten days for ten hours!" their arses started to go as they heard the doors slamming shut behind them, the keys jangling in the locks and the handcuffs snapping shut.

"The blokes a fucking hanging judge lad's," Walker said. A rueful expression planted on his face and he thought about hang-over's with melancholic remorse. He looked around the cell and thought ,home for the next five days.

Walker was interviewed by probation twenty minutes later; in the short time he had been locked up he had formed a plan on how to beat the situation. They would call Kathy for him and inform her he was now in jail, they would also pass over a message to call his employer and tell them he was sick and he would be back into work in a week. It could not have been simpler. The lady from probation nodded and said they would and could and wrote down a number. She promised Walker she would do it immediately. He suspected that she felt faintly sorry for him. Five hours later after a lunch served on a plastic tray Walker was handcuffed and lead to the prison van to start his sentence.

The journey to jail was nearly as long as the time he had to serve. Five days in jail and a seven hour drive to Durham prison. Walker couldn't get his head around the situation. Eight cons were all lead out of the

Reliance private security van and led a booking desk to handover their possessions before being told to wait in a holding room. There were eight of them sitting down looking glum. One lad cracked a joke and they laughed and started to talk.

Walker looked the part and joined in the banter, his thoughts turning to Silks and all his years in the system and his face didn't crack even though his stomach did. It wasn't the thought of jail. It was his job and career that caused his anxiety.

He showered received his grey sweats, prison issue boxer shorts and a hot meal and cup of tea from a sympathetic prisoner who looked like he had served more than five days in jail.

Walker was led to the wing office and asked if he wanted to see a doctor, did he have any medical problems. He spend five minutes on the landing soaking up his new environment before he was issued a phone card. The screw informed the small group they could make one call before they would be shown to their cells.

Walker used it to call Kathy and reinforce the importance of calling work, leaving a message on her answer phone. He did wonder why her mobile was turned off and slight clouds of concern passed by the sun. He rationalised that she wouldn't be so stupid as not to pass on the information. She had made her life with villains in the past and could be relied upon totally in a legal crisis.

Walker calmed his head and lay down on his bunk and counted down the hours to his release.

Monday came around and Walker hit the street with a travel warrant and enough money for a beer and a smoke when he landed back in Wolverhampton. He had slight misgiving when he turned on his phone and had ten messages in his inbox requesting that he call work and it was urgent. He dialled the number and spoke to the home manager, feigning pain in his voice and arranged a meeting with her for two days time. A message from Kathy popped up and it made him smile.

All he wanted was to get home, smoke a weed, drink a beer and sleep in his own bed. The boys were standing outside when he arrived home, they laughed and joked with him and patted him on the back before passing him over a twenty bag of green. He walked into the lounge and Kathy was perched on the sofa looking as beautiful as ever. She kissed him on the cheek and passed him a cold beer, laughing as he moaned about his five day bender.

She had done longer in the police cells she told him with a smile. "You did phone in work for me, yes Kathy?" "Yeah, yeah no problem." Walker smiled, the misgiving blown away as the weed and beer took hold of him.

The meeting with his line managers didn't go quiet as expected. Questions were asked which he couldn't provide answers to simple questions. "Why had he not phoned in work?" Walker shook his head and told them. "I was too ill to move, I left instructions with my partner to phone in, did you not received the call?"

They shook their head and looked gravely at him. "We did receive a call, Gary twenty four hours after you were meant to be on shift. Walker looked confused and stuttered, "Excuse me, what?"

"We received a call twenty four hours after you were due on shift, the shift when you were on-call officer. You are aware that in policies and procedures that the person who is sick is responsible for informing the home that they are unwell and cannot present to complete their shift, yes? We tried to contact you and your mobile was turned off, can you explain that please Gary?"

"I was too ill to receive calls." He knew he was a sitting duck in the water, he sounded as believable as a Nazi at Nuremburg.

"Your actions are simply unprofessional and not what we expect from our RMN team."

Walker could see the storm clouds gathering and resigned. He did not want a dismissal on his record. They accepted it without rancor and he left the office with his head down, his professional world pulled apart. He jumped into his cab shocked; the news hadn't really sunk in that he had just lost his job. He had arranged to pick Kathy up from work that morning but his first stop on the way was at the off sales, he needed a drink and he had an hour to kill before he was due to collect her. Walker needed time to think.

He sat quietly and pulled the tab from his can, drinking deeply. Walker was trying to make sense of the situation, the full implication of his resignation hadn't yet landed in his mind yet. The self-regulated defence mechanisms and alcohol numbed the initial agony, like Paracetamol did to tooth ache, but the pain wasn't ebbing away, it was building, a framework of historical angst .

He was alone, sitting in his 4x4 and consuming more than enough cider to fuel his anger before he made the journey over to where she, Kathy worked.

She glanced at him when she got in the truck unaware of the storm that was about to break. "You ok?" She asked. Walker certainly didn't look it. He had that look about him. His jam was set firm and his eyes were narrow.

"I'm fucking top dollar Kath, how is YOUR job going?"

Kathy knew Walker and knew that something was seriously on his mind and ignored the jibe. She didn't want to get into a stand up after she had just finished a night shift.

Walkers anger, like many storm's before would blow over as quickly has it had started. She saw an empty can on the floor as her eyes looked down and her stomach dipped.

"You called in work for me then. You wouldn't fuck that up would you eh? It's not like your fucking thick is it?"

"Yes, I called in for you, what with the attitude? It's a bit early to be drinking isn't it?"

Walker ignored her remarks and concentrated on the cross examination. "When? When exactly did you pick up the fucking phone and dial in the fucking number?"

"I don't remember""You don't fucking remember! Let me fucking tell you when!" Walker spat out the words with hate, his face red, his anger filling the car. Kathy was meant to call in work on Thursday the day he had been sentenced. Friday would have sufficed. Kathy had decided to have one too many on Friday night, having a happy clap with the Irish travellers that she knew. She didn't remember to phone until Saturday evening, eight hours after he was due on shift; eight hours to late to save his reputation, eight hours to late to save his job. Walker's anger boiled over and she knew he was close to breaking point and violence. Her head telling her to put as much distance between herself and Walker as she possibly could. Her boys were there but did not get involved, they listened as the words hit the ceiling and the doors slammed. Walker was a different bloke with a beer and an attitude. He drank some more and threatened her by text and abused her by phone.

Kathy didn't' return home for days at a time. She would walk round Wolverhampton in between shifts, sit on park benches and finally camp on a sofa, any sofa to avoid Walker. The boys didn't say a word and went about their business. Walker drank some more. On the odd occasion she did return he would spit in her face and hiss insults, before she left again.

After a month Walkers thirst had been quenched, his arms and head hurt as he had cut himself with anger and frustration. He knew he was becoming unwell again, his mind had splintered and he could no longer rationalise the way forward. A tiny orb, a micro light in the dark kept burning and sang to him to stop the slide and fight back.

 They were dark days and he fought the demons that had been realised back into his head.

He remembered the desolate days of his previous suicide attempt and fought back, his fear of becoming unwell his motivation to fight. In the space of a week he had lost the woman he loved, his liberty and his job. It was a horrendous mess and Walker knew it. He couldn't approach Silks when he was ill. Silks didn't get mental illness.

Walker needed a shoulder and not the truth and lay on his bed for hours. Not moving, his head on his pillow, his stare fixed on the window. Day became night, the stars receded and the sun came out. The world moved forward, Walker was stuck in a time capsule. Transported back to 2001. He used all his experience and the strength that had grown within him to fight the depression, to make a move forward. Slowly and surly he recovered.

He was in a house that didn't want him, in a life he didn't want, with people that he didn't belong with.

 Finally when Kathy came home, he left her alone and nodded to her on the stairs as they passed one morning. After a week a truce was called and they spoke but their relationship was over.

She felt too guilty to throw him on the street, he had nowhere to go and was penniless, he had finally hit rock bottom.

Walker looked at the jobs pages to start the search for self respect. The fire in his belly burned brighter as he formulated a plan. He reasoned that he still had his pin number. He knew that it took five to six months for a CRB to reach the desk of any potential employers. In that time he could earn enough money to set himself up in a flat and prove his worth to his new employers, he picked up the phone and dialled some numbers. Walker had a plan, Walker always had a plan. Walker had to get out of her house. It was a nightmare existence for him living with the woman he had once loved, in a house where he not welcome. Kathy was a constant reminder of another battle lost and a further bridge burned when he looked at her sitting on the sofa as he ventured downstairs to eat. As he lay on his bed and fought his feeling, he would think of Natalie and her betrayal of him and he knew that time wasn't on his side, he had to escape the chains that hung round his neck.

Walker licked his fingers and turned the page over, his attention was drawn by an advert for the post of manager of a care home and applied for the post as a joke. Using it as tool to keep his hopes alive and his mind occupied. He filled in the application; he had nothing to lose he thought as he walked to the post box and slipped the letter inside.

Two weeks later a letter dropped onto the mat informing him that he had been invited to an informal interview with the owner, to have a look around the facility. Walker still didn't consider that he was a viable candidate to fill the role, he was only thinking of ways to fill in time in the endless boredom of his existence. It was a way to keep busy, a way to fight the ghosts from his past, isolated and alone in Kathy's bedroom.

He picked up the phone and made the necessary calls and arranged a time and date to meet with the owner. The owner was a man not unlike himself, big, straight talking and down to earth. They talked about mental health and their personal philosophy and Walker was invited back to spend a day with the team. His mood was lifted on the drive back to Kathy's, the fire in his head started to burn brighter as the thoughts he could be in the running for the job grew.

Walker went back to the home a week later and spent the day with the nurses and support staff. The owner was further impressed with the way Walker operated so he arranged a meeting with the operations director of a larger care company that was about to buy the facility off him.

He told Walker that he was his personal recommendation and it was between him and one other candidate. His excitement started to grow. The salary he would be started on were figures he never believed that he could ever earn. It would provide him with the lifestyle he had craved for, for so long. It would provide him with the title he deserved and the accolades his practise called for. Walker bought a new suit and looked like the smart professional when he arrived at Temple Court to meet the owner of the care group and its Operations Director. He continued to make the right noises and surprised himself with his intelligent answers.

He was sitting in a room with top professionals and he had to wear a long sleeved shirts to cover up the scars on him arm from where the knife had cut him just a few weeks previously. The Operations Director an attractive power dresser of a woman, nodded at his answers and agreed with his visions for the future as she invited him to head office for a final interview. The excitement continued to mount in his stomach as he told Silks that he might just be able to pull this one off. Walker could taste the pound notes in his mouth they were so close. As he lay alone in the double bed he had bought for him and Kathy to spend the rest of their life in, the thought that he must walk on the shoulders of angels kept him awake.

Three months ago he had been in jail and his life had hit a new low, now he was in the running to operate his own home. He sat down at table and revised the care standards act for a couple of hours before he gave up and threw the weighty document in the bin. He rehearsed his answerers as he made the drive over to meet with her, happy with the premise that he was there to sell himself.

He was calm and surprisingly confident as he was led to a leather chair parked outside her office. He waited two minutes until he was greeted with a large smile and a big thank you for coming. Walker sat behind her desk and answered some perfunctory questions, surprised at how easy they were. It was all cosmetic, and he knew it, after ten minutes the interview was stopped as she offered him her hand across the table and offered him the job.

Walker managed to remain calm and collected, negotiating his financial package and arranging start dates, when all he wanted was to run down the road and shout, jump and dance.

He held it together on the long drive home, his excitement near breaking point. She was sitting on the sofa as he arrived 'home' smoking a joint surrounded by her sons and their friends.

Walker smiled and thought, I didn't buy those expensive fucking big leather sofas to see how many we could fit on them at once. Instead he just walked through the living room and headed off upstairs to get changed. Kathy followed him up to the bedroom and asked him, "Did you get you get it then?"

"Yeah I did, I start Monday morning. I'm going out to celebrate."

Walker was now the manager of his own home, above the nurses, above the ward managers he was as high as a nurse could get. Walker had arrived on Broadway.

Walker's mum appeared happier than he did when he arrived at her house, she kissed him on the cheek and told him she was proud of him, he held back the tears as he called Victoria to inform her that her dad was top of his profession. Walker had made the journey in five years. A week into his new job Kathy had a fit. She told him it was due the stress of their break-up and having him living in the same house as her. He agreed and as he handed the keys over to her, they both knew that a story which should have been masterpiece had ended as just a brief chapter in another trashy romantic novel. Walker moved onto his mom's sofa and started flat hunting.

Walker found the initial stage of managing the home difficult. It wasn't nursing anymore, it was budgets, it was administration and it was hard work. Given a patient, he could work a minor miracle, given a health and safety risk assessment he could not.

The staff team resented the new owners and Walker was resented all the more for being the front man for the new regime. The job and stresses involved got harder and he would drive home with his head aching and his eyes in a fixed stare before he spent an hour pouring it all out to his mum.

He was making decisions that were outsider his normal scope and his work started to follow him to bed. His sleep was now down to three hours a night and he would be at work at six in the morning. The staff though his early arrival was dedication, he didn't tell them it was nerves and anxiety at fulfilling his new role.

Slowly he began to find his feet and win the team around; he was a quick learner and would listen to the staff's apprehensions about the new owners. He called a staff meeting to avoid a mutiny and like a solider took all incoming bullets. The team nodded their heads as they left agreeing at least he had the bottle to stand in front of them and give honest answers and not hide away in his office.

He remained visible and the nurses started to respond to his humour and obvious motivation to provide a better life for the patients. The team slowly became dedicated to him. Those employees who were loyal to the previous regime and tried to undermine his tenure were identified and disposed off quickly.

The staff came to like and respect Walker. He could laugh, joke and would clean up a toilet but they now knew him as fair manager, who did have a ruthless steak. His ability to make the residents feel at ease highlighted his personal motivation and the way he dealt with potential situations and dangerous and violent residents were noted. The home had a focus on forensic provision, ladies and gentlemen who had been detained in high security mental health hospitals and had served their time inside those high walls, moved into Temple Court. Walker knew how to care for them and the staff knew it. His administration was poor, he was lax at dealing with incoming e-mails from his bosses and completing budget returns but his clinical skills were not. He assessed and improved the procedures that governed the operations and the care aspect and the moral and feeling around the home continued to improve.

The relationship with head office continued to be strained as his inability to meet budgets continued. He wouldn't compromise on patient care he told the staff and fought cuts. Head office relented impressed at the improvement he made to the clinical operations of the home. He worked hard on his administration skills to reduce the anxiety that this process caused him and he worked harder than ever, his weeks became 80 hours long and his practise became refined. Professionals that presented to view the home where impressed with its *'feel'*, and the down to earth manager that talked English and had the patients best interests at heart. His worth in the local community increased his home a place where they wanted their clients to live. Walker started behavioural profiles and would forward monthly trends and analysis to consultant psychiatrists identifying points that him and his team would work on. He had become a leader to thirty employees and twenty clients, his social life suffered but he didn't care, the professional kudos he was receiving was better than any drug he had taken.

His drinking was under control. For the first time in his life he could go to the pub and have a couple of pints and leave without the need to get shit faced. He had finally found his niche in society.

Walker found a car that appealed to him and his mother arranged finance, a blue Jaguar now sat proudly in the garage, the car he had always dreamed that one day he would own was now his. Silks helped him locate an apartment in a new red brick development with wood floors, a fitted kitchen and a balcony that offered him a view of his beloved Wolverhampton. Italian leather sofas were delivered and his home took shape. It was his first real home since he had lived with Victoria and he looked at it proudly.

The lounge was bedecked with polished black and chrome furniture, glass cabinets and a large flat screen television took pride of place. Walker would sit back and view his life not sure how he had got here.

He still had worries, he knew it could all crumble when his CRB dropped on head office.

There was a chance he could lose his job but there was still a chance he wouldn't, and he worked harder and harder. His efforts were recognised by the powers that be and G.O.D would always leave with a smile on her face when she left Temple Court. Charmed by the no nonsense, cheeky chappie that was now Gary Walker.

On his way to work he would look at passengers in other cars and contemplate what they saw when they looked at the big man in the Jag. He knew where he had come from; he knew where he had been. He bought Victoria a car, happy that he could now give his child what proper dads did and look after their children instead of hurting them. When she moved out of Natalie' home into her own little house he took her shopping and bought her expensive soft furnishing and food. She had grown up into a beautiful young lady and she was now setting sail into the wide word.

Proudly he took her to lunch at nice restaurants, his head held high as he parked his Jaguar and escorted her inside.

Silks was happy for his mate. Walker wasn't around much anymore.When people would ask about him. Silks would tell them he was the gaffer and driving a Jag. People had always thought that the pair of them were too unstable to make amends in respectable life. Silks had his own building crew, and could earn in a month what some people earned in a year. Walker operated his own nursing home. When they did link up, mutual respect was offered and even though Walker was careful about the amount of alcohol he imbibed he would accept cocaine on rare occasions. He and Kathy remained friends, their relationship improving now they had space between them. She would visit him at his new apartment and they would smoke weed and giggle like naughty teenagers just as they did when they first met. Kathy would tell him he was a better person without the alcohol and maybe as friends they could make it back as lovers when the time was right. He knew her problems in finding employment and offered her a job. She accepted and started work on his support team. Walker did know where he had come from and he would never forget the journey he had made. He would take the memories to the places he was going. Walker and Kathy continued to see each other but she remained at arm's length, uneasy about going back into a relationship with him. Her life had been dogged by bad decision making when it came to men. She had thought that Walker different, but he had caused her more pain than many other men she had dated. Walker, as congruent to his previous character, would jump in the sea first and wonder if there where man eating sharks in proximity later.

He couldn't understand her reservations and was getting bored waiting for her to make a decision. Her Marlene Dietrich rendition of, *"I want to be alone"* was starting to melt his head.

A pretty blond nurse was leaving Temple court to find success at the hands of the N.H.S. She had shown interest in Walker and called him on the pretence of looking around his new flat Walker suspected her true motives. It was as an excuse to start up a relationship.

He kept an open mind and arranged a night when she could come over and share a bottle of wine. Walker decided that maybe a woman that had a good job, wanted a normal life and didn't come with more baggage than terminal five at Heathrow, would make a change for him. They shared one bottle and Walker opened another two as he prepared a *'quick supper'* and she fell for his patter and his charms. Walker could be funny, he possessed a quick wit and a good sense of humour at work. She laughed even harder when he dropped his one liner's and tales of his past, as they chilled together on his sofa.

Walker wanted a nice girl. She wanted a bad boy that had done well. It appeared peripherally that is was a marriage made in heaven. Walker persuaded her to stay on at Temple Court as a bank nurse. He knew it was a good management decision and it enhanced his status with G.O.D. He could work with her part time and fuck her part time, the delineation clear in his mind.

Samantha liked Walker, Walker wasn't bothered with her. She had money and paid her way and offered him a taste of normalised life. After a short space of time she started to get on his nerves with her Laura Ashley ways and wanting trips to the garden centre .

The boredom came down on his head like a cold November night. The final straw was when they were invited to one of her very middle class friends' house warming party. Walker was put on a leash and dragged round as the working class hooligan that had made good and joined acceptable society.

The bankers gathered round to view this curious exhibit and he answered a couple of stupid questions from *'proper football fans'* eager to learn about the battles they'd read about in the Mail.

Walker not impressed at being spoken to like a six year old exploded
when they arrived home after she took another snipe at him. Sam later
told him she saw, 'Madness in his eyes'. In the ensuing domestic Sam
told him she had never seen that level of aggression. Walker laughed it
off. If that was aggression, then she hadn't seen a lot in her life. Walker
didn't care. At this moment on his life he had a messianic step in his
stride.

Kathy saw them together at work and put two and two together and
came up with the right answer. Hurt and never to be out done, she
went on a mission to find a tit for tat partner and landed up in bed
with one of Wolverhampton's most notorious hooligans.

She professed her love for the new man and Walker laughed it off, not
convinced. Their relationship struggled like a match in a vacuum and
the flame finally burned out. Walker did miss her, but he didn't miss
the pain and conflict that she'd caused him.

Sam went the way of other women he had date, loving him and not
sure what he wanted. Walker always wanted a normal life. However
when his dreams were served on a plate to him he would send it back
to the kitchen. He was happiest when the women he was with caused
him problems in his head and he was swept away on a magic carpet of
passion and emotion.

His search for a replacement for Natalie was now at an end, his
odyssey finally completed. For the first time in his life he was happy to
be on his own. His work had become his wife.

Friday dawned just like any other day. Walker had been waiting for it
excitedly. Today he had the who's who of Welsh mental health services
coming to Temple Court. He was entertaining the top psychiatrist of
the region, a renowned psychologist, and a solicitor from the home
office, they all arriving to meet with him Gary Walker ex hooligan, ex
addict. If he could finally seal a big deal and get them to sign on the
dotted line, he would land the big fish, a complex man who could be in
line for *'Britain's maddest man'* award. This man had been in the
system for years with no improvement in his fixed delusional paranoid
framework.

Walker had spent hours in his office typing on his computer and
drinking gallons of coffee, cross referencing previous risk assessments
and care plans. Putting together a comprehensive package that
included: costs, individual development time, care pathways and
psycho-social development plans. They had been submitted and met

with home office approval. They were a work of mental health art and Walker was proud of them. He would sit back and read them back to himself unsure whether he had actually written the words on the page as they looked back up at him.

Today was d-day, if they agreed to the package after a final round of inspections today, the client would be his. He would earn the company £150,000 a year for the foreseeable future.

The resident would never be well enough for a return to independent living, he would be theirs forever. This was the cost of private mental health care in modern Britain £3,000 a week to make sure that the mentally ill were looked after and had a home. Walker would use the money he had made them to complete the revamp of his community rehabilitation team and take his home to another dimension.

Finally he would hit 100% bed occupancy and that would finally get head office off his back, assure his future with the company and at the same time nail down his bonus award that would increase his annual income to £50,000 a year.

The home looked and smelled wonderful. His best cook provided a buffet lunch fit for the occasion and the clients that constantly caused him problems with their 'challenging' and 'complex' behaviour had been taken to the seaside for a day out under the close scrutiny of his most trusted nurse and three other members of staff. This day had been planned meticulously and nothing had being left to chance. He dressed in his best suit and packed his brief-case full of care plans and mental health action plans ready for inspection. His walk was full of confidence as he left his flat. As he looked up to the skies as went outside he saw that the morning was as bright as his mood.

He decided to play some upbeat songs instead of listening to talk sport and headed off to work, gunning his Jag and appreciating the power, singing loudly to himself.

When he arrived and signed in, he looked around the home and went to the conference room. His staff had done him proud, all his hard work and the portfolios he had spent hours creating were laid out neatly, they were in place just as he had requested. His chest swelled with pride and he went around to all staff and thanked them personally for their hard work, making merry with a few residents on his tour of inspection.

When Walker was happy, the home was a bright and merry place to live and work.

The meeting was a success; the team from Wales were impressed with the way the home operated. Walker spoke with passion and good sense about his personal philosophy and how the home was a reflection of it. He spoke with eloquence, he spoke without the need for psycho-babble and he spoke from the heart. It was his finest moment as a nurse.

As the team from Wales loaded up their cars and made ready to leave the West Midlands, Walker stood on the steps of Temple Court and waved them goodbye; with the contract safely in his hand with a scheduled admission date.

Turning around he looked at his empire, at the big Victorian house with its bright modern annex that had become his home and his favourite place in the world, it was the zenith of his career. As he walked back to the office he danced and shook hands with his residents .

His face told the story as he sat down on the leather sofa in his office and looked at the team as he called them all in, he punched the air in delight and exclaimed loudly. "Yes we fucking did it people. I'm so proud of you all, thank you all so much. Give me the phone Loz, let's call the fuhrer and tell her the good news".

He phoned head office and purred as he informed G.O.D that they had hit 100% bed status and she stroked his ego in return. He danced with his staff in the office and assured them that their request for a pay rise couldn't of been hurt by today's events.

When he had a moment he called Mandy his long time friend and invited her round for dinner, telling her: Vodka, smoked salmon and fillet steak were on the menu he had some good news and he wanted to celebrate. He bounced proudly around the supermarket with his manager's badge standing out on his lapel, proving his status and worth to society as he filled his trolley and planed his cooking method. Walker was drinking a can of strongbow and Mandy were sipping on a cold glass, both comfortable on his Italian sofa, discussing his plans for the future. In the morning he was heading home, back to his original stomping ground, his journey around Wolverhampton complete. A striking development had just been opened close to where his mother lived and where he had raised Victoria, they had units remaining and Walkers was returning home.

Next on the agenda was a trip to the Jaguar show room. He wanted a DF and he wanted one now. The car was now in his price range and obtainable. His mobile phone rang and broke up the party. Walker's mother was identified on his caller ID. He answered and listened to her. Mandy saw him turn white and stutter into the phone, she knew that the plan was going wrong somehow.

Walker got off the phone and dived for the vodka bottle pouring himself a neat measure of nearly a third of a pint and drinking it in one go. Mandy was unsure of what to do and looked at him.

"I've been struck off Mandy" Walker said, his ashen face showing a gradual degree of increasing pain.

"What!" she looked confused. "What D'you mean?"

"My mom was just re-registering my PIN number and the NMC have told her that I have been struck off for *'continued criminal behaviour'*. Walker was in shock, he didn't know anything about a fitness to practise hearing, let alone being removed from the register. His phone rang again a few moments later, identifying a London number. He answered and attempted to make sense of the destruction raining down upon him.

He turned to Mandy and blew out his cheeks, "Apparently they were investigating me from time, since the crash.

When I went to jail it was the last nail in my coffin. They send the paperwork to the wrong address and I'm fucked. I can appeal to the high court but that will take thousands. I can apply for my number back in five years."

Walker downed more vodka and his head went into his hands. Mandy didn't know what to do. When the glass hit the wall and she was covered with shards, she called Silks. The only man that could deal with Walker, the only man he would listen to when he lost the plot. Within ten minutes Silks landed at Walkers apartment and spoke gently to his mate.

Walker wanted to kill Kathy, kill the world. Silks sat down and let him pour it out, stopping only to tell Mandy to build him a joint. He wanted Walker knocked out, he was talking madness and sometimes in Silks experience, he would act on these crazy, irrational thoughts.

Victoria received a phone call, her dad had not sounded like this since the day he was taken into hospital and she was worried.

Silks spoke to her gently reassuring her that he and Mandy were going to look after him. Gradually the tears subsided and the cannabis took hold and Walker slipped into the darkness.

When he awoke in the morning he looked out of the window and the sun was shining, tacked onto a shimmering blue sky.

He had a plan.

Walkers always had a plan.

EPILOGUE.

Walker sat down on his sofa, the fallout from his life running in slow motion through his mind, like an old silent movie. He rubbed his eyes as he reviewed his life shaking his head to the silent audience. He had been struck off the nursing register for criminal behaviour. Was he a criminal he asked the question? Walker had hardly been a career criminal throughout his life, he had made money but his offences were not serious. He was an offender that was a given, there wasn't an argument for the defence, but they were wrong about him. His philosophy had been to help and give his heart to the clients in his care as he had walked the same path in life as them.

He had loved three women and scared of rejection pushed them away, his behaviour and his mind never at peace or harmony. For the first time in his life, he was content to be alone. His drug use and problems with alcohol beaten. Those days of addiction long since passed and consigned to history.

He had earned and spent a fortune on his quest for the highlife and all he had to show was a few quid in his bank balance all that stood between him and the clients he had once served.

Nurses from all over England were called to task and asked to explain their poor practise in a clinical setting and how they treated their patients with neglect. They were slapped on the wrist and allowed to continue with their lives. He had been an advocate for his clients, his clients had all loved or at least respected him, knowing his passion and commitment to help them. Yet because he had trouble coping with events in his personal life, he had been given the harshest possible punishment. He found their decision myopic and ill-conceived. His value system was based on a hatred for bullies and people that abused their positions over the weak and vulnerable. The judge that sent him to jail may as well of given him a life sentence that day because that was the result. His career was over before it really began. The people that knew him well, knew of his loyalty and his kindness and his sense of humour.

Where had he gone wrong? All through his life he had struggled, struggled with his mental health and his emotions, yet he had made the journey from service user to service manager, from drug user to drug counsellor. He had raised his daughter when her mother had deserted them both. He looked up to the skies and thought that God did work in mysterious ways and once again asked him for guidance. Walker was tired of the constant battle that was his life. He thought he had finally won the war, how many more times would he have to fight back? Did he have one more round left in the tank?

Walker had a decision to make, he thought of Silks and Kathy and the lessons they had taught him and the resilience and back bone they had encouraged and brought out in him. He thought of Victoria, the person he loved more than anything else in the world.

His anger started to boil and he wiped the tears away. He wasn't about to let the establishment beat him, he would fight back and start again. Walker turned on his lap top and started to write.............

The End.

Printed in Great Britain
by Amazon.co.uk, Ltd.,
Marston Gate.